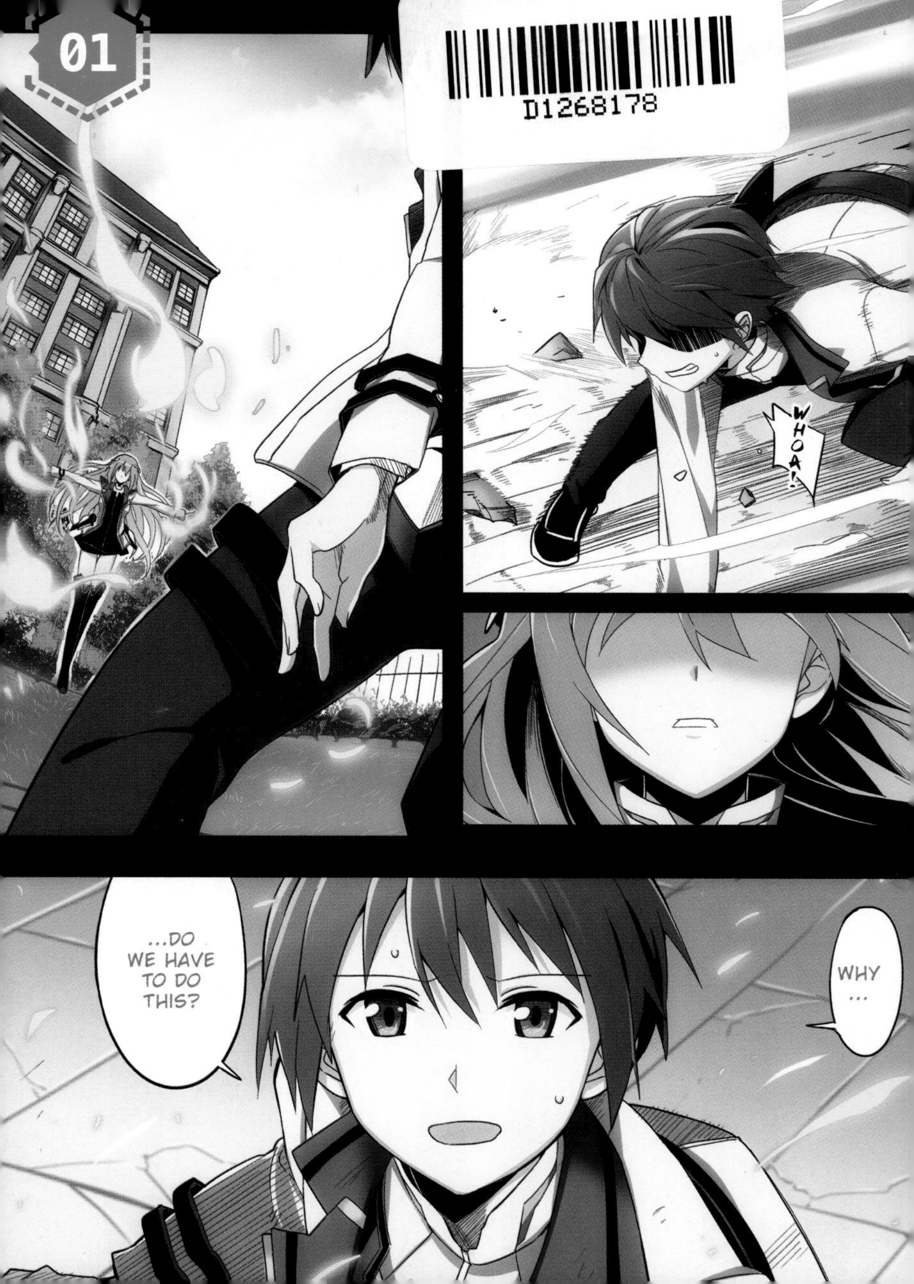
01
WHOA!
WHY...
...DO WE HAVE TO DO THIS?

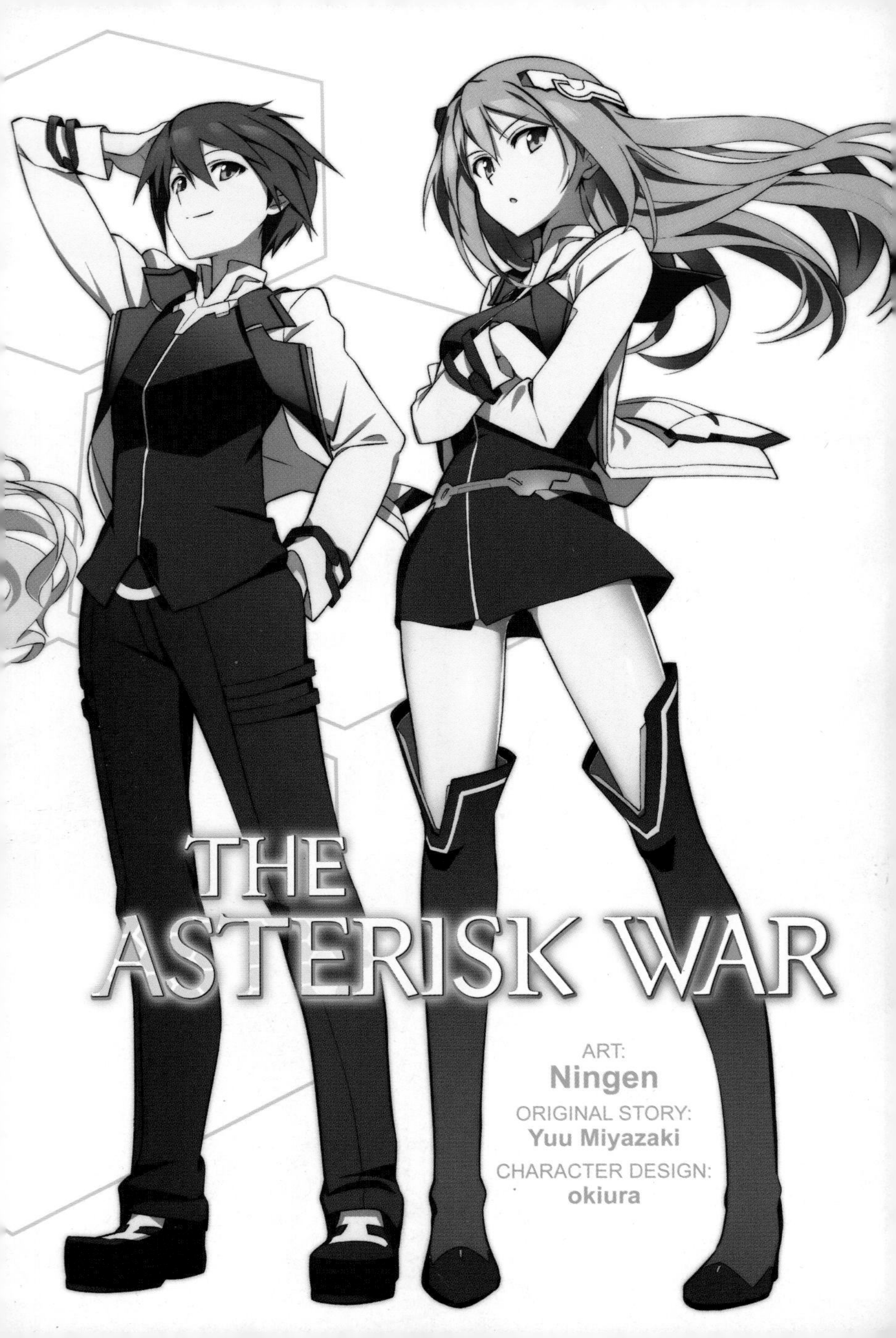

THE ASTERISK WAR

ART:
Ningen

ORIGINAL STORY:
Yuu Miyazaki

CHARACTER DESIGN:
okiura

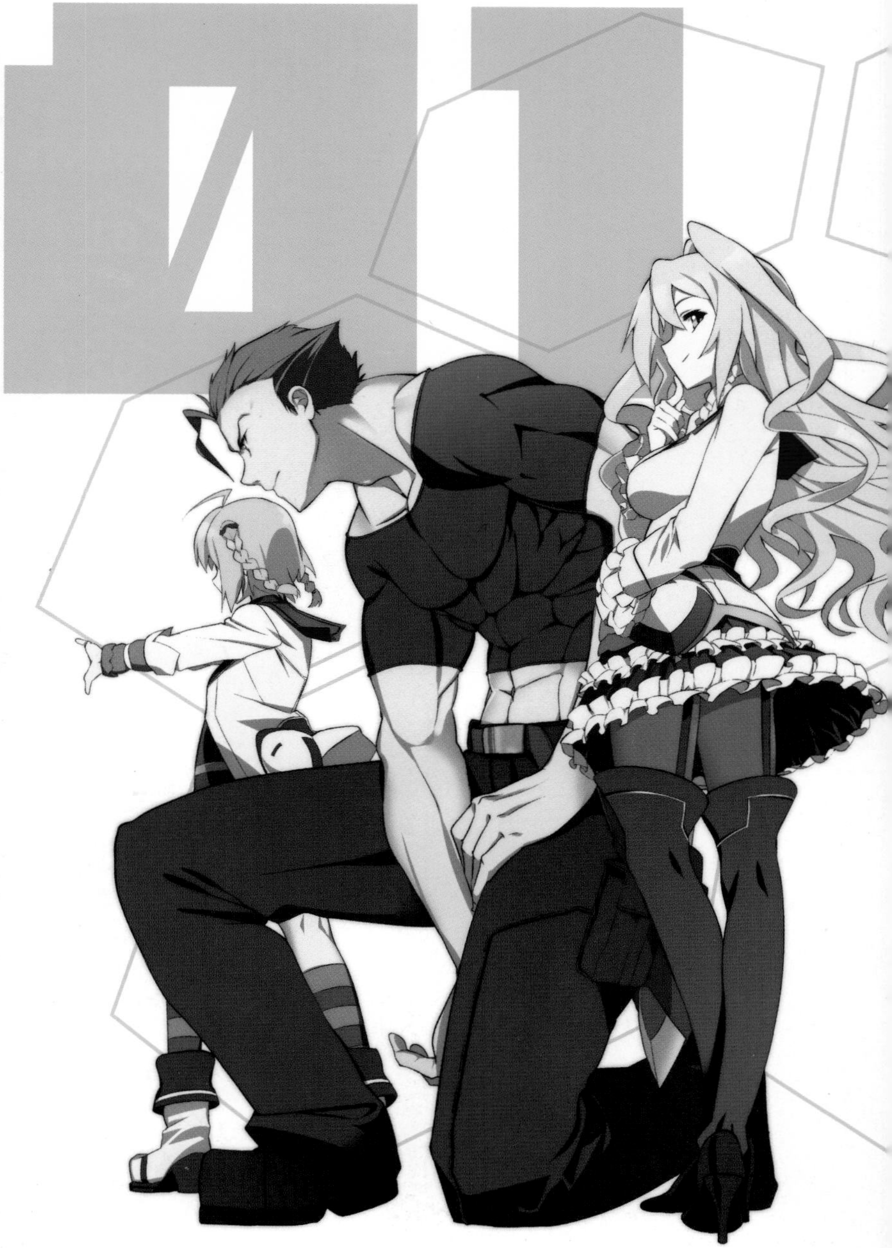

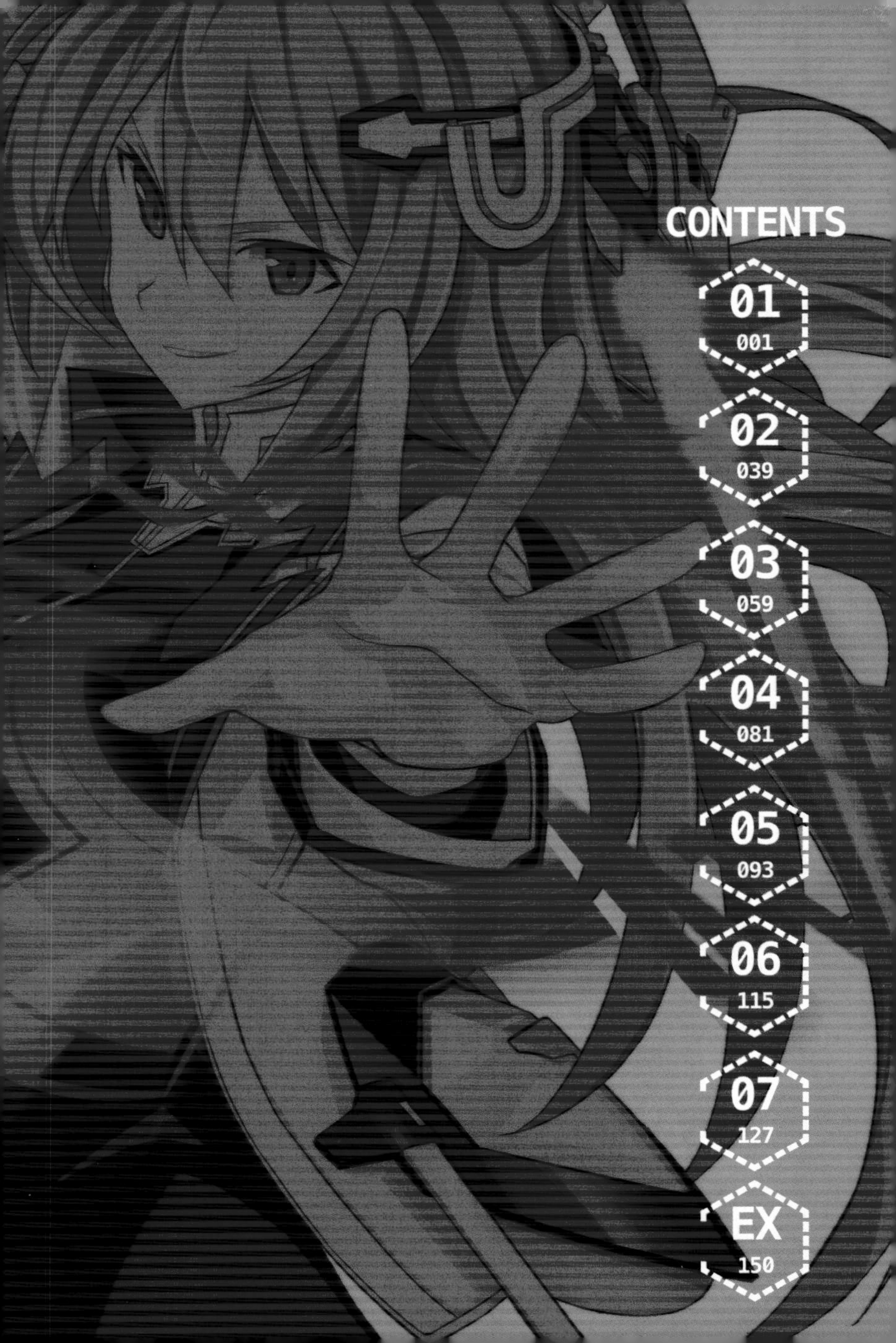

CONTENTS

THE ASTERISK WAR

01

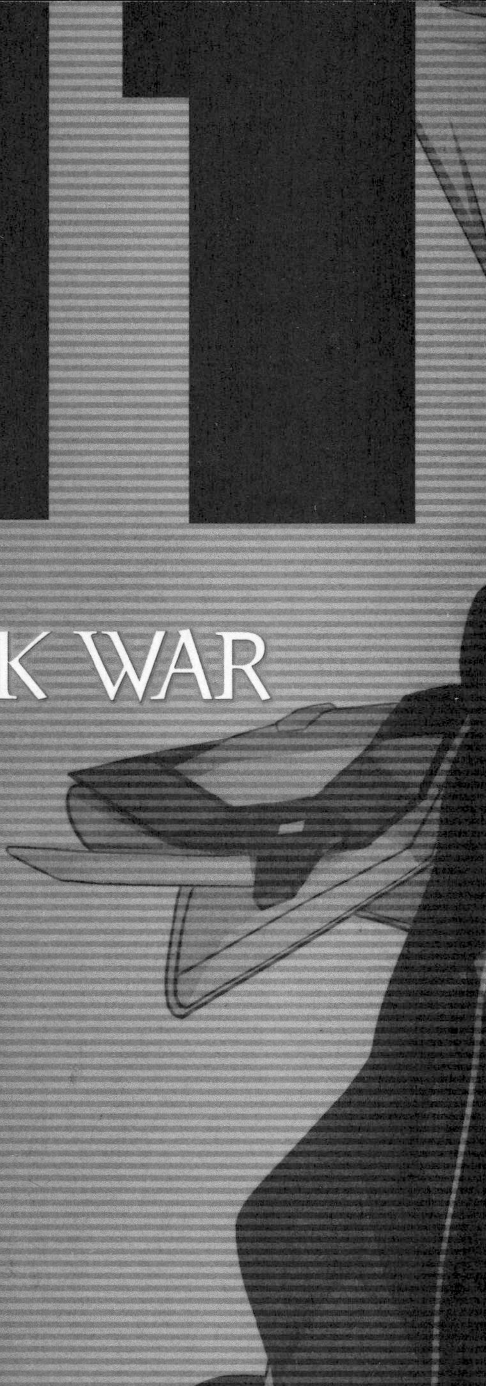

ART: **Ningen**
ORIGINAL STORY: **Yuu Miyazaki**
CHARACTER DESIGN: **okiura**

THE ASTERISK WAR

CHARACTERS

Ayato Amagiri

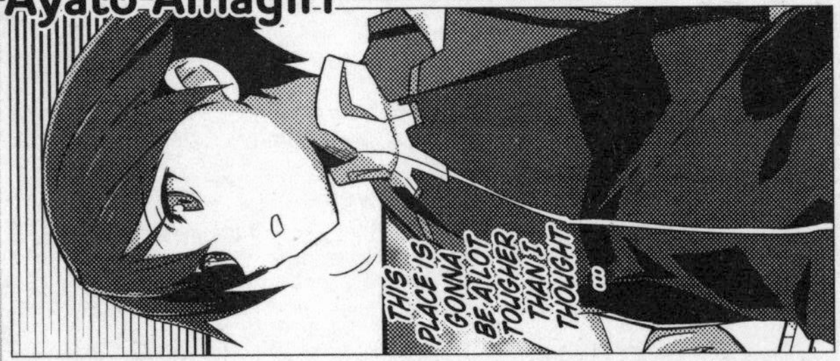
THIS PLACE IS GONNA BE A LOT TOUGHER THAN I THOUGHT...

Transferred into Seidoukan Academy High School on a special scholarship. A skilled swordsman who has been training since he was small in his family's Amagiri Shinmei Sword Style.

Saya Sasamiya

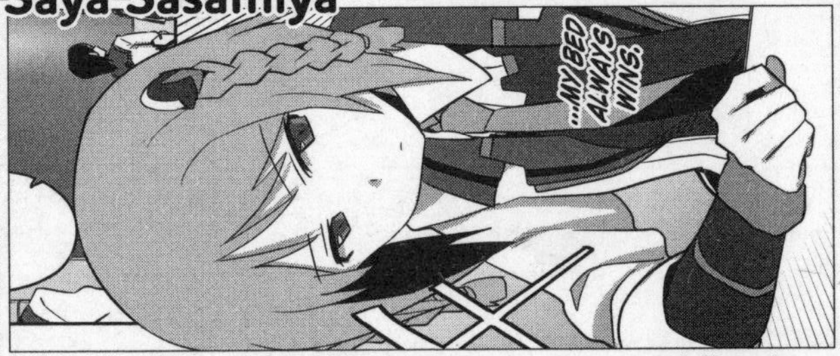
...MY BED ALWAYS WINS.

In the same grade as Ayato. They've known each other since they were small. Always sleepy due to bad circulation. At the request of her father, a scientist in meteoric engineering, she came to Asterisk to advertise the gun he invented. A firm believer that bigger is better when it comes to firearms, and an expert in the subject.

Julis-Alexia von Riessfeld

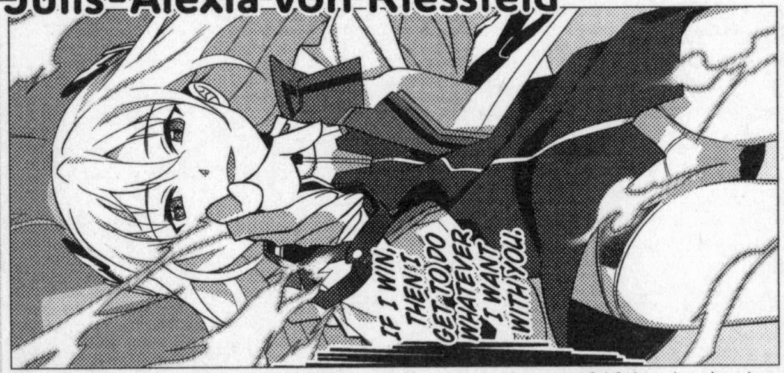
IF I WIN, THEN I GET TO DO WHATEVER I WANT WITH YOU.

A Page One student, ranked fifth at Seidoukan Academy, and a powerful fighter bearing the epithet "Glűhen Rose—Witch of the Resplendent Flames." Proud and short-tempered, but also conscientious and kind.

Claudia Enfield

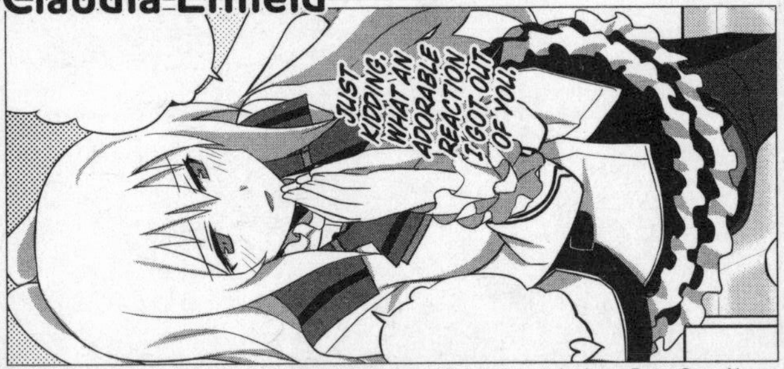
JUST KIDDING. WHAT AN ADORABLE REACTION I GOT OUT OF YOU.

President of the Seidoukan Academy Student Council and also ranked as a Page One. Always smiling, gentle, and polite—but describes herself as blackhearted.

THE WORLD OF ASTERISK

Rikka: the Academy City on the Water

A city that floats on the surface of the North Kanto crater lake, surrounded by six schools. Its hexagonal shape earned it the nickname Asterisk.

Seidoukan Academy

The school our main characters attend, ranked fifth in Asterisk. Seidoukan used to dominate in all three Festa events but has recently been in a slump. A campus culture that emphasizes students' independence attracts many Dantes and Stregas as students.

Queenvale Academy for Young Ladies

The only all-girls' school, Queenvale is consistently ranked last, and the matriculation requirement of "good looks" makes it an odd sort of academy. Their beauty is on a level with top-class idols, and despite the rankings, they have plenty of fans, even from other schools.

St. Gallardworth Academy

One of the top-ranking schools ever since its founding, Gallardworth also boasts the most overall victories in Asterisk. The rigid culture there values discipline and loyalty above all else, and in principle, even duels are forbidden. They are on poor terms with Le Wolfe.

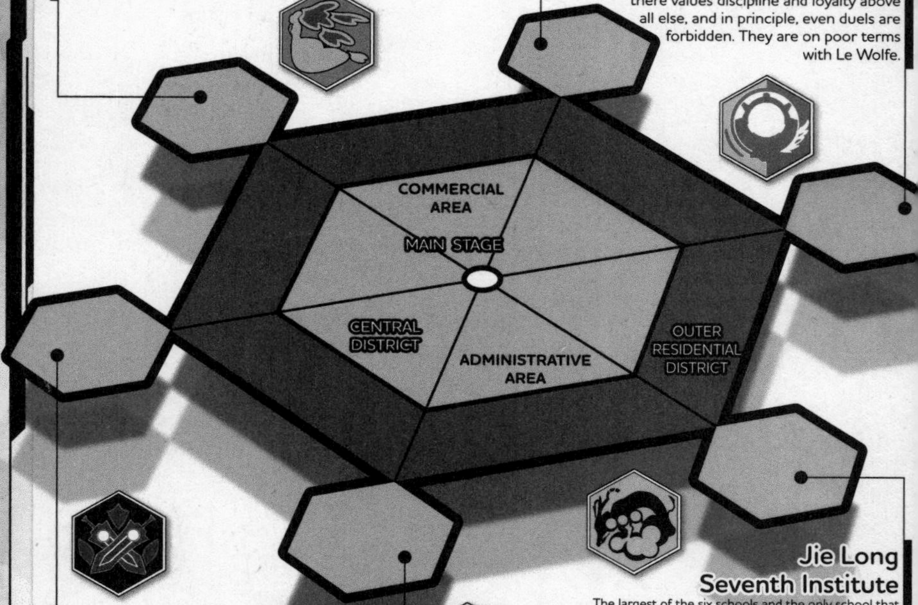
COMMERCIAL AREA
MAIN STAGE
CENTRAL DISTRICT
ADMINISTRATIVE AREA
OUTER RESIDENTIAL DISTRICT

Jie Long Seventh Institute

The largest of the six schools and the only school that has never once fallen to last place in the overall rankings. Bureaucracy clashes with a laissez-faire attitude, making the school culture rather chaotic. The atmosphere has strong Far Eastern leanings, and they boast their own martial art technique known as Star Xianshu.

Le Wolfe Black Institute

Ferociously strong when it comes to one-on-one battles, Le Wolfe has a tremendously belligerent culture, to the point of encouraging duels with students from other schools. The place is practically lawless, and more than a few students end up in mercenary or criminal activity. Whenever there's commotion in the city, Le Wolfe students are likely to be involved.

Allekant Académie

Specializing in meteoric engineering, Allekant is the only one of the six schools with an actual research department. Their technological expertise shows in the quality of their Lux weapons, which far surpass those of the other schools. With a culture driven by results, they have rapidly progressed to the rank of second place in the last several years.

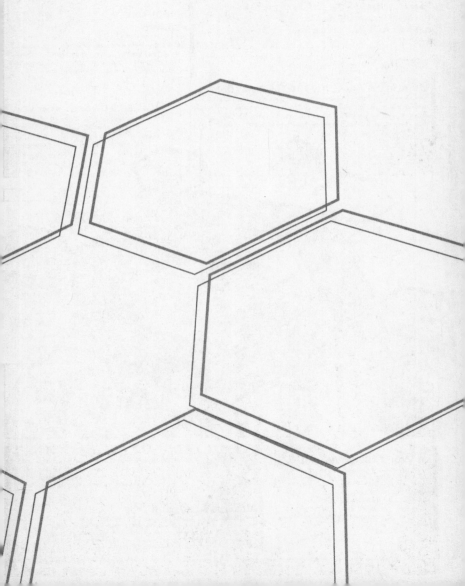

THE
ASTERISK WAR

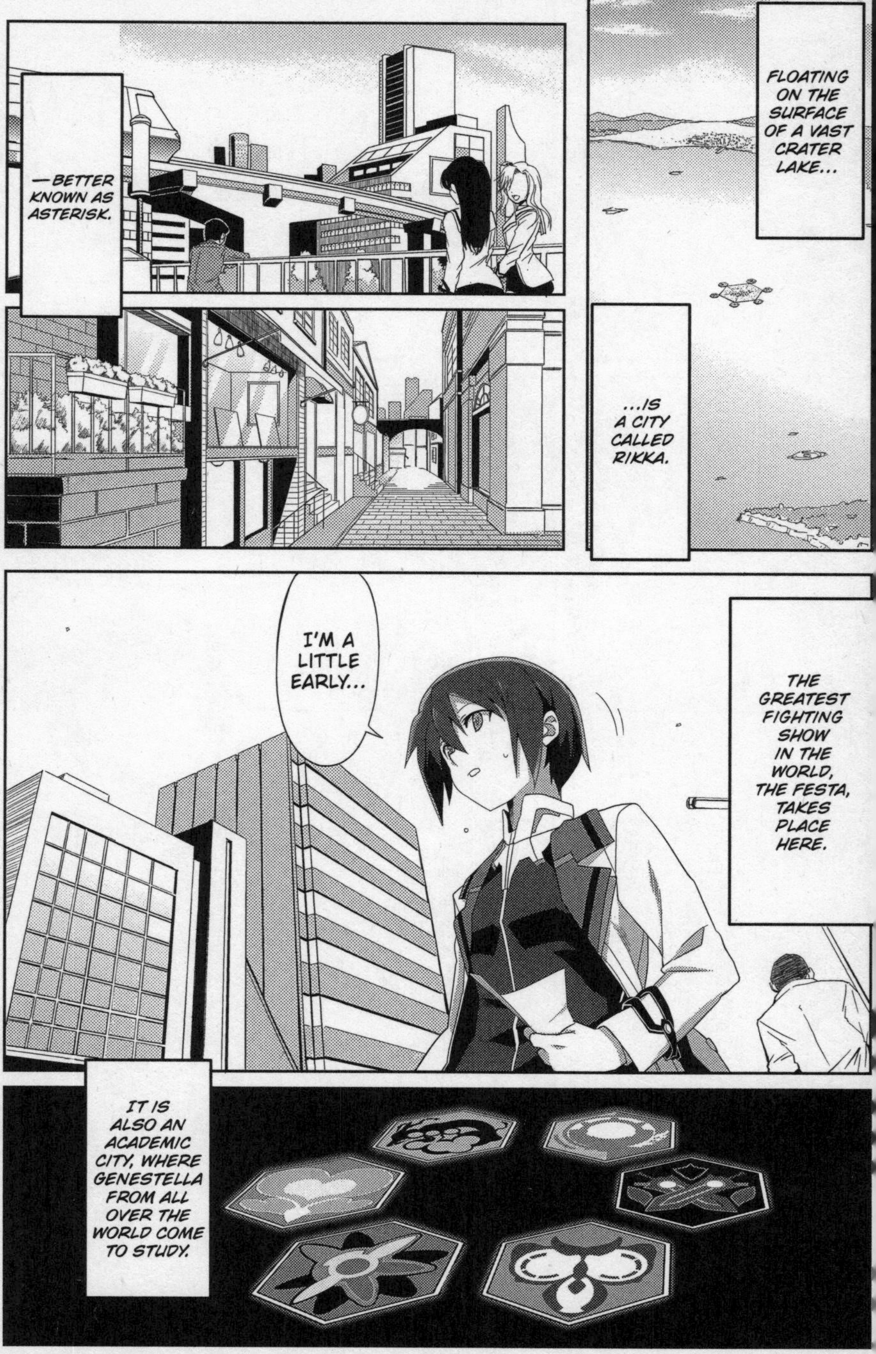

FLOATING ON THE SURFACE OF A VAST CRATER LAKE...
...IS A CITY CALLED RIKKA.
—BETTER KNOWN AS ASTERISK.
THE GREATEST FIGHTING SHOW IN THE WORLD, THE FESTA, TAKES PLACE HERE.
I'M A LITTLE EARLY...
IT IS ALSO AN ACADEMIC CITY, WHERE GENESTELLA FROM ALL OVER THE WORLD COME TO STUDY.

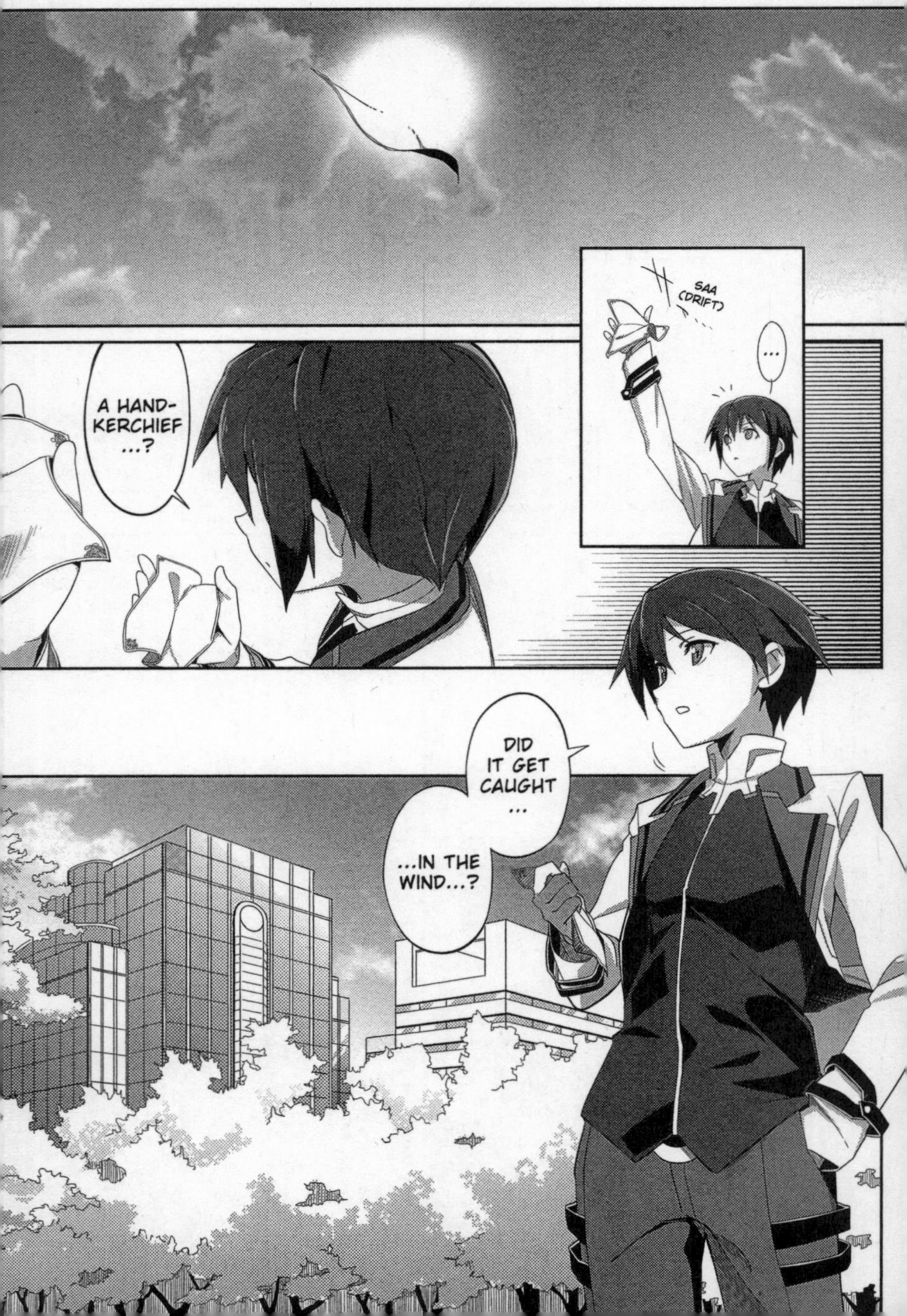
SAA (DRIFT)
...
A HAND-KERCHIEF ...?
DID IT GET CAUGHT ...
...IN THE WIND...?

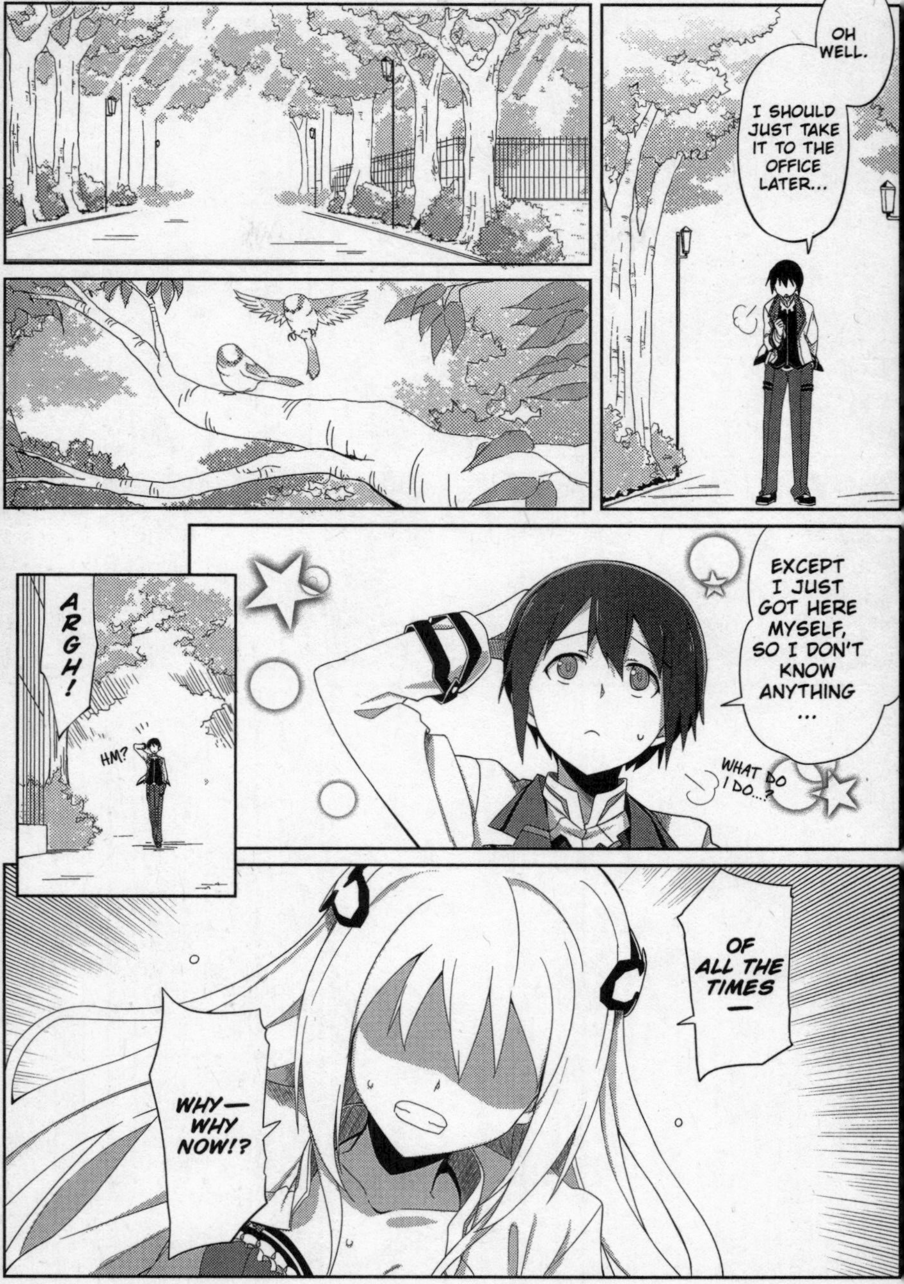
OH WELL.
I SHOULD JUST TAKE IT TO THE OFFICE LATER...
EXCEPT I JUST GOT HERE MYSELF, SO I DON'T KNOW ANYTHING ...
WHAT DO I DO...?
ARGH!
HM?
OF ALL THE TIMES —
WHY— WHY NOW!?

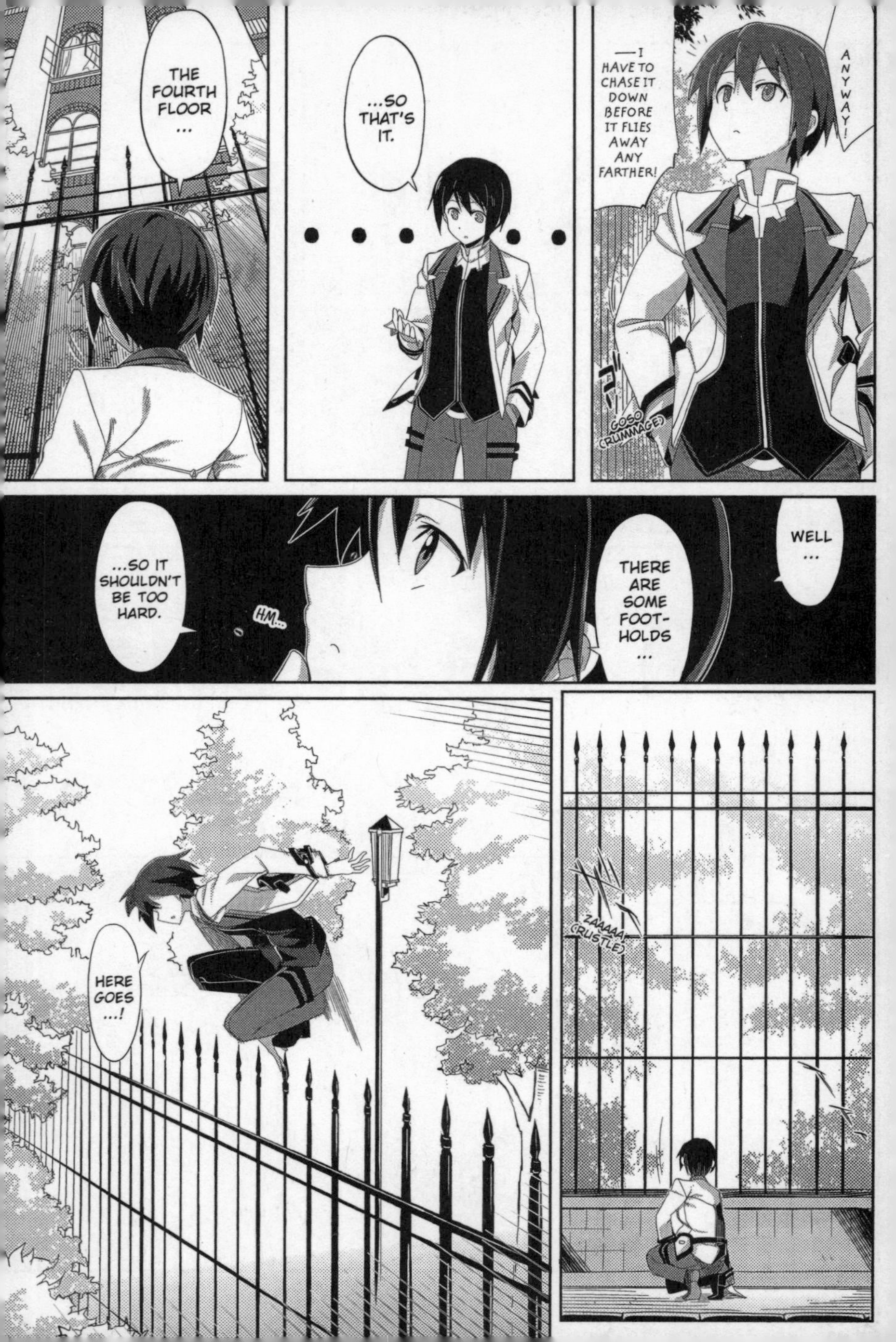
ANYWAY!
—I HAVE TO CHASE IT DOWN BEFORE IT FLIES AWAY ANY FARTHER!
GOSO (RUMMAGE)
...SO THAT'S IT.
THE FOURTH FLOOR ...
WELL ...
THERE ARE SOME FOOT-HOLDS ...
HM...
...SO IT SHOULDN'T BE TOO HARD.
ZAAAAA (RUSTLE)
HERE GOES ...!

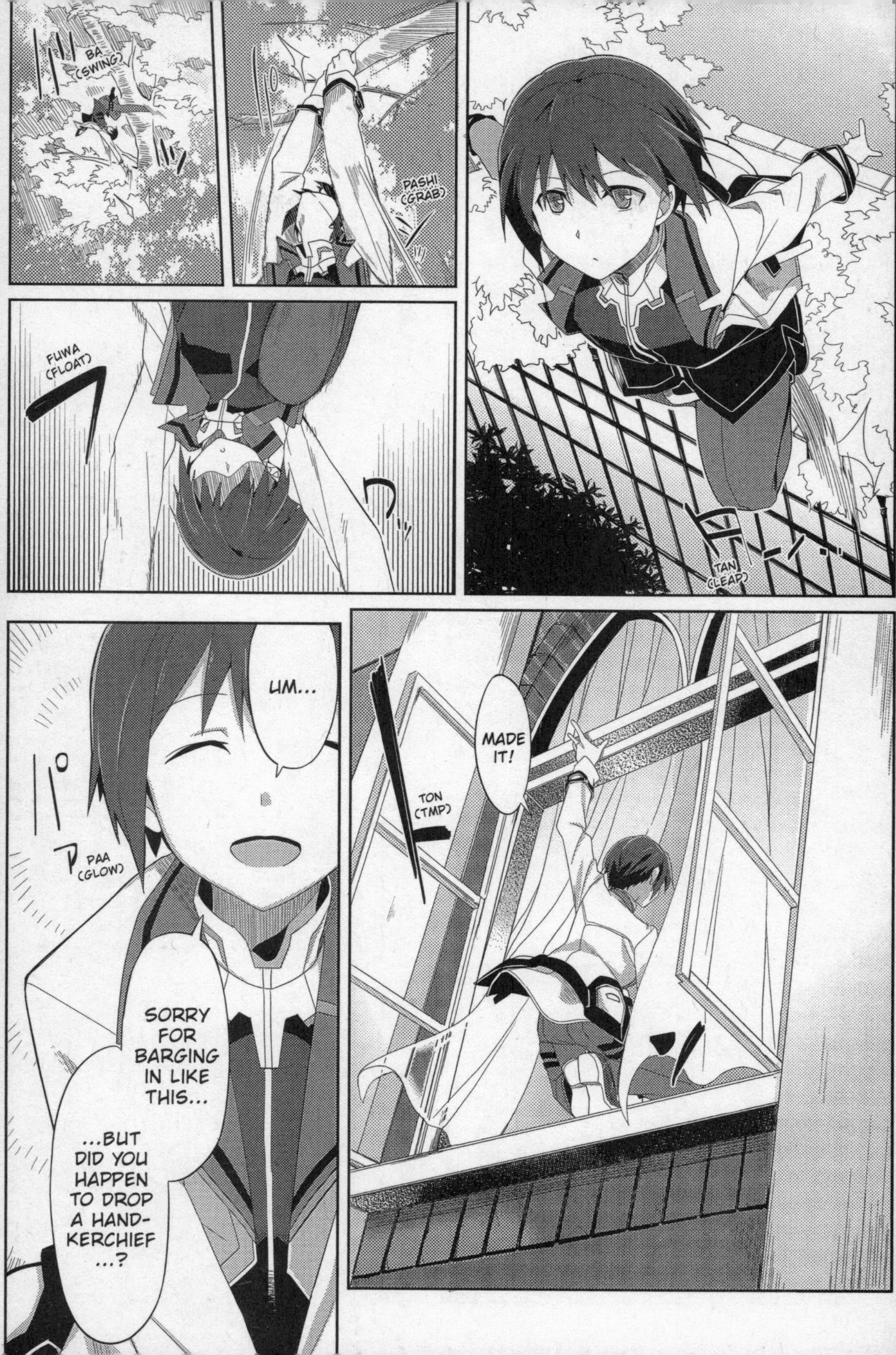
TAN (LEAP)
PASHI (GRAB)
BA (SWING)
FUWA (FLOAT)
MADE IT!
TON (TMP)
UM...
PAA (GLOW)
SORRY FOR BARGING IN LIKE THIS...
...BUT DID YOU HAPPEN TO DROP A HAND-KERCHIEF ...?

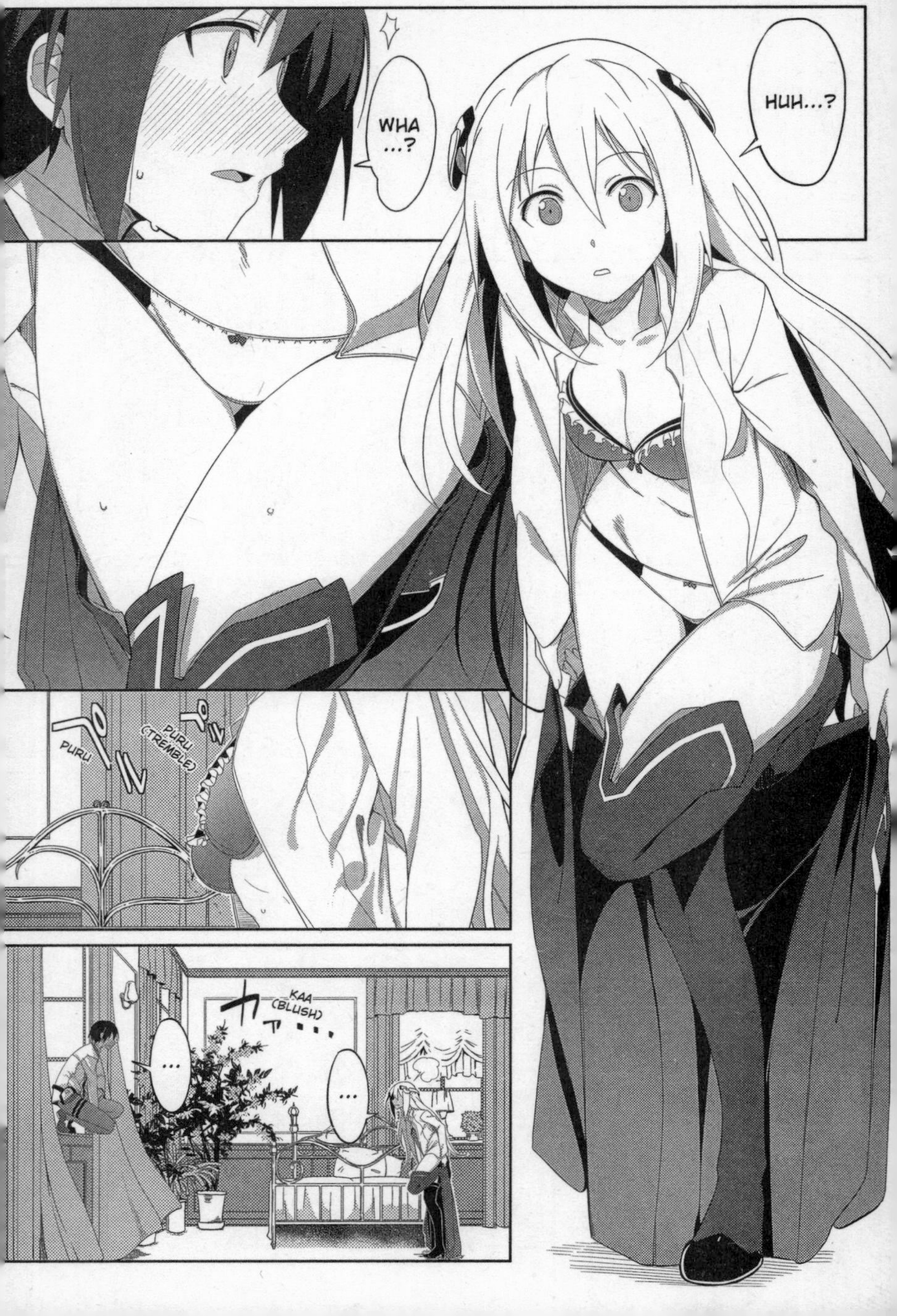
HUH...?
WHA ...?
PURU (TREMBLE)
PURU
KAA (BLUSH)
...
...

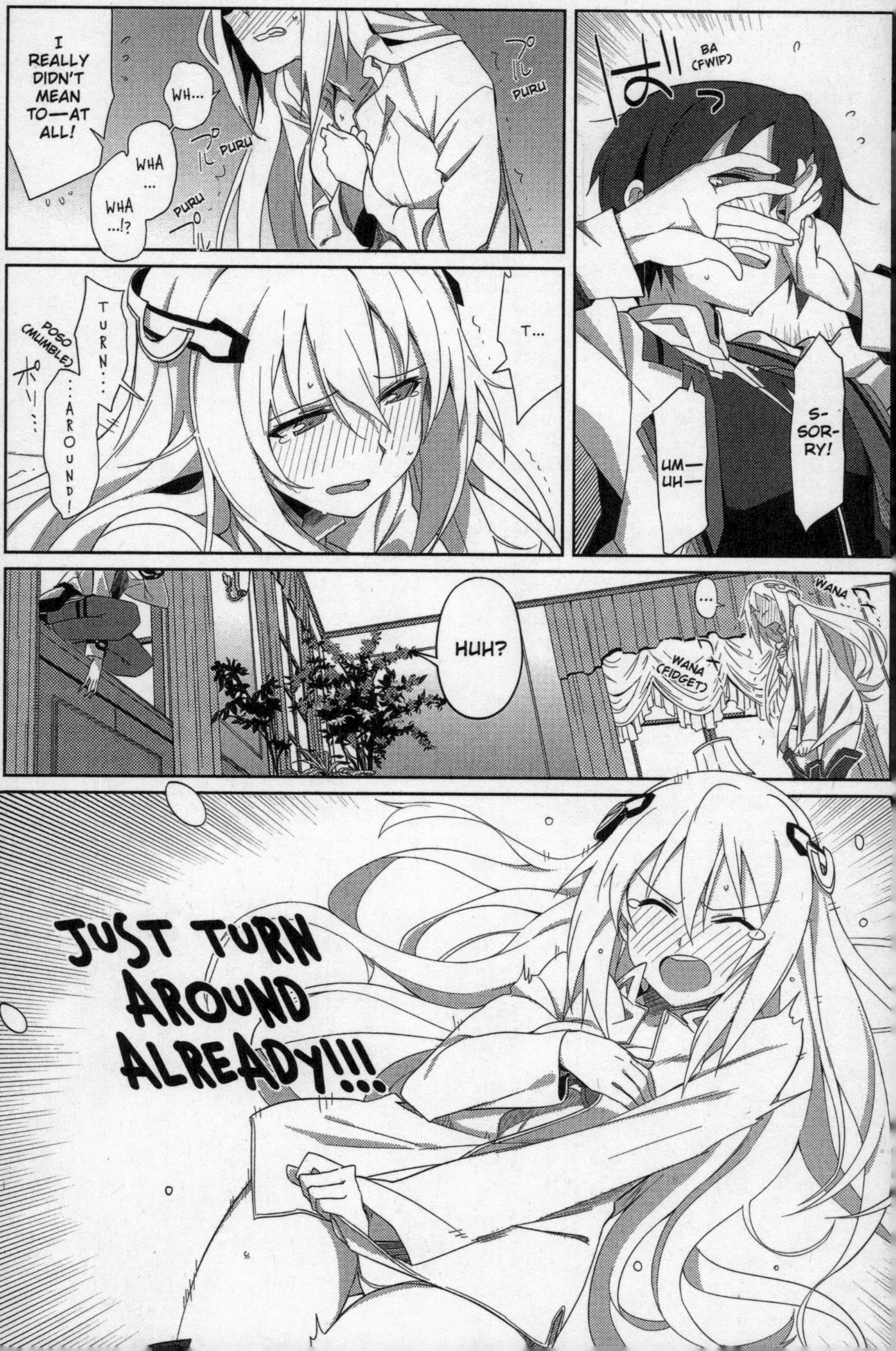
BA (FWIP)
S-SORRY!
UM— UH—
PURU
WH...
I REALLY DIDN'T MEAN TO—AT ALL!
PURU
WHA ... WHA ...!?
PURU
T...
TURN...
...AROUND!
POSO (MUMBLE)
WANA
...
WANA (FIDGET)
HUH?
JUST TURN AROUND ALREADY!!!

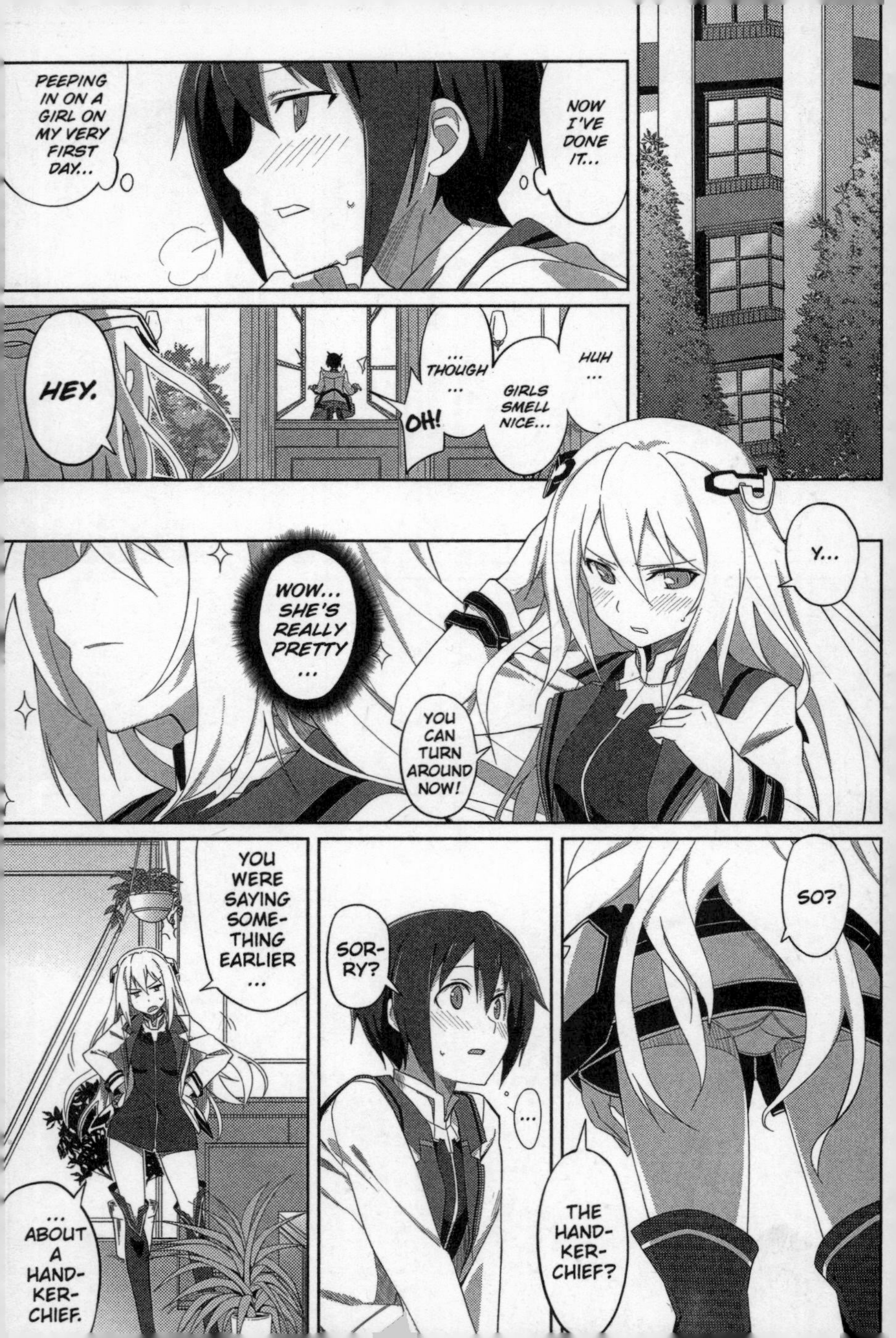
NOW I'VE DONE IT...
PEEPING IN ON A GIRL ON MY VERY FIRST DAY...
HUH ... GIRLS SMELL NICE...
... THOUGH ...
OH!
HEY.
Y...
YOU CAN TURN AROUND NOW!
WOW... SHE'S REALLY PRETTY ...
SO?
THE HAND-KER-CHIEF?
SOR-RY?
...
YOU WERE SAYING SOME-THING EARLIER ...
... ABOUT A HAND-KER-CHIEF.

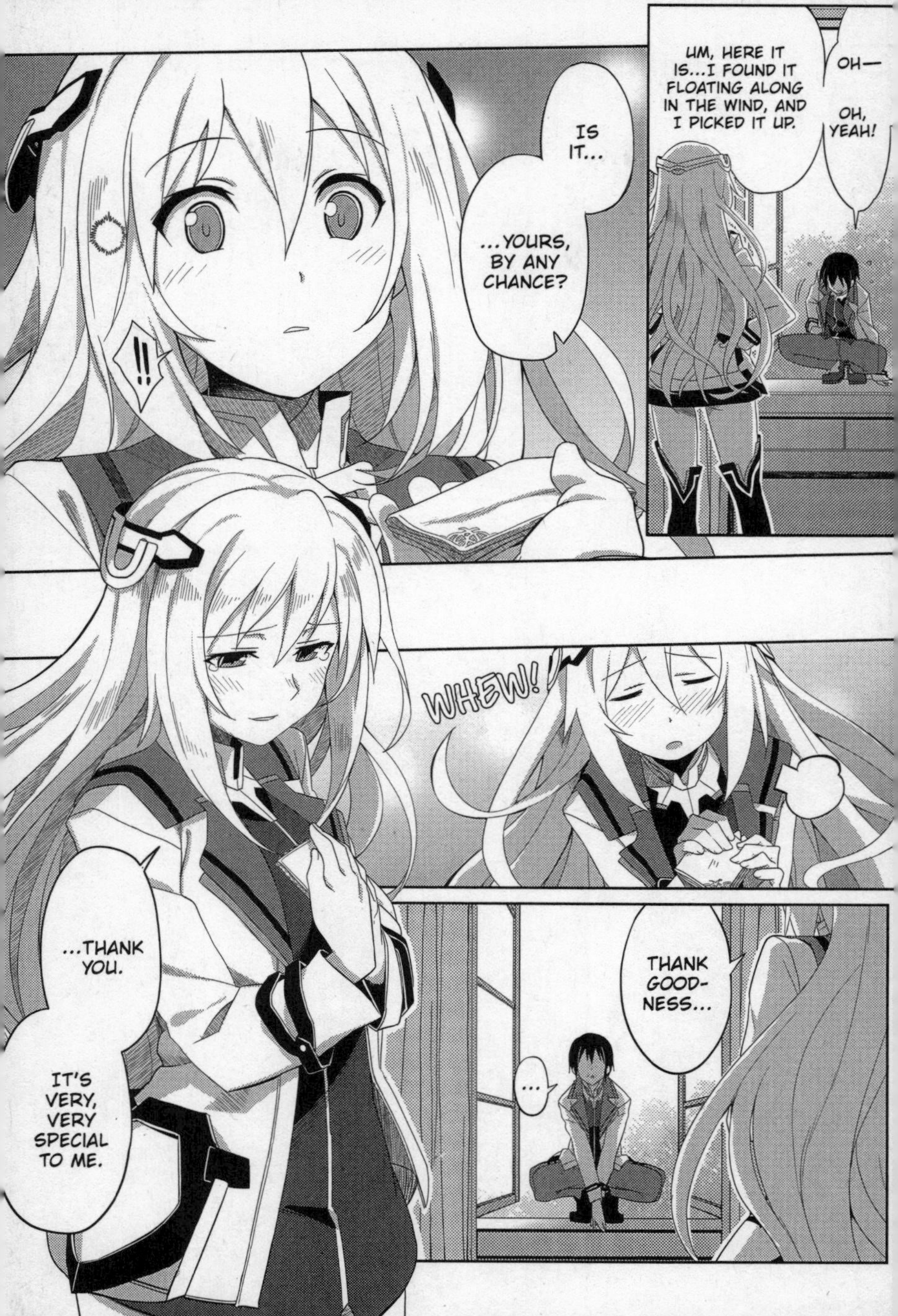
OH— OH, YEAH!
UM, HERE IT IS...I FOUND IT FLOATING ALONG IN THE WIND, AND I PICKED IT UP.
IS IT...
...YOURS, BY ANY CHANCE?
!!
WHEW!
THANK GOODNESS...
...
...THANK YOU.
IT'S VERY, VERY SPECIAL TO ME.

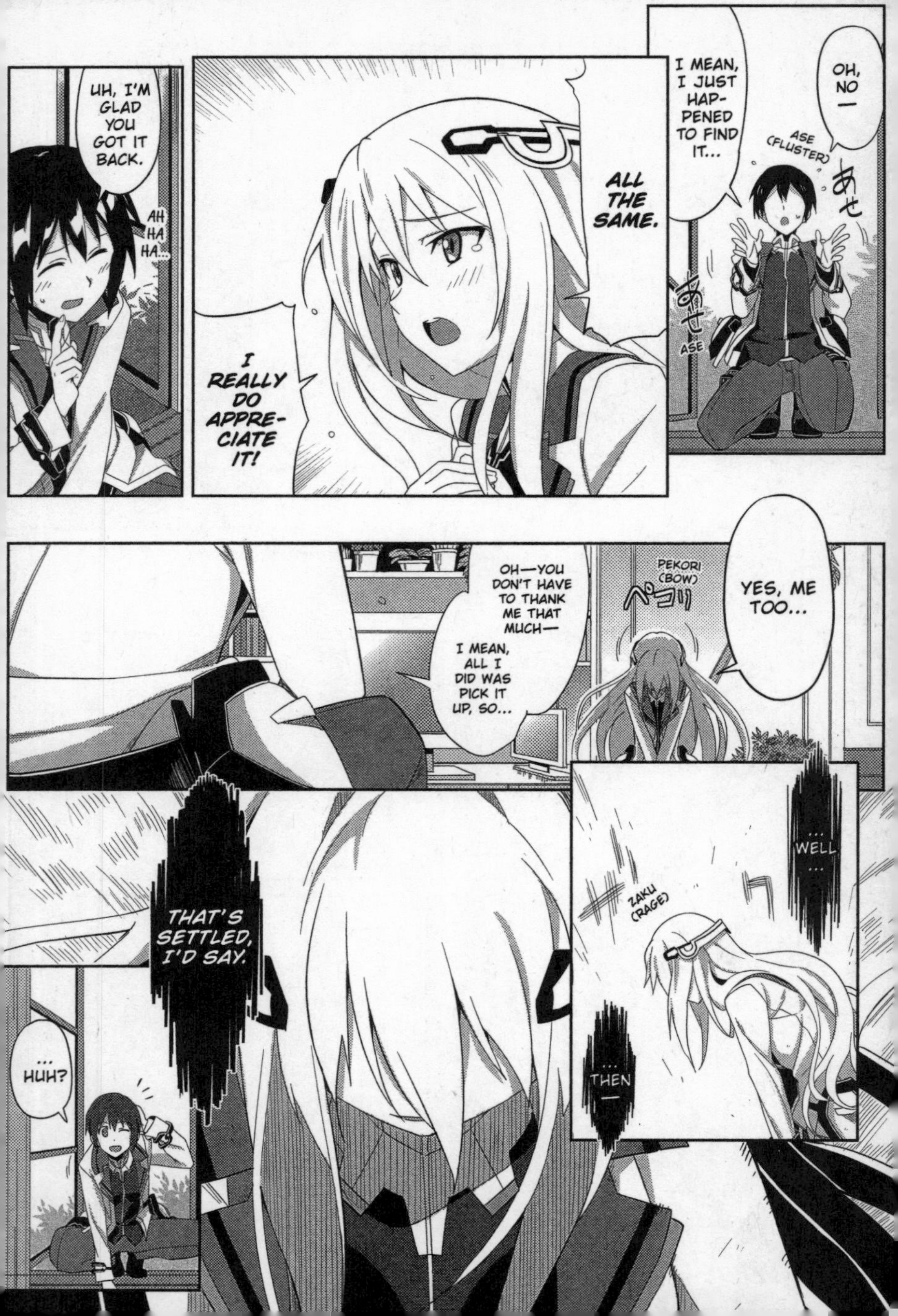
OH, NO—
I MEAN, I JUST HAP-PENED TO FIND IT...
ASE (FLUSTER)
あせ
あせ
ASE
ALL THE SAME.
I REALLY DO APPRE-CIATE IT!
UH, I'M GLAD YOU GOT IT BACK.
AH HA HA...
YES, ME TOO...
PEKORI (BOW)
ペコリ
OH—YOU DON'T HAVE TO THANK ME THAT MUCH—
I MEAN, ALL I DID WAS PICK IT UP, SO...
...WELL...
ZAKU (RAGE)
...THEN—
THAT'S SETTLED, I'D SAY.
...HUH?

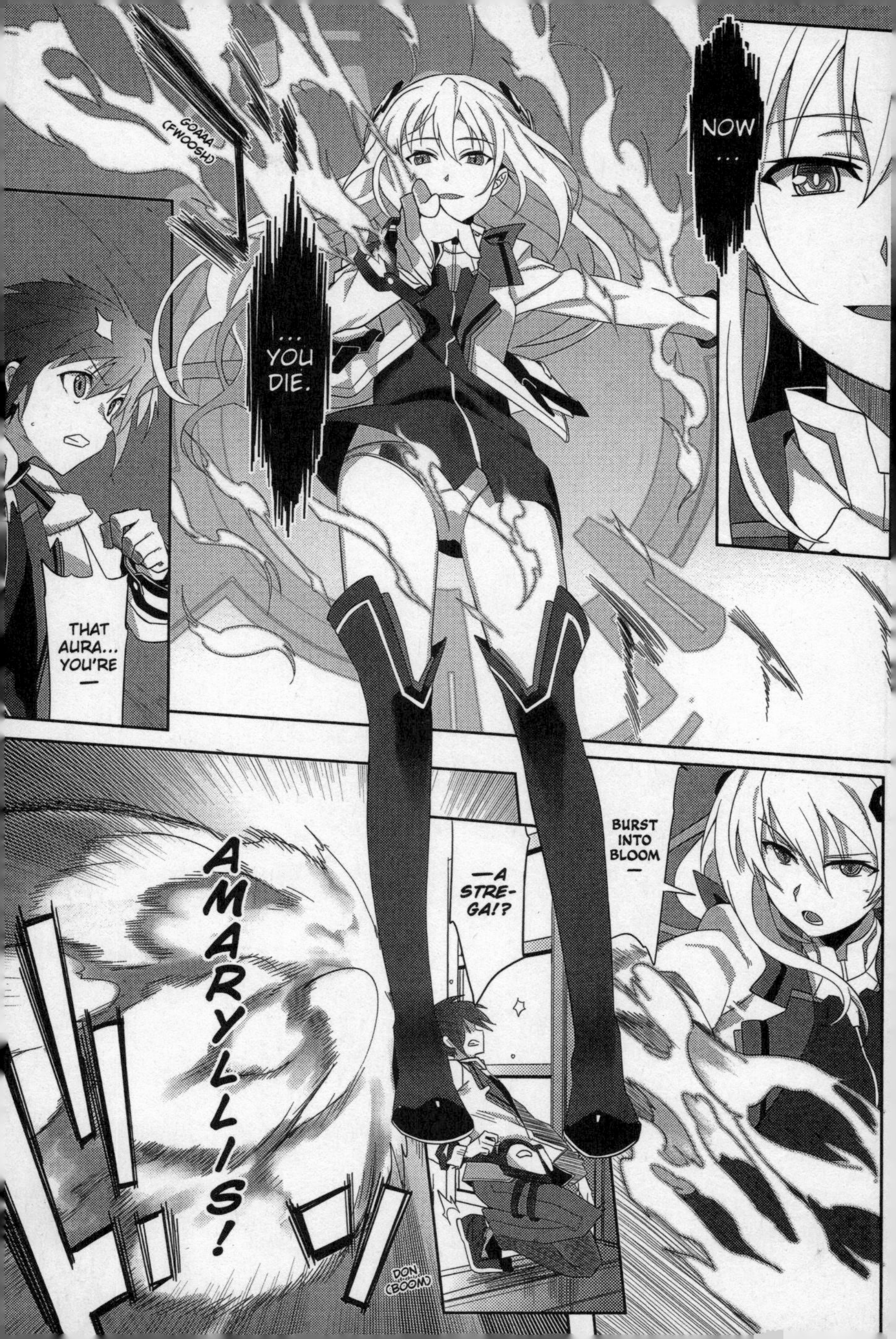
NOW ...
... YOU DIE.
GOAAA (FWOOSH)
THAT AURA... YOU'RE —
BURST INTO BLOOM —
—A STREGA!?
AMARYLLIS!
DON (BOOM)

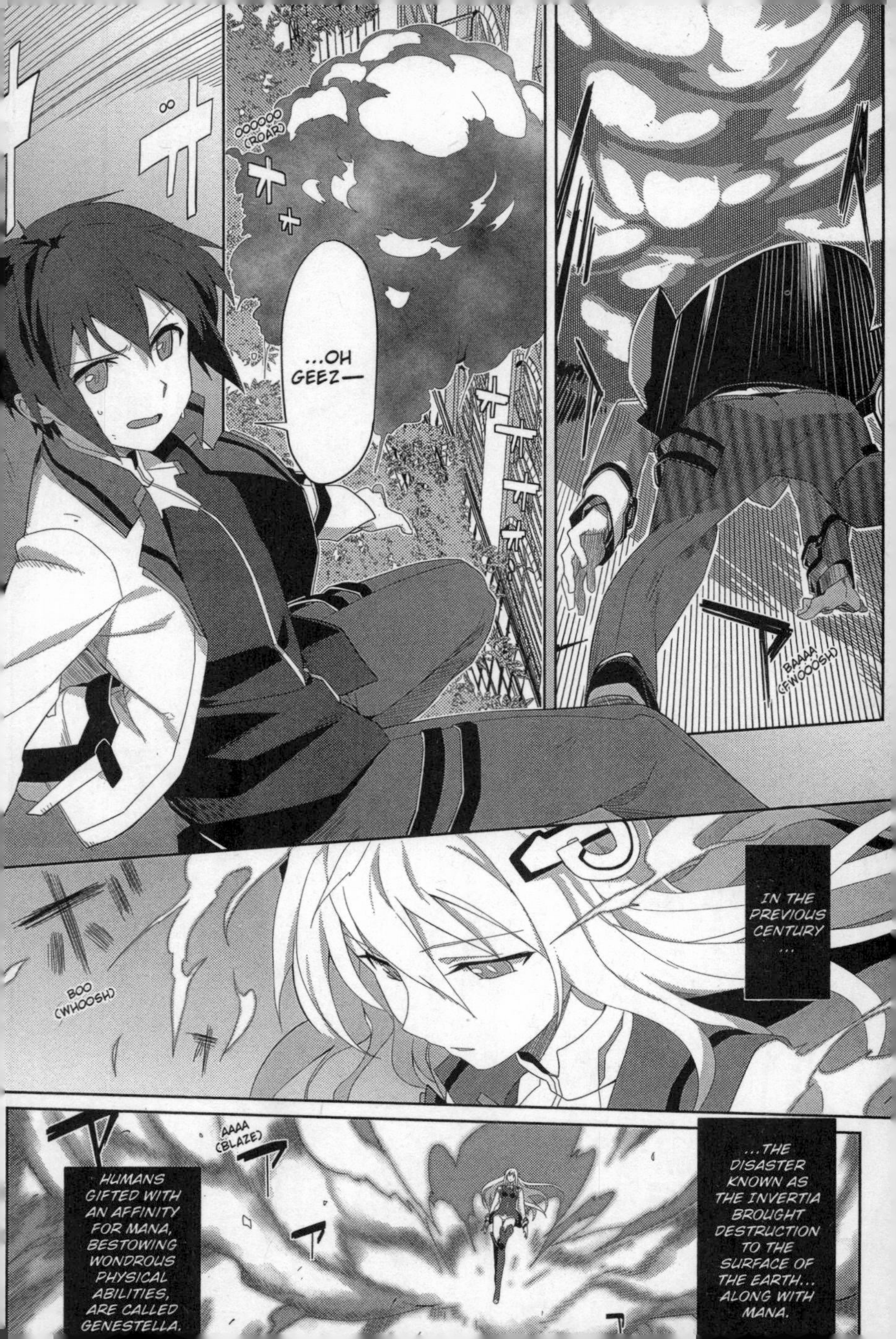
BAAAA (FWOOOSH)
OOOOOO (ROAR)
...OH GEEZ—
IN THE PREVIOUS CENTURY...
BOO (WHOOSH)
...THE DISASTER KNOWN AS THE INVERTIA BROUGHT DESTRUCTION TO THE SURFACE OF THE EARTH... ALONG WITH MANA.
AAAA (BLAZE)
HUMANS GIFTED WITH AN AFFINITY FOR MANA, BESTOWING WONDROUS PHYSICAL ABILITIES, ARE CALLED GENESTELLA.

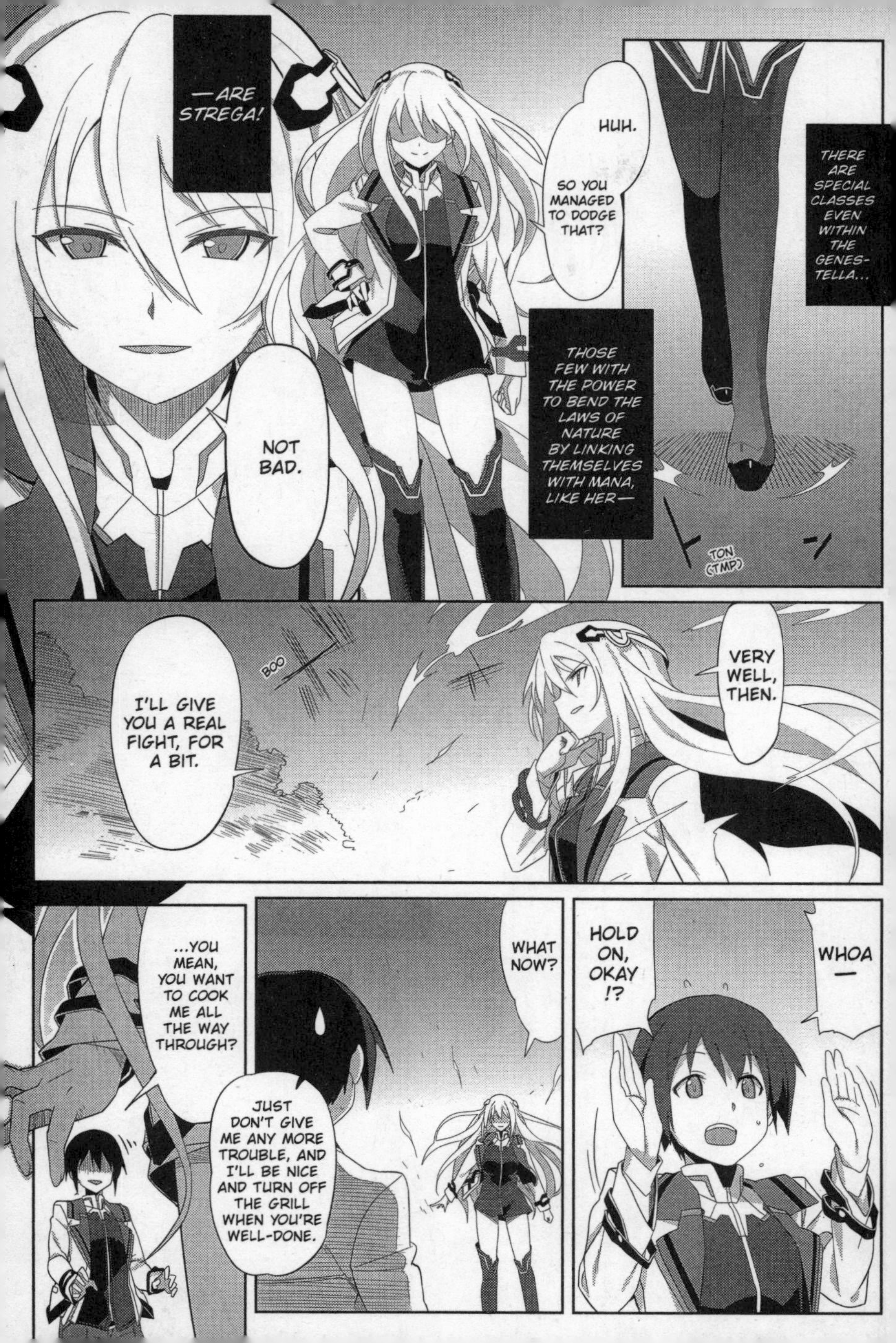

THERE ARE SPECIAL CLASSES EVEN WITHIN THE GENES-TELLA...
TON (TMP)
HUH.
SO YOU MANAGED TO DODGE THAT?
THOSE FEW WITH THE POWER TO BEND THE LAWS OF NATURE BY LINKING THEMSELVES WITH MANA, LIKE HER—
—ARE STREGA!
NOT BAD.
VERY WELL, THEN.
BOO
I'LL GIVE YOU A REAL FIGHT, FOR A BIT.
WHOA—
HOLD ON, OKAY!?
WHAT NOW?
JUST DON'T GIVE ME ANY MORE TROUBLE, AND I'LL BE NICE AND TURN OFF THE GRILL WHEN YOU'RE WELL-DONE.
...YOU MEAN, YOU WANT TO COOK ME ALL THE WAY THROUGH?

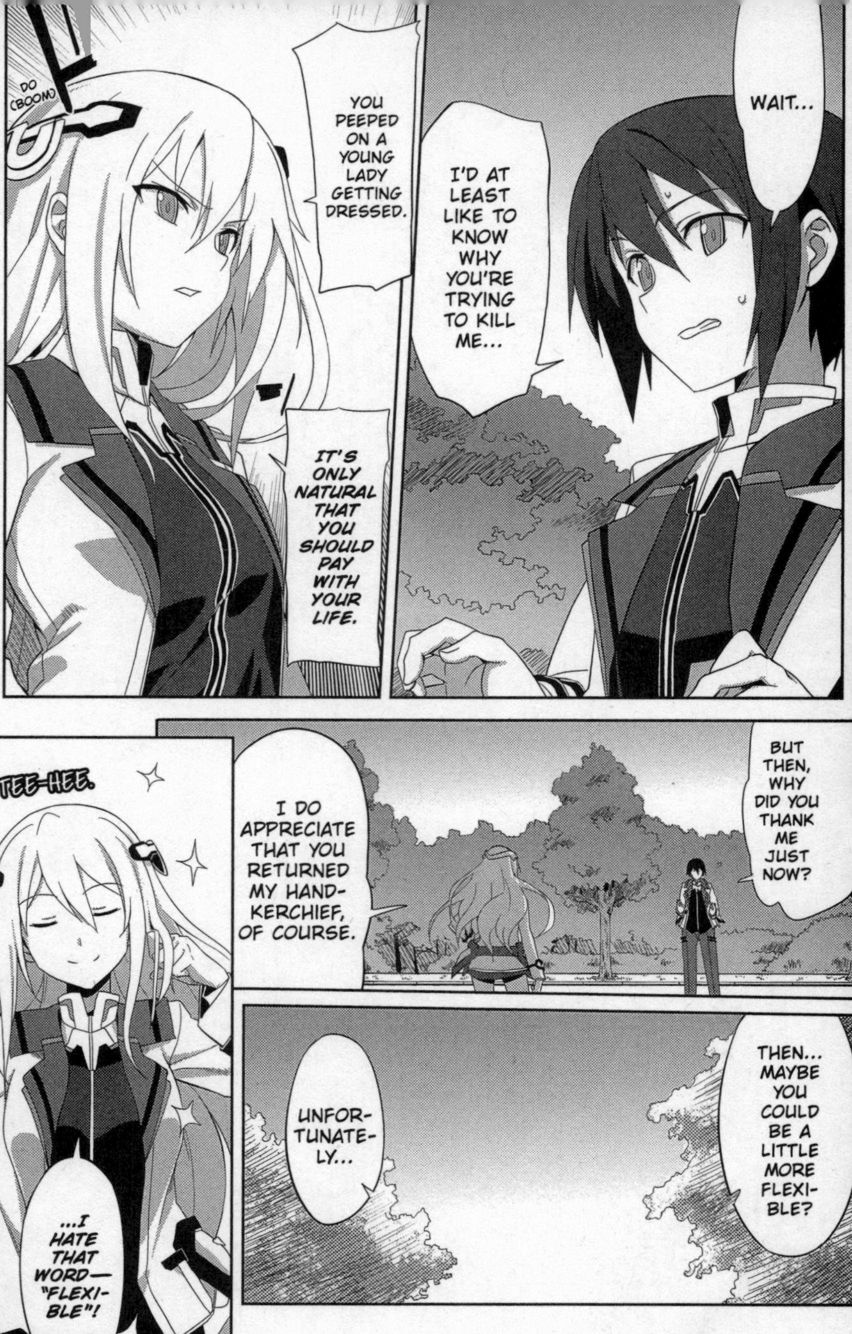
WAIT...
I'D AT LEAST LIKE TO KNOW WHY YOU'RE TRYING TO KILL ME...
DO (BOOM)
YOU PEEPED ON A YOUNG LADY GETTING DRESSED.
IT'S ONLY NATURAL THAT YOU SHOULD PAY WITH YOUR LIFE.
BUT THEN, WHY DID YOU THANK ME JUST NOW?
I DO APPRECIATE THAT YOU RETURNED MY HANDKERCHIEF, OF COURSE.
THEN... MAYBE YOU COULD BE A LITTLE MORE FLEXIBLE?
UNFORTUNATELY...
TEE-HEE.
...I HATE THAT WORD—"FLEXIBLE"!

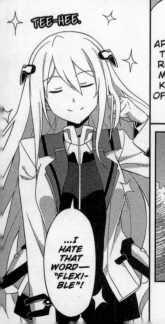

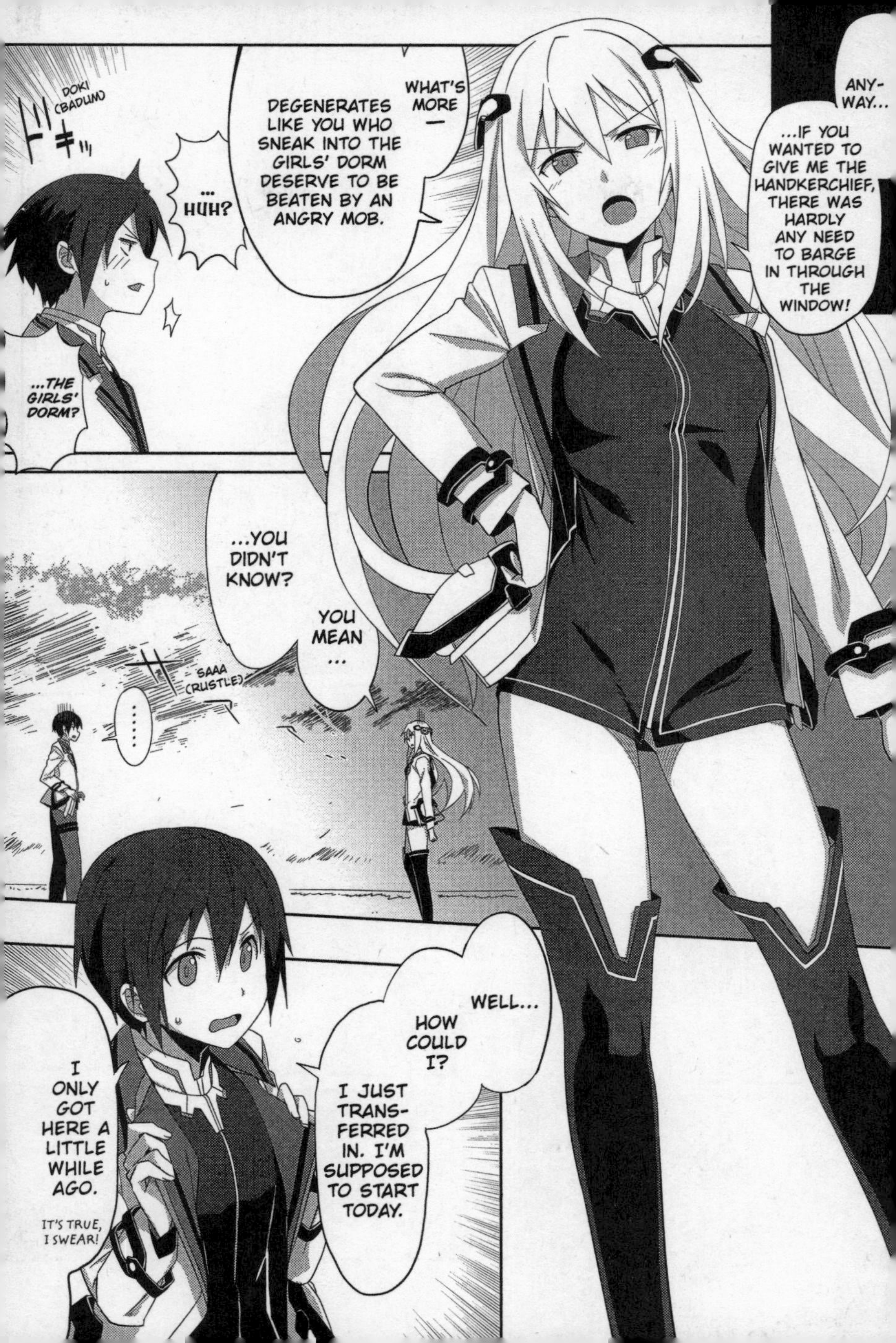
ANY-WAY...
...IF YOU WANTED TO GIVE ME THE HANDKERCHIEF, THERE WAS HARDLY ANY NEED TO BARGE IN THROUGH THE WINDOW!
WHAT'S MORE —
DEGENERATES LIKE YOU WHO SNEAK INTO THE GIRLS' DORM DESERVE TO BE BEATEN BY AN ANGRY MOB.
ドキッ
DOKI (BADUM)
...HUH?
...THE GIRLS' DORM?
...YOU DIDN'T KNOW?
YOU MEAN ...
SAAA (RUSTLE)
......
WELL...
HOW COULD I?
I JUST TRANSFERRED IN. I'M SUPPOSED TO START TODAY.
I ONLY GOT HERE A LITTLE WHILE AGO.
IT'S TRUE, I SWEAR!

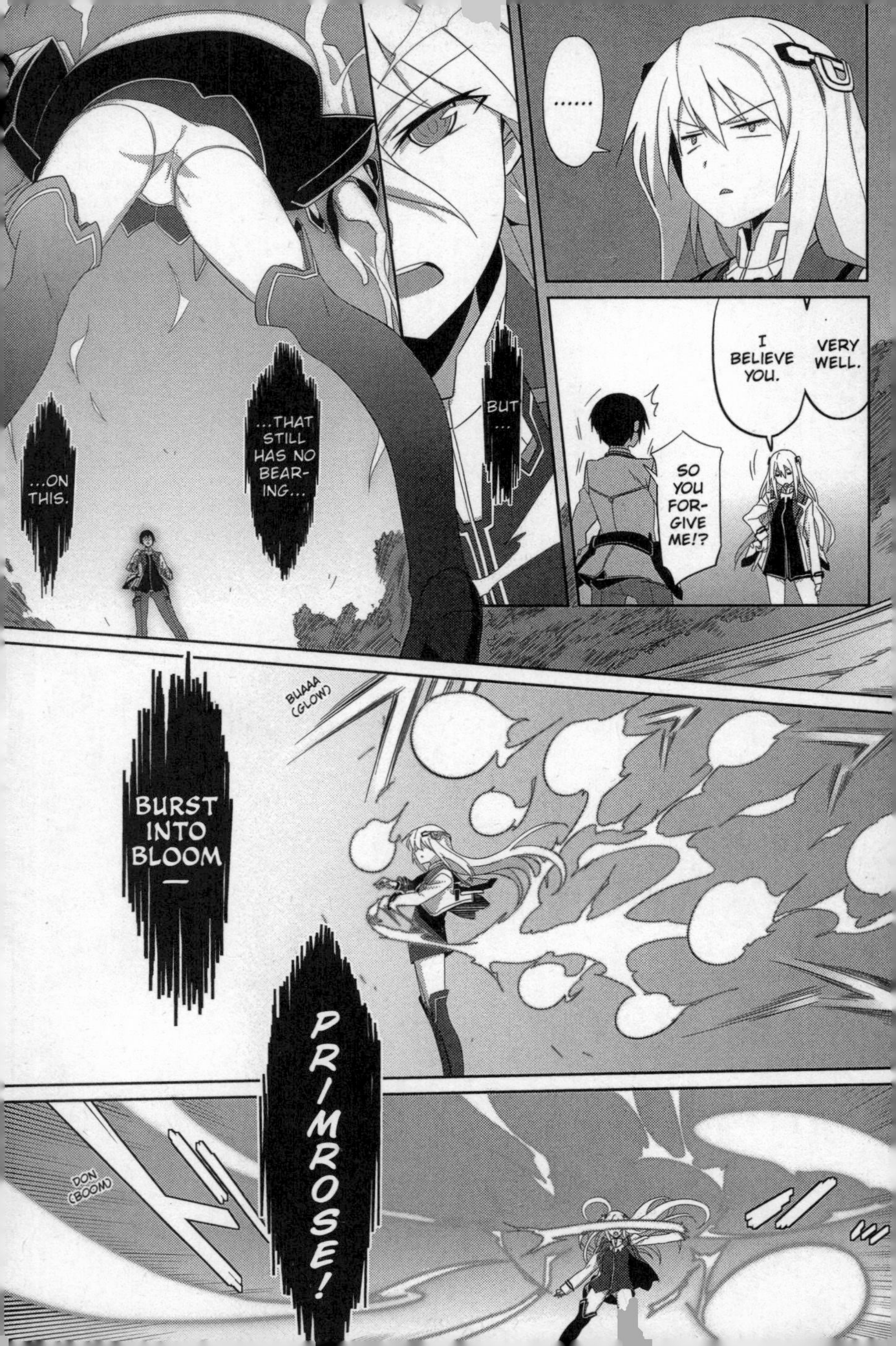
......
VERY WELL.
I BELIEVE YOU.
SO YOU FORGIVE ME!?
BUT...
...THAT STILL HAS NO BEARING...
...ON THIS.
BUAAA (GLOW)
BURST INTO BLOOM —
PRIMROSE!
DON (BOOM)

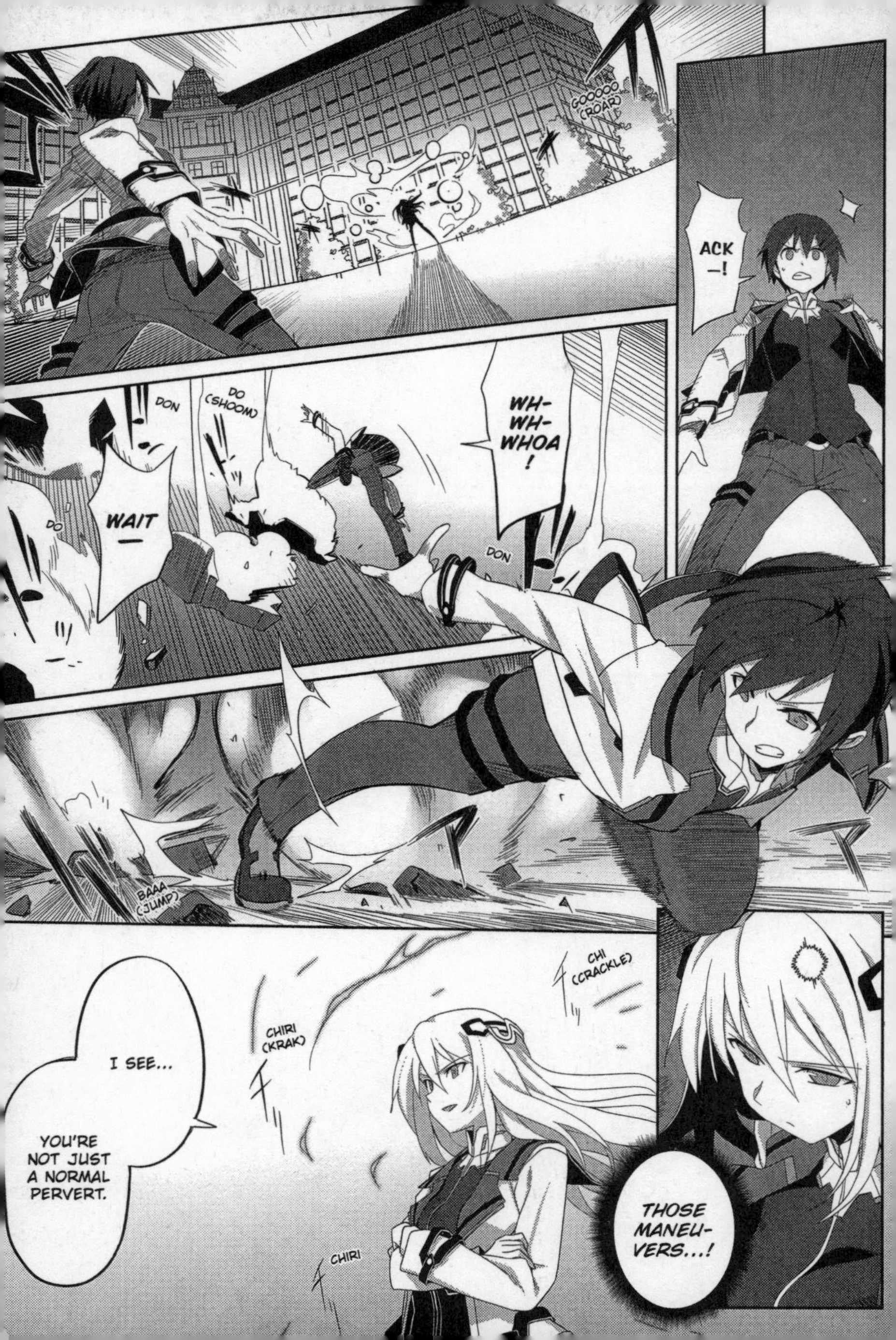
ACK —!
GOOOOO (ROAR)
WH-WH-WHOA!
DO (SHOOM)
DON
DON
WAIT —
DO
BAAA (JUMP)
CHI (CRACKLE)
THOSE MANEUVERS...!
CHIRI (KRAK)
I SEE...
YOU'RE NOT JUST A NORMAL PERVERT.
CHIRI

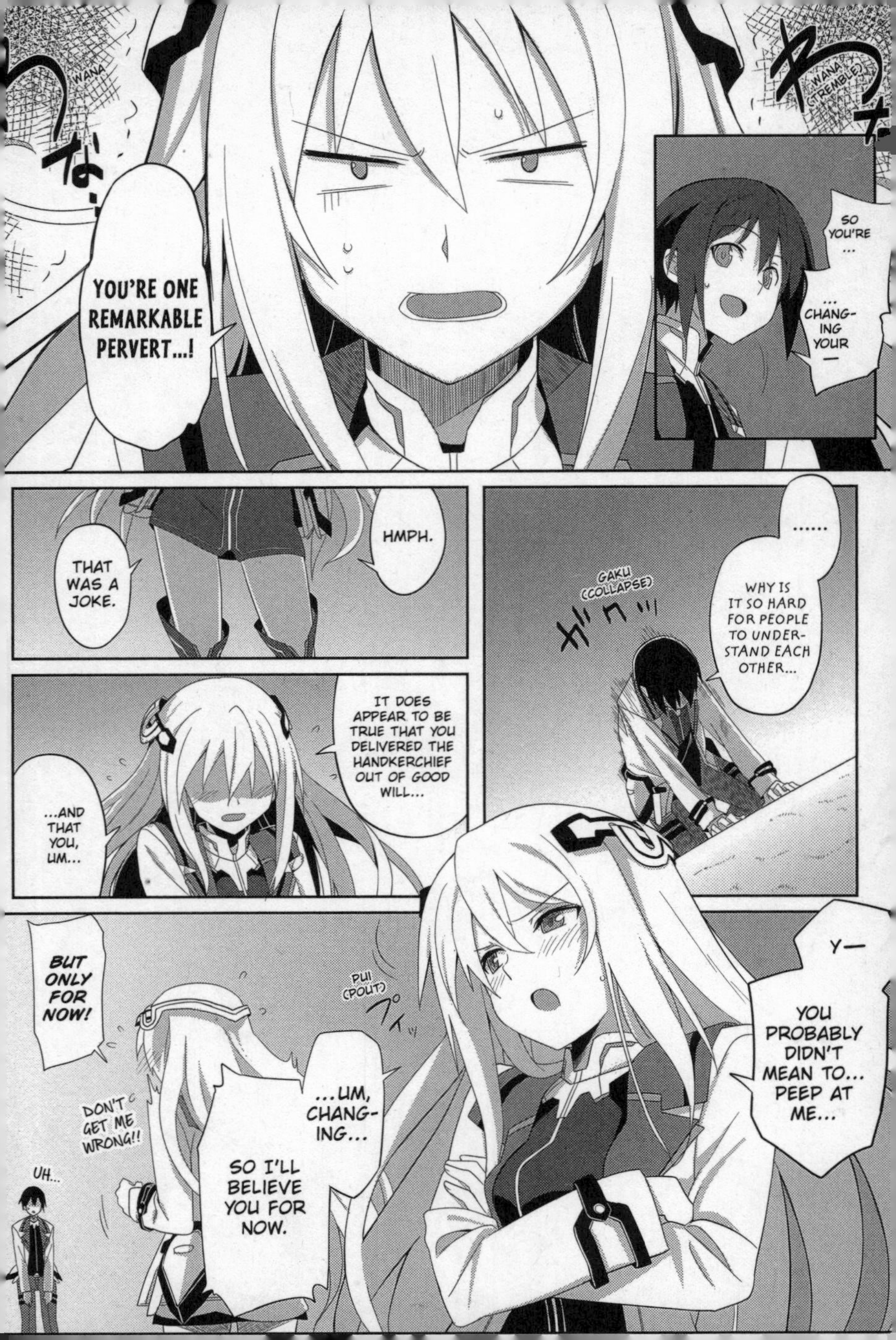
WANA (TREMBLE)
SO YOU'RE ...
... CHANG-ING YOUR —
WANA
YOU'RE ONE REMARKABLE PERVERT...!
......
GAKU (COLLAPSE)
WHY IS IT SO HARD FOR PEOPLE TO UNDER-STAND EACH OTHER...
HMPH.
THAT WAS A JOKE.
IT DOES APPEAR TO BE TRUE THAT YOU DELIVERED THE HANDKERCHIEF OUT OF GOOD WILL...
...AND THAT YOU, UM...
Y—
YOU PROBABLY DIDN'T MEAN TO... PEEP AT ME...
...UM, CHANG-ING...
SO I'LL BELIEVE YOU FOR NOW.
PUI (POUT)
BUT ONLY FOR NOW!
DON'T GET ME WRONG!!
UH...

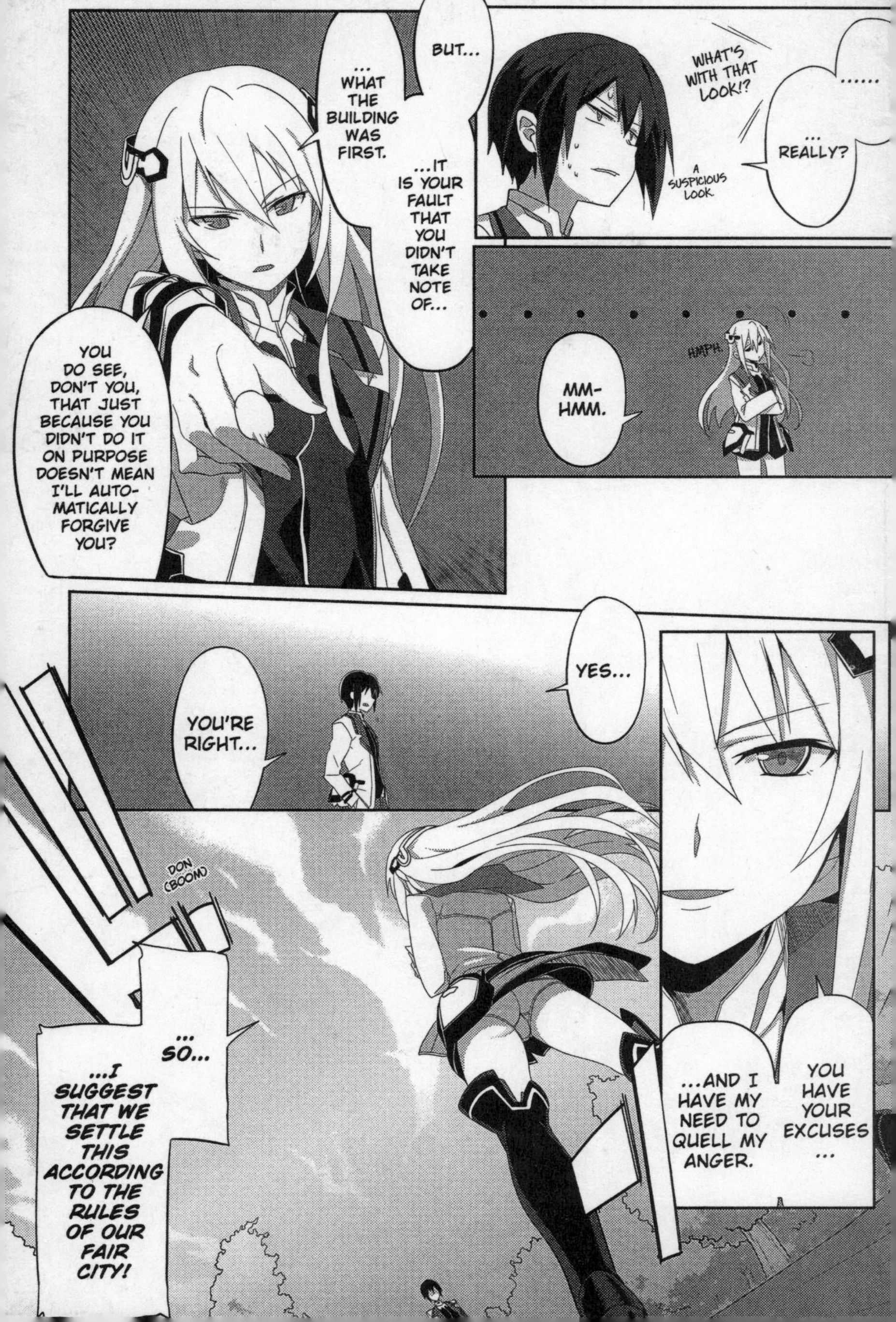
......
... REALLY?
WHAT'S WITH THAT LOOK!?
A SUSPICIOUS LOOK
HMPH.
MM-HMM.
BUT...
... WHAT THE BUILDING WAS FIRST.
...IT IS YOUR FAULT THAT YOU DIDN'T TAKE NOTE OF...
YOU DO SEE, DON'T YOU, THAT JUST BECAUSE YOU DIDN'T DO IT ON PURPOSE DOESN'T MEAN I'LL AUTO-MATICALLY FORGIVE YOU?
YOU HAVE YOUR EXCUSES ...
...AND I HAVE MY NEED TO QUELL MY ANGER.
YES...
YOU'RE RIGHT...
DON (BOOM)
... SO...
...I SUGGEST THAT WE SETTLE THIS ACCORDING TO THE RULES OF OUR FAIR CITY!

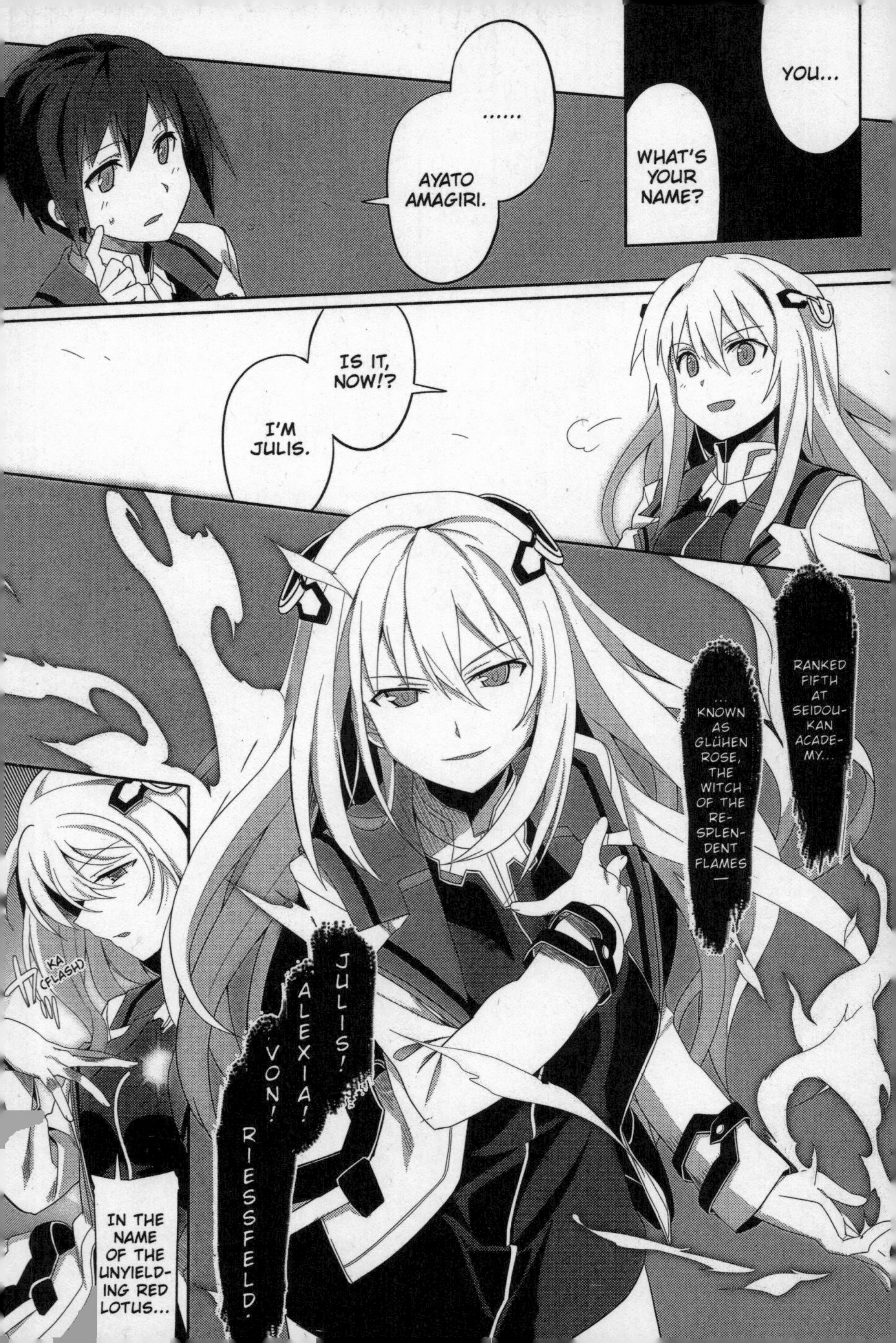
YOU...
WHAT'S YOUR NAME?
......
AYATO AMAGIRI.
IS IT, NOW!?
I'M JULIS.
RANKED FIFTH AT SEIDOU-KAN ACADE-MY...
...KNOWN AS GLÜHEN ROSE, THE WITCH OF THE RE-SPLEN-DENT FLAMES—
JULIS! ALEXIA! VON! RIESSFELD.
KA (FLASH)
IN THE NAME OF THE UNYIELD-ING RED LOTUS...

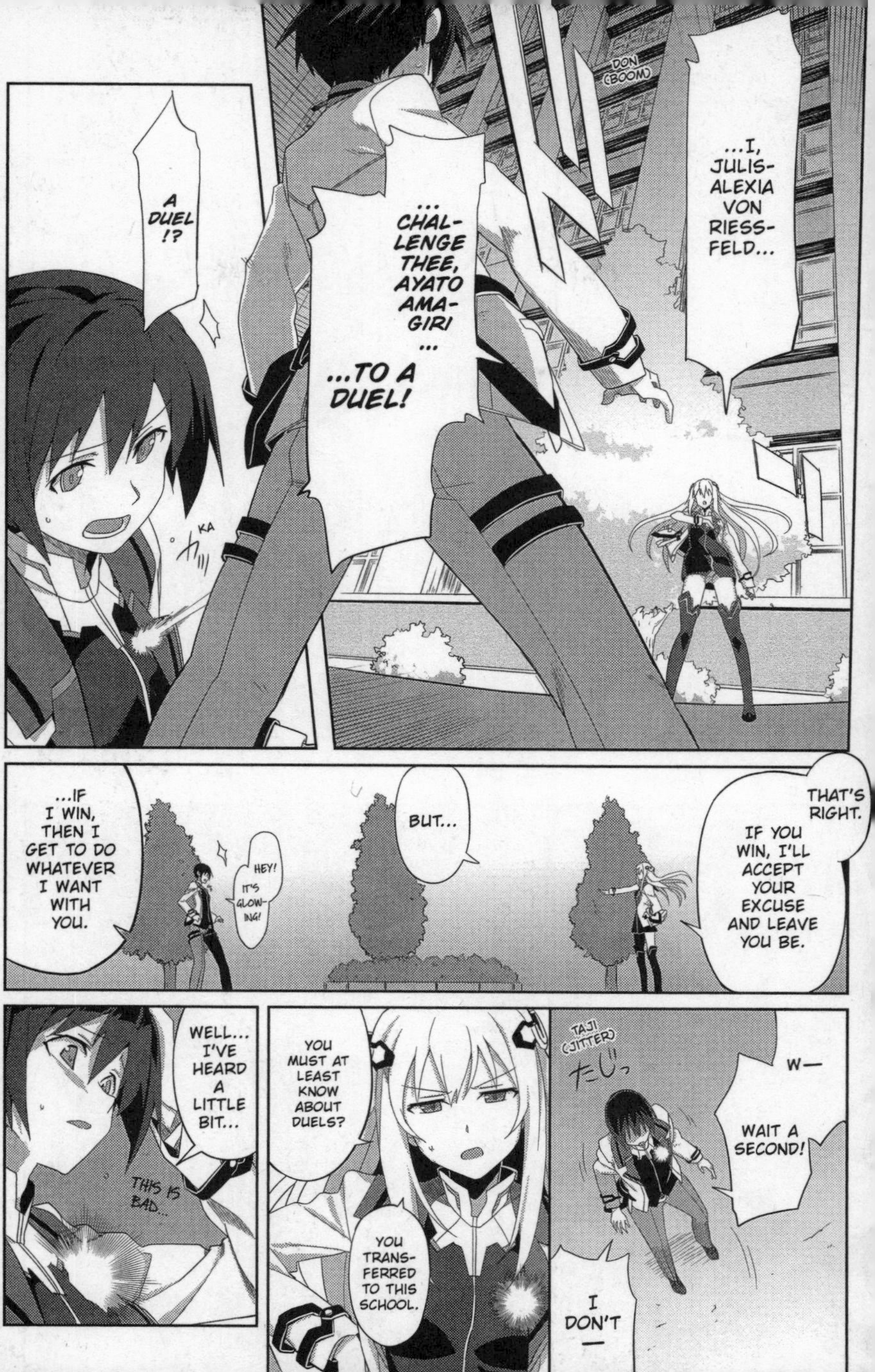
DON (BOOM)
...I, JULIS-ALEXIA VON RIESS-FELD...
...CHALLENGE THEE, AYATO AMAGIRI ... ...TO A DUEL!
A DUEL!?
KA
THAT'S RIGHT. IF YOU WIN, I'LL ACCEPT YOUR EXCUSE AND LEAVE YOU BE.
BUT...
HEY! IT'S GLOWING!
...IF I WIN, THEN I GET TO DO WHATEVER I WANT WITH YOU.
TAJI (JITTER)
たじっ
W—
WAIT A SECOND!
I DON'T —
YOU MUST AT LEAST KNOW ABOUT DUELS?
YOU TRANSFERRED TO THIS SCHOOL.
WELL... I'VE HEARD A LITTLE BIT...
THIS IS BAD...

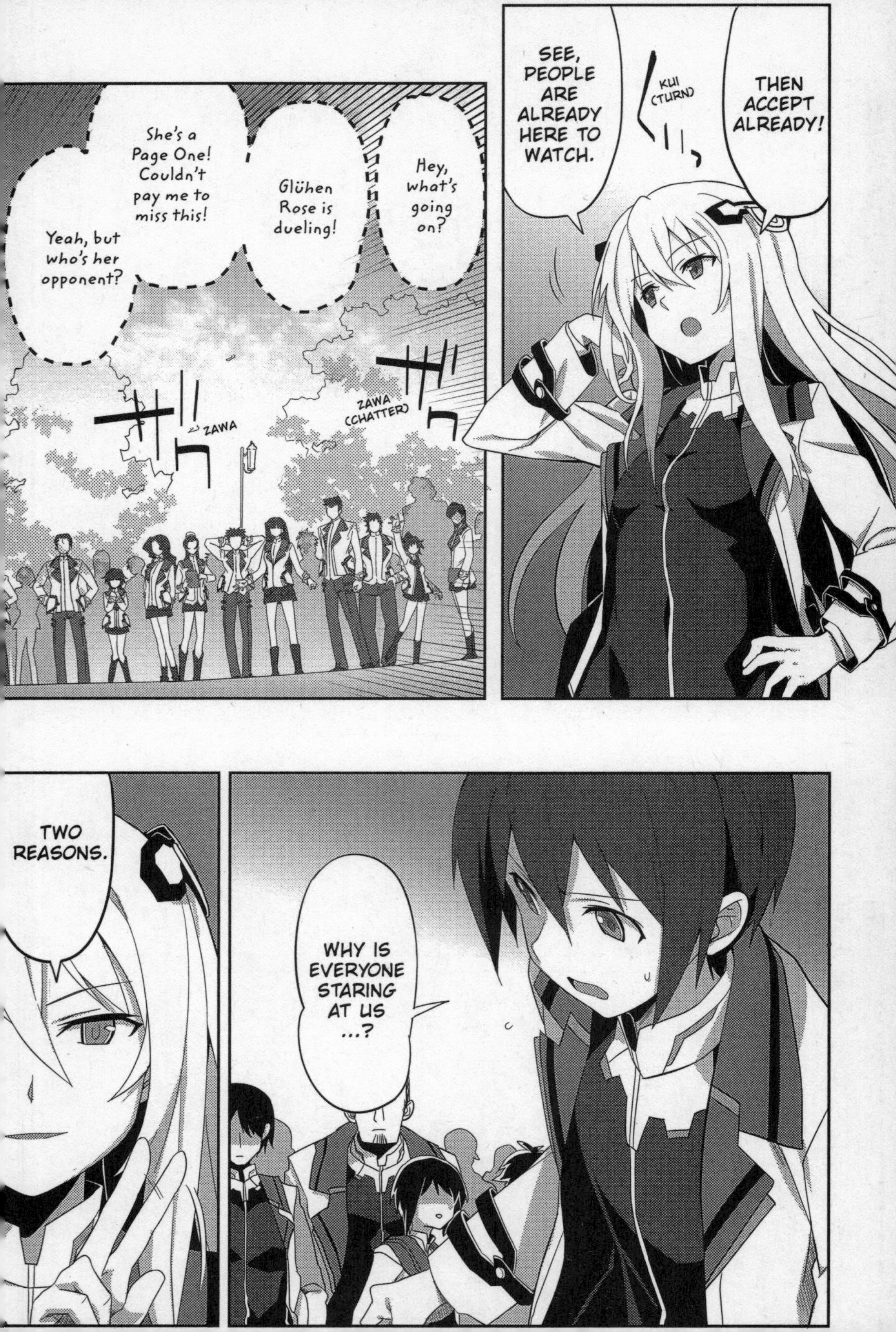
THEN ACCEPT ALREADY!
KUI (TURN)
SEE, PEOPLE ARE ALREADY HERE TO WATCH.
Hey, what's going on?
Glühen Rose is dueling!
She's a Page One! Couldn't pay me to miss this!
Yeah, but who's her opponent?
ZAWA (CHATTER)
ZAWA
WHY IS EVERYONE STARING AT US ...?
TWO REASONS.

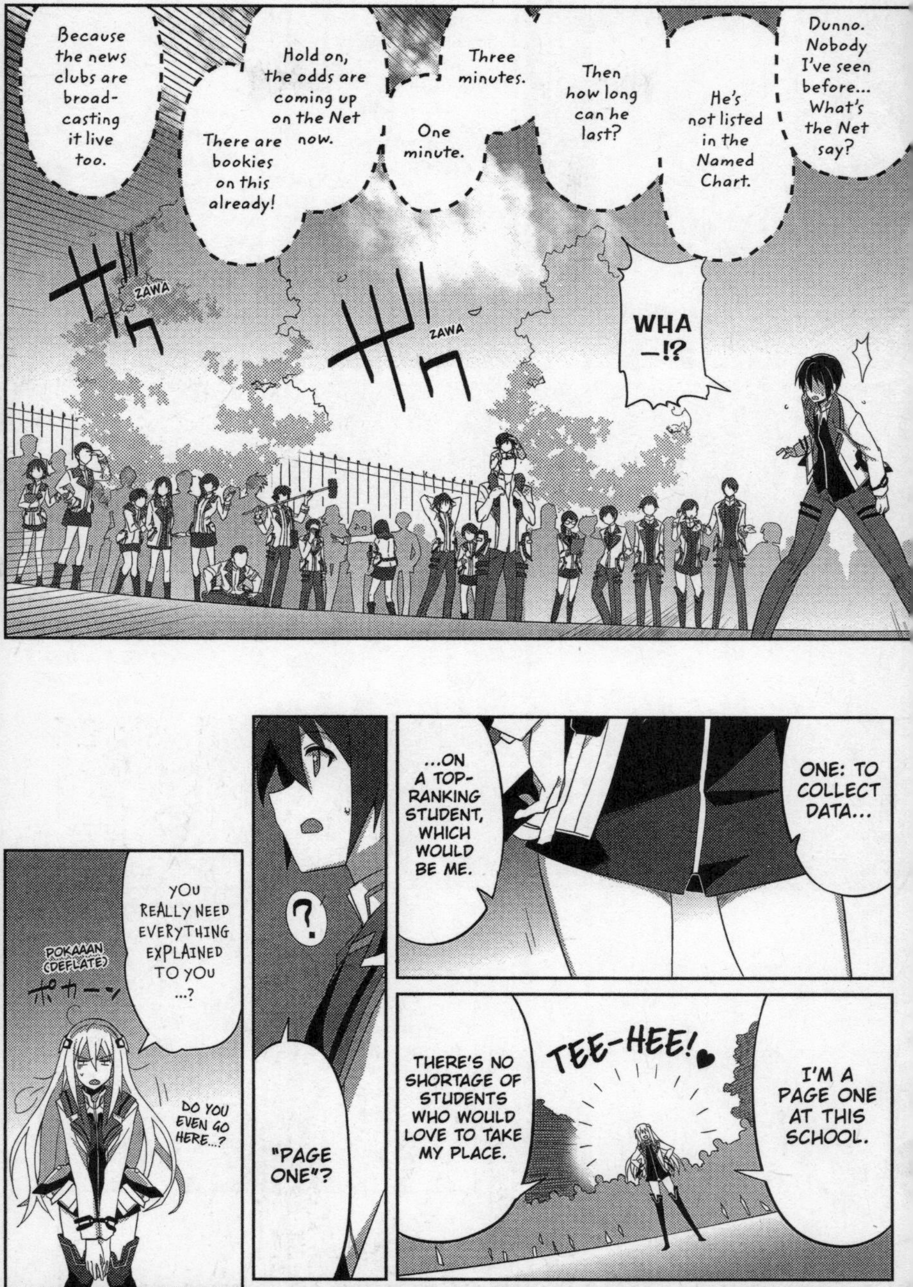
Dunno. Nobody I've seen before... What's the Net say?
He's not listed in the Named Chart.
Then how long can he last?
Three minutes.
One minute.
Hold on, the odds are coming up on the Net now.
There are bookies on this already!
Because the news clubs are broadcasting it live too.
WHA—!?
ZAWA
ZAWA
ONE: TO COLLECT DATA...
...ON A TOP-RANKING STUDENT, WHICH WOULD BE ME.
I'M A PAGE ONE AT THIS SCHOOL.
TEE-HEE!♥
THERE'S NO SHORTAGE OF STUDENTS WHO WOULD LOVE TO TAKE MY PLACE.
?
"PAGE ONE"?
YOU REALLY NEED EVERYTHING EXPLAINED TO YOU ...?
POKAAAN (DEFLATE)
ポカーン
DO YOU EVEN GO HERE...?

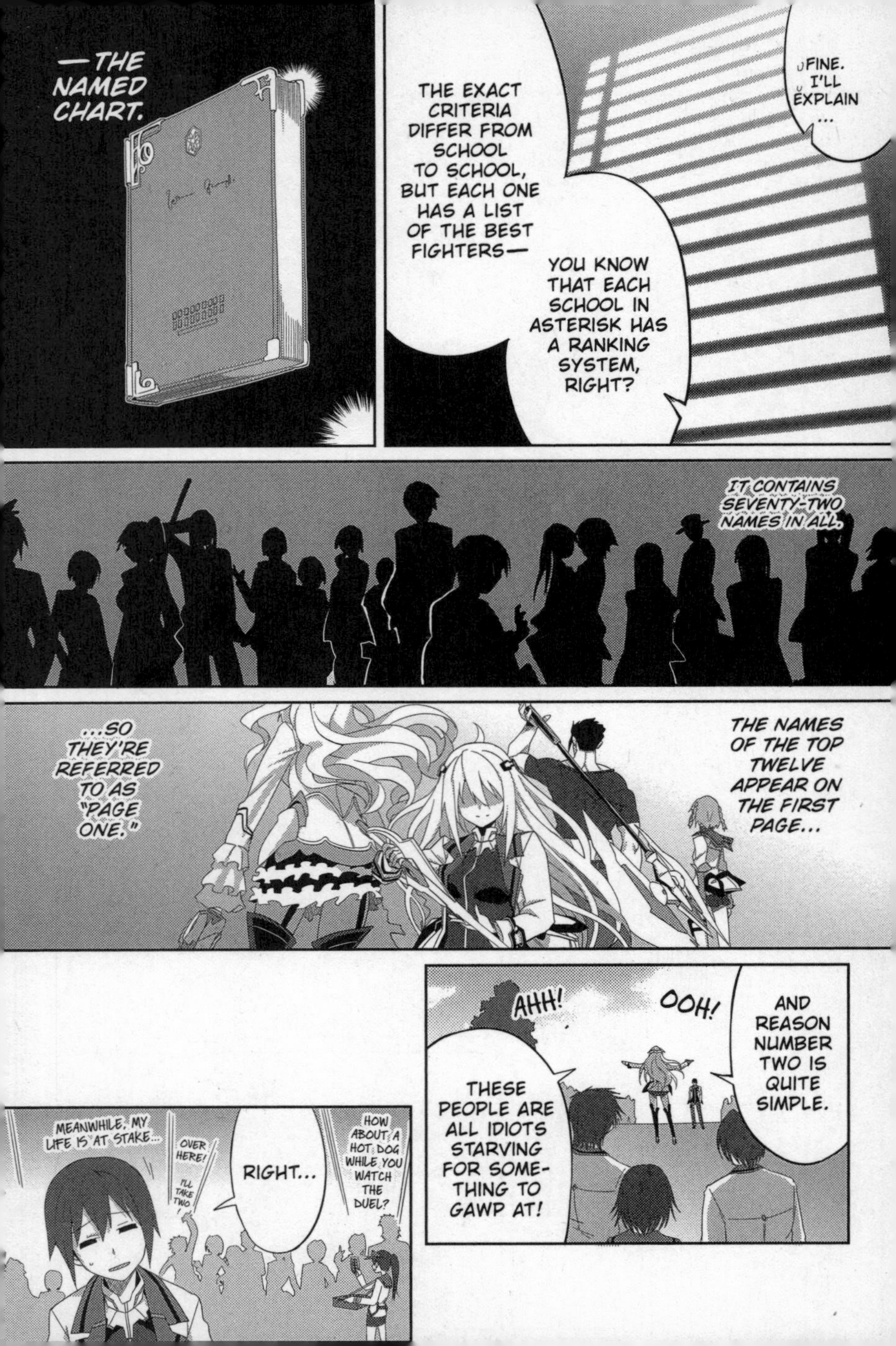
FINE. I'LL EXPLAIN...
YOU KNOW THAT EACH SCHOOL IN ASTERISK HAS A RANKING SYSTEM, RIGHT?
THE EXACT CRITERIA DIFFER FROM SCHOOL TO SCHOOL, BUT EACH ONE HAS A LIST OF THE BEST FIGHTERS—
—THE NAMED CHART.
IT CONTAINS SEVENTY-TWO NAMES IN ALL.
THE NAMES OF THE TOP TWELVE APPEAR ON THE FIRST PAGE...
...SO THEY'RE REFERRED TO AS "PAGE ONE."
AND REASON NUMBER TWO IS QUITE SIMPLE.
OOH!
AHH!
THESE PEOPLE ARE ALL IDIOTS STARVING FOR SOME-THING TO GAWP AT!
HOW ABOUT A HOT DOG WHILE YOU WATCH THE DUEL?
RIGHT...
I'LL TAKE TWO!
OVER HERE!
MEANWHILE, MY LIFE IS AT STAKE...

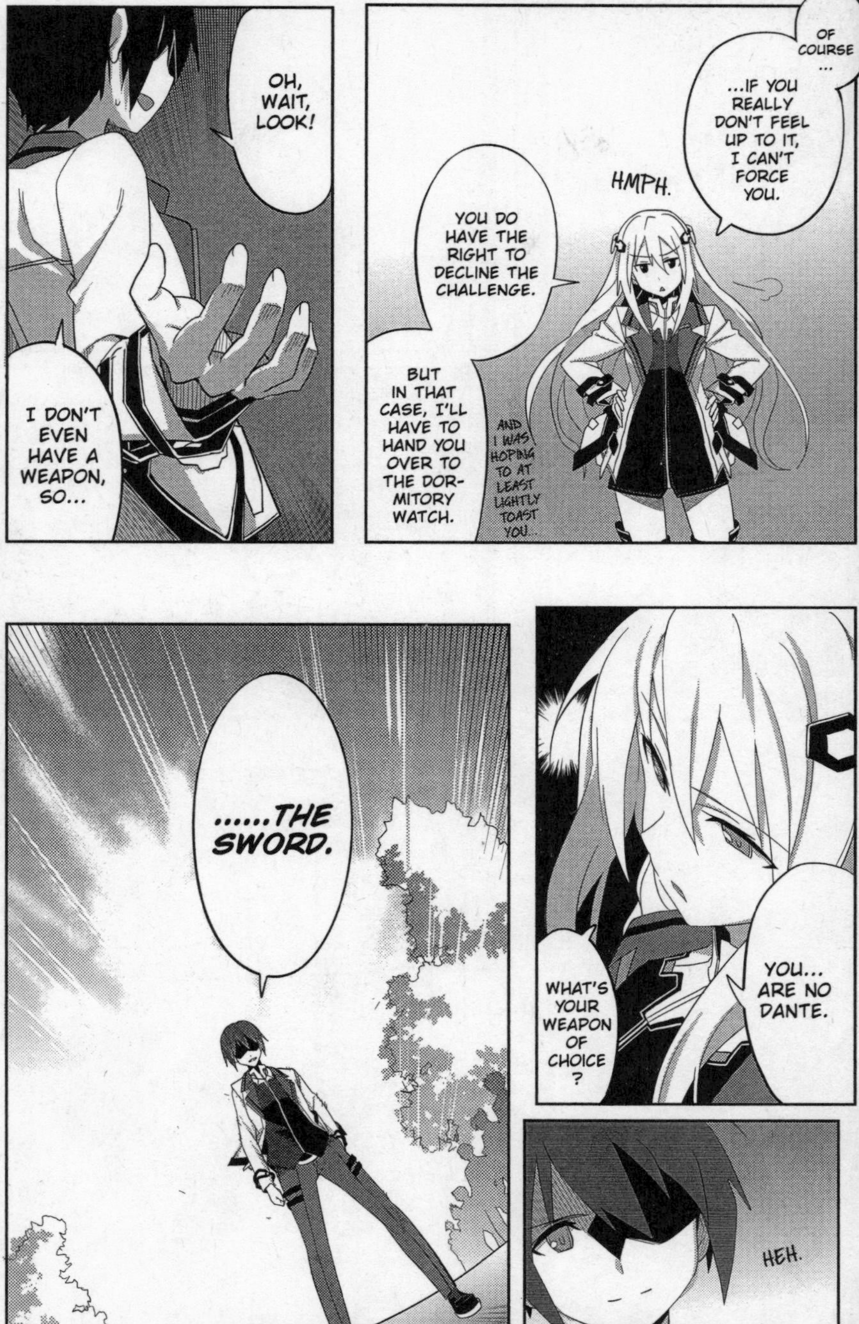
OF COURSE...
...IF YOU REALLY DON'T FEEL UP TO IT, I CAN'T FORCE YOU.
HMPH.
YOU DO HAVE THE RIGHT TO DECLINE THE CHALLENGE.
BUT IN THAT CASE, I'LL HAVE TO HAND YOU OVER TO THE DORMITORY WATCH.
AND I WAS HOPING TO AT LEAST LIGHTLY TOAST YOU...
OH, WAIT, LOOK!
I DON'T EVEN HAVE A WEAPON, SO...
YOU... ARE NO DANTE.
WHAT'S YOUR WEAPON OF CHOICE?
HEH.
......THE SWORD.

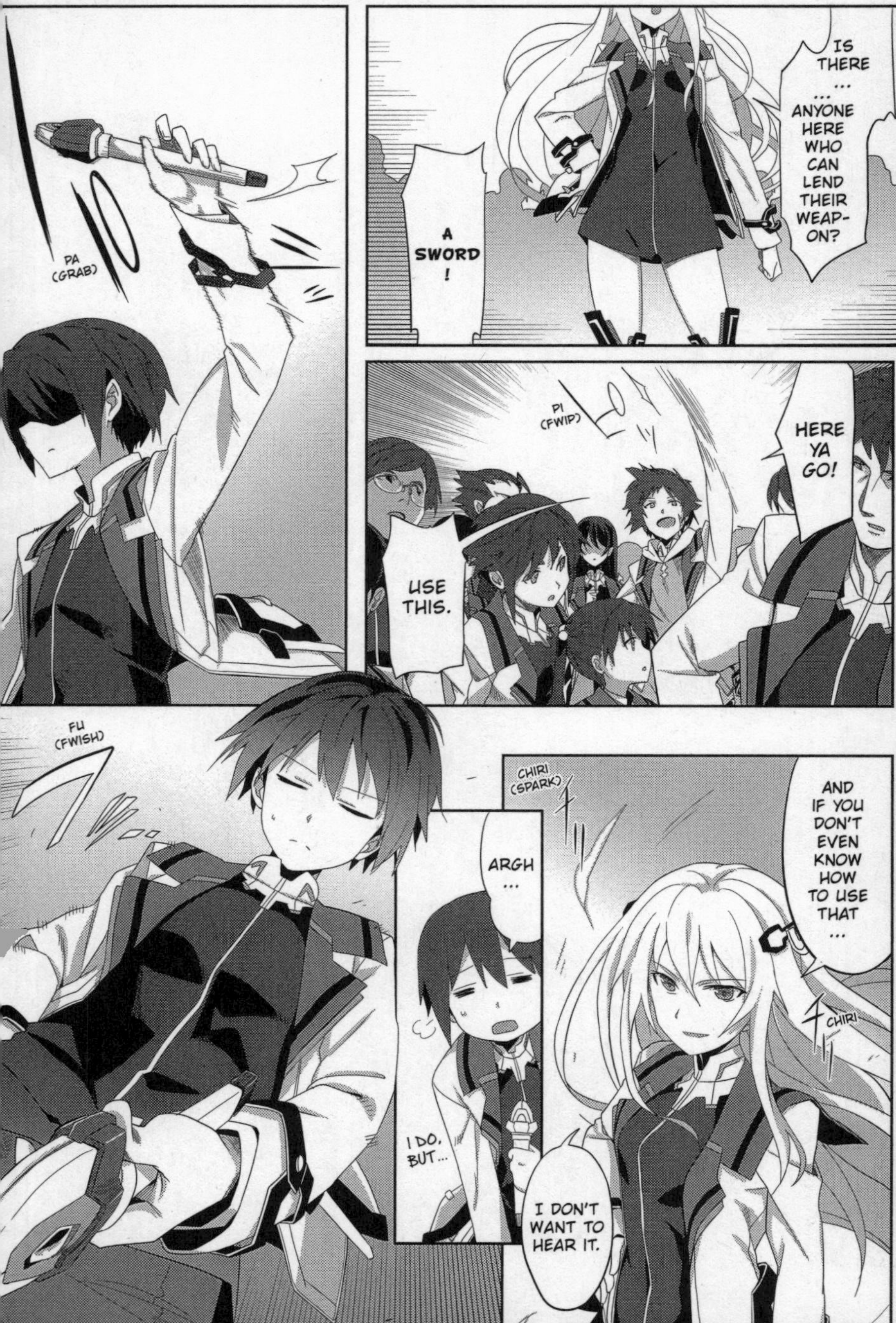
IS THERE ... ... ANYONE HERE WHO CAN LEND THEIR WEAP-ON?
A SWORD!
HERE YA GO!
PI (FWIP)
USE THIS.
PA (GRAB)
CHIRI (SPARK)
AND IF YOU DON'T EVEN KNOW HOW TO USE THAT ...
CHIRI
I DO, BUT...
I DON'T WANT TO HEAR IT.
ARGH ...
FU (FWISH)

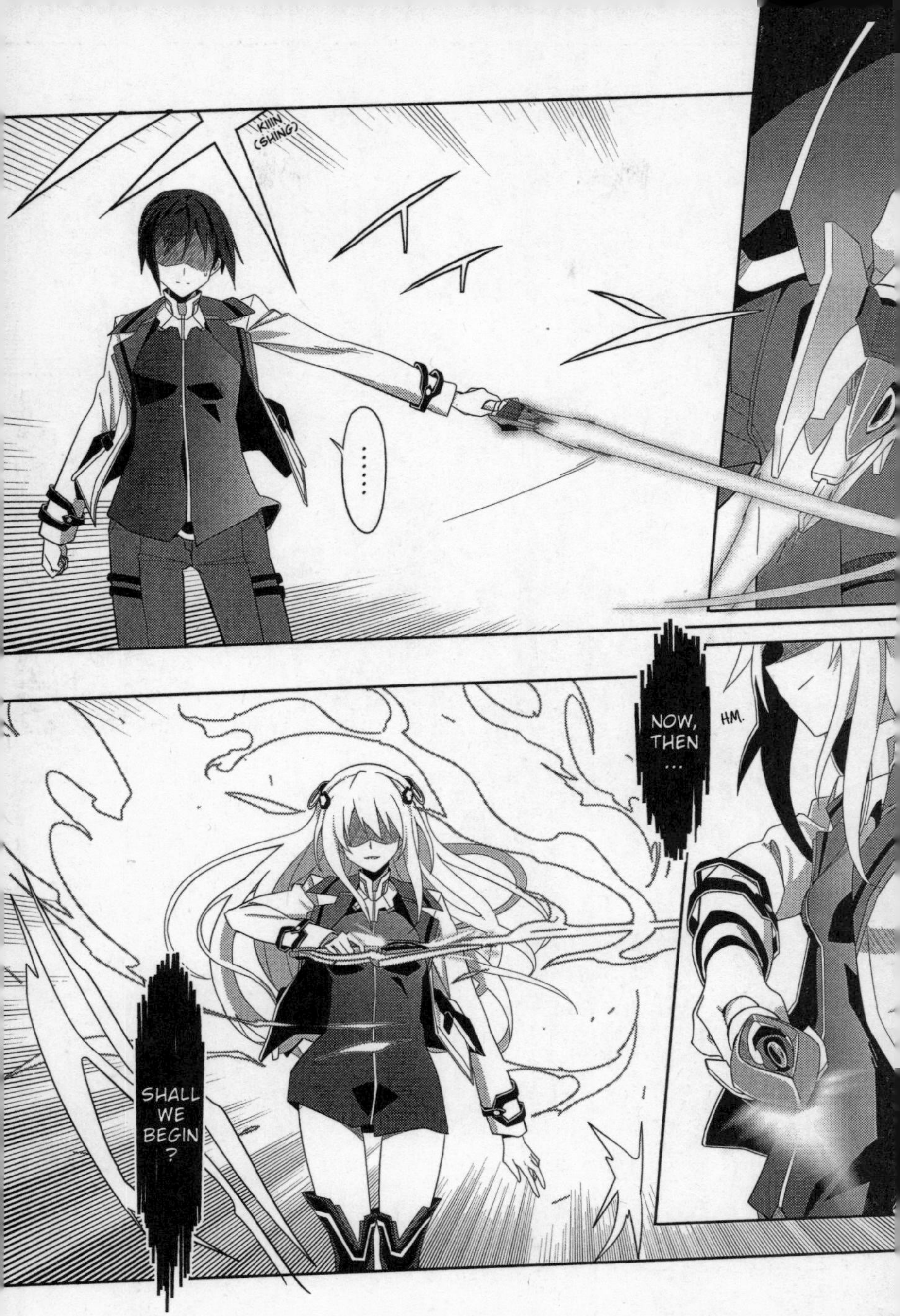
KIIIN (SHING)
......
HM.
NOW, THEN ...
SHALL WE BEGIN ?

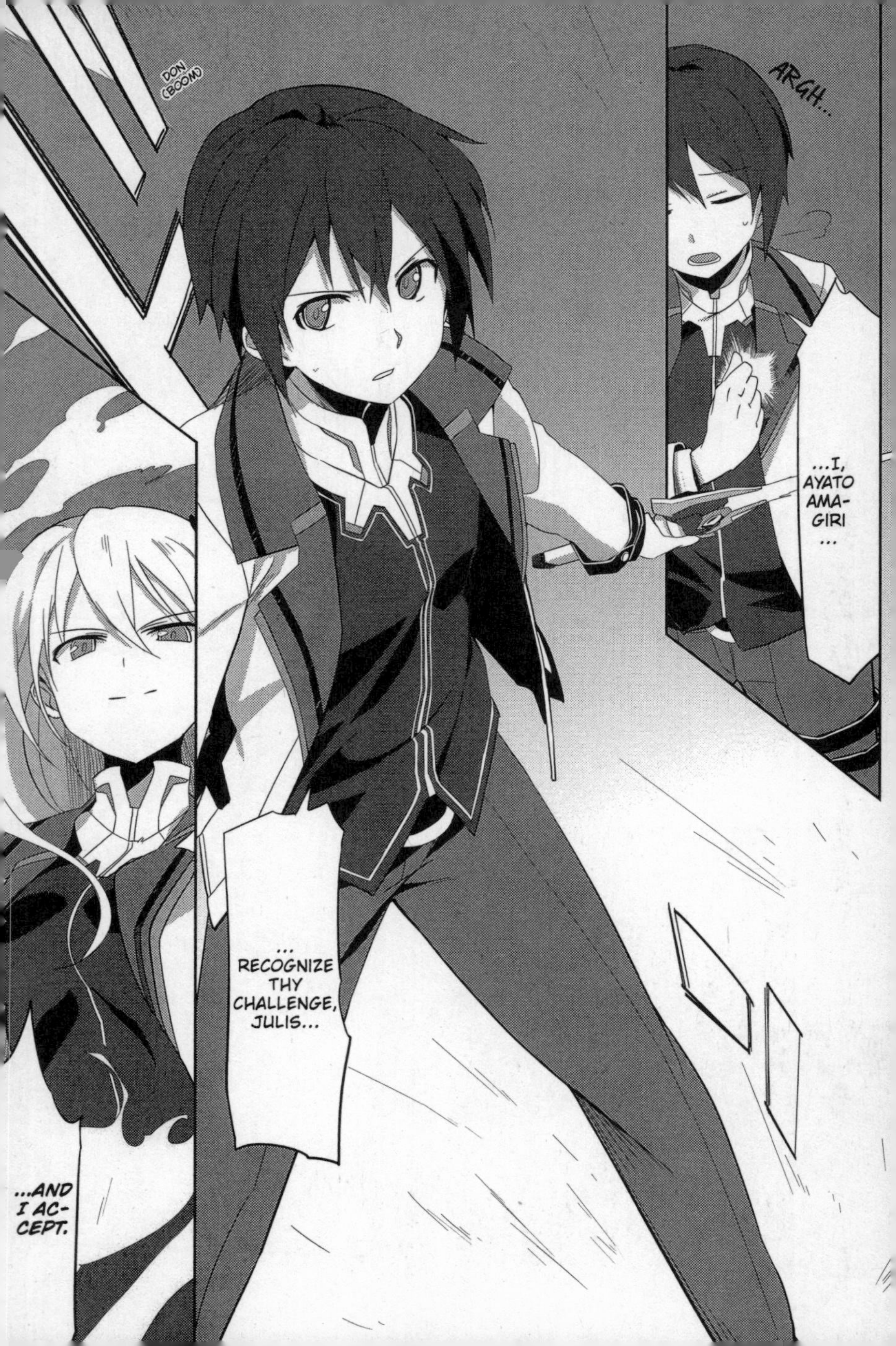
ARGH...
...I, AYATO AMAGIRI ...
DON (BOOM)
... RECOGNIZE THY CHALLENGE, JULIS...
...AND I ACCEPT.

THE ASTERISK WAR

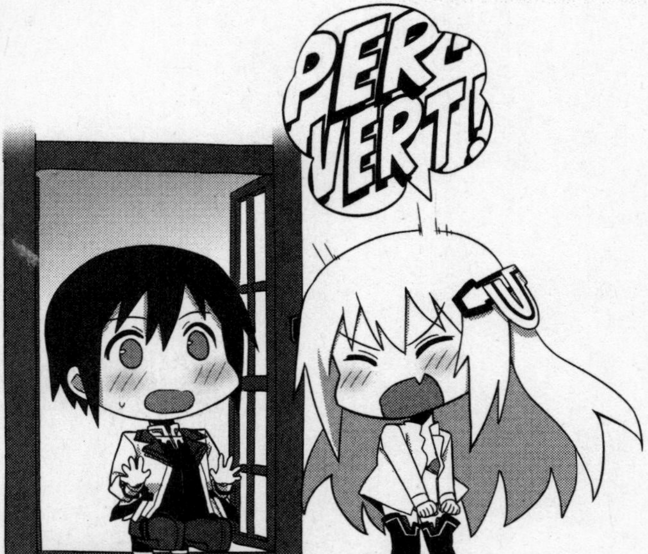
PERVERT!

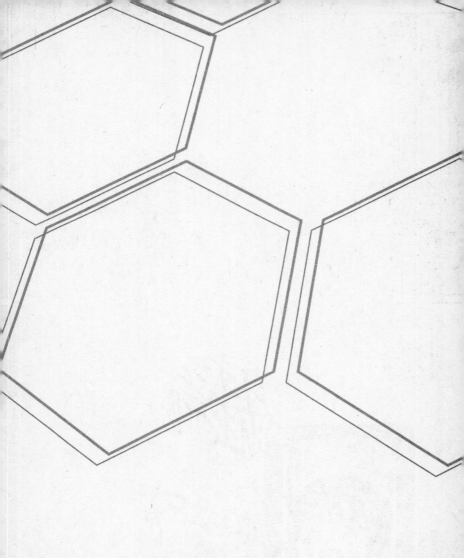

THE
ASTERISK WAR

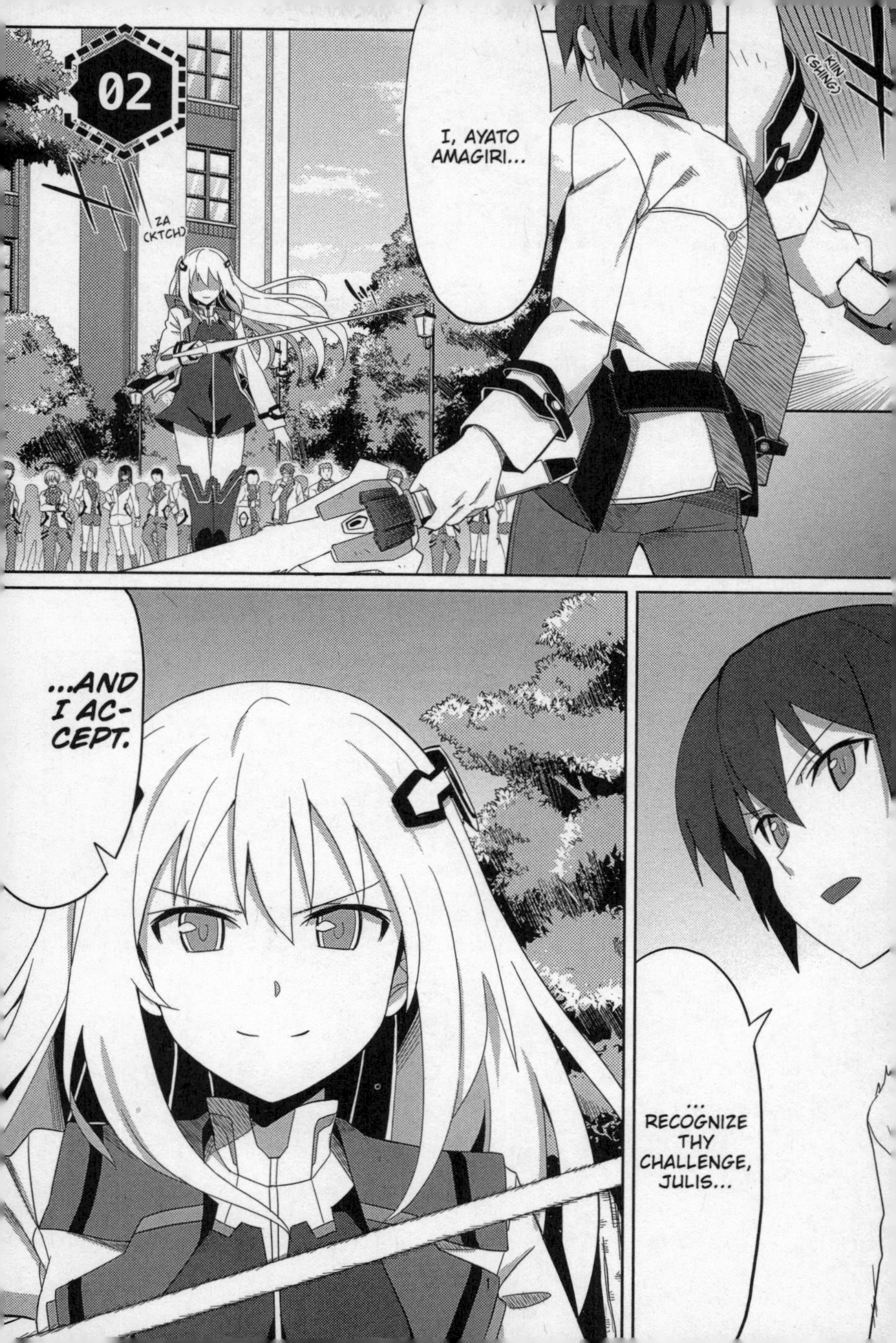
KIN (SHING)
I, AYATO AMAGIRI...
02
ZA (KTCH)
...RECOGNIZE THY CHALLENGE, JULIS...
...AND I AC-CEPT.

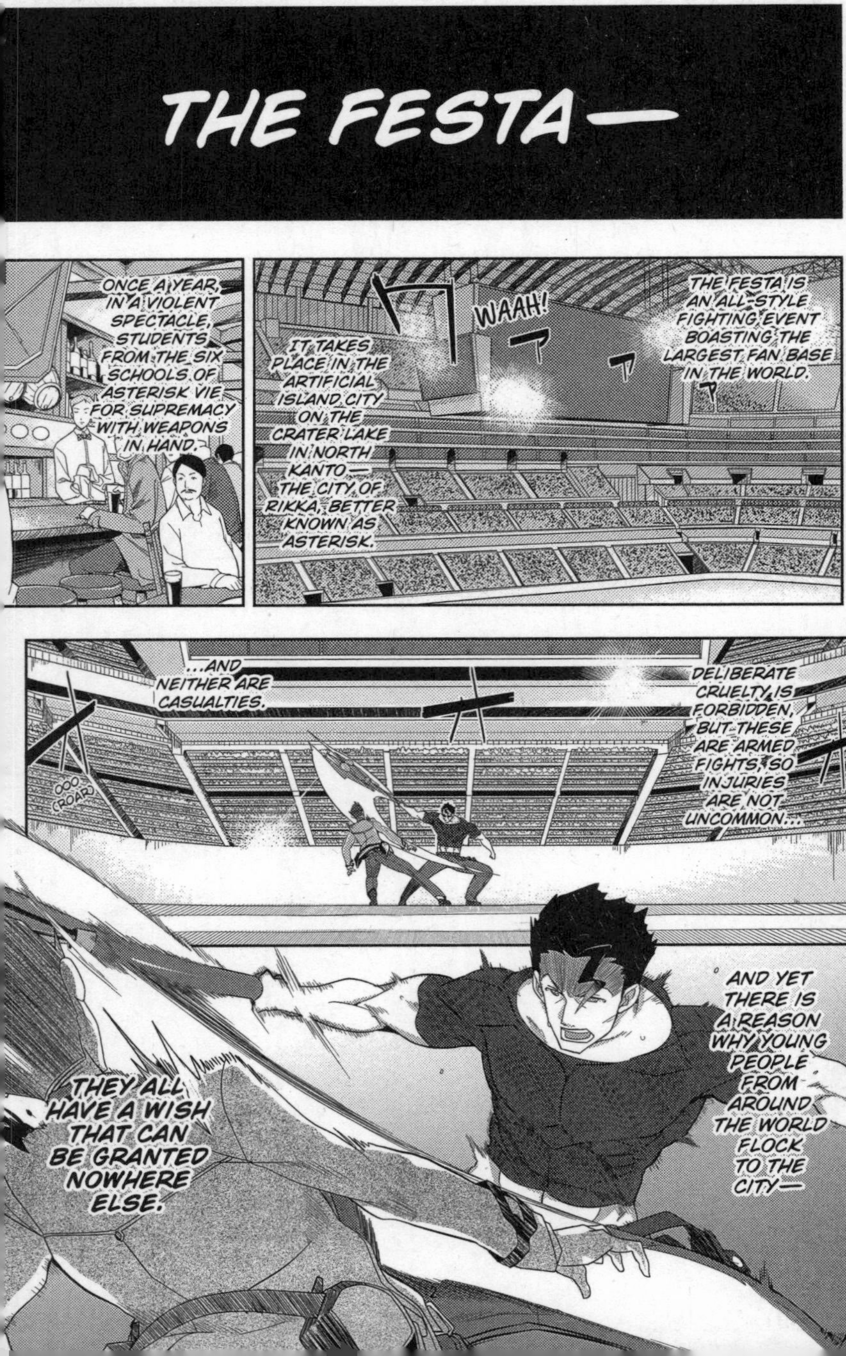
THE FESTA—
THE FESTA IS AN ALL-STYLE FIGHTING EVENT BOASTING THE LARGEST FAN BASE IN THE WORLD.
WAAH!
IT TAKES PLACE IN THE ARTIFICIAL ISLAND CITY ON THE CRATER LAKE IN NORTH KANTO— THE CITY OF RIKKA, BETTER KNOWN AS ASTERISK.
ONCE A YEAR, IN A VIOLENT SPECTACLE, STUDENTS FROM THE SIX SCHOOLS OF ASTERISK VIE FOR SUPREMACY WITH WEAPONS IN HAND.
DELIBERATE CRUELTY IS FORBIDDEN, BUT THESE ARE ARMED FIGHTS, SO INJURIES ARE NOT UNCOMMON...
...AND NEITHER ARE CASUALTIES.
OOO (ROAR)
AND YET THERE IS A REASON WHY YOUNG PEOPLE FROM AROUND THE WORLD FLOCK TO THE CITY—
THEY ALL HAVE A WISH THAT CAN BE GRANTED NOWHERE ELSE.

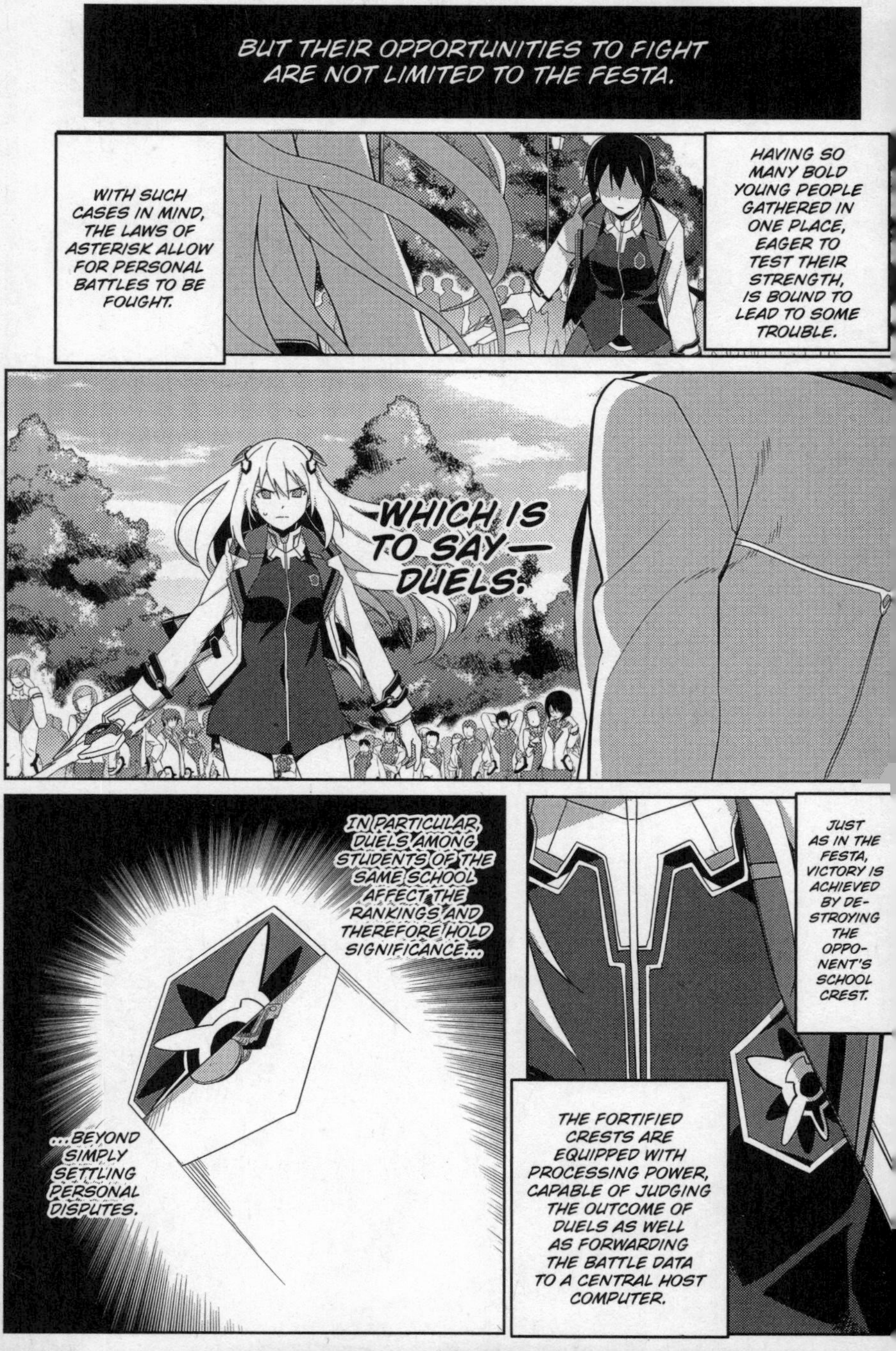
BUT THEIR OPPORTUNITIES TO FIGHT ARE NOT LIMITED TO THE FESTA.
HAVING SO MANY BOLD YOUNG PEOPLE GATHERED IN ONE PLACE, EAGER TO TEST THEIR STRENGTH, IS BOUND TO LEAD TO SOME TROUBLE.
WITH SUCH CASES IN MIND, THE LAWS OF ASTERISK ALLOW FOR PERSONAL BATTLES TO BE FOUGHT.
WHICH IS TO SAY— DUELS.
JUST AS IN THE FESTA, VICTORY IS ACHIEVED BY DE-STROYING THE OPPO-NENT'S SCHOOL CREST.
THE FORTIFIED CRESTS ARE EQUIPPED WITH PROCESSING POWER, CAPABLE OF JUDGING THE OUTCOME OF DUELS AS WELL AS FORWARDING THE BATTLE DATA TO A CENTRAL HOST COMPUTER.
IN PARTICULAR, DUELS AMONG STUDENTS OF THE SAME SCHOOL AFFECT THE RANKINGS AND THEREFORE HOLD SIGNIFICANCE...
...BEYOND SIMPLY SETTLING PERSONAL DISPUTES.

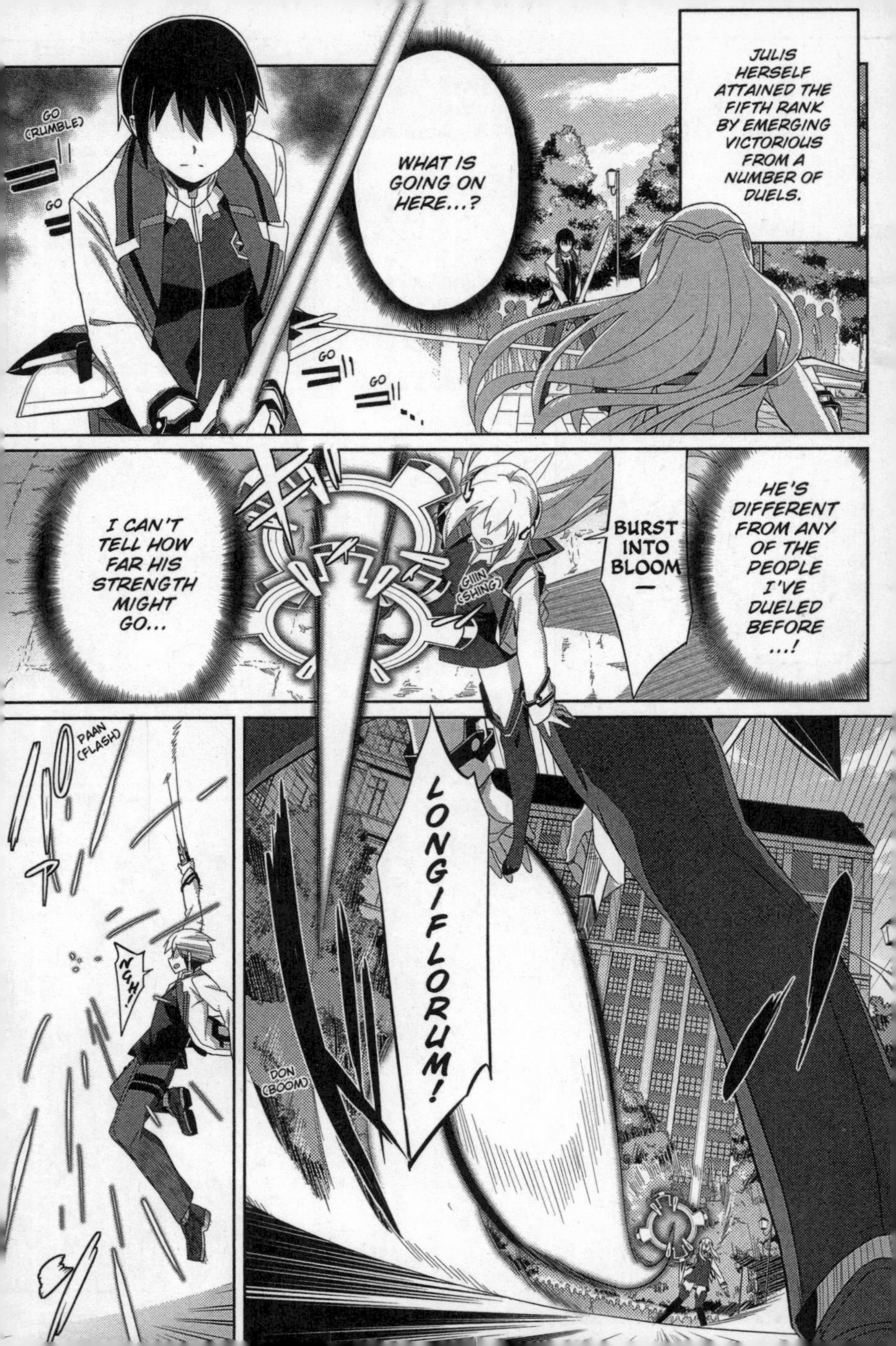

JULIS HERSELF ATTAINED THE FIFTH RANK BY EMERGING VICTORIOUS FROM A NUMBER OF DUELS.
WHAT IS GOING ON HERE...?
GO (RUMBLE)
GO
GO
GO
HE'S DIFFERENT FROM ANY OF THE PEOPLE I'VE DUELED BEFORE ...!
BURST INTO BLOOM —
GIIIN (SHING)
I CAN'T TELL HOW FAR HIS STRENGTH MIGHT GO...
LONGIFLORUM!
DON (BOOM)
PAAN (FLASH)
NGH!

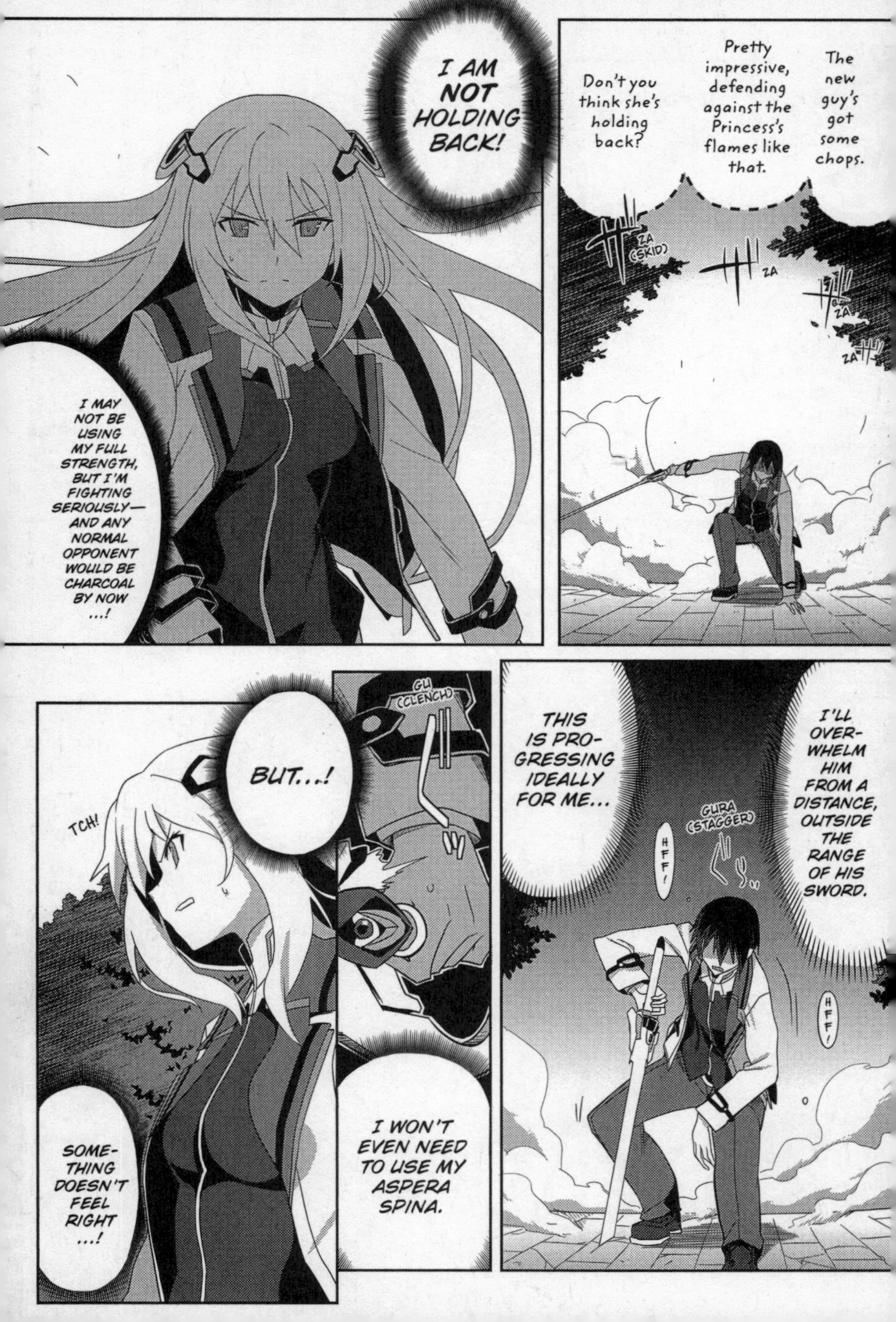
The new guy's got some chops.
Pretty impressive, defending against the Princess's flames like that.
Don't you think she's holding back?
ZA (SKID)
ZA
ZA
ZA
I AM NOT HOLDING BACK!
I MAY NOT BE USING MY FULL STRENGTH, BUT I'M FIGHTING SERIOUSLY—AND ANY NORMAL OPPONENT WOULD BE CHARCOAL BY NOW ...!
I'LL OVER-WHELM HIM FROM A DISTANCE, OUTSIDE THE RANGE OF HIS SWORD.
THIS IS PRO-GRESSING IDEALLY FOR ME...
GURA (STAGGER)
HFF!
HFF!
I WON'T EVEN NEED TO USE MY ASPERA SPINA.
GU (CLENCH)
BUT...!
TCH!
SOME-THING DOESN'T FEEL RIGHT ...!

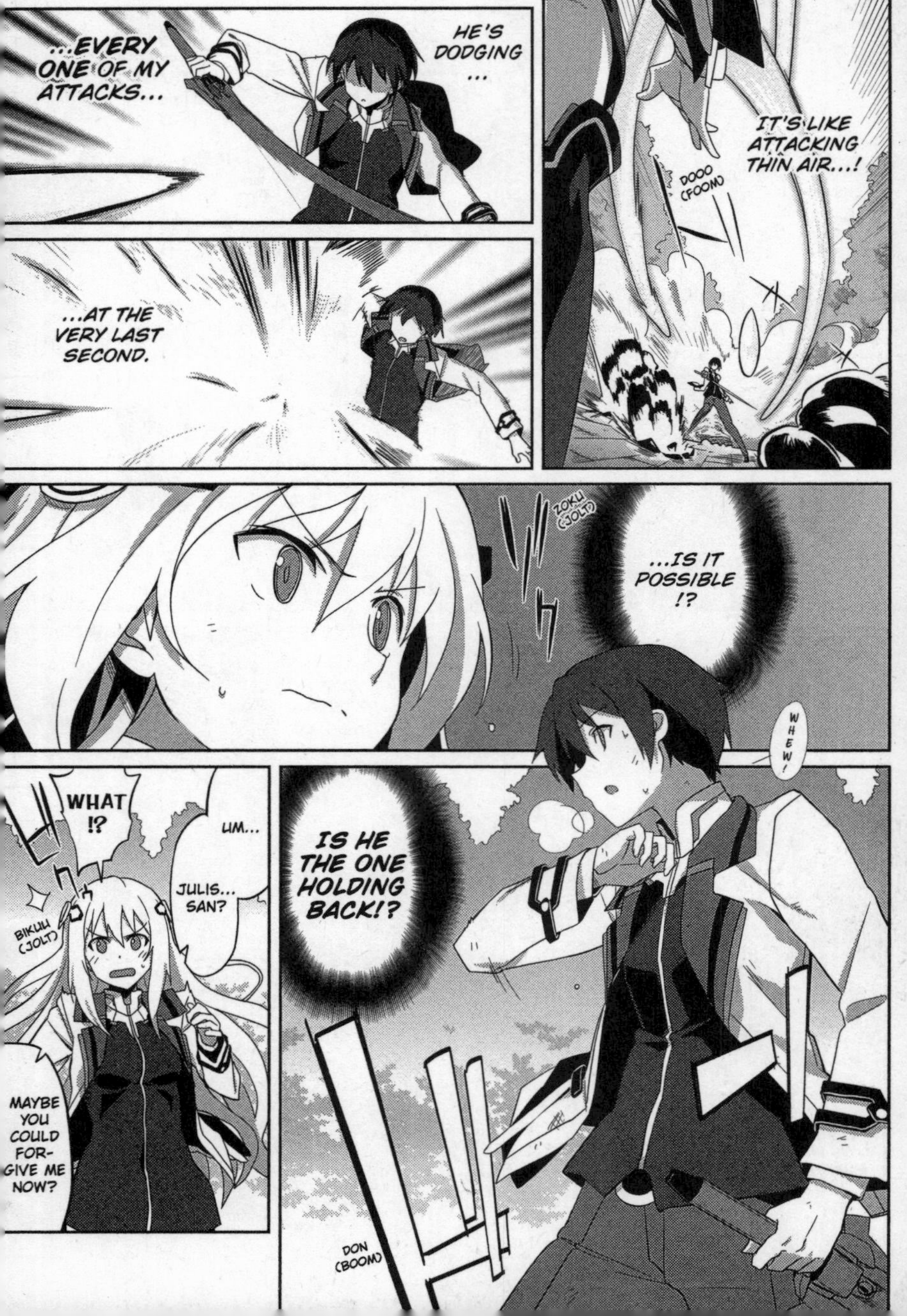
IT'S LIKE ATTACKING THIN AIR...!
DOOO (FOOM)
HE'S DODGING ...
...EVERY ONE OF MY ATTACKS...
...AT THE VERY LAST SECOND.
ZOKU (JOLT)
...IS IT POSSIBLE !?
WHEW!
IS HE THE ONE HOLDING BACK!?
DON (BOOM)
UM...
JULIS... SAN?
WHAT !?
BIKUU (JOLT)
MAYBE YOU COULD FOR-GIVE ME NOW?

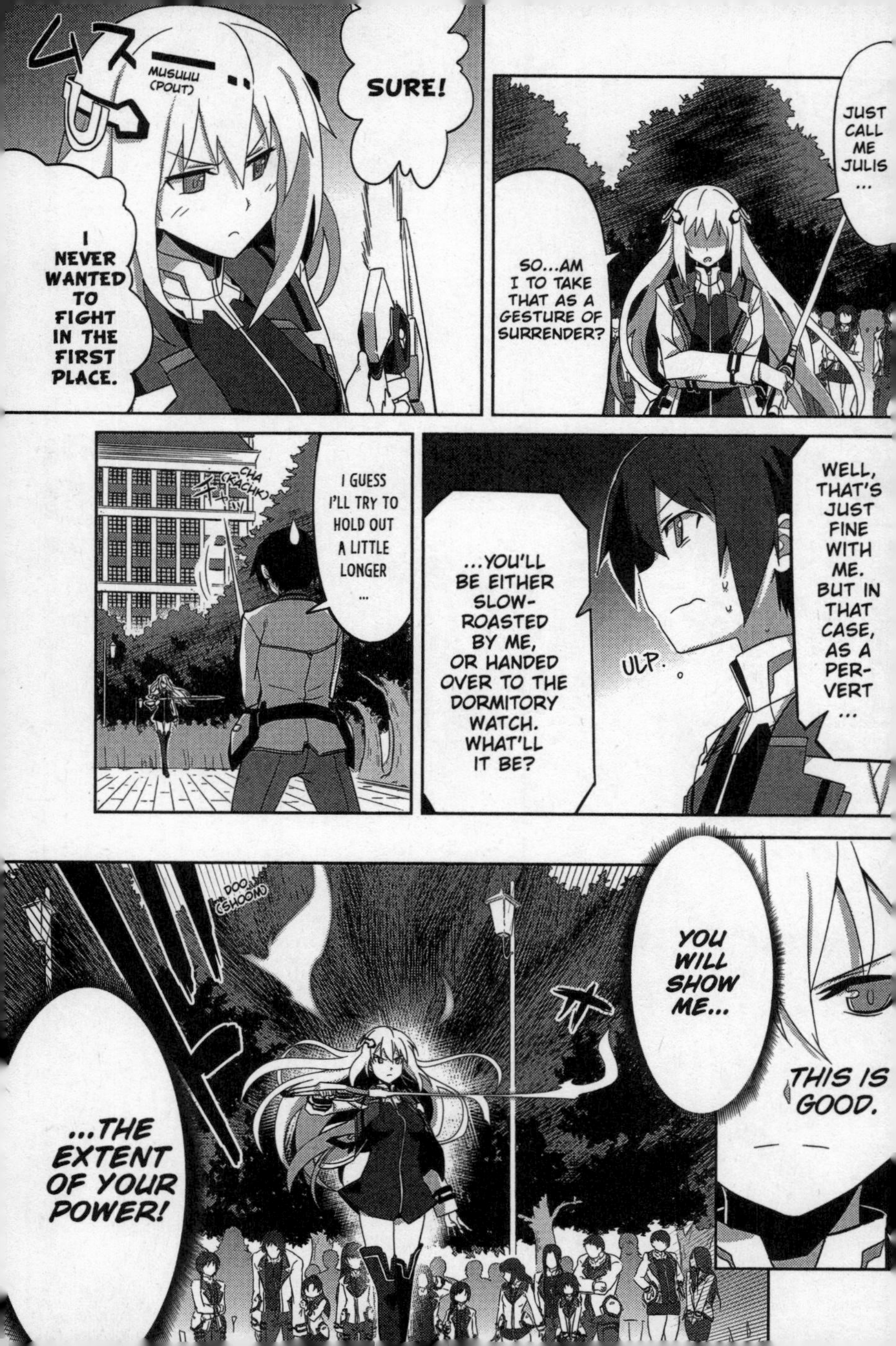

JUST CALL ME JULIS...
SO...AM I TO TAKE THAT AS A GESTURE OF SURRENDER?
SURE!
MUSUUU (POUT)
I NEVER WANTED TO FIGHT IN THE FIRST PLACE.
WELL, THAT'S JUST FINE WITH ME. BUT IN THAT CASE, AS A PER-VERT...
...YOU'LL BE EITHER SLOW-ROASTED BY ME, OR HANDED OVER TO THE DORMITORY WATCH. WHAT'LL IT BE?
ULP.
CHA (KACHK)
I GUESS I'LL TRY TO HOLD OUT A LITTLE LONGER...
YOU WILL SHOW ME...
THIS IS GOOD.
DOO (SHOOM)
...THE EXTENT OF YOUR POWER!

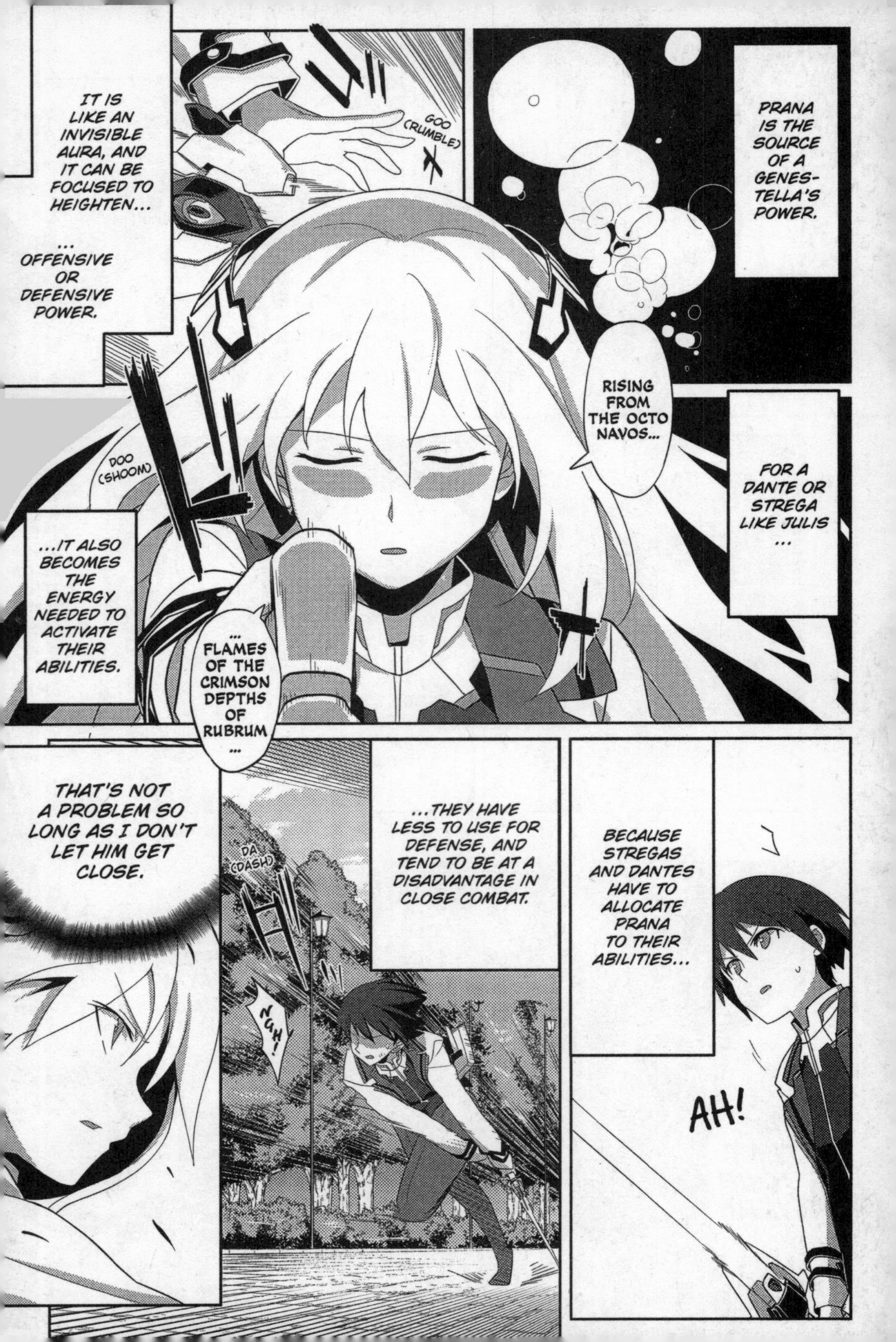
PRANA IS THE SOURCE OF A GENES-TELLA'S POWER.
IT IS LIKE AN INVISIBLE AURA, AND IT CAN BE FOCUSED TO HEIGHTEN...
...OFFENSIVE OR DEFENSIVE POWER.
GOO (RUMBLE)
FOR A DANTE OR STREGA LIKE JULIS...
RISING FROM THE OCTO NAVOS...
DOO (SHOOM)
...IT ALSO BECOMES THE ENERGY NEEDED TO ACTIVATE THEIR ABILITIES.
...FLAMES OF THE CRIMSON DEPTHS OF RUBRUM...
BECAUSE STREGAS AND DANTES HAVE TO ALLOCATE PRANA TO THEIR ABILITIES...
AH!
...THEY HAVE LESS TO USE FOR DEFENSE, AND TEND TO BE AT A DISADVANTAGE IN CLOSE COMBAT.
DA (DASH)
NGH!
THAT'S NOT A PROBLEM SO LONG AS I DON'T LET HIM GET CLOSE.

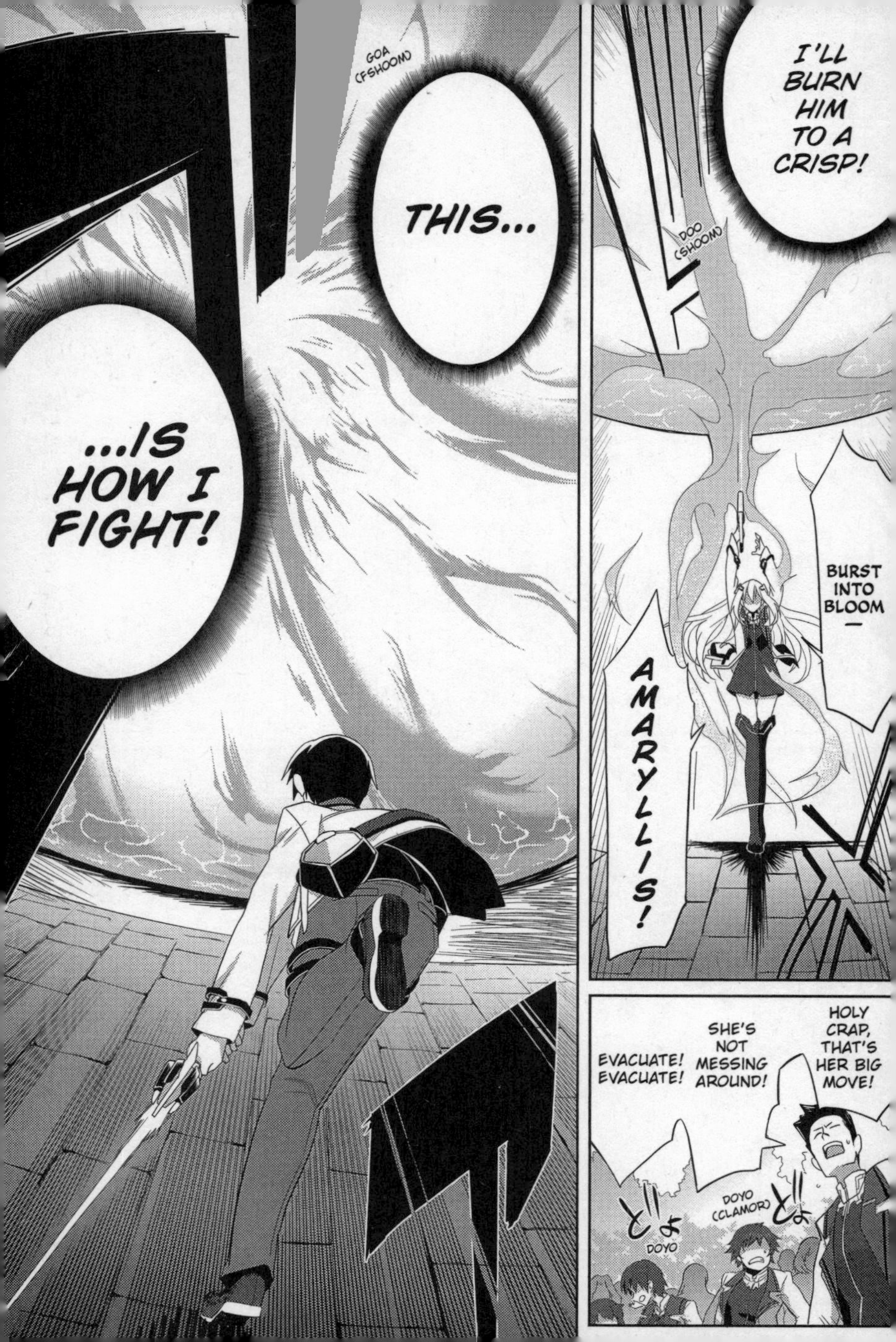
I'LL BURN HIM TO A CRISP!
DOO (SHOOM)
BURST INTO BLOOM—
AMARYLLIS!
HOLY CRAP, THAT'S HER BIG MOVE!
SHE'S NOT MESSING AROUND!
EVACUATE! EVACUATE!
どよ
DOYO (CLAMOR)
どよ
DOYO
GOA (FSHOOM)
THIS...
...IS HOW I FIGHT!

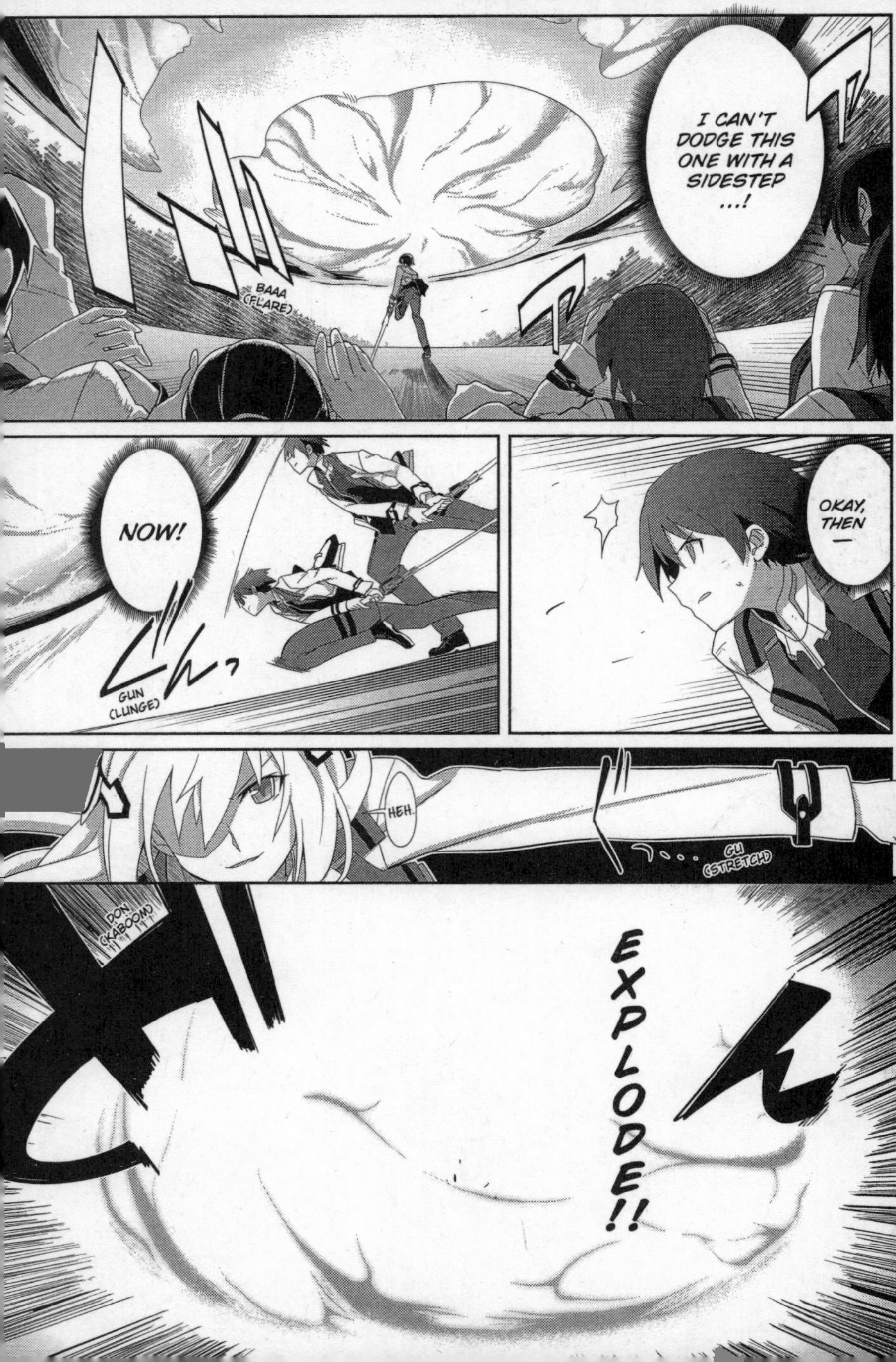
I CAN'T DODGE THIS ONE WITH A SIDESTEP ...!
BAAA (FLARE)
OKAY, THEN —
NOW!
GUN (LUNGE)
HEH.
GU (STRETCH)
DON (KABOOM)
EXPLODE!!

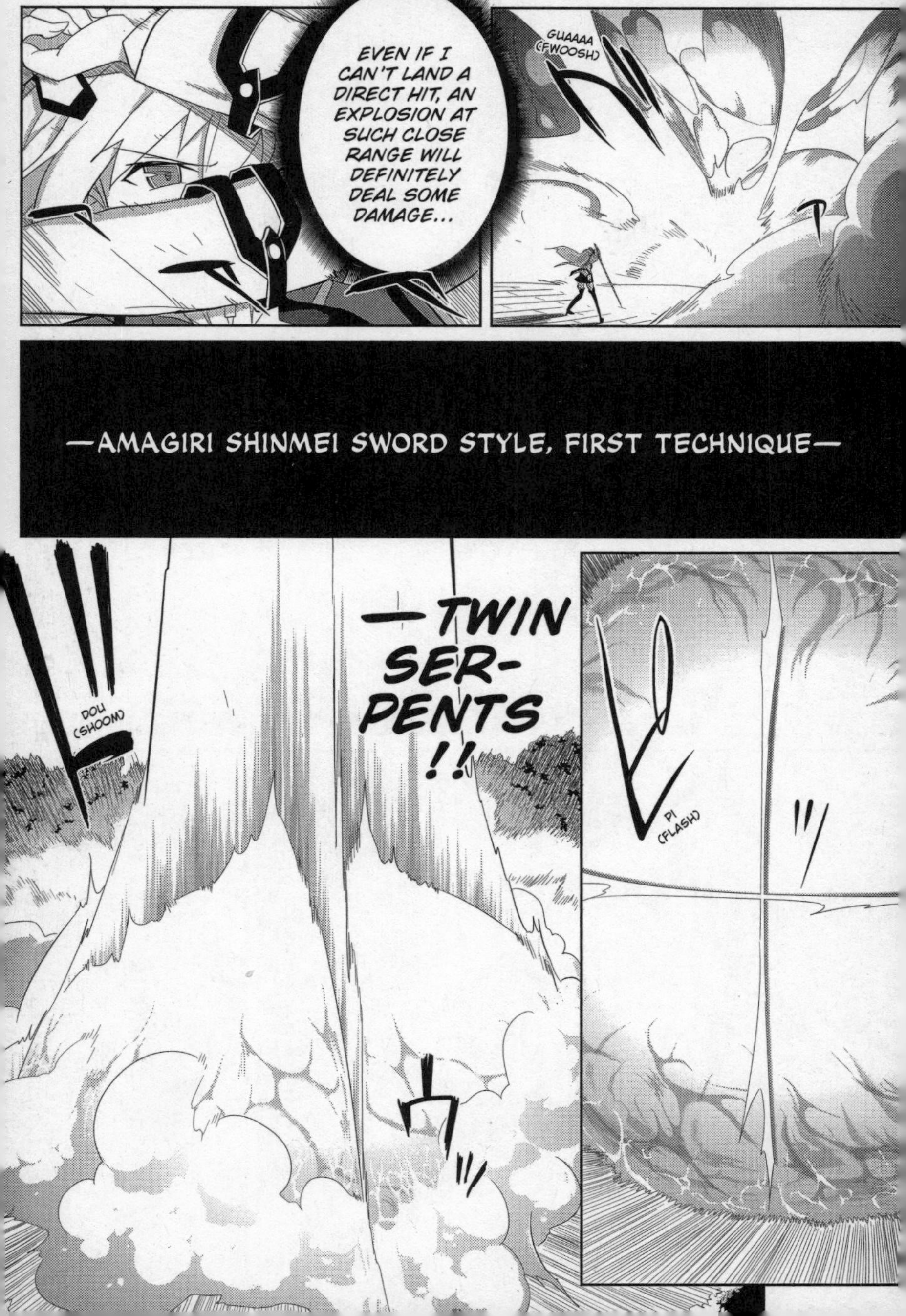
GUAAAA (FWOOSH)
EVEN IF I CAN'T LAND A DIRECT HIT, AN EXPLOSION AT SUCH CLOSE RANGE WILL DEFINITELY DEAL SOME DAMAGE...
—AMAGIRI SHINMEI SWORD STYLE, FIRST TECHNIQUE—
PI (FLASH)
DOU (SHOOM)
—TWIN SERPENTS!!

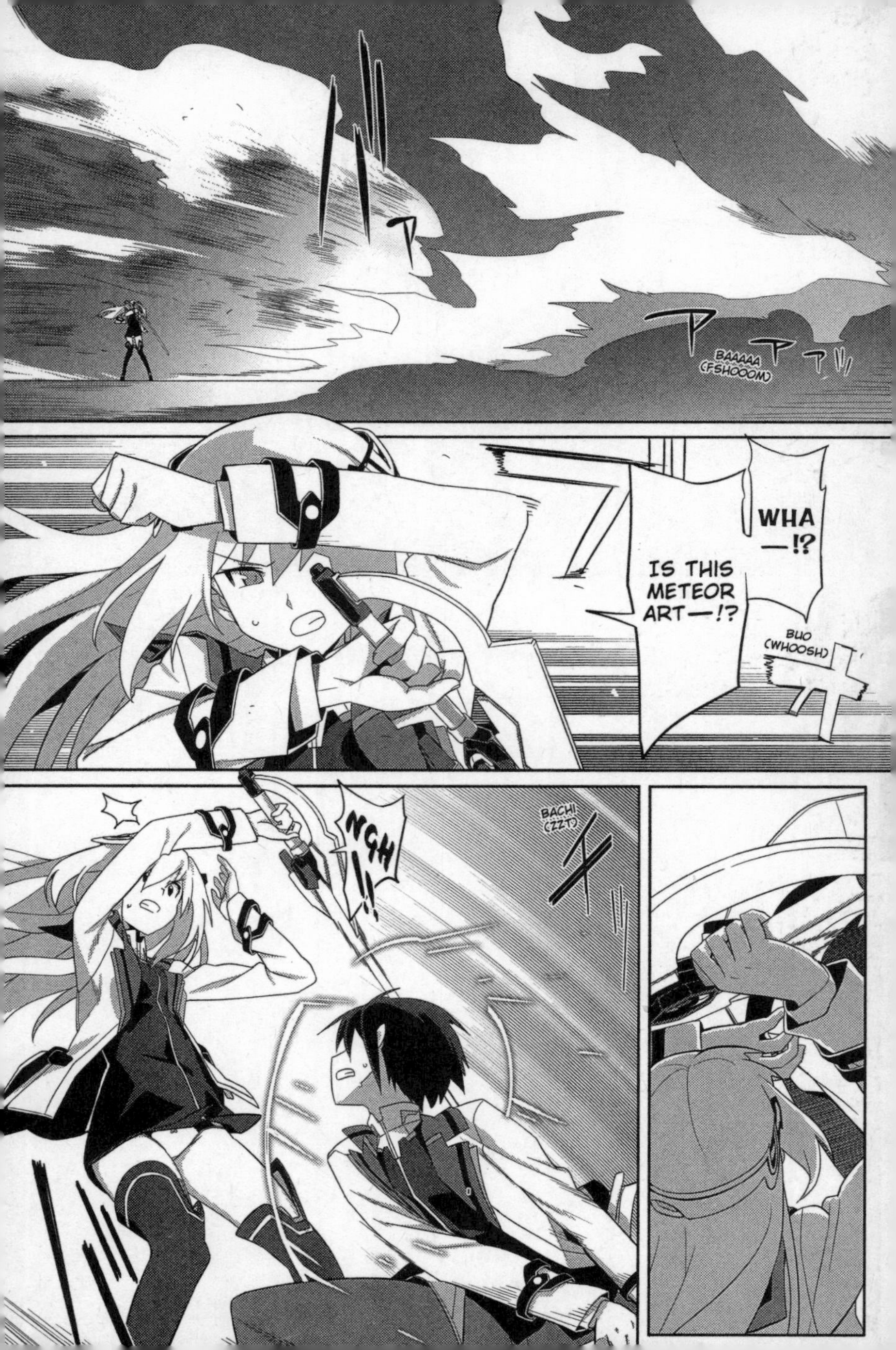
BAAAAA (FSHOOOM)
WHA—!?
IS THIS METEOR ART—!?
BUO (WHOOSH)
BACHI (ZZT)
NGH—!!

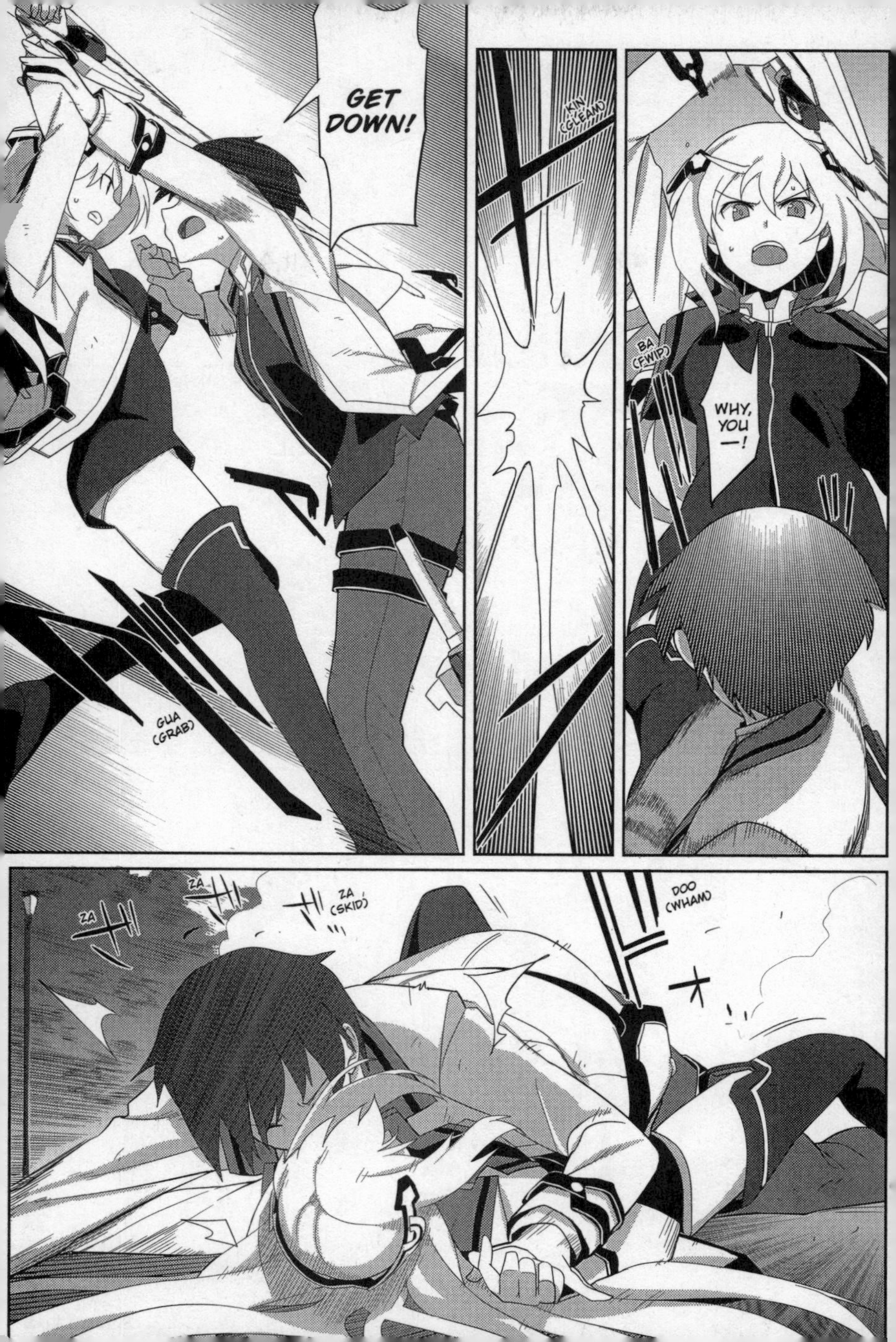
BA (FWIP)
WHY, YOU—!
KIN (GLEAM)
GET DOWN!
GUA (GRAB)
DOO (WHAM)
ZA (SKID)
ZA
ZA

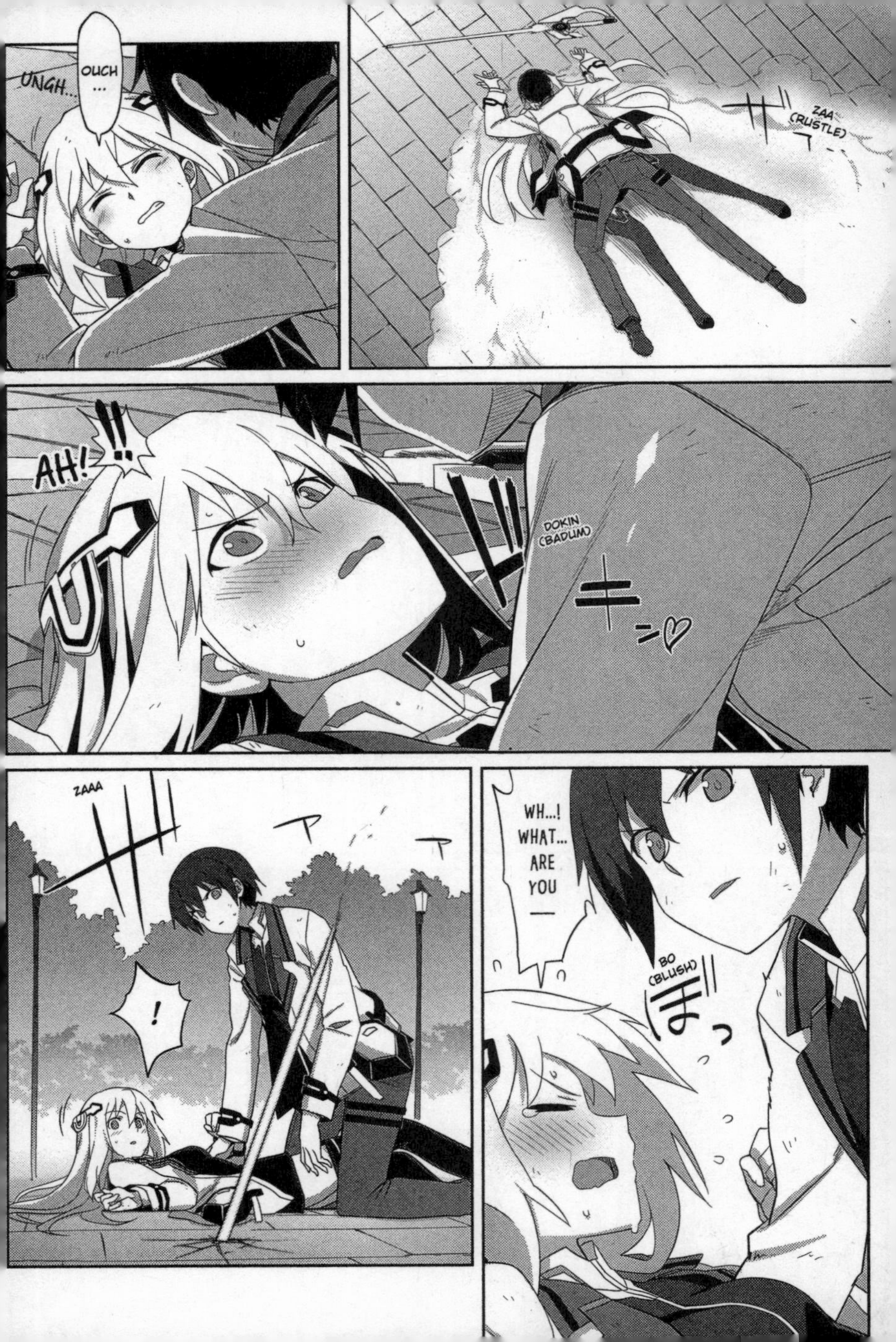
ZAA (RUSTLE)
OUCH ...
UNGH...
AH!
DOKIN (BADUM)
WH...! WHAT... ARE YOU —
BO (BLUSH)
ZAAA
!

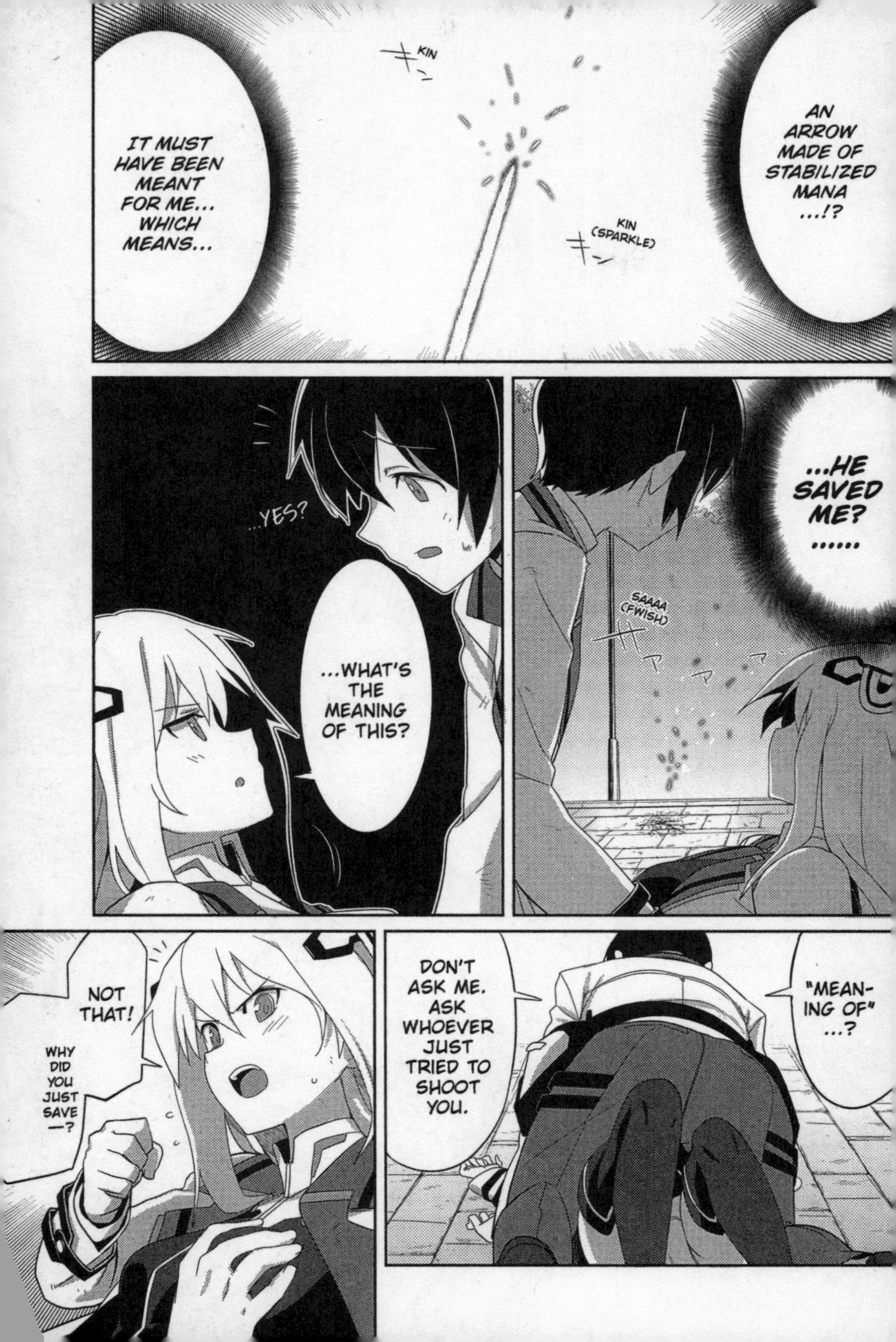
AN ARROW MADE OF STABILIZED MANA ...!?
KIN
KIN (SPARKLE)
IT MUST HAVE BEEN MEANT FOR ME... WHICH MEANS...
...HE SAVED ME? ......
SAAAA (FWISH)
...YES?
...WHAT'S THE MEANING OF THIS?
"MEAN-ING OF" ...?
DON'T ASK ME. ASK WHOEVER JUST TRIED TO SHOOT YOU.
NOT THAT!
WHY DID YOU JUST SAVE —?

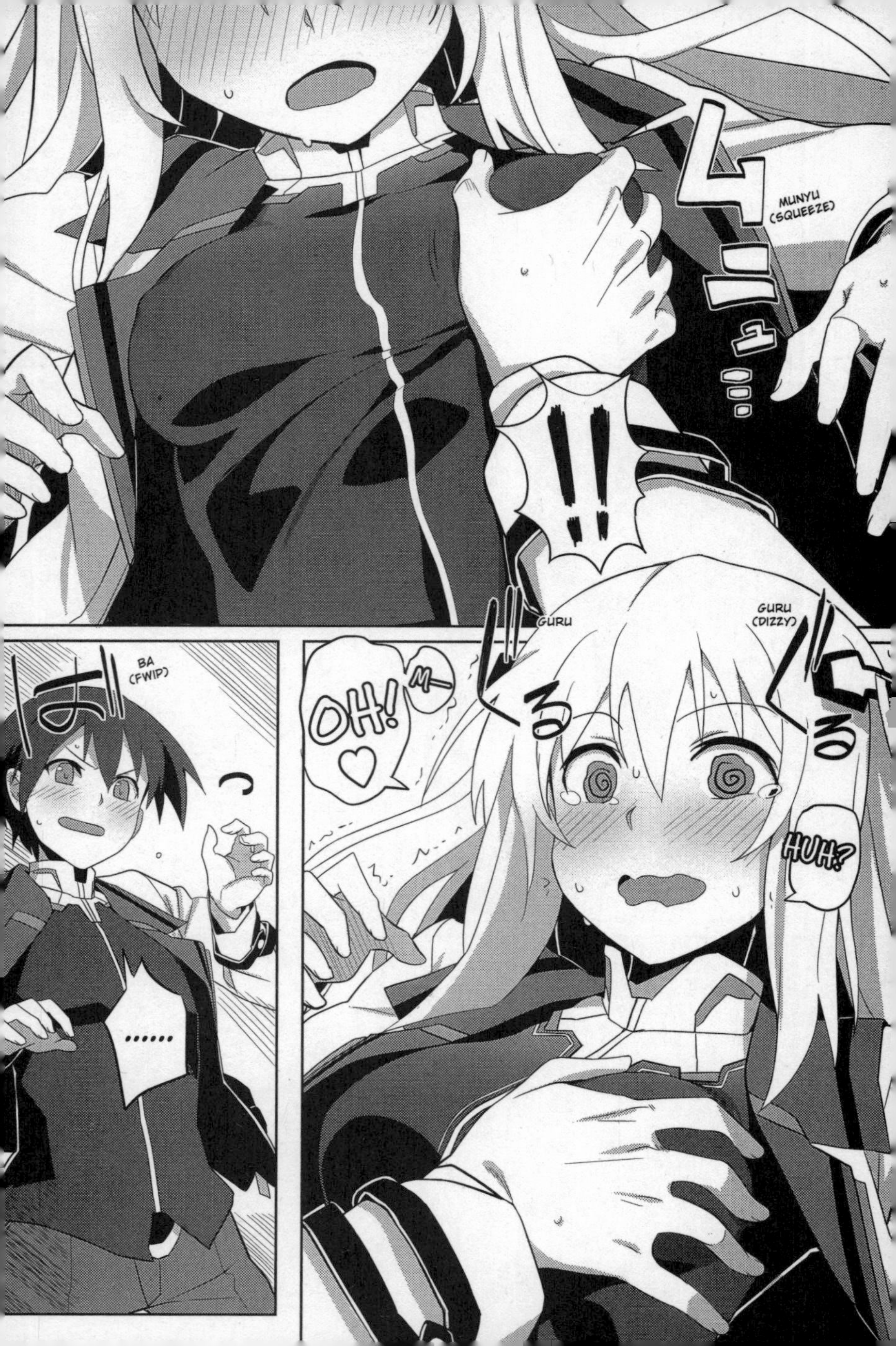
MUNYU (SQUEEZE)
!!
GURU (DIZZY)
GURU
HUH?
M—
OH! ♥
BA (FWIP)
......

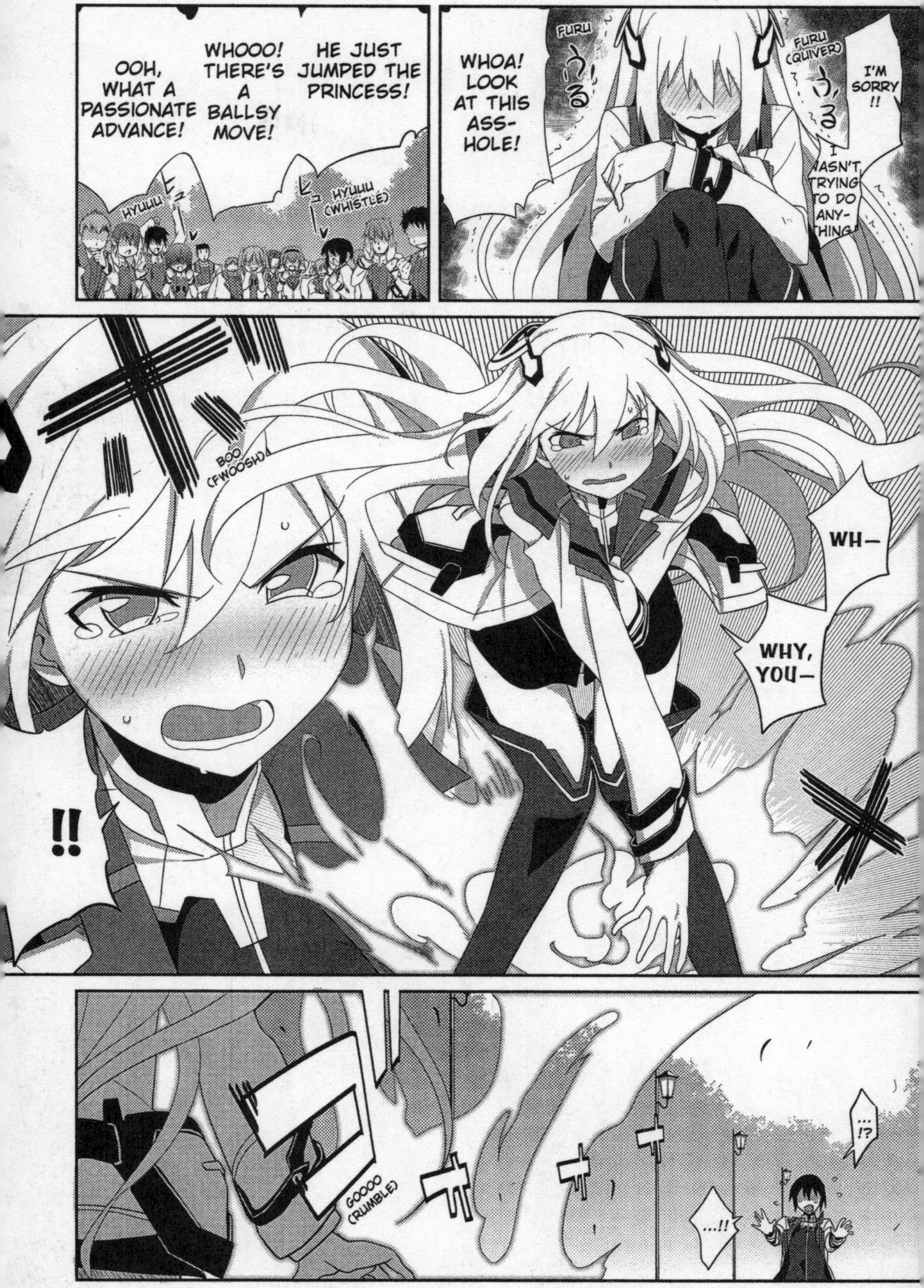

FURU (QUIVER)
ふる
I'M SORRY!!
I WASN'T TRYING TO DO ANYTHING!
FURU
ふる
WHOA! LOOK AT THIS ASS-HOLE!
HE JUST JUMPED THE PRINCESS!
WHOOOO! THERE'S A BALLSY MOVE!
OOH, WHAT A PASSIONATE ADVANCE!
HYUUU (WHISTLE)
HYUUU
WH—
WHY, YOU—
BOO (FWOOSH)
!!
...!?
...!!
GOOOO (RUMBLE)

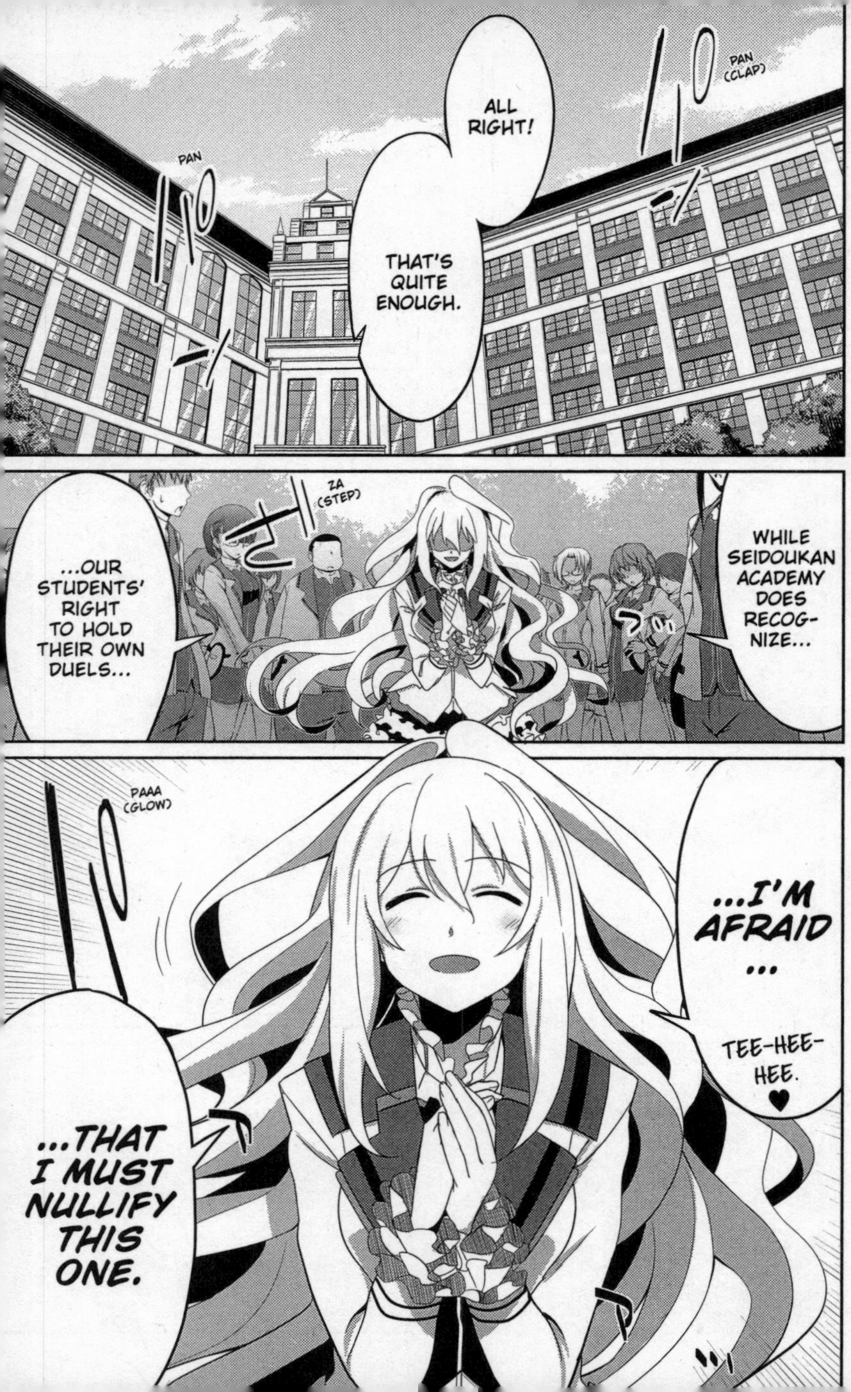
PAN (CLAP)
ALL RIGHT!
THAT'S QUITE ENOUGH.
PAN
WHILE SEIDOUKAN ACADEMY DOES RECOG-NIZE...
ZA (STEP)
...OUR STUDENTS' RIGHT TO HOLD THEIR OWN DUELS...
...I'M AFRAID...
TEE-HEE-HEE. ♥
PAAA (GLOW)
...THAT I MUST NULLIFY THIS ONE.

THE ASTERISK WAR

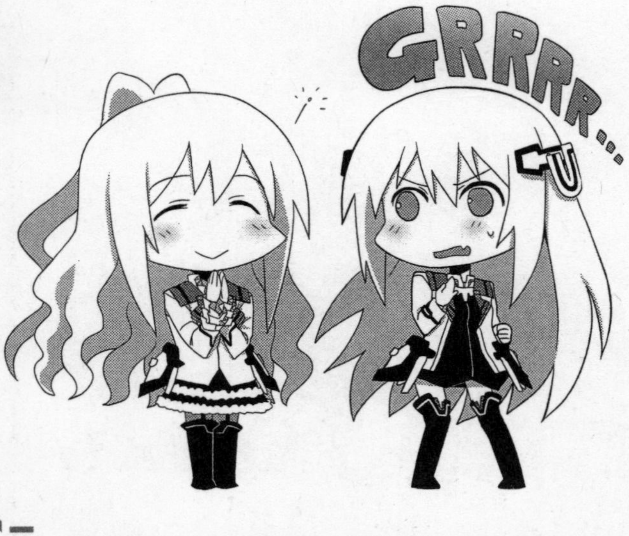
GRRRR...

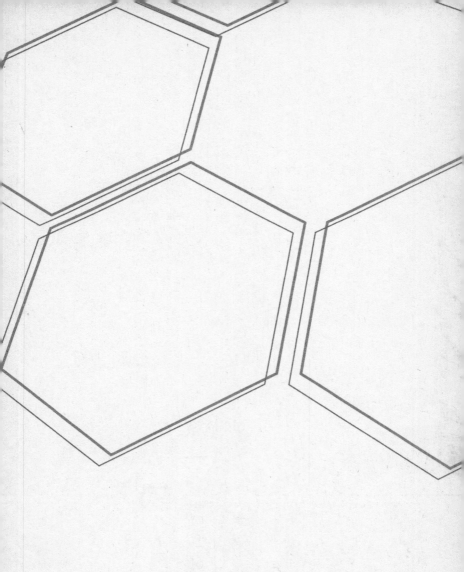

THE
ASTERISK WAR

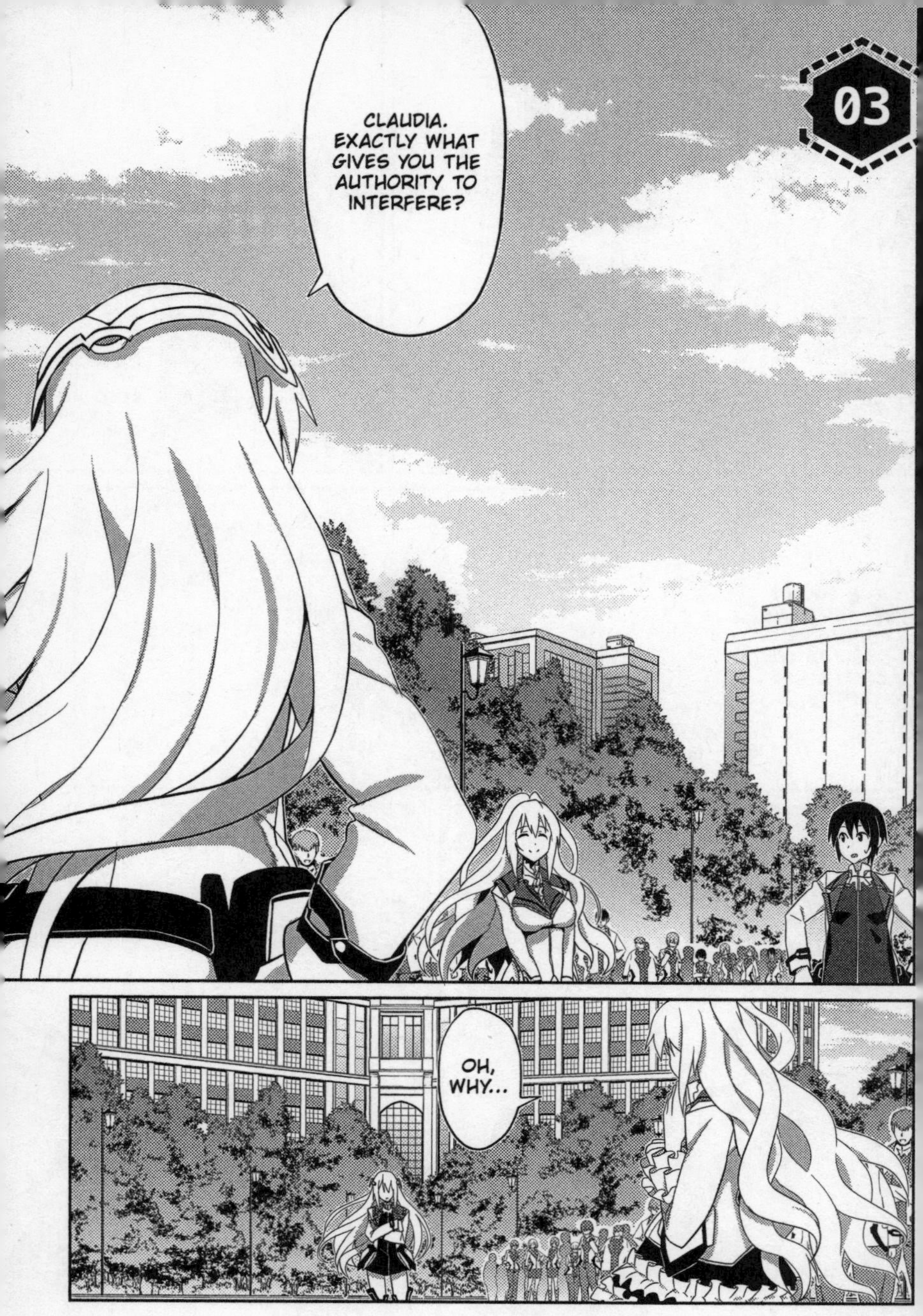
03
CLAUDIA. EXACTLY WHAT GIVES YOU THE AUTHORITY TO INTERFERE?
OH, WHY...

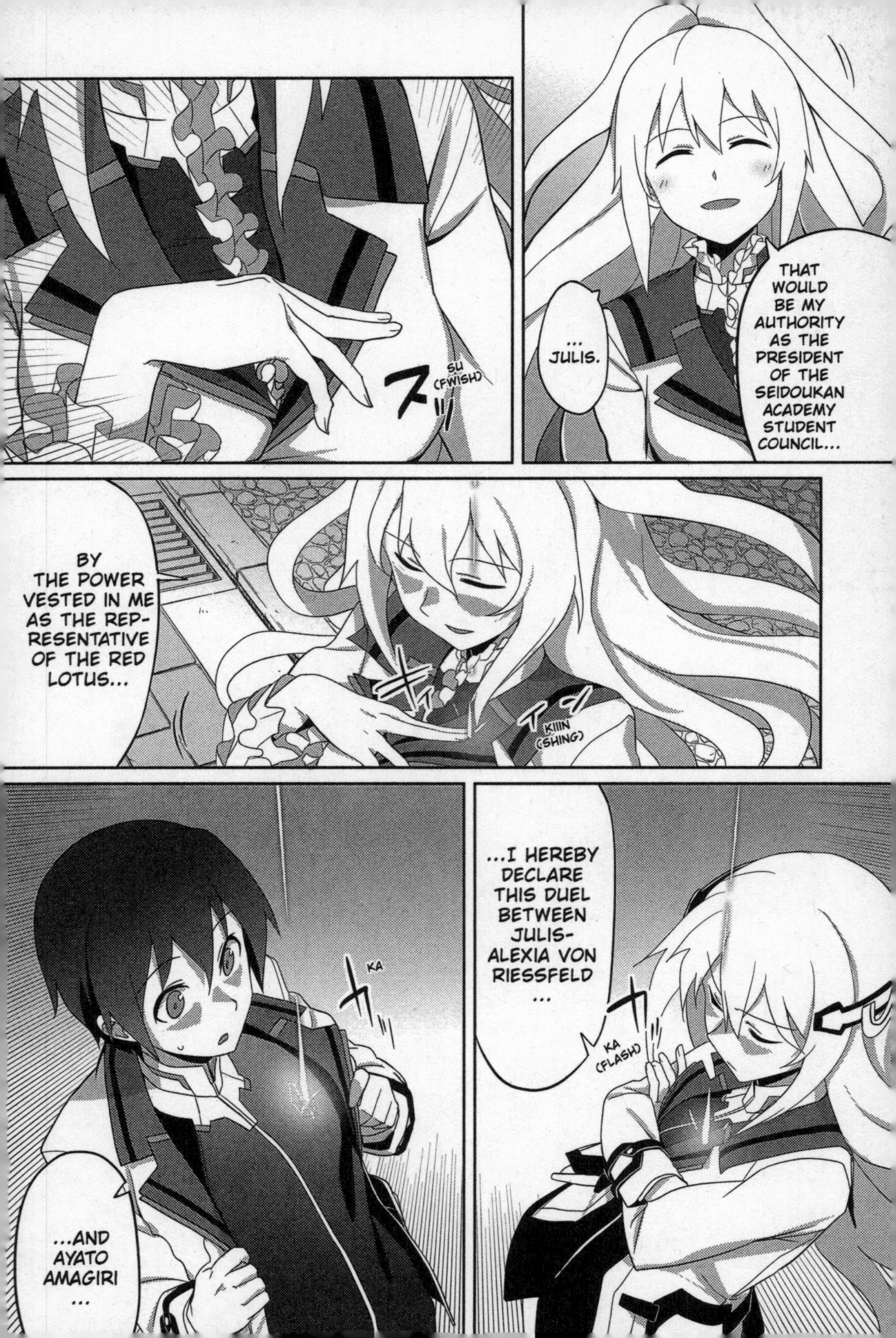
THAT WOULD BE MY AUTHORITY AS THE PRESIDENT OF THE SEIDOUKAN ACADEMY STUDENT COUNCIL...
... JULIS.
SU (FWISH)
BY THE POWER VESTED IN ME AS THE REP-RESENTATIVE OF THE RED LOTUS...
KIIN (SHING)
...I HEREBY DECLARE THIS DUEL BETWEEN JULIS-ALEXIA VON RIESSFELD ...
KA (FLASH)
KA
...AND AYATO AMAGIRI ...

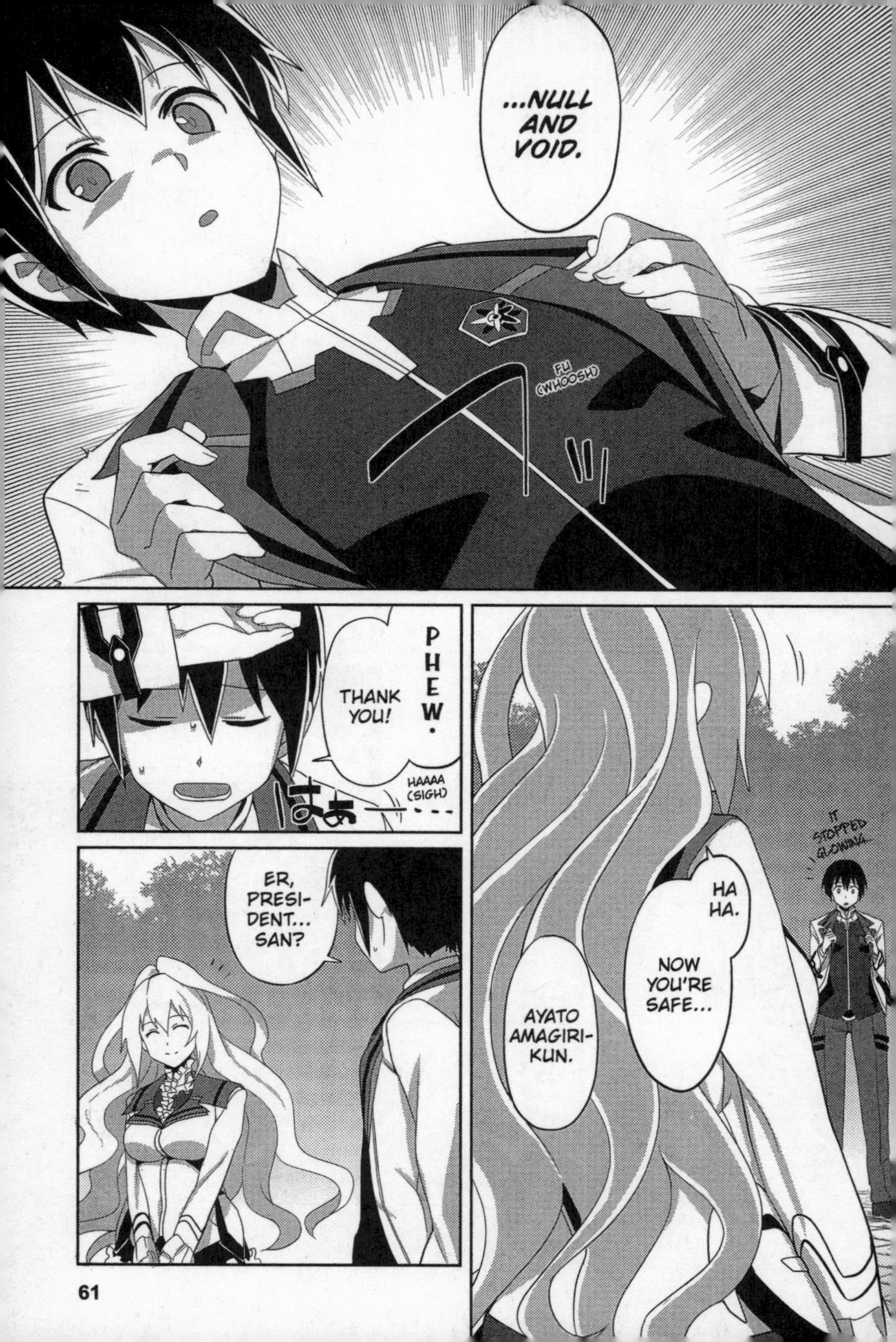
...NULL AND VOID.
FU (WHOOSH)
HA HA.
NOW YOU'RE SAFE...
AYATO AMAGIRI-KUN.
IT STOPPED GLOWING...
PHEW.
THANK YOU!
HAAAA (SIGH)
ER, PRESIDENT... SAN?

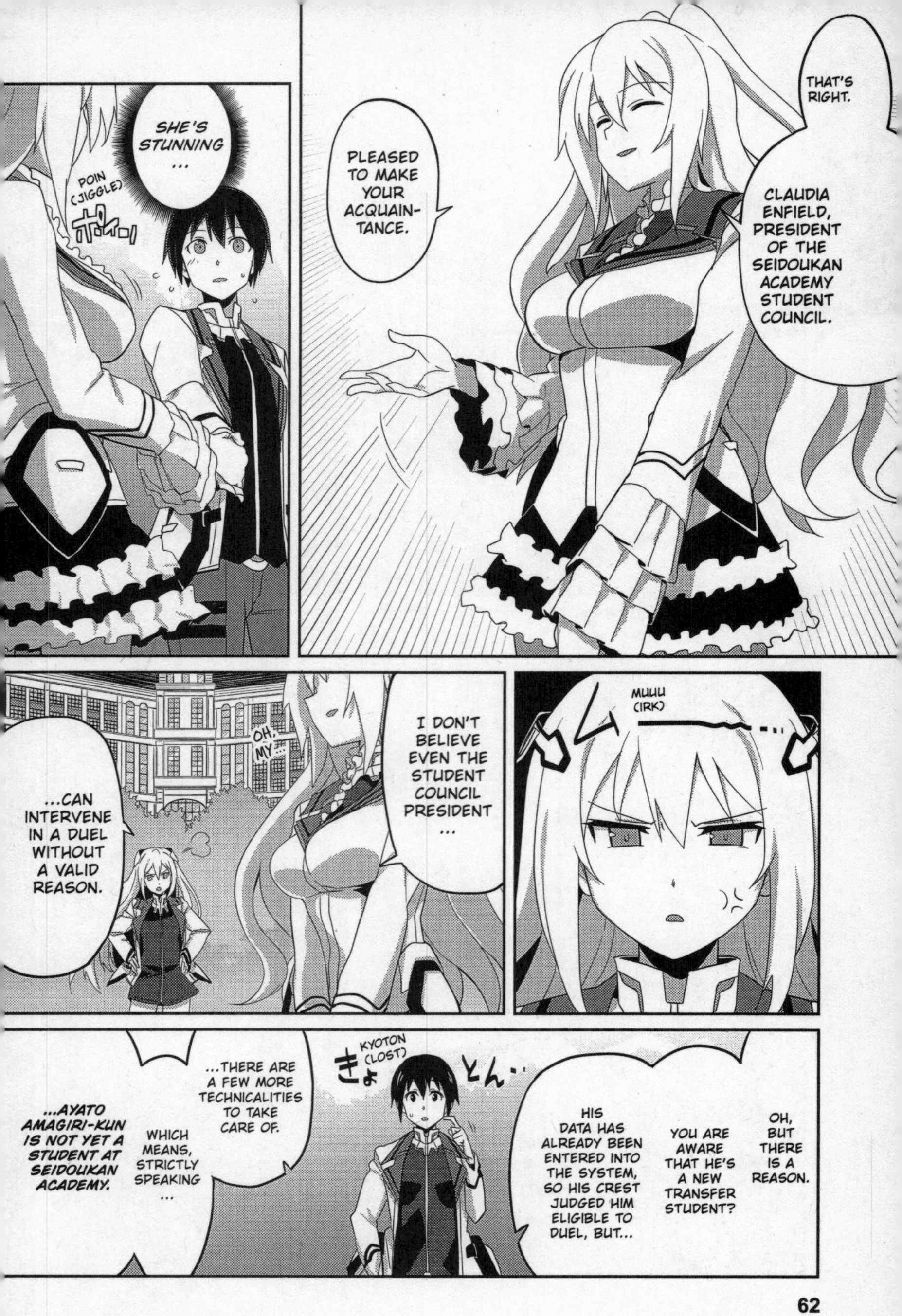
THAT'S RIGHT.
CLAUDIA ENFIELD, PRESIDENT OF THE SEIDOUKAN ACADEMY STUDENT COUNCIL.
PLEASED TO MAKE YOUR ACQUAINTANCE.
SHE'S STUNNING...
POIN (JIGGLE)
MUUU (IRK)
I DON'T BELIEVE EVEN THE STUDENT COUNCIL PRESIDENT...
OH, MY...
...CAN INTERVENE IN A DUEL WITHOUT A VALID REASON.
OH, BUT THERE IS A REASON.
YOU ARE AWARE THAT HE'S A NEW TRANSFER STUDENT?
HIS DATA HAS ALREADY BEEN ENTERED INTO THE SYSTEM, SO HIS CREST JUDGED HIM ELIGIBLE TO DUEL, BUT...
KYOTON (LOST)
きょとん
...THERE ARE A FEW MORE TECHNICALITIES TO TAKE CARE OF.
WHICH MEANS, STRICTLY SPEAKING...
...AYATO AMAGIRI-KUN IS NOT YET A STUDENT AT SEIDOUKAN ACADEMY.

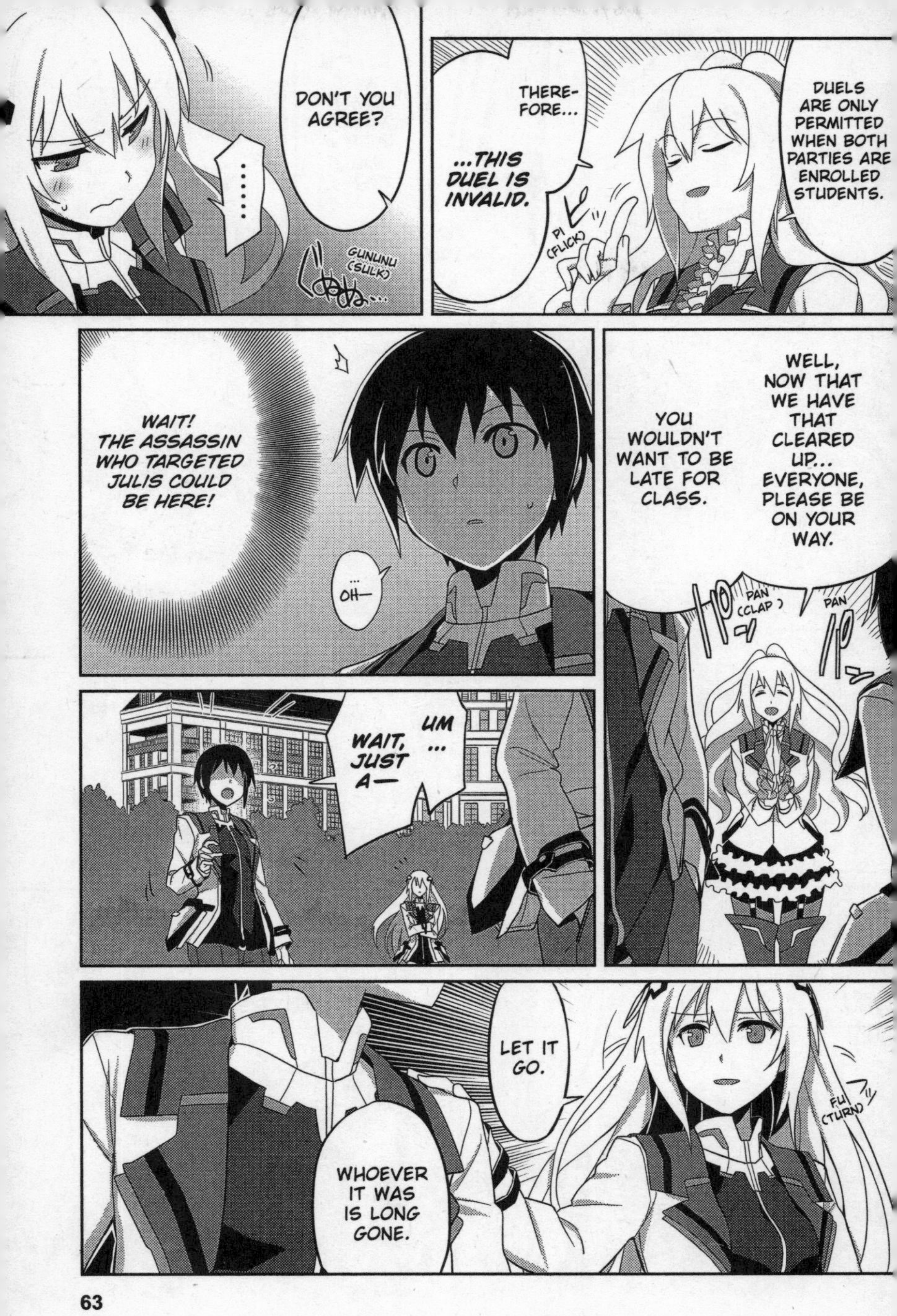
DUELS ARE ONLY PERMITTED WHEN BOTH PARTIES ARE ENROLLED STUDENTS.
THERE-FORE...
...THIS DUEL IS INVALID.
PI (FLICK)
DON'T YOU AGREE?
......
GUNUNU (SULK)
WELL, NOW THAT WE HAVE THAT CLEARED UP... EVERYONE, PLEASE BE ON YOUR WAY.
YOU WOULDN'T WANT TO BE LATE FOR CLASS.
PAN (CLAP)
PAN
...OH—
WAIT! THE ASSASSIN WHO TARGETED JULIS COULD BE HERE!
UM...
WAIT, JUST A—
LET IT GO.
FU (TURN)
WHOEVER IT WAS IS LONG GONE.

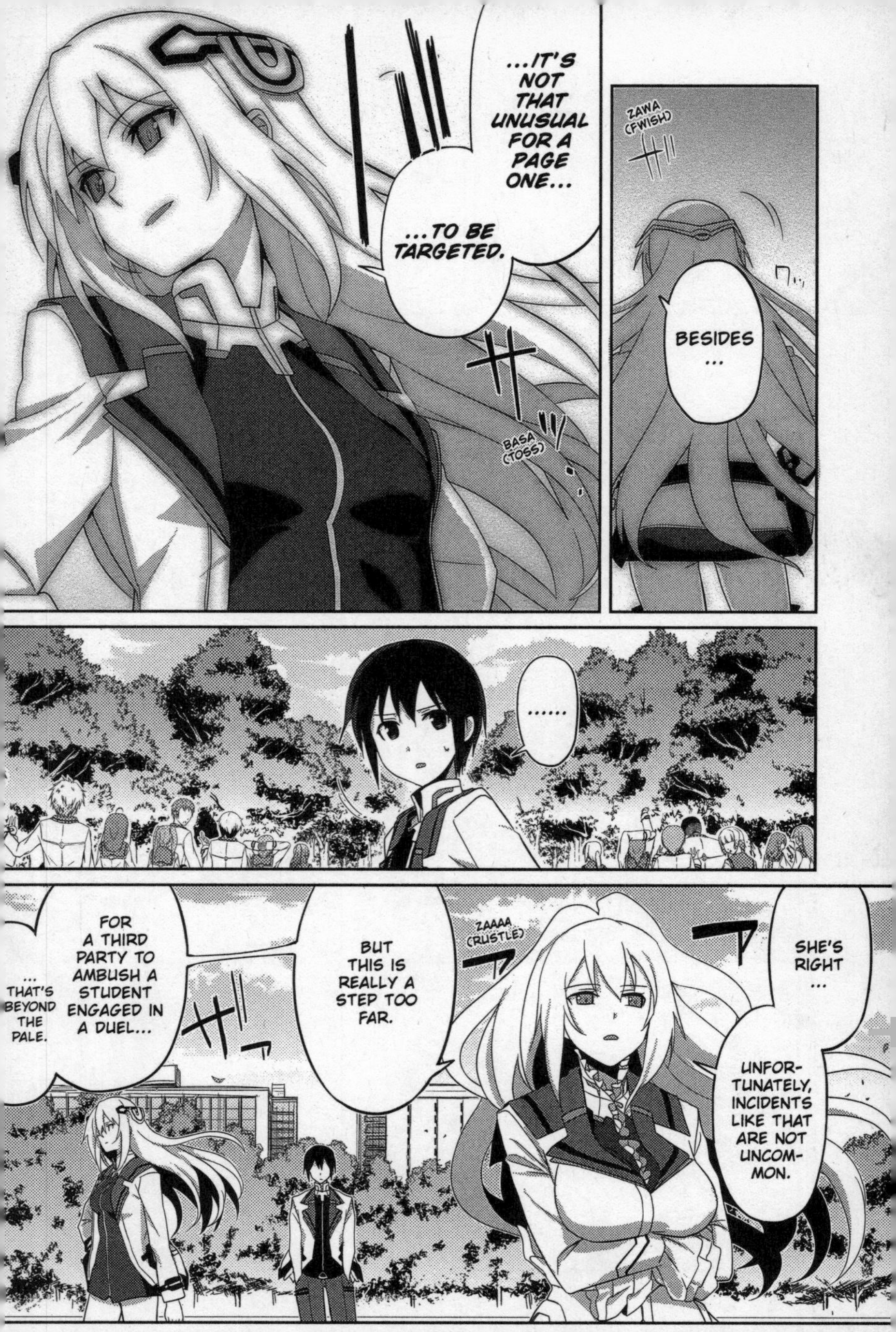
ZAWA (FWISH)
BESIDES...
...IT'S NOT THAT UNUSUAL FOR A PAGE ONE...
...TO BE TARGETED.
BASA (TOSS)
......
SHE'S RIGHT...
UNFORTUNATELY, INCIDENTS LIKE THAT ARE NOT UNCOMMON.
ZAAAA (RUSTLE)
BUT THIS IS REALLY A STEP TOO FAR.
FOR A THIRD PARTY TO AMBUSH A STUDENT ENGAGED IN A DUEL...
...THAT'S BEYOND THE PALE.

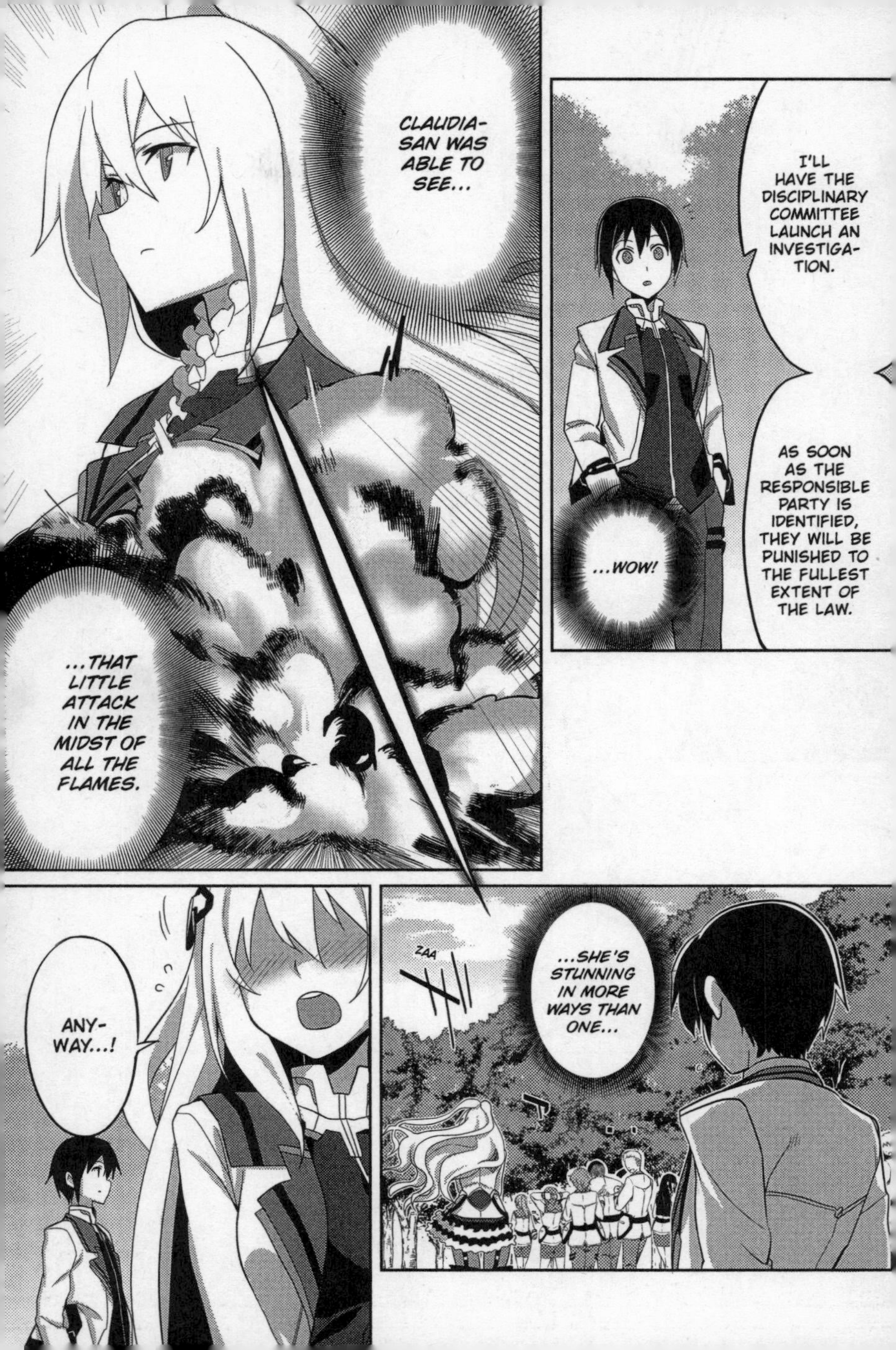
I'LL HAVE THE DISCIPLINARY COMMITTEE LAUNCH AN INVESTIGATION.
AS SOON AS THE RESPONSIBLE PARTY IS IDENTIFIED, THEY WILL BE PUNISHED TO THE FULLEST EXTENT OF THE LAW.
...WOW!
CLAUDIA-SAN WAS ABLE TO SEE...
...THAT LITTLE ATTACK IN THE MIDST OF ALL THE FLAMES.
ZAA
...SHE'S STUNNING IN MORE WAYS THAN ONE...
ANYWAY...!

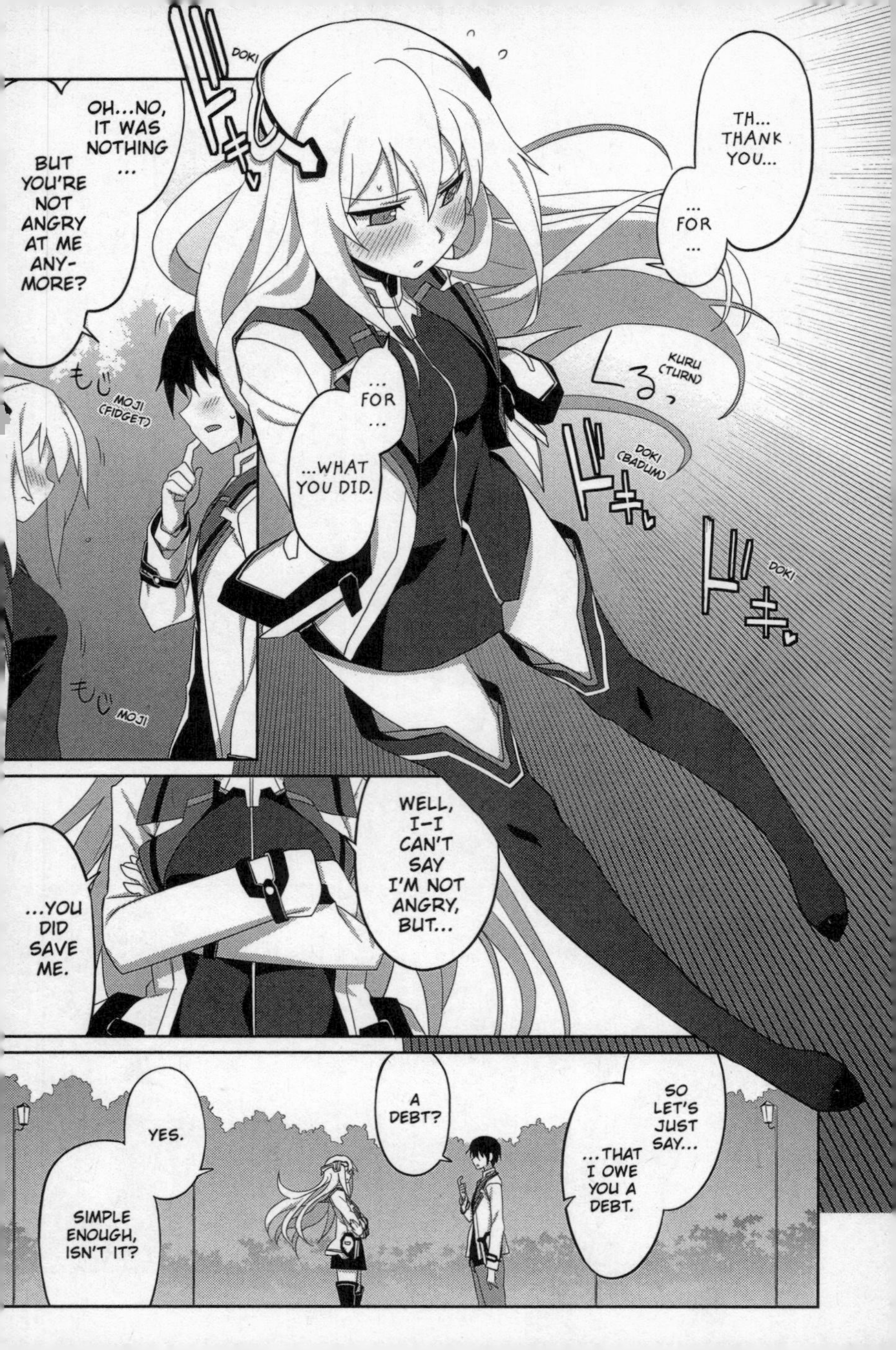
DOKI
TH... THANK YOU...
... FOR ...
KURU (TURN)
DOKI (BADUM)
DOKI
... FOR ...
...WHAT YOU DID.
OH...NO, IT WAS NOTHING ...
BUT YOU'RE NOT ANGRY AT ME ANY-MORE?
MOJI (FIDGET)
MOJI
WELL, I-I CAN'T SAY I'M NOT ANGRY, BUT...
...YOU DID SAVE ME.
SO LET'S JUST SAY...
...THAT I OWE YOU A DEBT.
A DEBT?
YES.
SIMPLE ENOUGH, ISN'T IT?

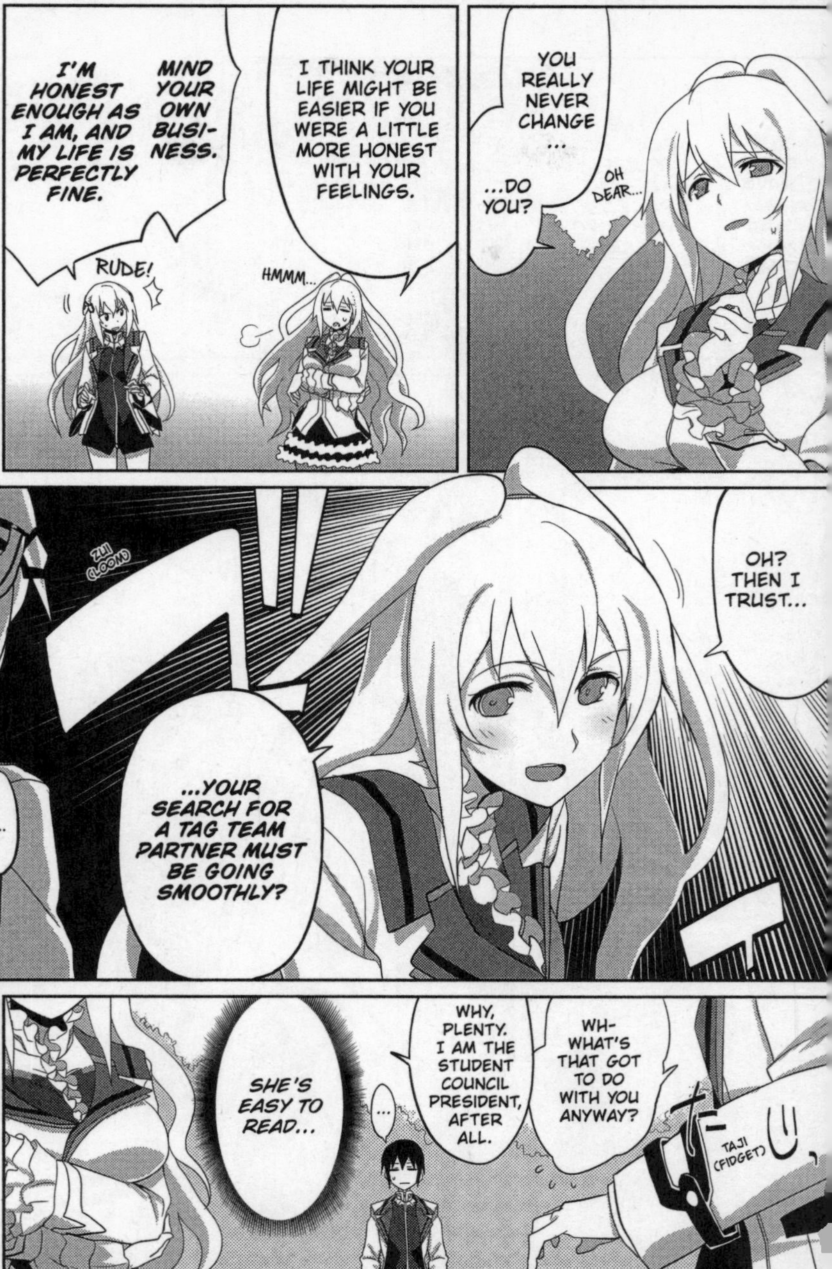
YOU REALLY NEVER CHANGE...
...DO YOU?
OH DEAR...
I THINK YOUR LIFE MIGHT BE EASIER IF YOU WERE A LITTLE MORE HONEST WITH YOUR FEELINGS.
MIND YOUR OWN BUSI-NESS.
I'M HONEST ENOUGH AS I AM, AND MY LIFE IS PERFECTLY FINE.
HMMM...
RUDE!
OH? THEN I TRUST...
...YOUR SEARCH FOR A TAG TEAM PARTNER MUST BE GOING SMOOTHLY?
ZUI (LOOM)
UM... WELL...
WH-WHAT'S THAT GOT TO DO WITH YOU ANYWAY?
TAJI (FIDGET)
WHY, PLENTY. I AM THE STUDENT COUNCIL PRESIDENT, AFTER ALL.
...
SHE'S EASY TO READ...

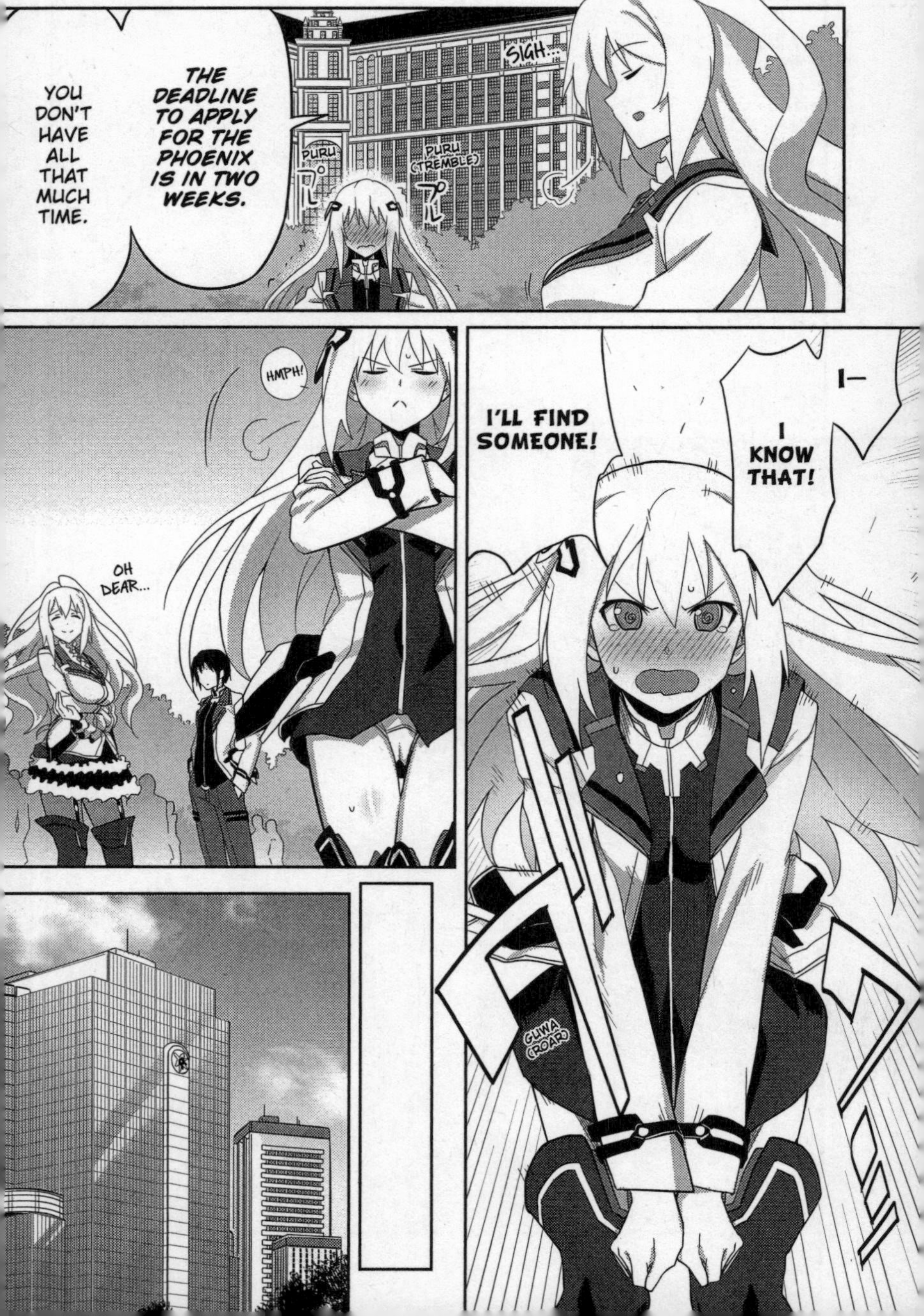
SIGH...
PURU (TREMBLE)
PURU
THE DEADLINE TO APPLY FOR THE PHOENIX IS IN TWO WEEKS.
YOU DON'T HAVE ALL THAT MUCH TIME.
I—
I KNOW THAT!
I'LL FIND SOMEONE!
GUWA (ROAR)
HMPH!
OH DEAR...

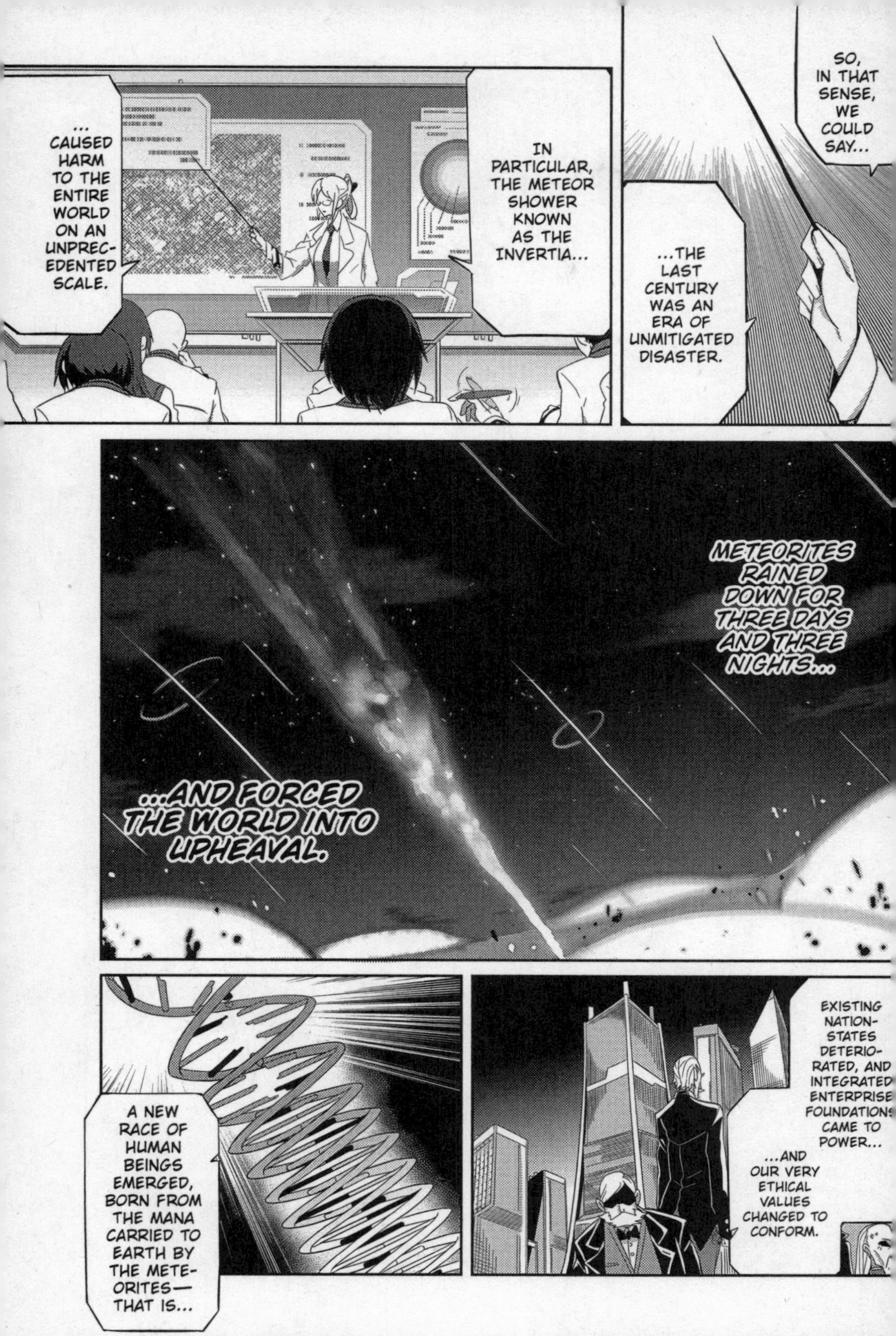
SO, IN THAT SENSE, WE COULD SAY...
...THE LAST CENTURY WAS AN ERA OF UNMITIGATED DISASTER.
IN PARTICULAR, THE METEOR SHOWER KNOWN AS THE INVERTIA...
...CAUSED HARM TO THE ENTIRE WORLD ON AN UNPREC-EDENTED SCALE.
METEORITES RAINED DOWN FOR THREE DAYS AND THREE NIGHTS...
...AND FORCED THE WORLD INTO UPHEAVAL.
EXISTING NATION-STATES DETERIO-RATED, AND INTEGRATED ENTERPRISE FOUNDATIONS CAME TO POWER...
...AND OUR VERY ETHICAL VALUES CHANGED TO CONFORM.
A NEW RACE OF HUMAN BEINGS EMERGED, BORN FROM THE MANA CARRIED TO EARTH BY THE METE-ORITES—THAT IS...

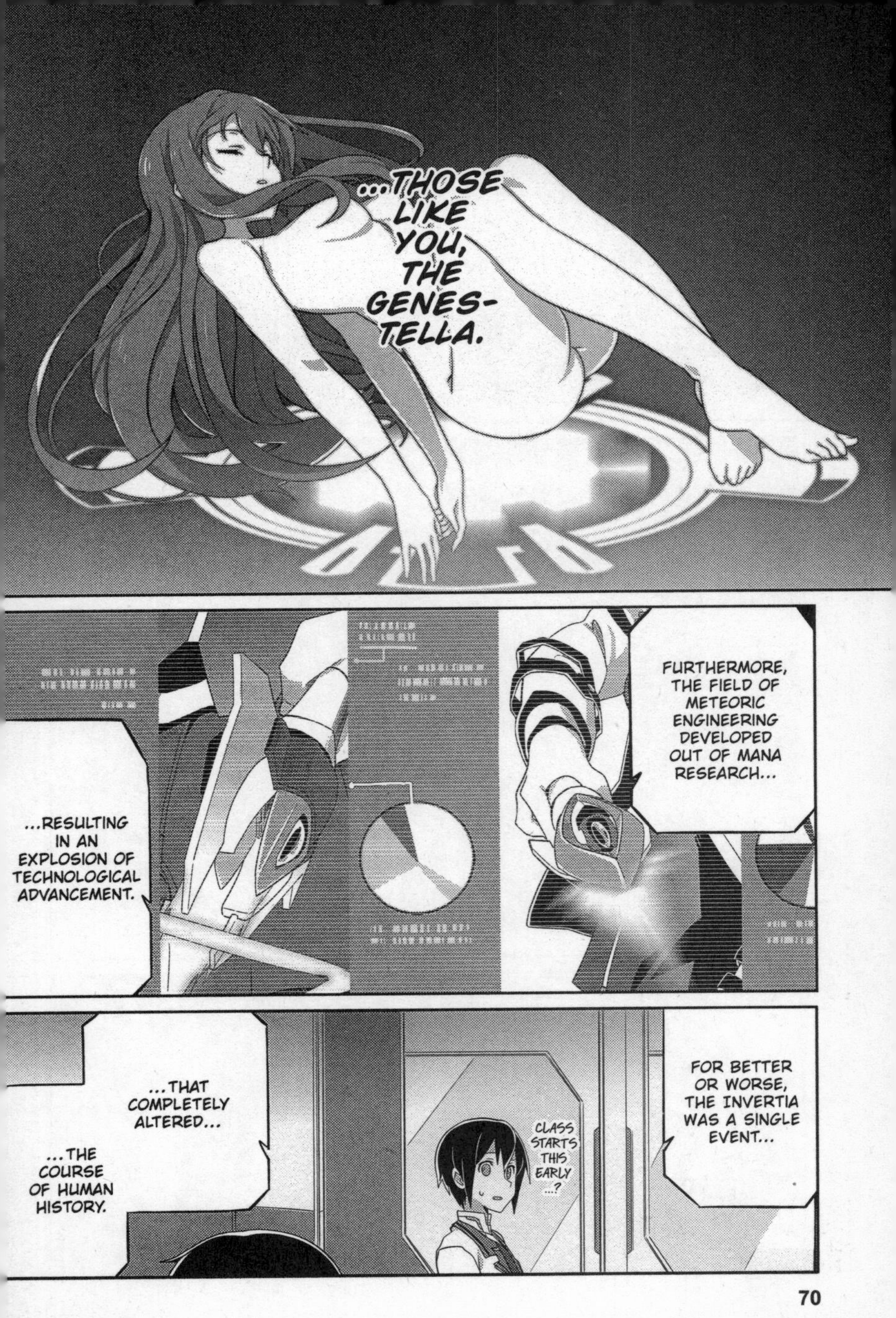
...THOSE LIKE YOU, THE GENES-TELLA.
FURTHERMORE, THE FIELD OF METEORIC ENGINEERING DEVELOPED OUT OF MANA RESEARCH...
...RESULTING IN AN EXPLOSION OF TECHNOLOGICAL ADVANCEMENT.
FOR BETTER OR WORSE, THE INVERTIA WAS A SINGLE EVENT...
CLASS STARTS THIS EARLY ...?
...THAT COMPLETELY ALTERED...
...THE COURSE OF HUMAN HISTORY.

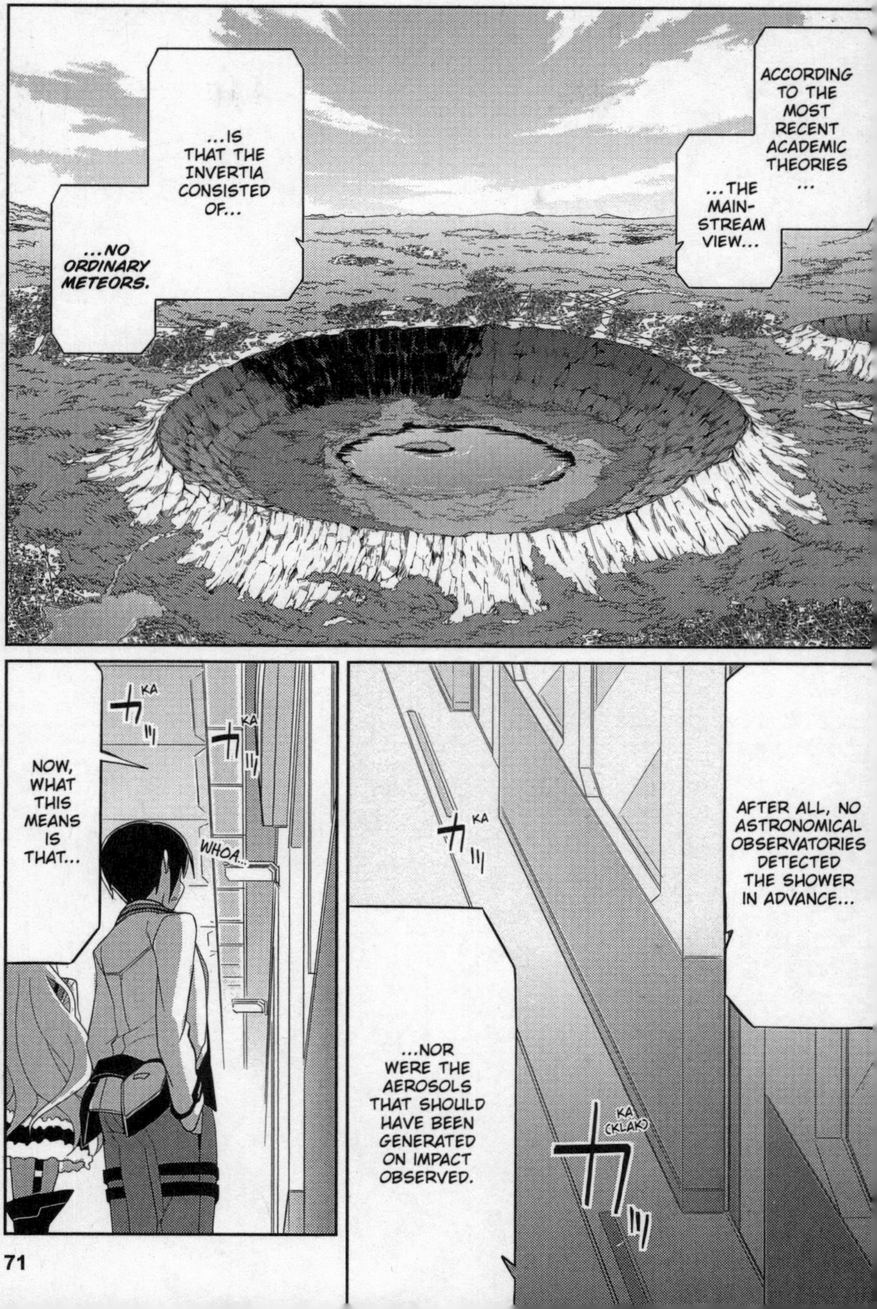
ACCORDING TO THE MOST RECENT ACADEMIC THEORIES...
...THE MAIN-STREAM VIEW...
...IS THAT THE INVERTIA CONSISTED OF...
...NO ORDINARY METEORS.
AFTER ALL, NO ASTRONOMICAL OBSERVATORIES DETECTED THE SHOWER IN ADVANCE...
カッ KA
...NOR WERE THE AEROSOLS THAT SHOULD HAVE BEEN GENERATED ON IMPACT OBSERVED.
カッ KA (KLAK)
カッ KA
カッ KA
NOW, WHAT THIS MEANS IS THAT...
WHOA...

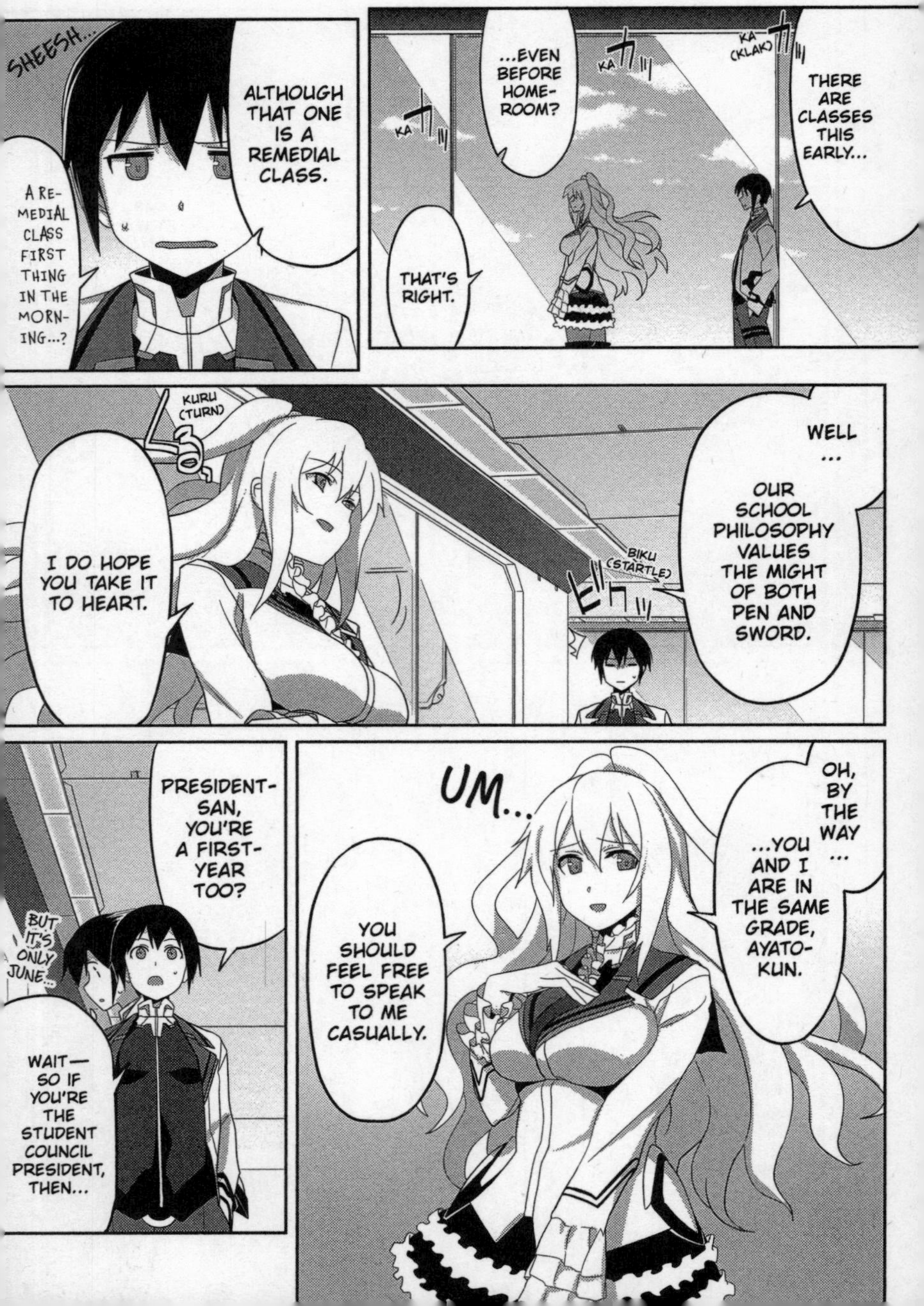
THERE ARE CLASSES THIS EARLY...
KA (KLAK)
KA
...EVEN BEFORE HOME-ROOM?
KA
THAT'S RIGHT.
ALTHOUGH THAT ONE IS A REMEDIAL CLASS.
SHEESH...
A RE-MEDIAL CLASS FIRST THING IN THE MORN-ING...?
WELL... OUR SCHOOL PHILOSOPHY VALUES THE MIGHT OF BOTH PEN AND SWORD.
BIKU (STARTLE)
KURU (TURN)
I DO HOPE YOU TAKE IT TO HEART.
OH, BY THE WAY... ...YOU AND I ARE IN THE SAME GRADE, AYATO-KUN.
UM...
YOU SHOULD FEEL FREE TO SPEAK TO ME CASUALLY.
PRESIDENT-SAN, YOU'RE A FIRST-YEAR TOO?
BUT IT'S ONLY JUNE...
WAIT— SO IF YOU'RE THE STUDENT COUNCIL PRESIDENT, THEN...

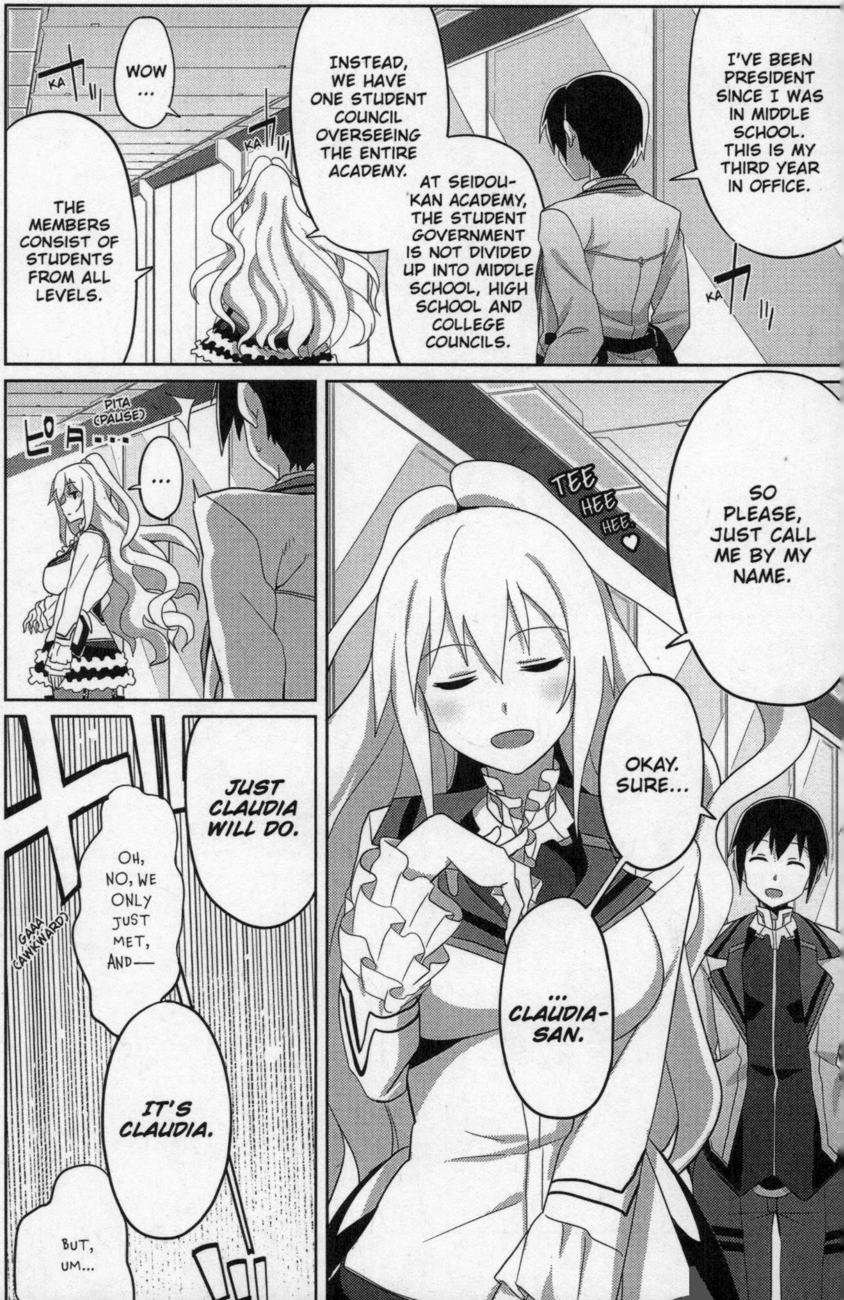
I'VE BEEN PRESIDENT SINCE I WAS IN MIDDLE SCHOOL. THIS IS MY THIRD YEAR IN OFFICE.
KA
INSTEAD, WE HAVE ONE STUDENT COUNCIL OVERSEEING THE ENTIRE ACADEMY.
KA
AT SEIDOU-KAN ACADEMY, THE STUDENT GOVERNMENT IS NOT DIVIDED UP INTO MIDDLE SCHOOL, HIGH SCHOOL AND COLLEGE COUNCILS.
WOW ...
KA
THE MEMBERS CONSIST OF STUDENTS FROM ALL LEVELS.
SO PLEASE, JUST CALL ME BY MY NAME.
TEE HEE HEE.♥
OKAY. SURE...
... CLAUDIA-SAN.
PITA (PAUSE)
ピタ…
...
JUST CLAUDIA WILL DO.
OH, NO, WE ONLY JUST MET, AND—
GAAA (AWKWARD)
IT'S CLAUDIA.
BUT, UM...

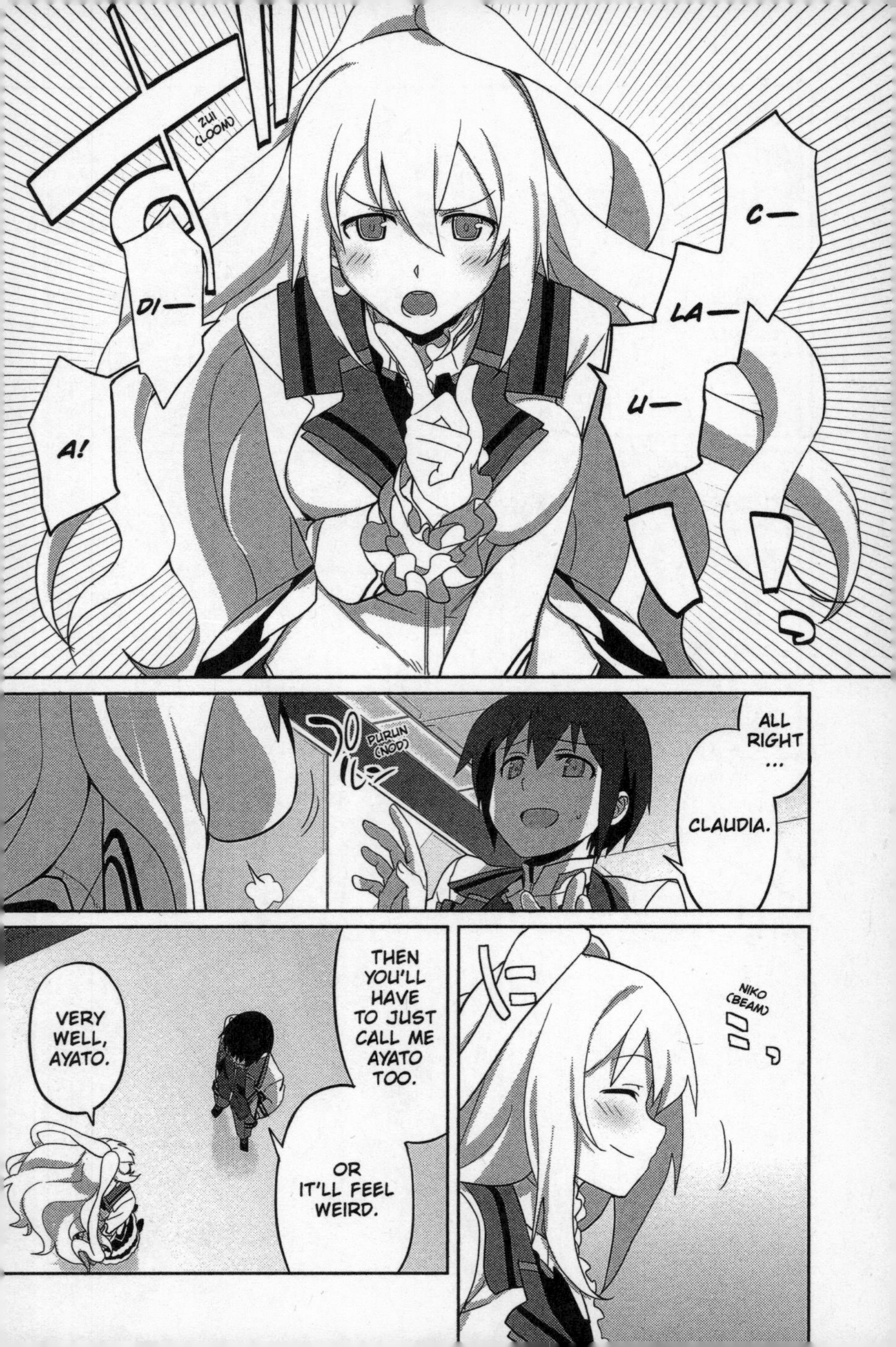
ZUI (LOOM)
C—
LA—
U—
DI—
A!
ALL RIGHT...
CLAUDIA.
PURUN (NOD)
NIKO (BEAM)
THEN YOU'LL HAVE TO JUST CALL ME AYATO TOO.
OR IT'LL FEEL WEIRD.
VERY WELL, AYATO.

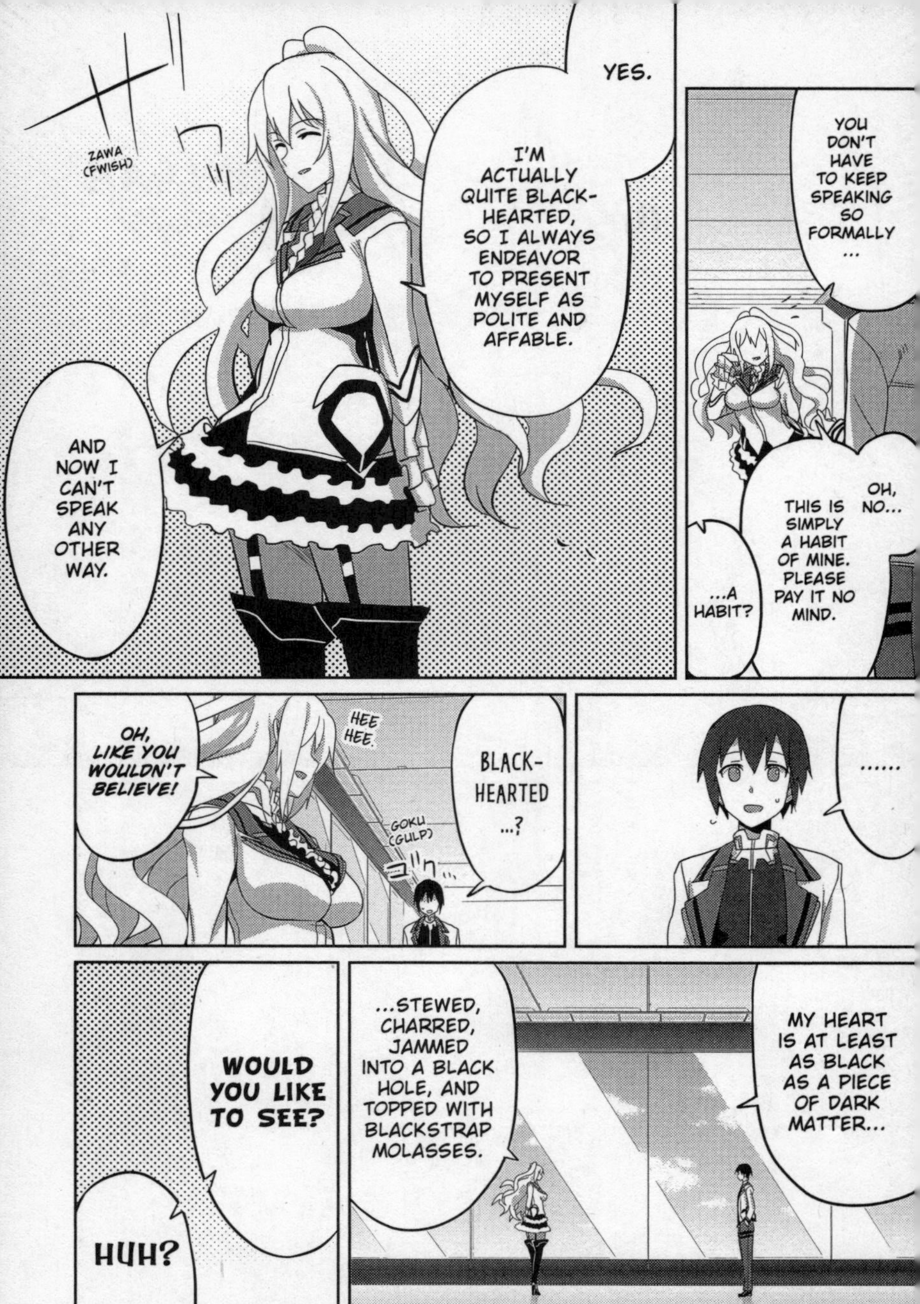
YOU DON'T HAVE TO KEEP SPEAKING SO FORMALLY ...
OH, NO...
THIS IS SIMPLY A HABIT OF MINE. PLEASE PAY IT NO MIND.
...A HABIT?
YES.
I'M ACTUALLY QUITE BLACK-HEARTED, SO I ALWAYS ENDEAVOR TO PRESENT MYSELF AS POLITE AND AFFABLE.
ZAWA (FWISH)
AND NOW I CAN'T SPEAK ANY OTHER WAY.
......
BLACK-HEARTED ...?
HEE HEE.
GOKU (GULP)
OH, LIKE YOU WOULDN'T BELIEVE!
MY HEART IS AT LEAST AS BLACK AS A PIECE OF DARK MATTER...
...STEWED, CHARRED, JAMMED INTO A BLACK HOLE, AND TOPPED WITH BLACKSTRAP MOLASSES.
WOULD YOU LIKE TO SEE?
HUH?

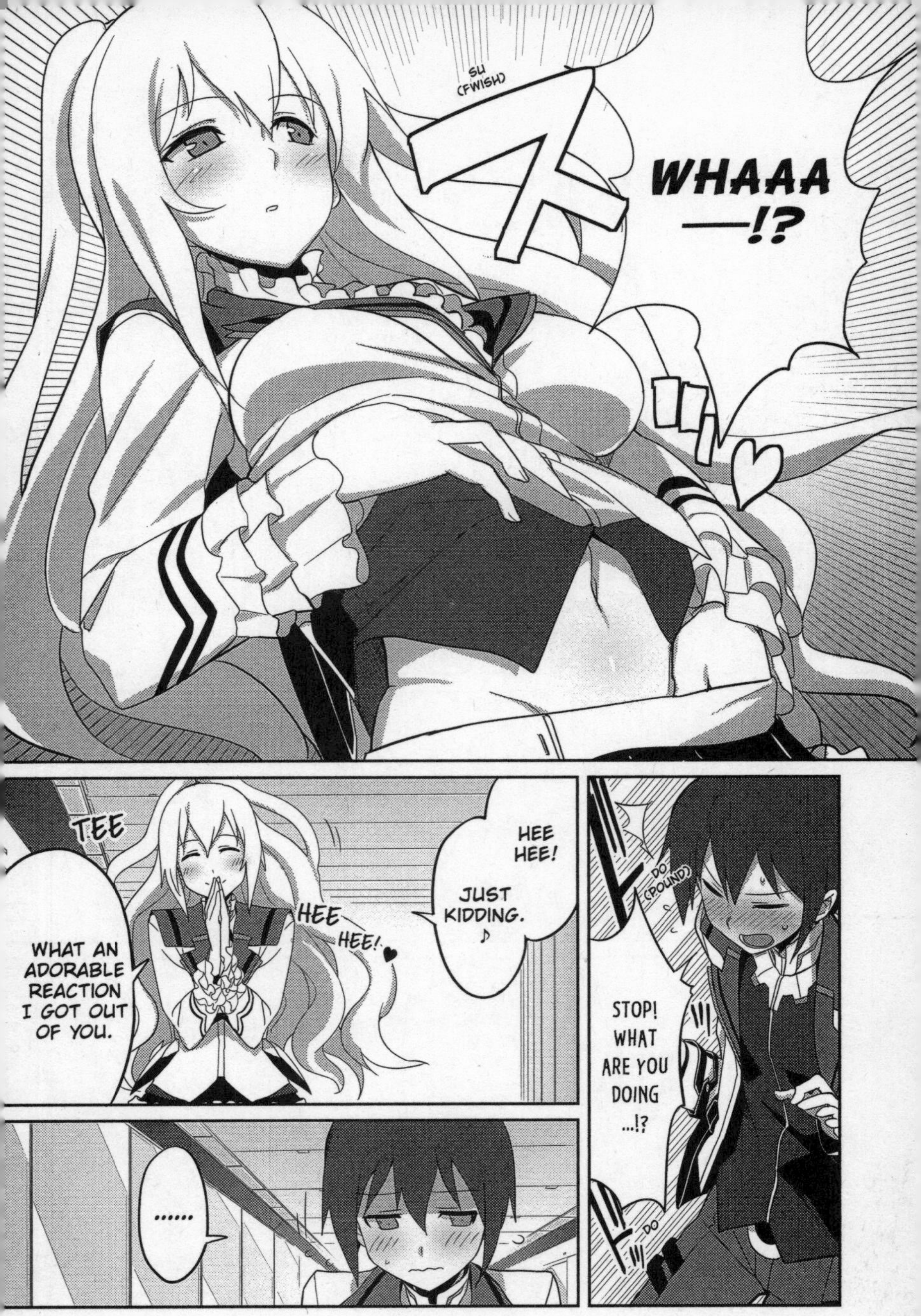

SU (FWISH)
WHAAA —!?
DO (POUND)
STOP! WHAT ARE YOU DOING ...!?
DO
HEE HEE! JUST KIDDING. ♪
HEE HEE! ♥
TEE
WHAT AN ADORABLE REACTION I GOT OUT OF YOU.
......

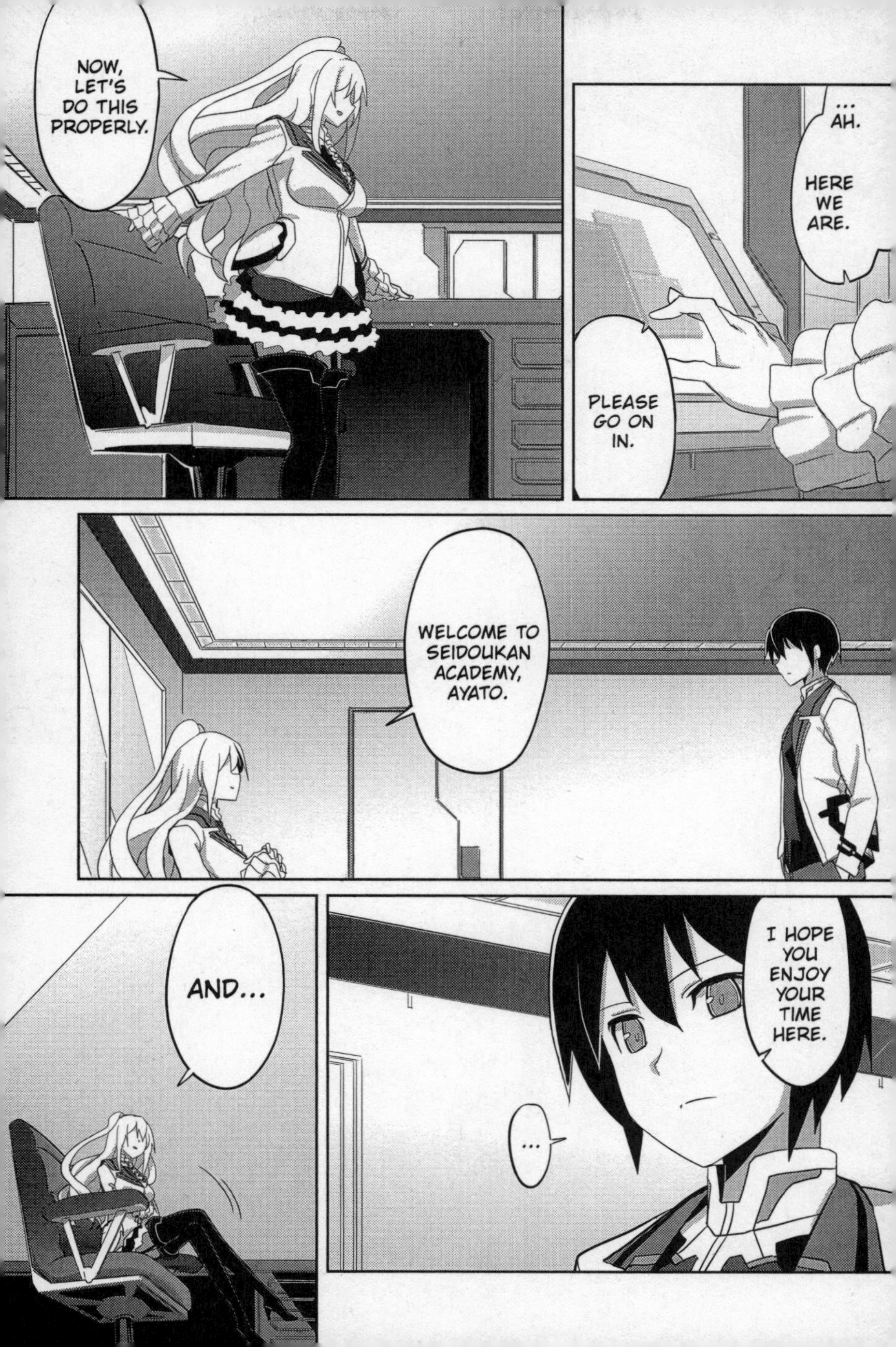

... AH.
HERE WE ARE.
PLEASE GO ON IN.
NOW, LET'S DO THIS PROPERLY.
WELCOME TO SEIDOUKAN ACADEMY, AYATO.
I HOPE YOU ENJOY YOUR TIME HERE.
...
AND...

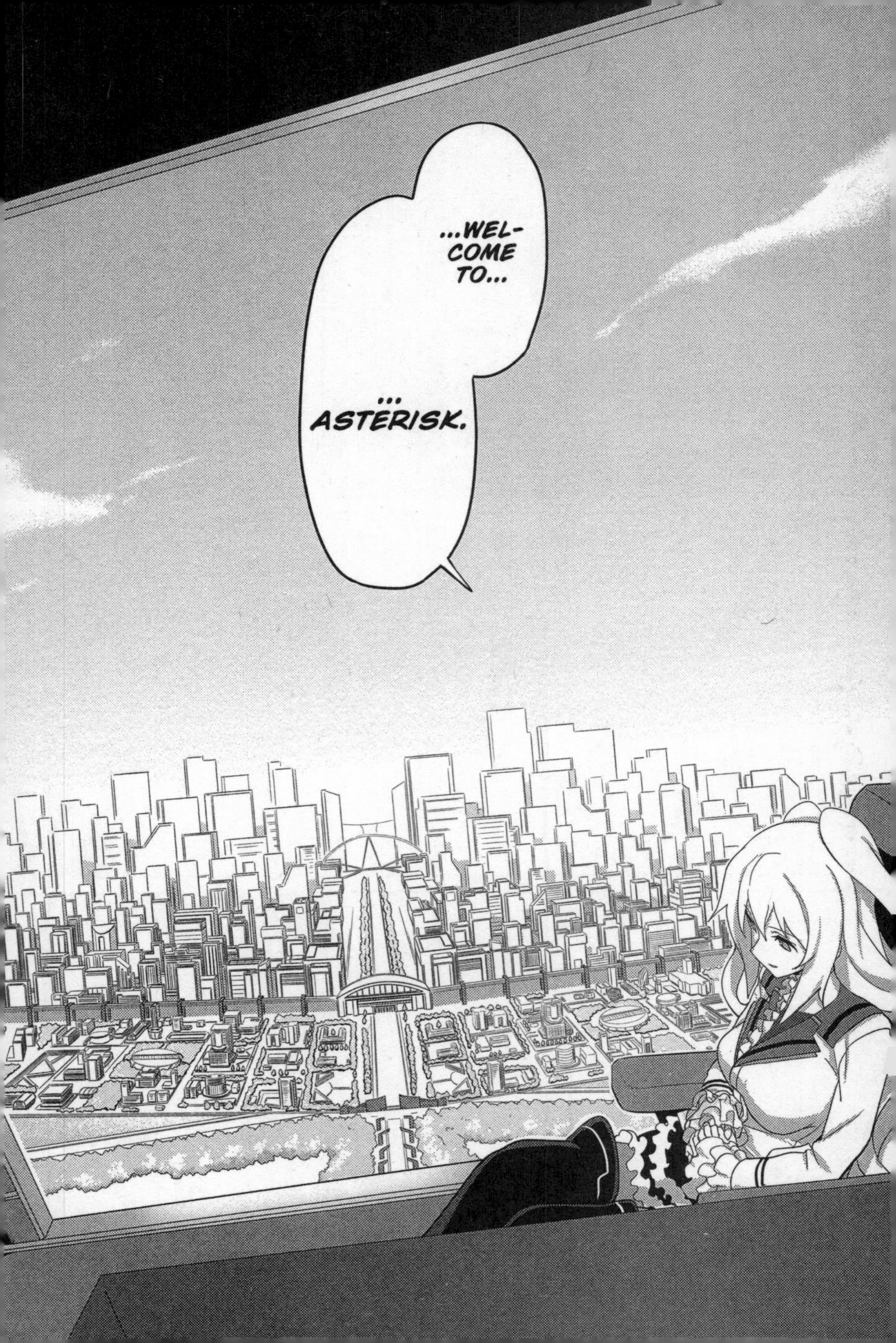
...WEL-
COME
TO...
... ASTERISK.

THE
ASTERISK WAR

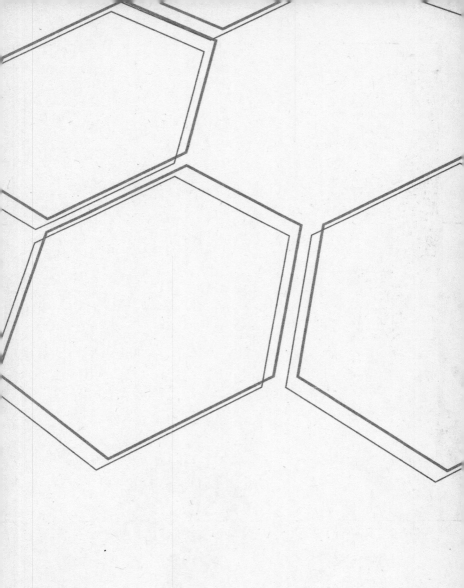

THE
ASTERISK WAR

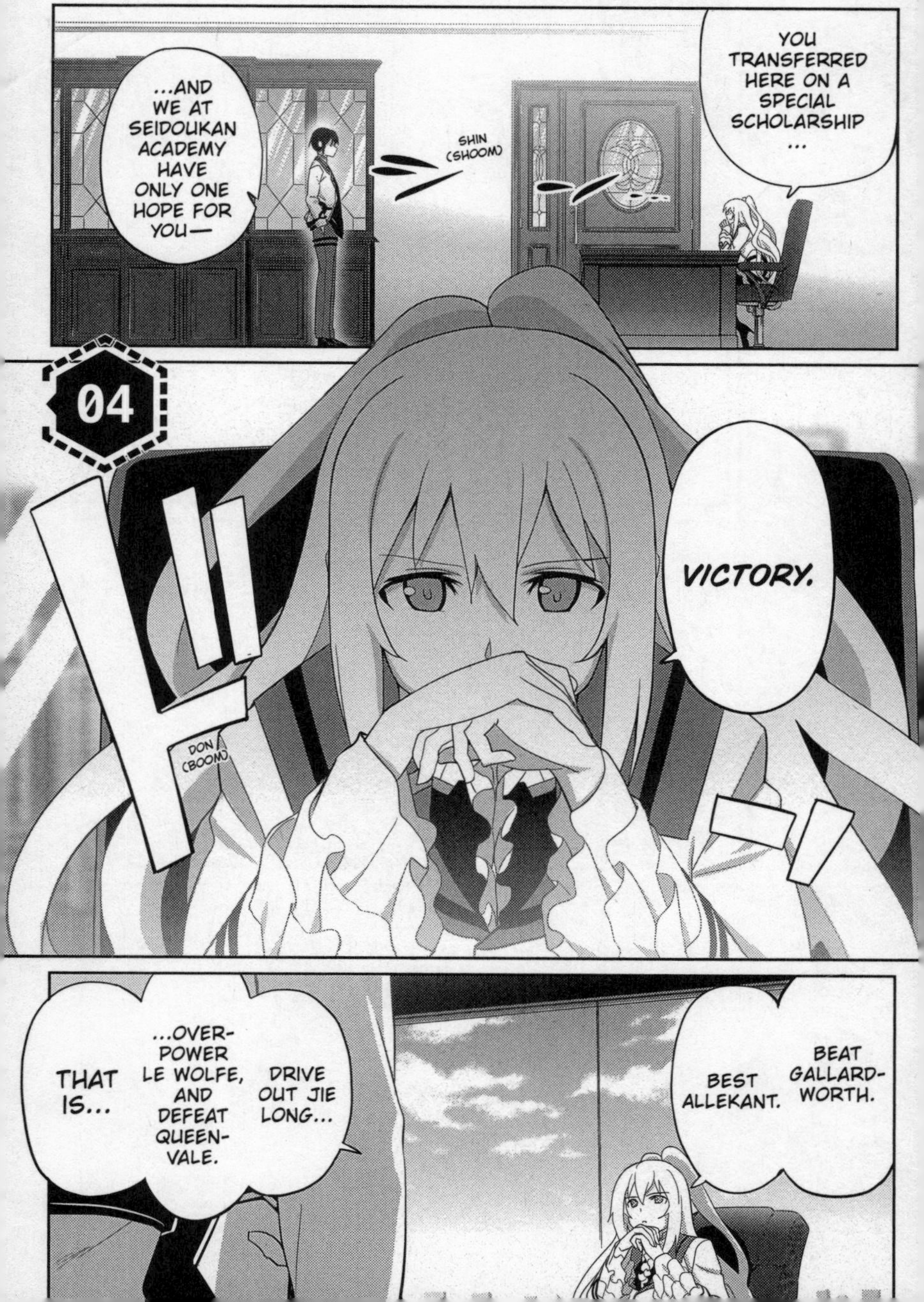
YOU TRANSFERRED HERE ON A SPECIAL SCHOLARSHIP ...
SHIN (SHOOM)
...AND WE AT SEIDOUKAN ACADEMY HAVE ONLY ONE HOPE FOR YOU—
04
VICTORY.
DON (BOOM)
BEAT GALLARD-WORTH.
BEST ALLEKANT.
DRIVE OUT JIE LONG...
...OVER-POWER LE WOLFE, AND DEFEAT QUEEN-VALE.
THAT IS...

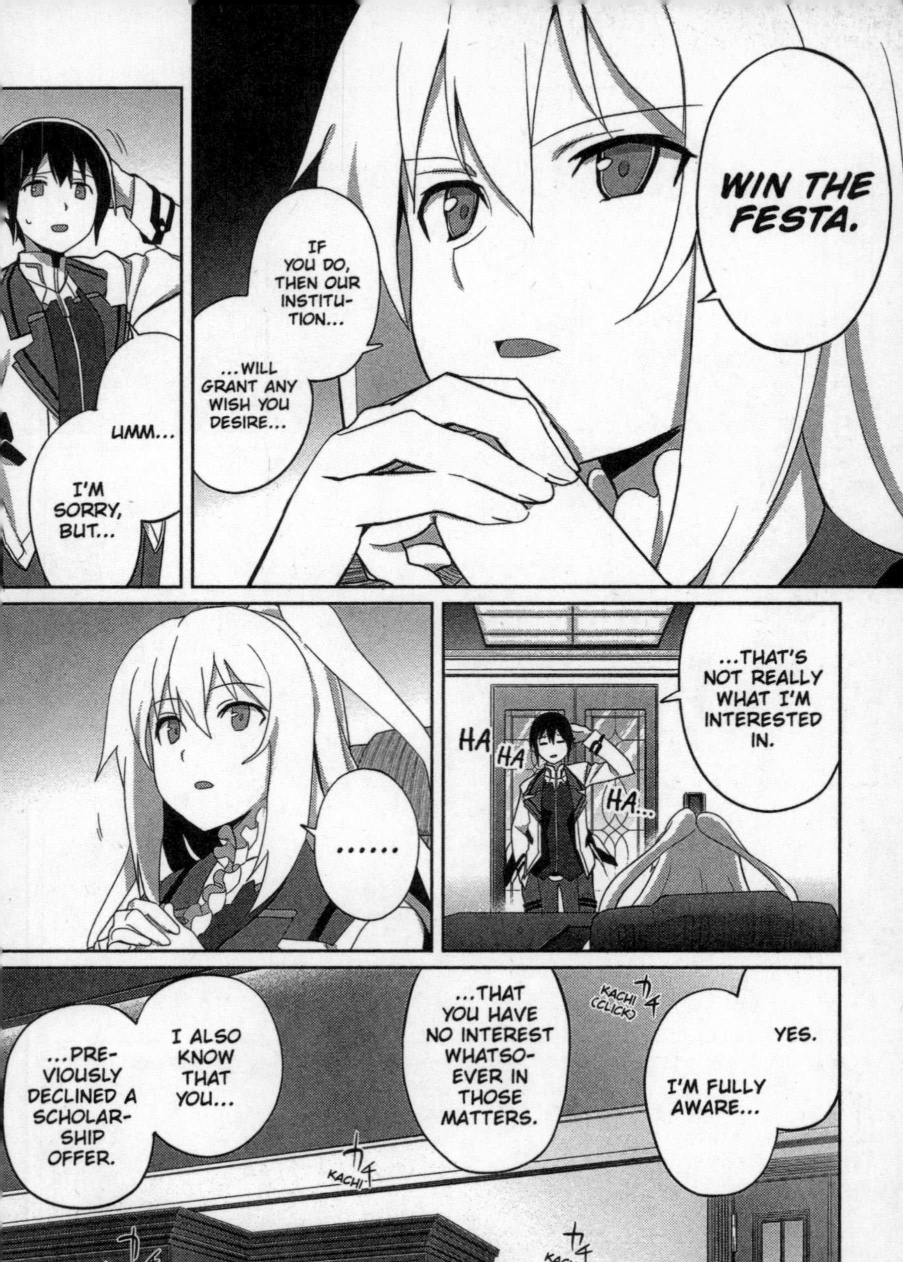
WIN THE FESTA.
IF YOU DO, THEN OUR INSTITUTION...
...WILL GRANT ANY WISH YOU DESIRE...
UMM...
I'M SORRY, BUT...
...THAT'S NOT REALLY WHAT I'M INTERESTED IN.
HA HA HA...
......
KACHI (CLICK)
YES.
I'M FULLY AWARE...
...THAT YOU HAVE NO INTEREST WHATSOEVER IN THOSE MATTERS.
KACHI
I ALSO KNOW THAT YOU...
...PREVIOUSLY DECLINED A SCHOLARSHIP OFFER.
KACHI
KACHI

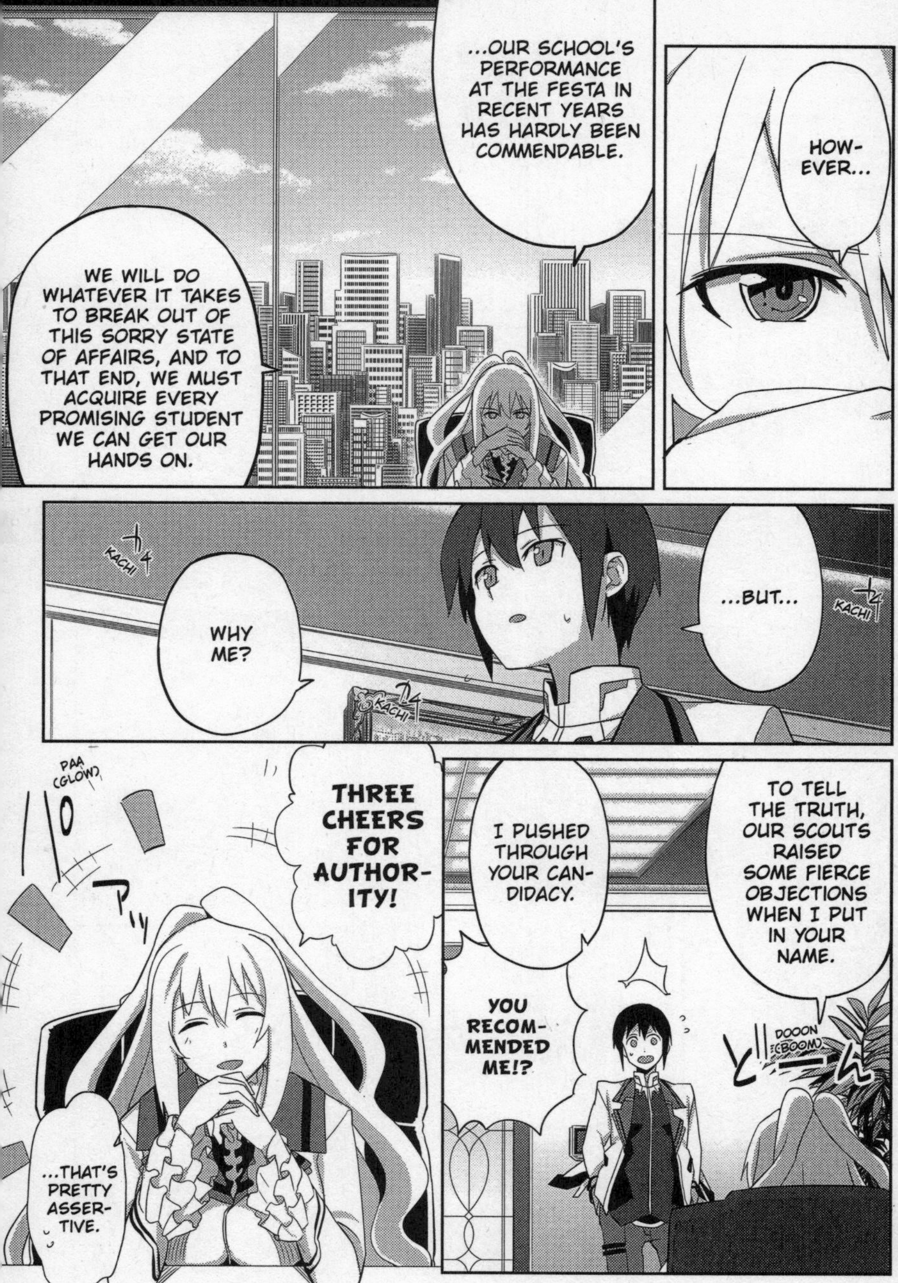
HOW-EVER...
...OUR SCHOOL'S PERFORMANCE AT THE FESTA IN RECENT YEARS HAS HARDLY BEEN COMMENDABLE.
WE WILL DO WHATEVER IT TAKES TO BREAK OUT OF THIS SORRY STATE OF AFFAIRS, AND TO THAT END, WE MUST ACQUIRE EVERY PROMISING STUDENT WE CAN GET OUR HANDS ON.
...BUT...
KACHI
WHY ME?
KACHI
KACHI
TO TELL THE TRUTH, OUR SCOUTS RAISED SOME FIERCE OBJECTIONS WHEN I PUT IN YOUR NAME.
I PUSHED THROUGH YOUR CAN-DIDACY.
DOOON (BOOM)
YOU RECOM-MENDED ME!?
THREE CHEERS FOR AUTHOR-ITY!
PAA (GLOW)
...THAT'S PRETTY ASSER-TIVE.

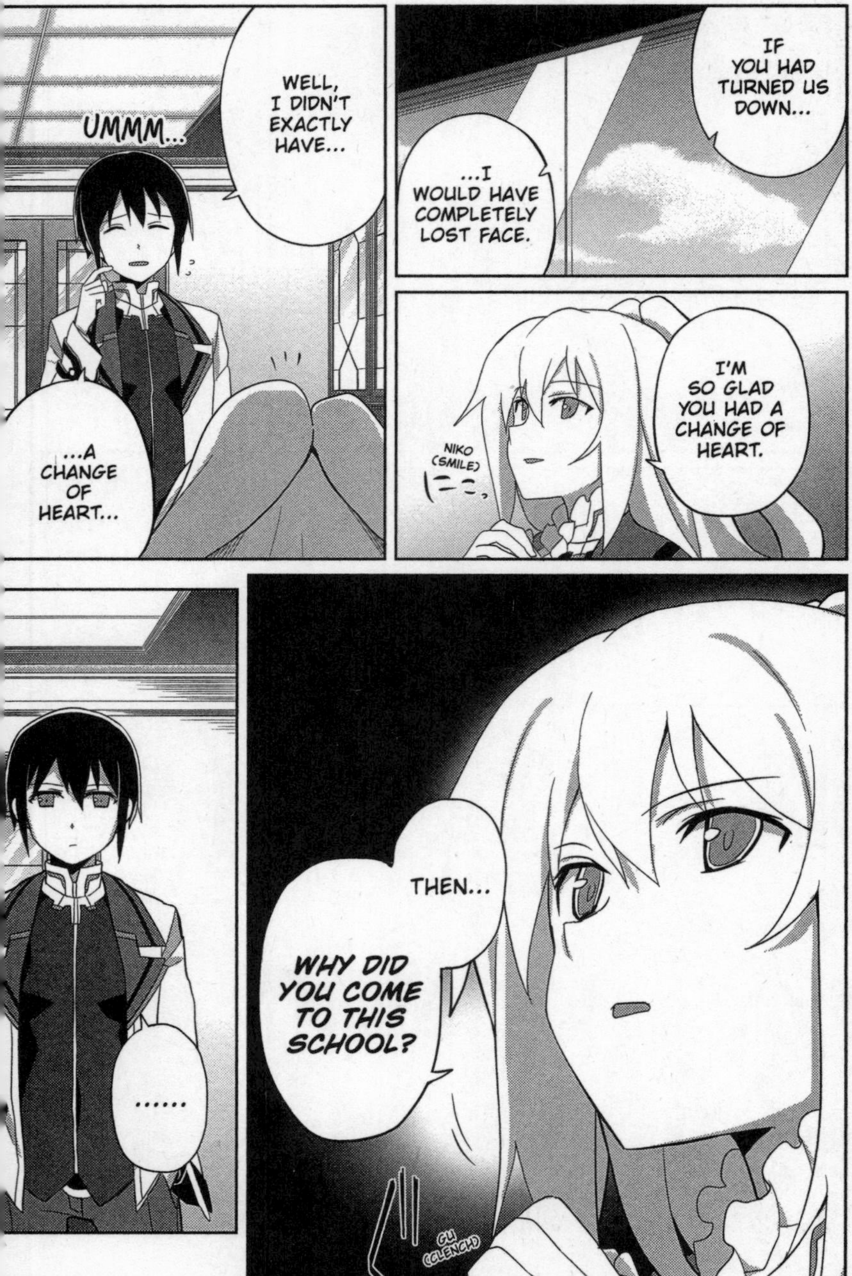
IF YOU HAD TURNED US DOWN...
...I WOULD HAVE COMPLETELY LOST FACE.
I'M SO GLAD YOU HAD A CHANGE OF HEART.
NIKO (SMILE)
UMMM...
WELL, I DIDN'T EXACTLY HAVE...
...A CHANGE OF HEART...
THEN...
WHY DID YOU COME TO THIS SCHOOL?
GU (CLENCH)
......

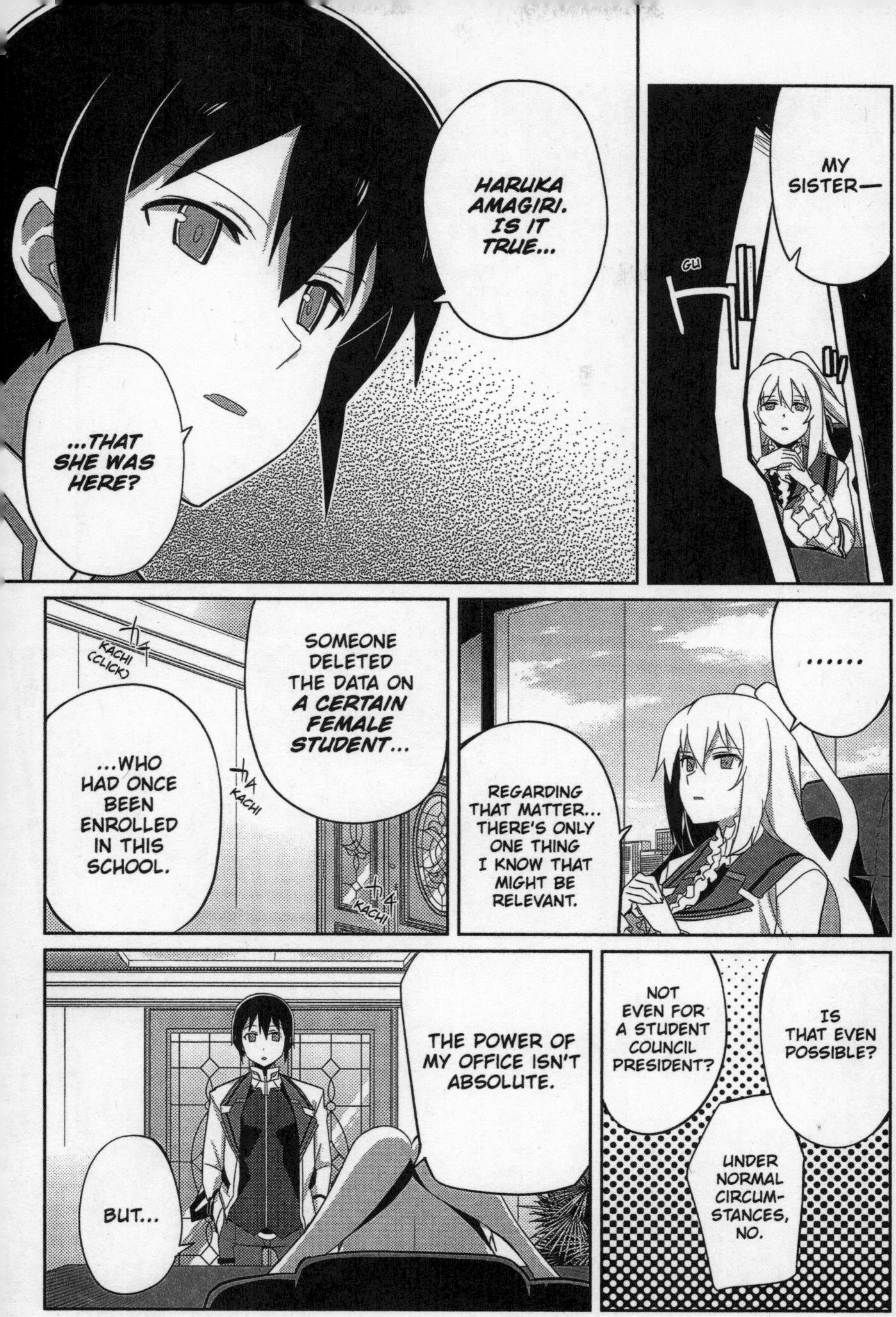

MY SISTER—
GU
HARUKA AMAGIRI. IS IT TRUE...
...THAT SHE WAS HERE?
......
REGARDING THAT MATTER... THERE'S ONLY ONE THING I KNOW THAT MIGHT BE RELEVANT.
KACHI (CLICK)
SOMEONE DELETED THE DATA ON A CERTAIN FEMALE STUDENT...
...WHO HAD ONCE BEEN ENROLLED IN THIS SCHOOL.
KACHI
KACHI
IS THAT EVEN POSSIBLE?
NOT EVEN FOR A STUDENT COUNCIL PRESIDENT?
UNDER NORMAL CIRCUM-STANCES, NO.
THE POWER OF MY OFFICE ISN'T ABSOLUTE.
BUT...

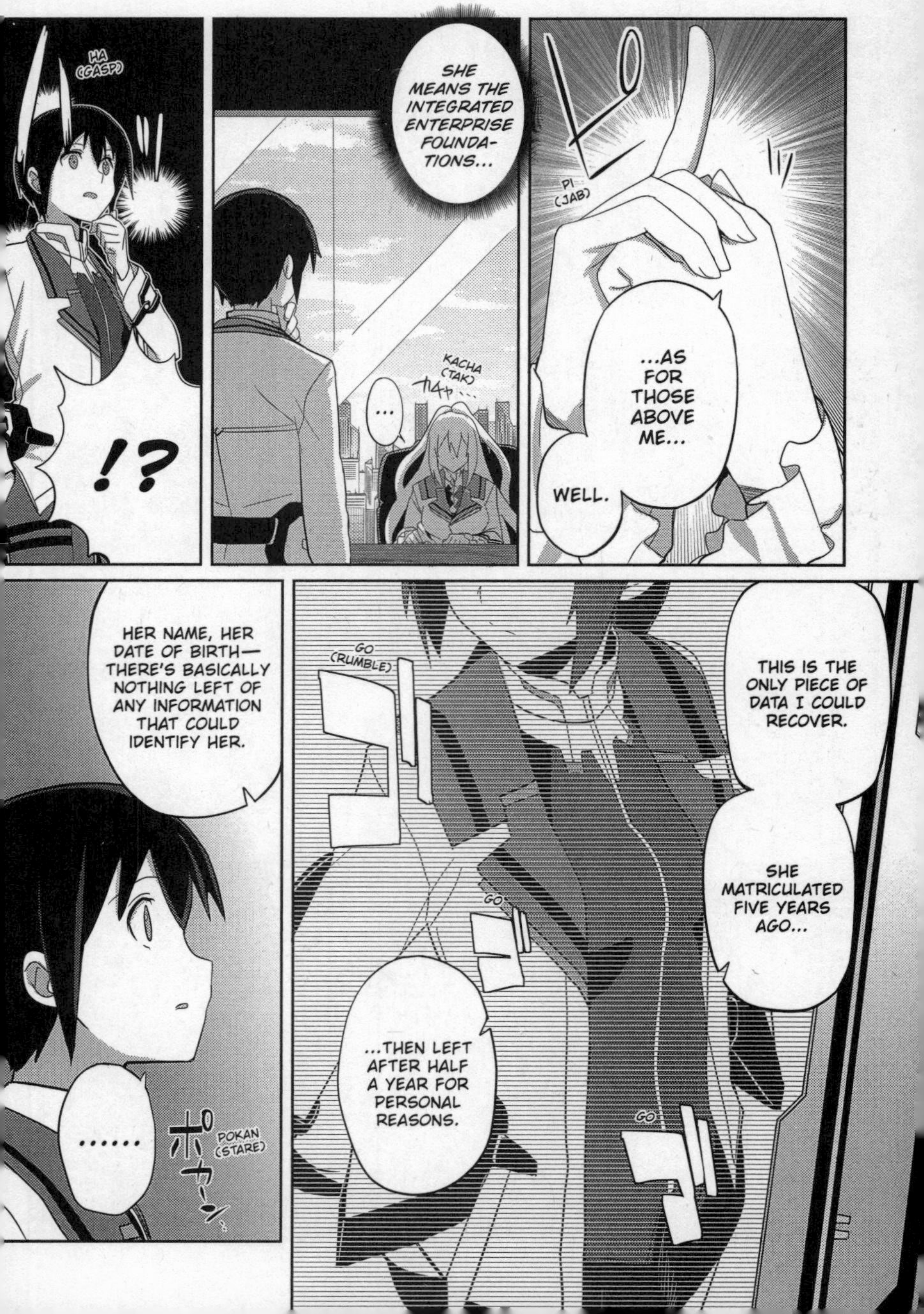
PI (JAB)
...AS FOR THOSE ABOVE ME...
WELL.
SHE MEANS THE INTEGRATED ENTERPRISE FOUNDA-TIONS...
KACHA (TAK)
...
HA (GASP)
!?
THIS IS THE ONLY PIECE OF DATA I COULD RECOVER.
GO (RUMBLE)
SHE MATRICULATED FIVE YEARS AGO...
GO
...THEN LEFT AFTER HALF A YEAR FOR PERSONAL REASONS.
GO
HER NAME, HER DATE OF BIRTH—THERE'S BASICALLY NOTHING LEFT OF ANY INFORMATION THAT COULD IDENTIFY HER.
......
POKAN (STARE)

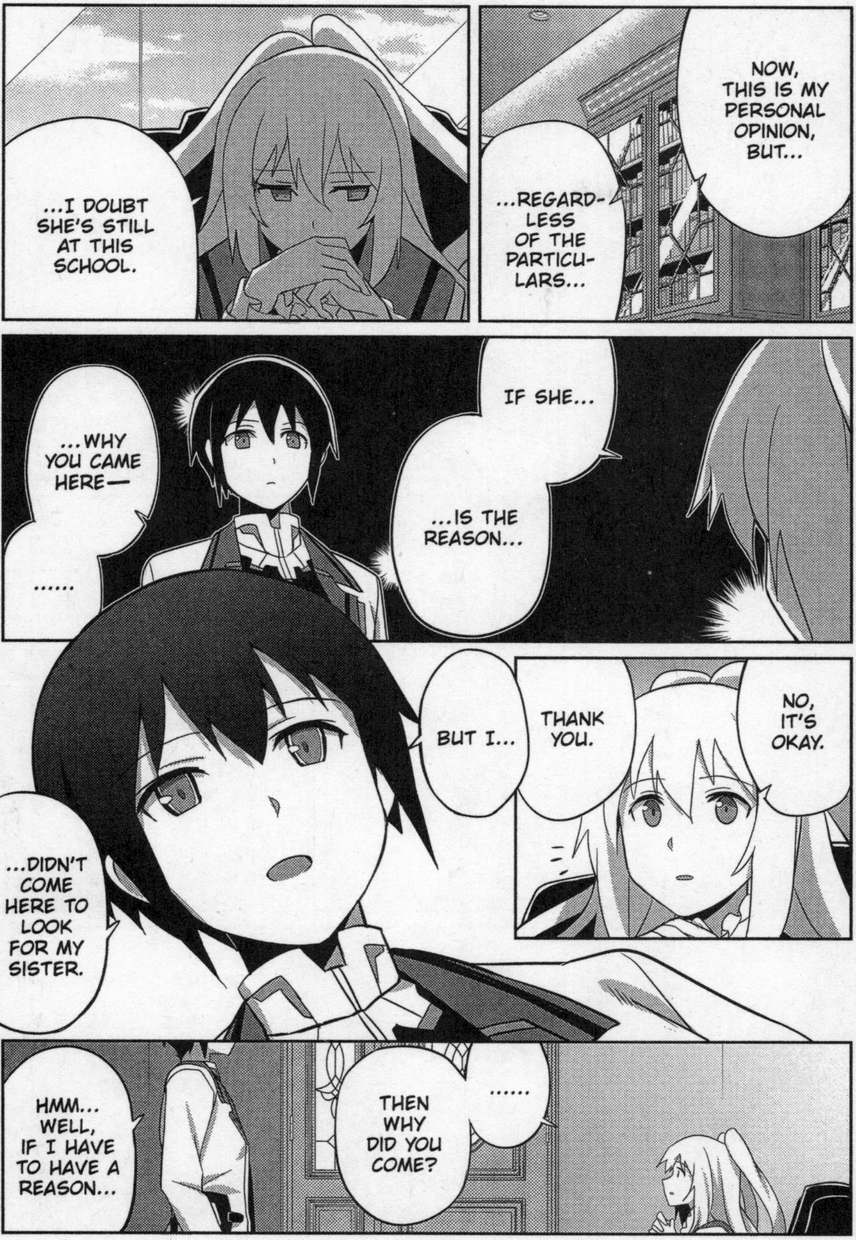
NOW, THIS IS MY PERSONAL OPINION, BUT...
...REGARD-LESS OF THE PARTICU-LARS...
...I DOUBT SHE'S STILL AT THIS SCHOOL.
IF SHE...
...IS THE REASON...
...WHY YOU CAME HERE—
......
NO, IT'S OKAY.
THANK YOU.
BUT I...
...DIDN'T COME HERE TO LOOK FOR MY SISTER.
......
THEN WHY DID YOU COME?
HMM... WELL, IF I HAVE TO HAVE A REASON...

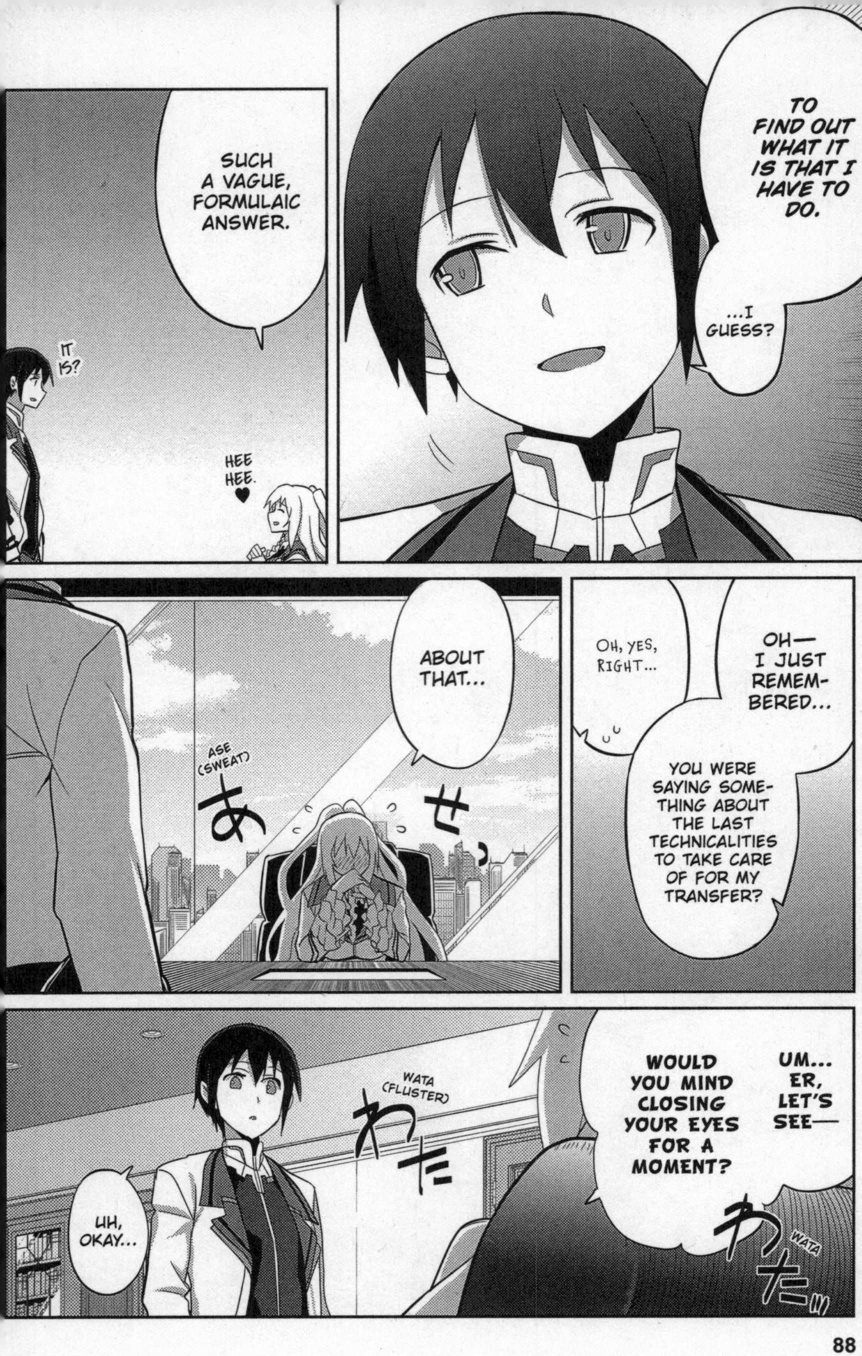
TO FIND OUT WHAT IT IS THAT I HAVE TO DO.
...I GUESS?
SUCH A VAGUE, FORMULAIC ANSWER.
IT IS?
HEE HEE. ♥
OH— I JUST REMEMBERED...
YOU WERE SAYING SOMETHING ABOUT THE LAST TECHNICALITIES TO TAKE CARE OF FOR MY TRANSFER?
OH, YES, RIGHT...
ABOUT THAT...
ASE (SWEAT)
あせっ
UM... ER, LET'S SEE—
WOULD YOU MIND CLOSING YOUR EYES FOR A MOMENT?
WATA
わた
WATA (FLUSTER)
わた
UH, OKAY...

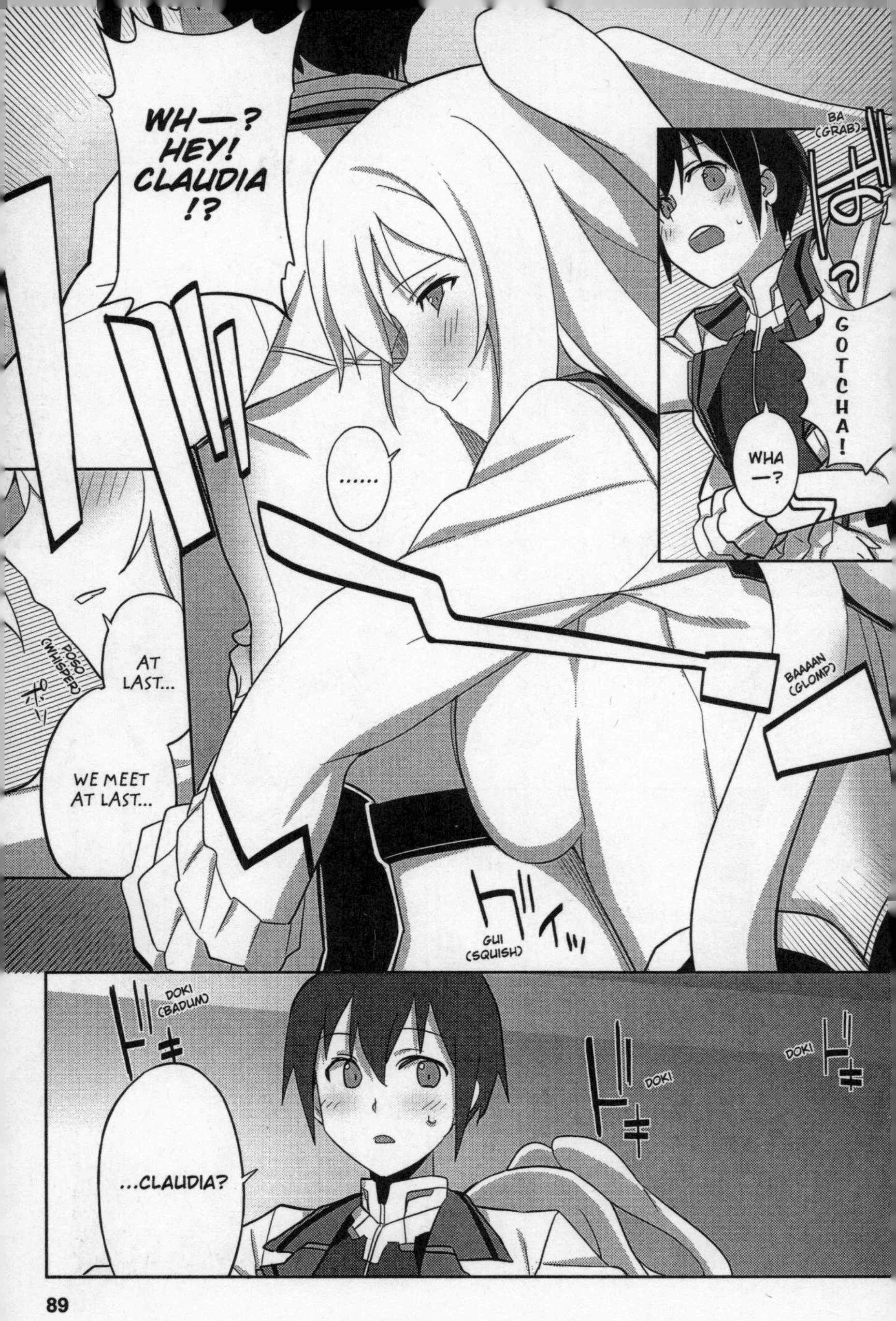

BA (GRAB)
GOTCHA!
WHA—?
BAAAAN (GLOMP)
WH—? HEY! CLAUDIA!?
......
POSO (WHISPER)
AT LAST...
WE MEET AT LAST...
GUI (SQUISH)
DOKI
DOKI
DOKI (BADUM)
...CLAUDIA?

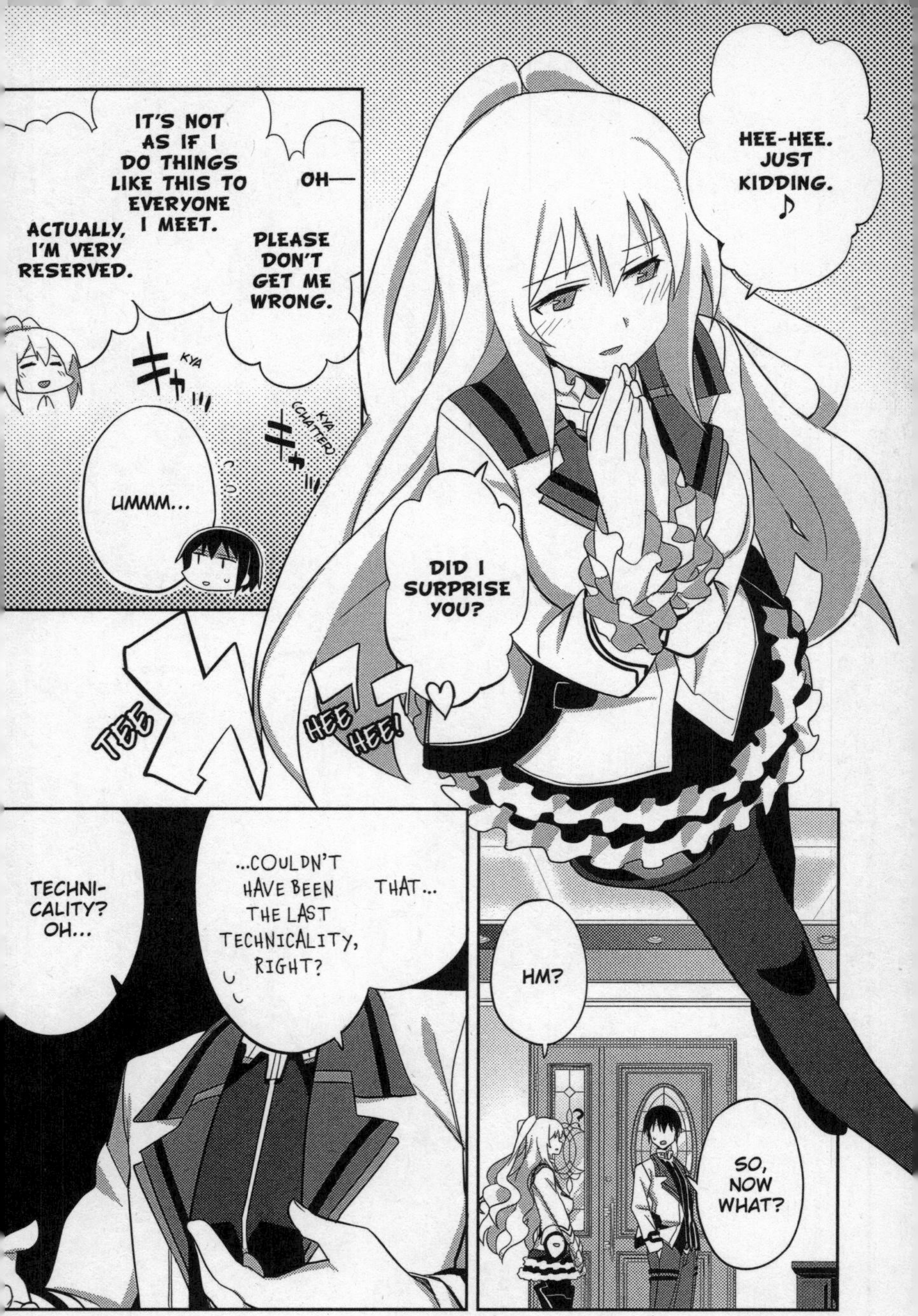
HEE-HEE. JUST KIDDING. ♪
DID I SURPRISE YOU?
HEE HEE!
TEE
OH— PLEASE DON'T GET ME WRONG.
IT'S NOT AS IF I DO THINGS LIKE THIS TO EVERYONE I MEET.
ACTUALLY, I'M VERY RESERVED.
KYA CHATTER
KYA
UMMM...
SO, NOW WHAT?
HM?
THAT...
...COULDN'T HAVE BEEN THE LAST TECHNICALITY, RIGHT?
TECHNICALITY? OH...

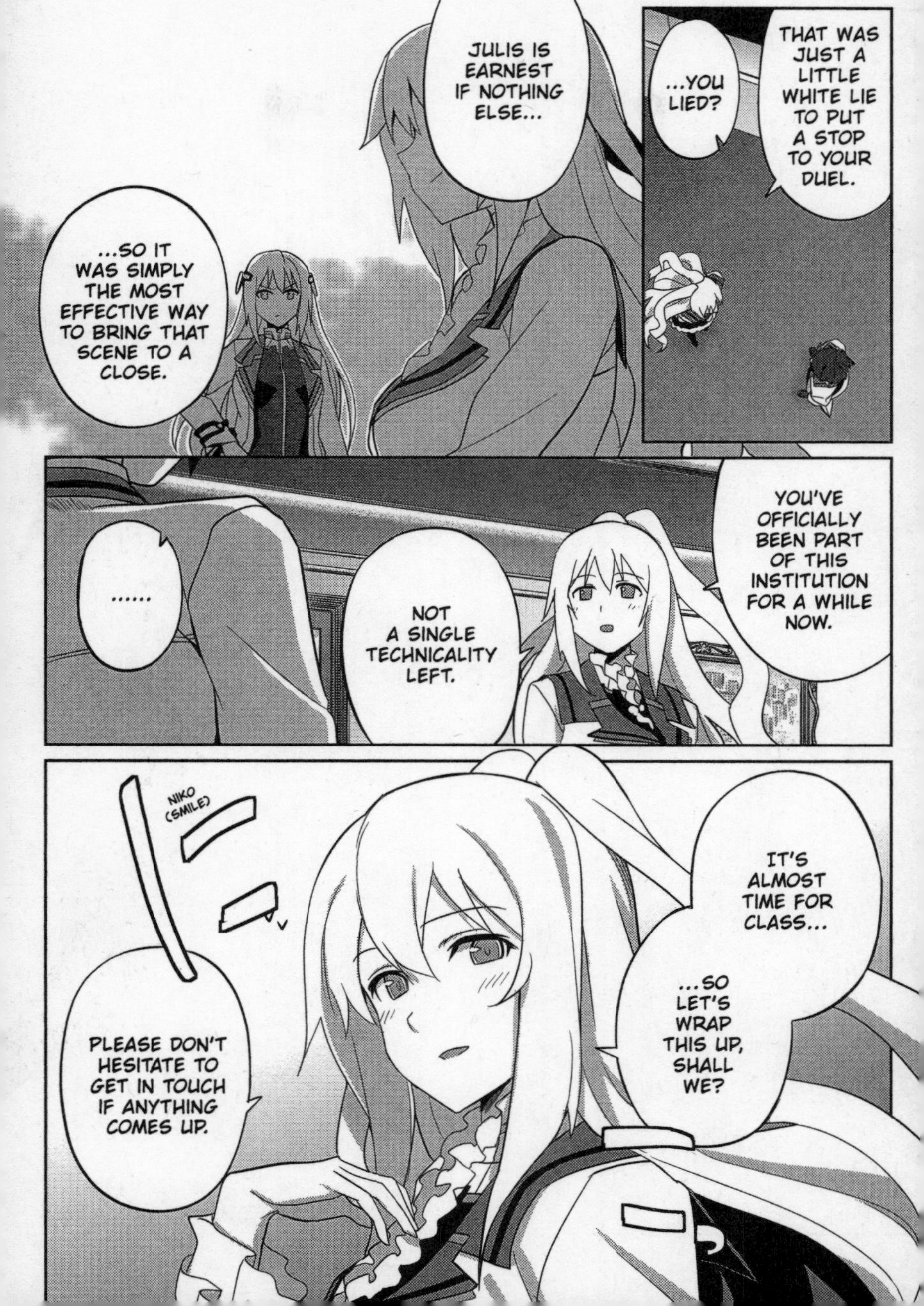
THAT WAS JUST A LITTLE WHITE LIE TO PUT A STOP TO YOUR DUEL.
...YOU LIED?
JULIS IS EARNEST IF NOTHING ELSE...
...SO IT WAS SIMPLY THE MOST EFFECTIVE WAY TO BRING THAT SCENE TO A CLOSE.
YOU'VE OFFICIALLY BEEN PART OF THIS INSTITUTION FOR A WHILE NOW.
NOT A SINGLE TECHNICALITY LEFT.
......
IT'S ALMOST TIME FOR CLASS...
...SO LET'S WRAP THIS UP, SHALL WE?
NIKO (SMILE)
PLEASE DON'T HESITATE TO GET IN TOUCH IF ANYTHING COMES UP.

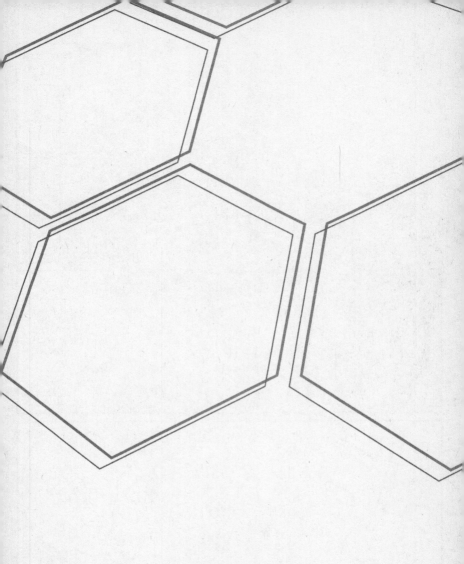

THE
ASTERISK WAR

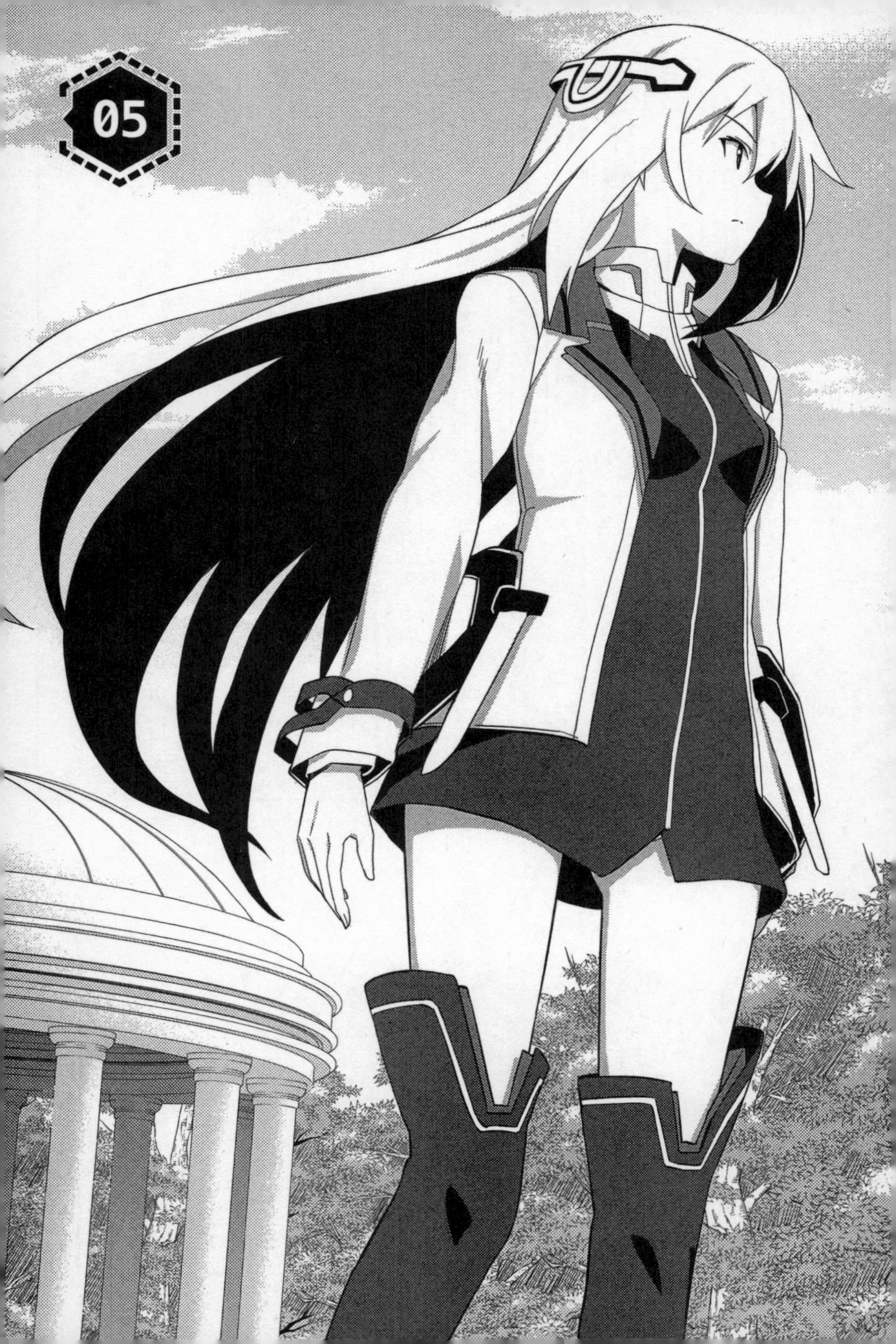
05

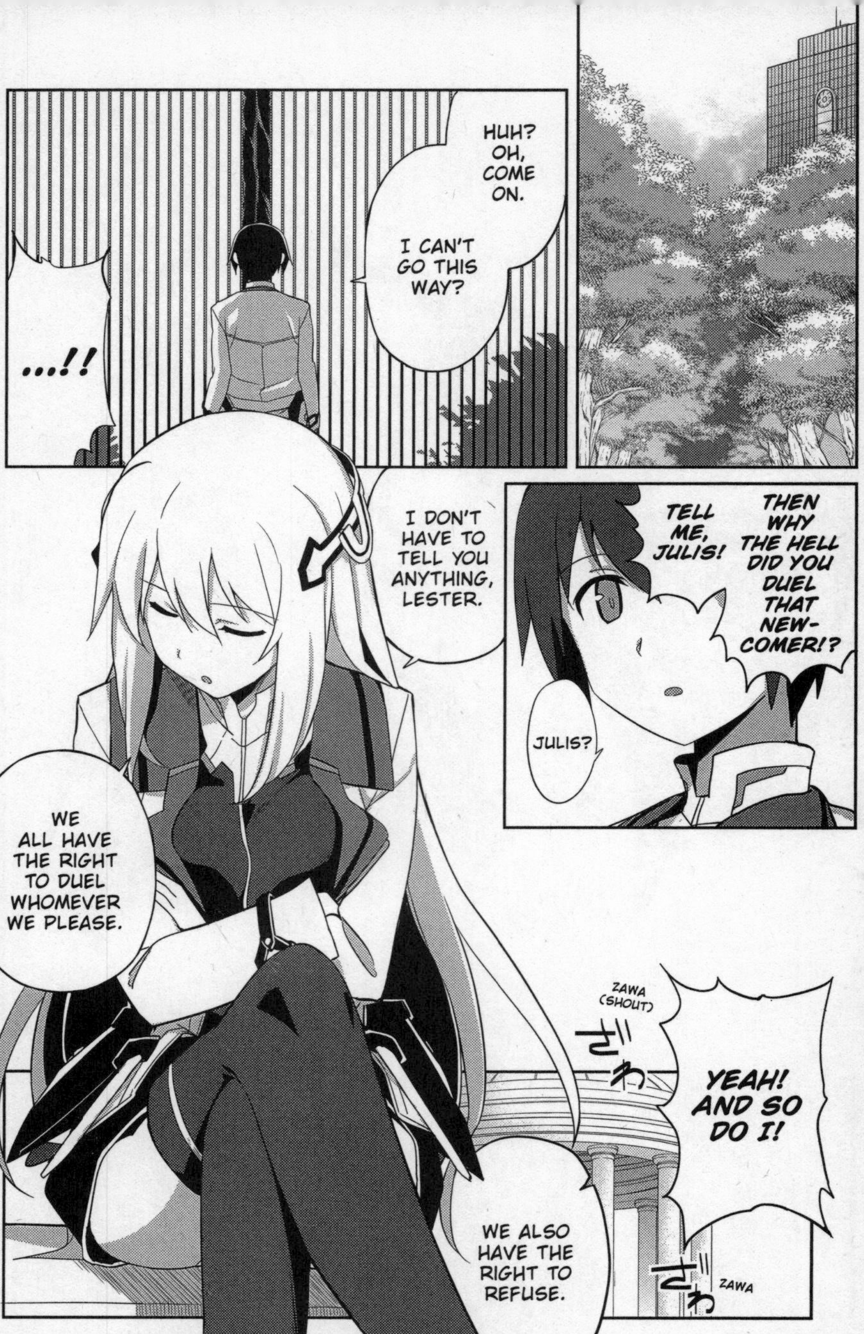
HUH? OH, COME ON.
I CAN'T GO THIS WAY?
...!!
THEN WHY THE HELL DID YOU DUEL THAT NEW-COMER!?
TELL ME, JULIS!
JULIS?
I DON'T HAVE TO TELL YOU ANYTHING, LESTER.
WE ALL HAVE THE RIGHT TO DUEL WHOMEVER WE PLEASE.
ざわ
ZAWA (SHOUT)
YEAH! AND SO DO I!
WE ALSO HAVE THE RIGHT TO REFUSE.
ざわ
ZAWA

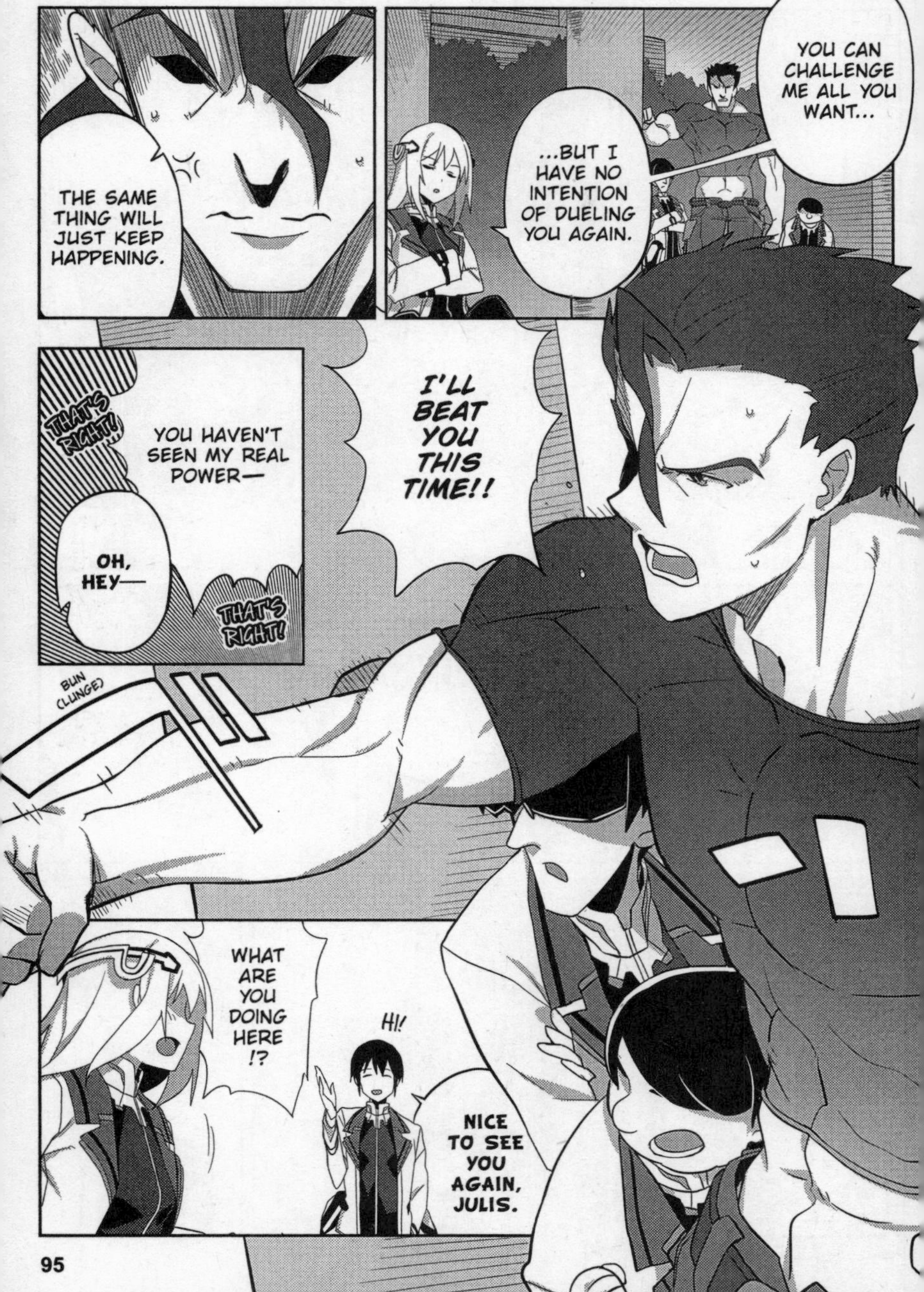
YOU CAN CHALLENGE ME ALL YOU WANT...
...BUT I HAVE NO INTENTION OF DUELING YOU AGAIN.
THE SAME THING WILL JUST KEEP HAPPENING.
I'LL BEAT YOU THIS TIME!!
THAT'S RIGHT!
YOU HAVEN'T SEEN MY REAL POWER—
THAT'S RIGHT!
OH, HEY—
BUN (LUNGE)
NICE TO SEE YOU AGAIN, JULIS.
HI!
WHAT ARE YOU DOING HERE!?

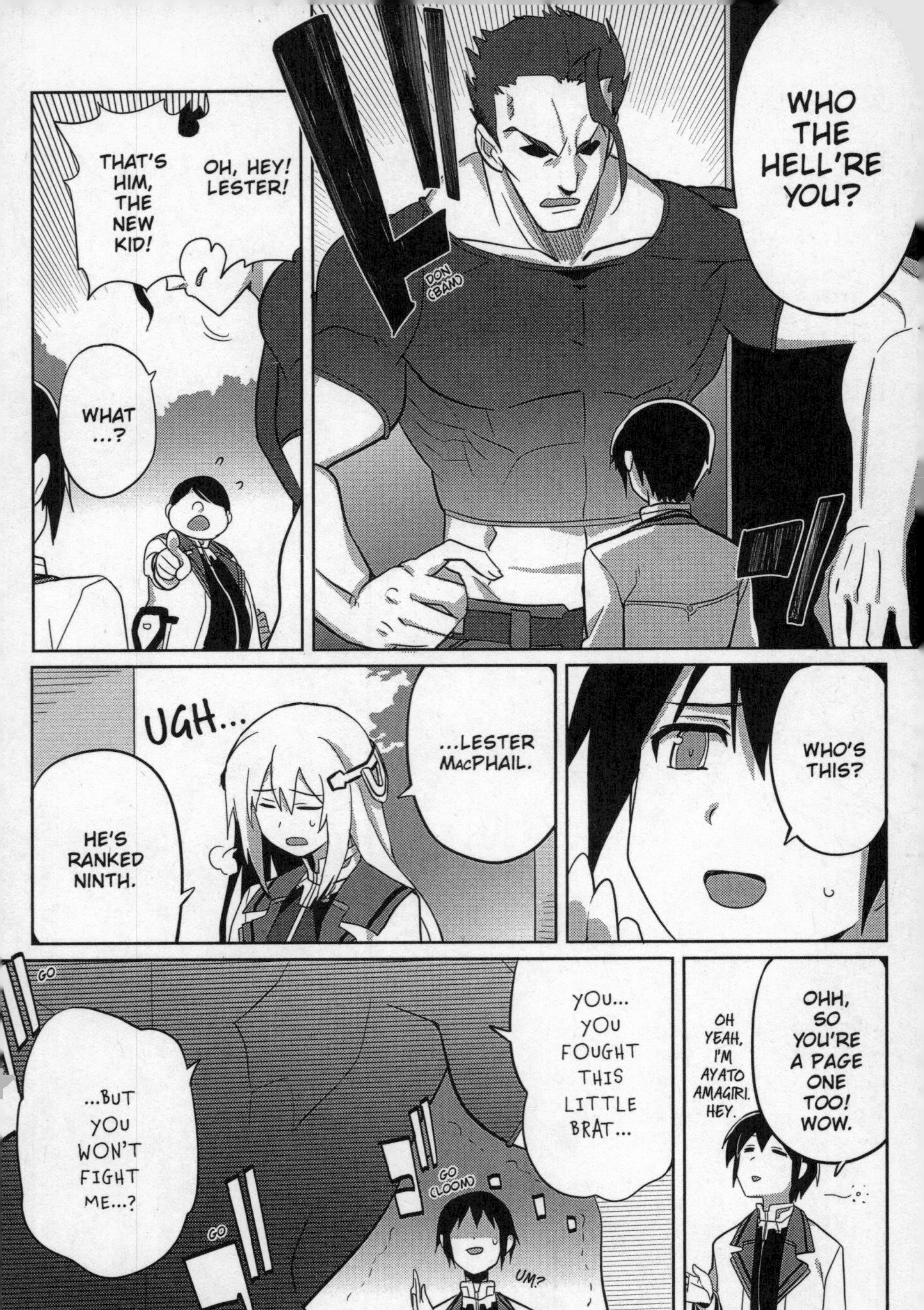
WHO THE HELL'RE YOU?
DON (BAM)
OH, HEY! LESTER!
THAT'S HIM, THE NEW KID!
WHAT...?
WHO'S THIS?
...LESTER MacPHAIL.
UGH...
HE'S RANKED NINTH.
OHH, SO YOU'RE A PAGE ONE TOO! WOW.
OH YEAH, I'M AYATO AMAGIRI. HEY.
YOU... YOU FOUGHT THIS LITTLE BRAT...
GO
...BUT YOU WON'T FIGHT ME...?
GO (LOOM)
GO
UM?

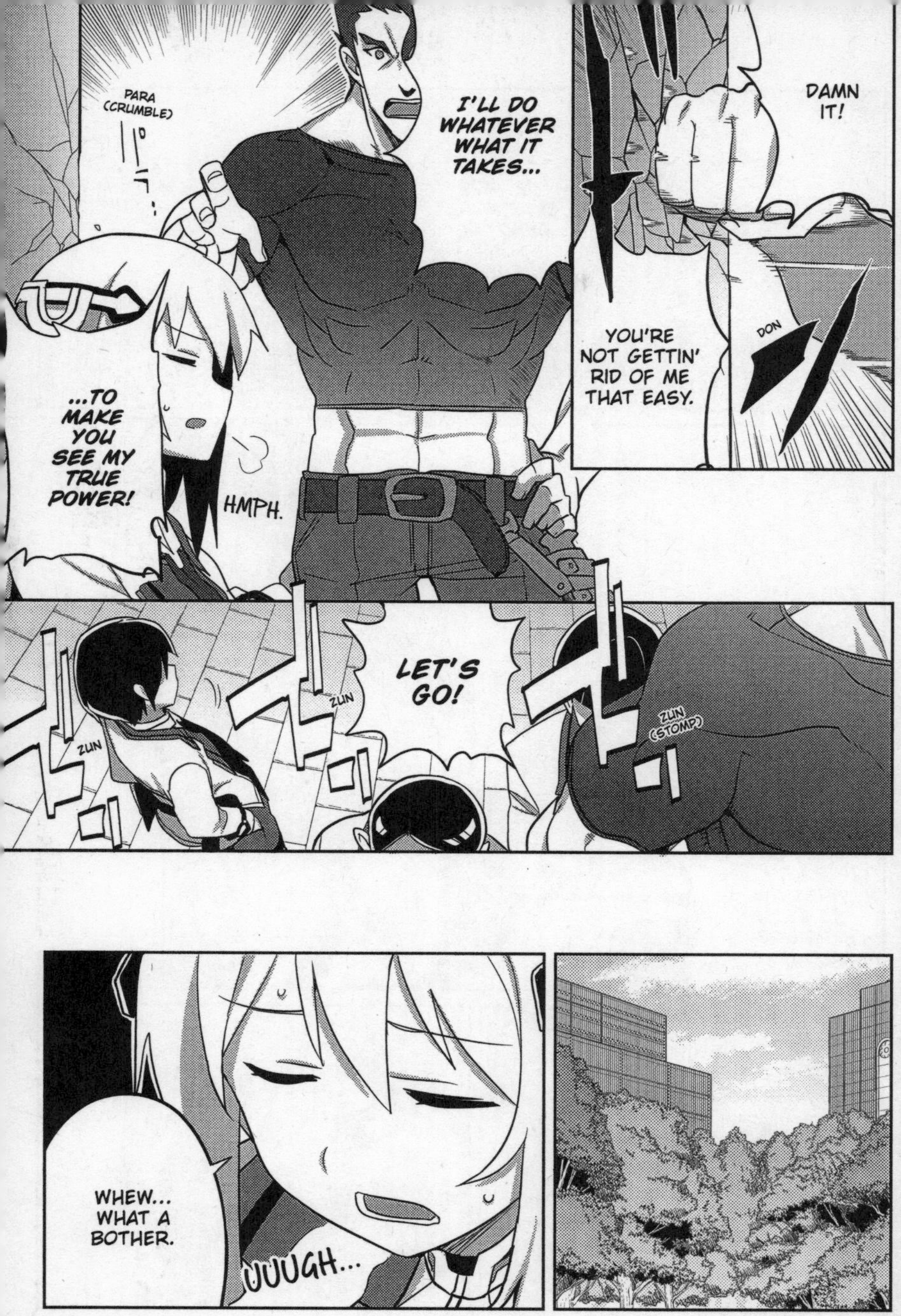
DAMN IT!
YOU'RE NOT GETTIN' RID OF ME THAT EASY.
DON
I'LL DO WHATEVER WHAT IT TAKES...
PARA (CRUMBLE)
...TO MAKE YOU SEE MY TRUE POWER!
HMPH.
ZUN (STOMP)
LET'S GO!
ZUN
ZUN
WHEW... WHAT A BOTHER.
UUUGH...

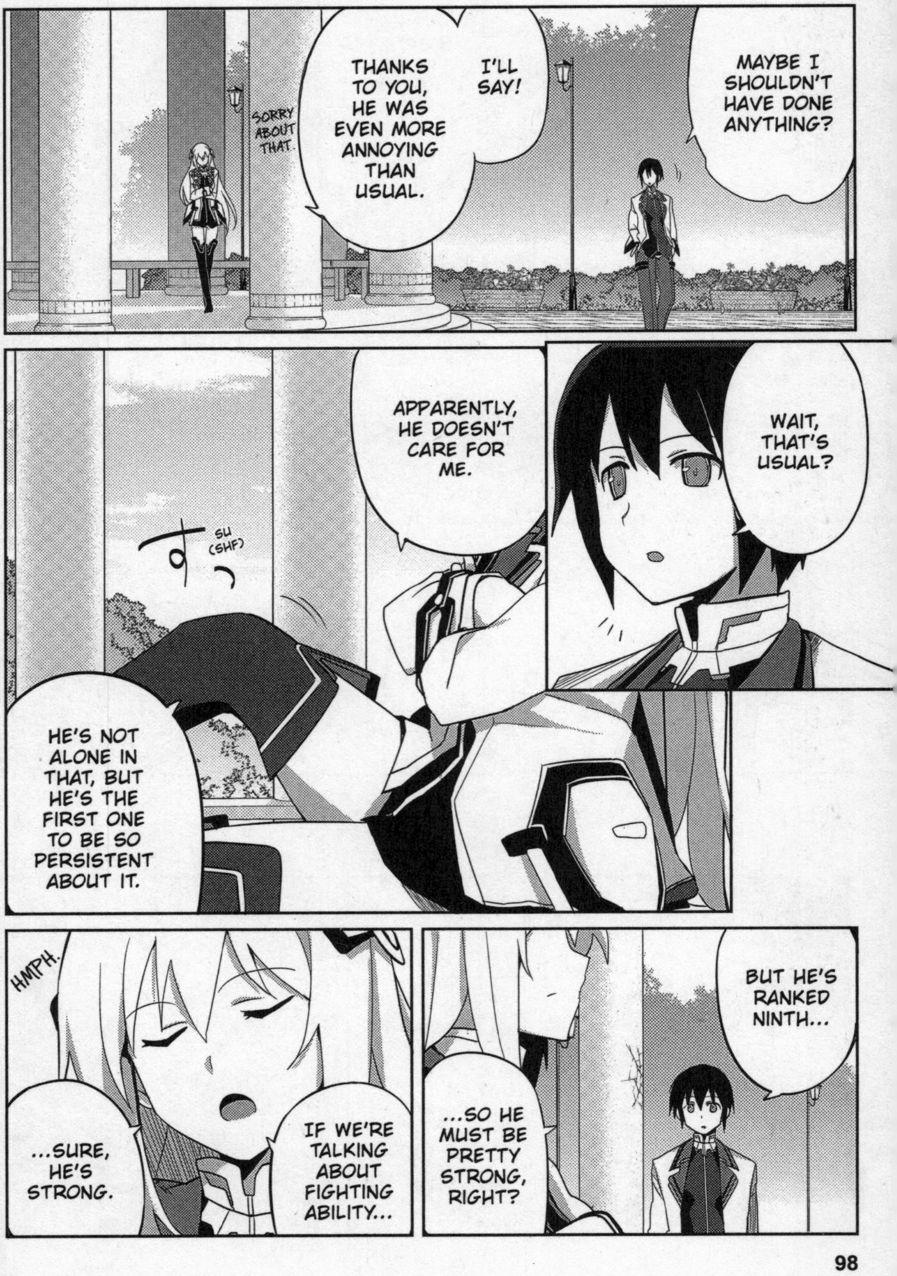
MAYBE I SHOULDN'T HAVE DONE ANYTHING?
I'LL SAY!
THANKS TO YOU, HE WAS EVEN MORE ANNOYING THAN USUAL.
SORRY ABOUT THAT.
WAIT, THAT'S USUAL?
APPARENTLY, HE DOESN'T CARE FOR ME.
SU (SHF)
HE'S NOT ALONE IN THAT, BUT HE'S THE FIRST ONE TO BE SO PERSISTENT ABOUT IT.
BUT HE'S RANKED NINTH...
...SO HE MUST BE PRETTY STRONG, RIGHT?
HMPH.
IF WE'RE TALKING ABOUT FIGHTING ABILITY...
...SURE, HE'S STRONG.

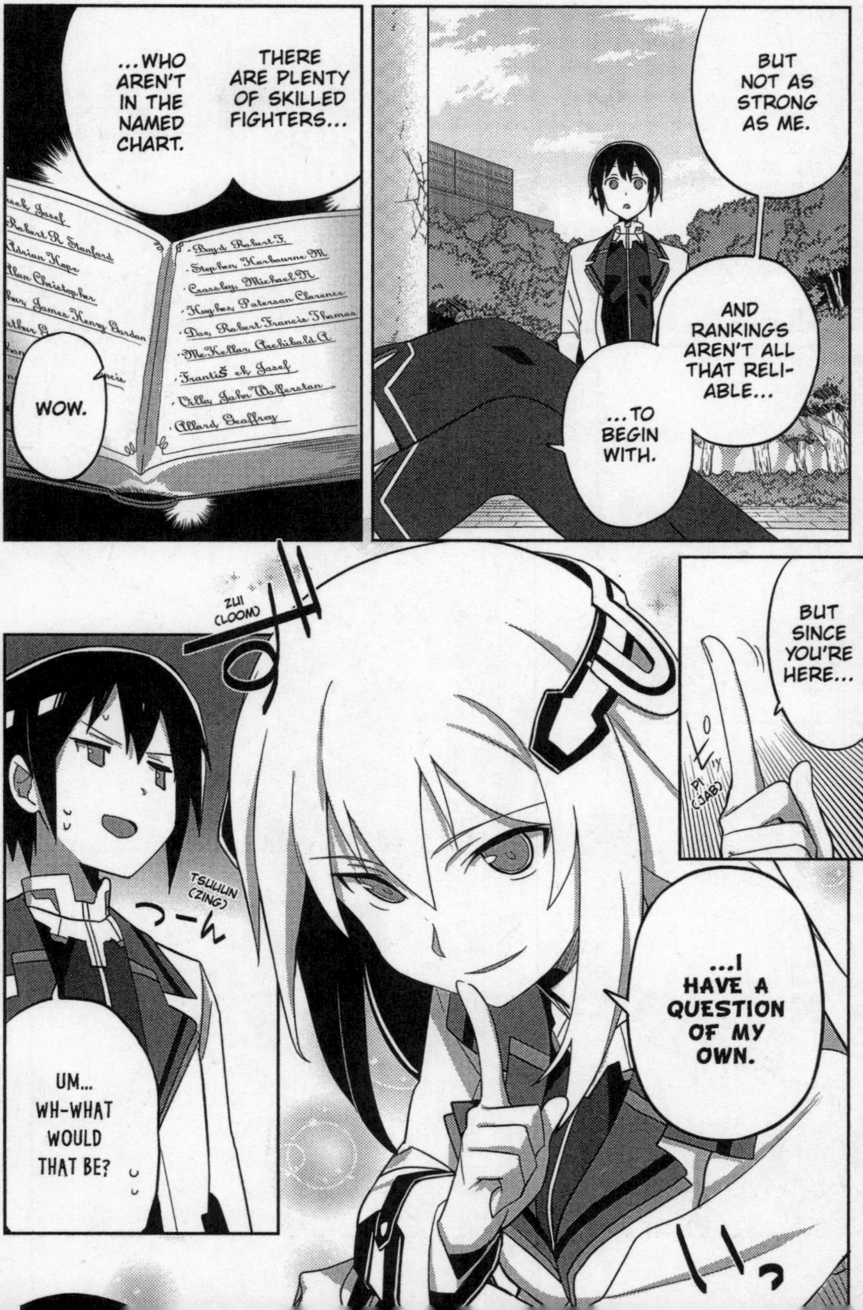
BUT NOT AS STRONG AS ME.
AND RANKINGS AREN'T ALL THAT RELI-ABLE...
...TO BEGIN WITH.
THERE ARE PLENTY OF SKILLED FIGHTERS...
...WHO AREN'T IN THE NAMED CHART.
Boyd Robert F.
Stephen Harbourne M
Crossley Michael N
Hughes Paterson Clarence
Day Robert Francis Thomas
McKellar Archibald A
František Josef
Villa John Walferstan
Allard Geoffrey
WOW.
BUT SINCE YOU'RE HERE...
PI (JAB)
ZUI (LOOM)
...I HAVE A QUESTION OF MY OWN.
TSUUUN (ZING)
UM... WH-WHAT WOULD THAT BE?

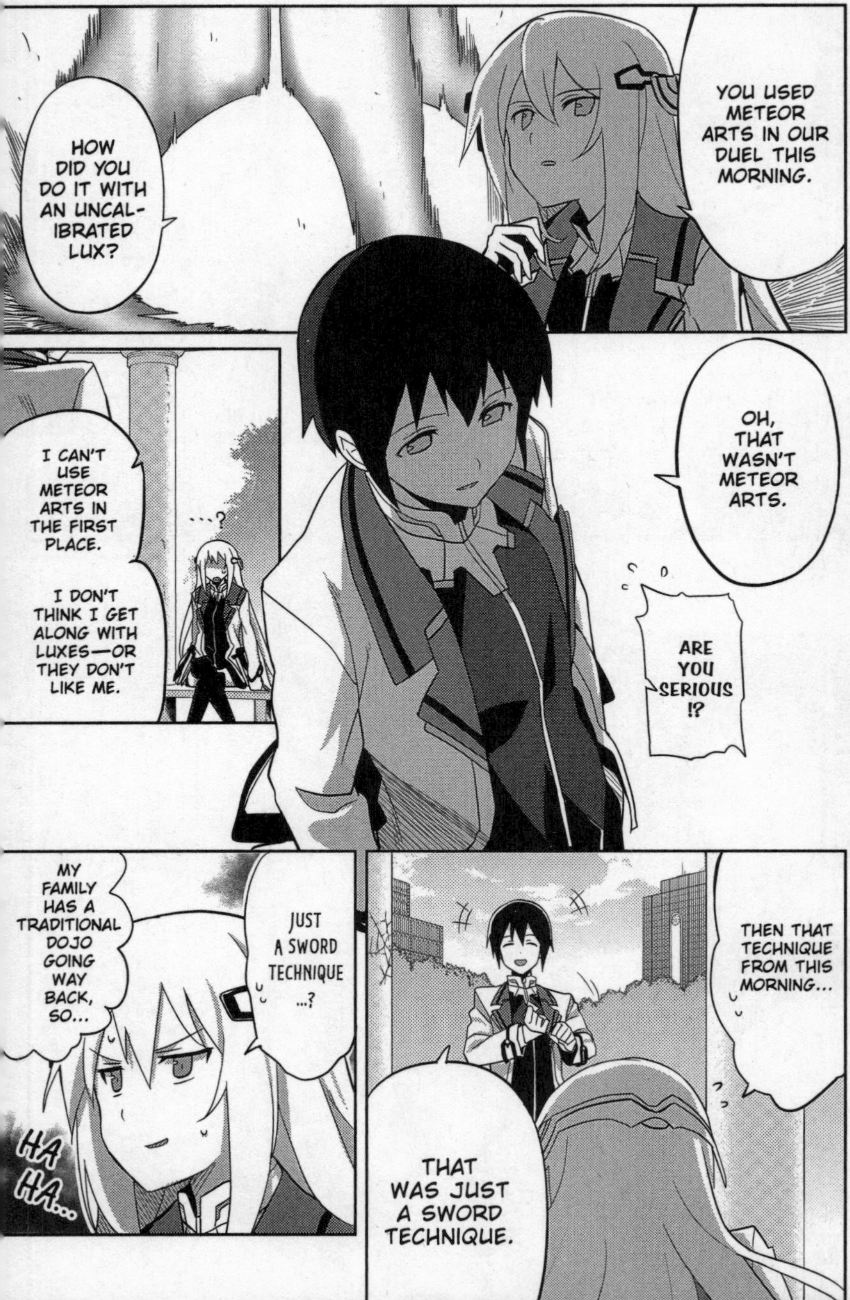
YOU USED METEOR ARTS IN OUR DUEL THIS MORNING.
HOW DID YOU DO IT WITH AN UNCAL-IBRATED LUX?
OH, THAT WASN'T METEOR ARTS.
ARE YOU SERIOUS!?
...?
I CAN'T USE METEOR ARTS IN THE FIRST PLACE.
I DON'T THINK I GET ALONG WITH LUXES—OR THEY DON'T LIKE ME.
THEN THAT TECHNIQUE FROM THIS MORNING...
THAT WAS JUST A SWORD TECHNIQUE.
JUST A SWORD TECHNIQUE ...?
MY FAMILY HAS A TRADITIONAL DOJO GOING WAY BACK, SO...
HA HA...

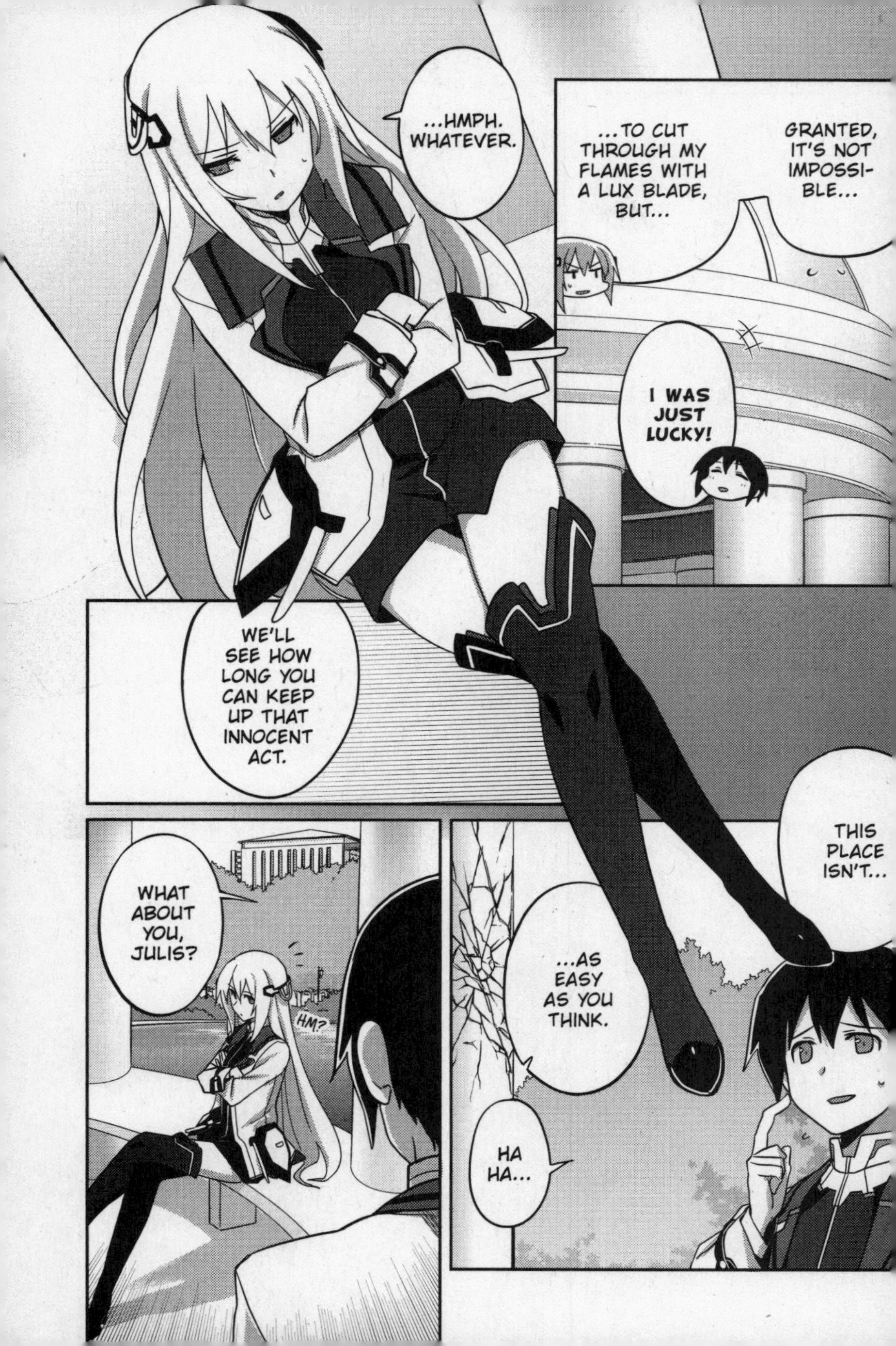
GRANTED, IT'S NOT IMPOSSI-BLE...
...TO CUT THROUGH MY FLAMES WITH A LUX BLADE, BUT...
I WAS JUST LUCKY!
...HMPH. WHATEVER.
WE'LL SEE HOW LONG YOU CAN KEEP UP THAT INNOCENT ACT.
THIS PLACE ISN'T...
...AS EASY AS YOU THINK.
HA HA...
WHAT ABOUT YOU, JULIS?
HM?

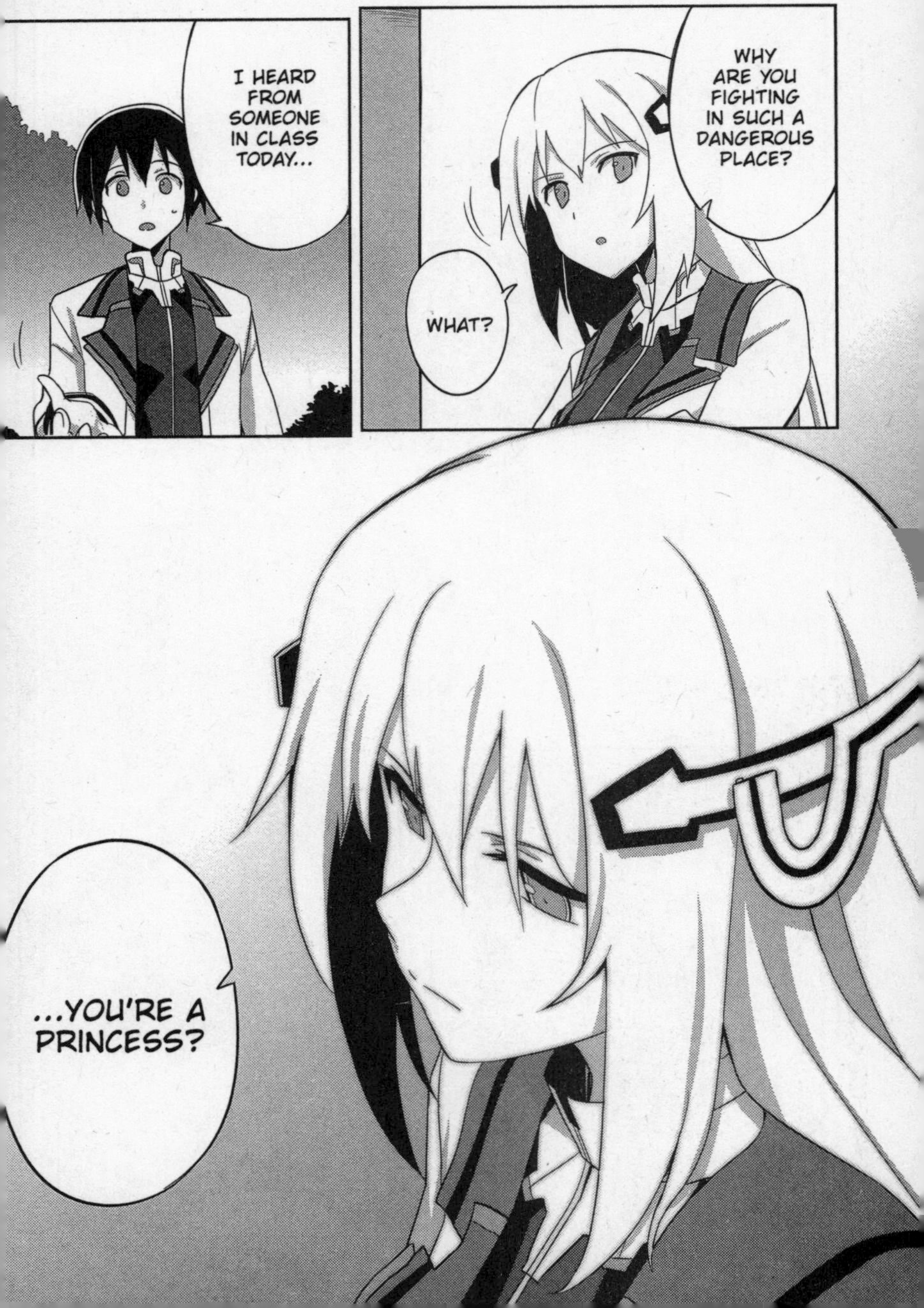
WHY ARE YOU FIGHTING IN SUCH A DANGEROUS PLACE?
WHAT?
I HEARD FROM SOMEONE IN CLASS TODAY...
...YOU'RE A PRINCESS?

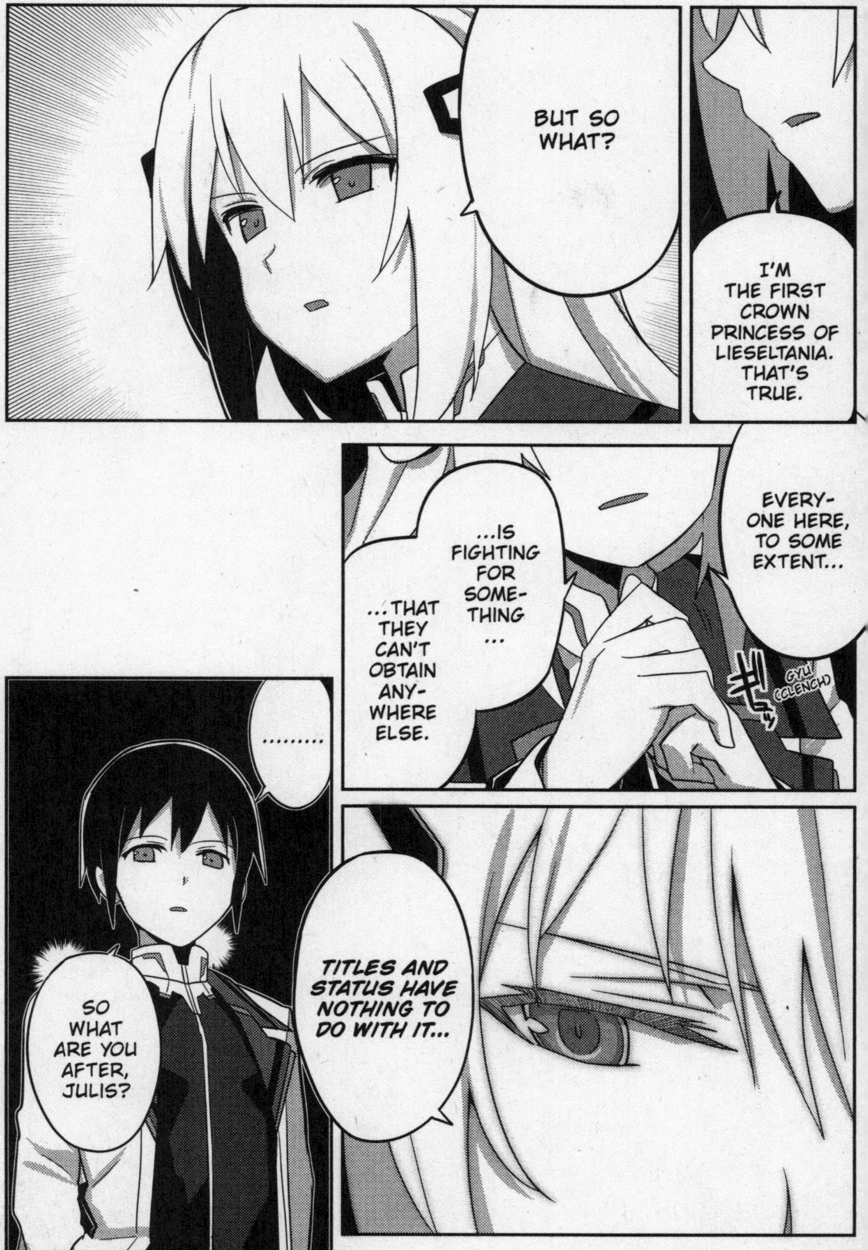
I'M THE FIRST CROWN PRINCESS OF LIESELTANIA. THAT'S TRUE.
BUT SO WHAT?
EVERY-ONE HERE, TO SOME EXTENT...
...IS FIGHTING FOR SOME-THING...
...THAT THEY CAN'T OBTAIN ANY-WHERE ELSE.
GYU! (CLENCH)
TITLES AND STATUS HAVE NOTHING TO DO WITH IT...
....
SO WHAT ARE YOU AFTER, JULIS?

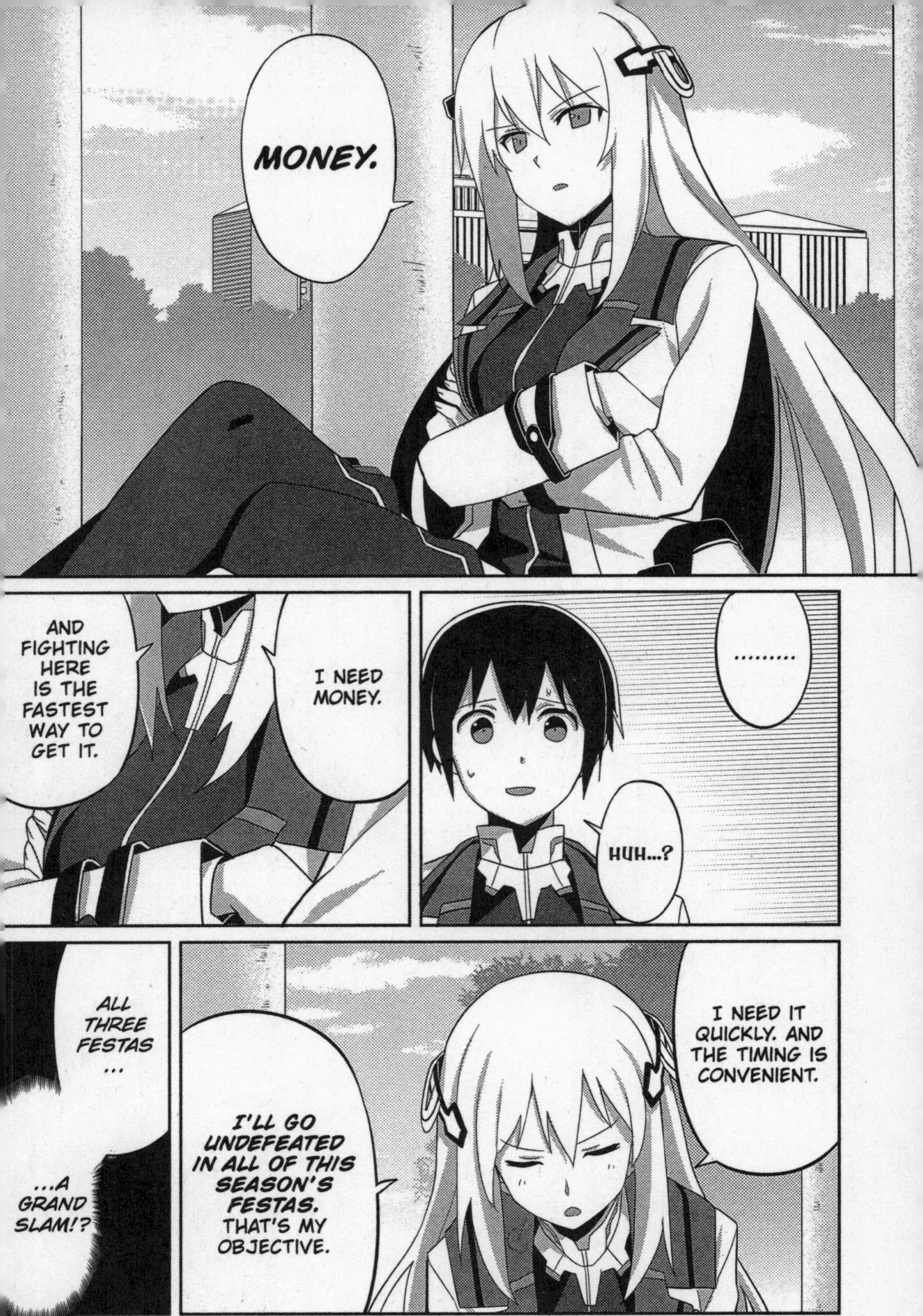
MONEY.
....
HUH...?
I NEED MONEY.
AND FIGHTING HERE IS THE FASTEST WAY TO GET IT.
I NEED IT QUICKLY. AND THE TIMING IS CONVENIENT.
I'LL GO UNDEFEATED IN ALL OF THIS SEASON'S FESTAS. THAT'S MY OBJECTIVE.
ALL THREE FESTAS ...
...A GRAND SLAM!?

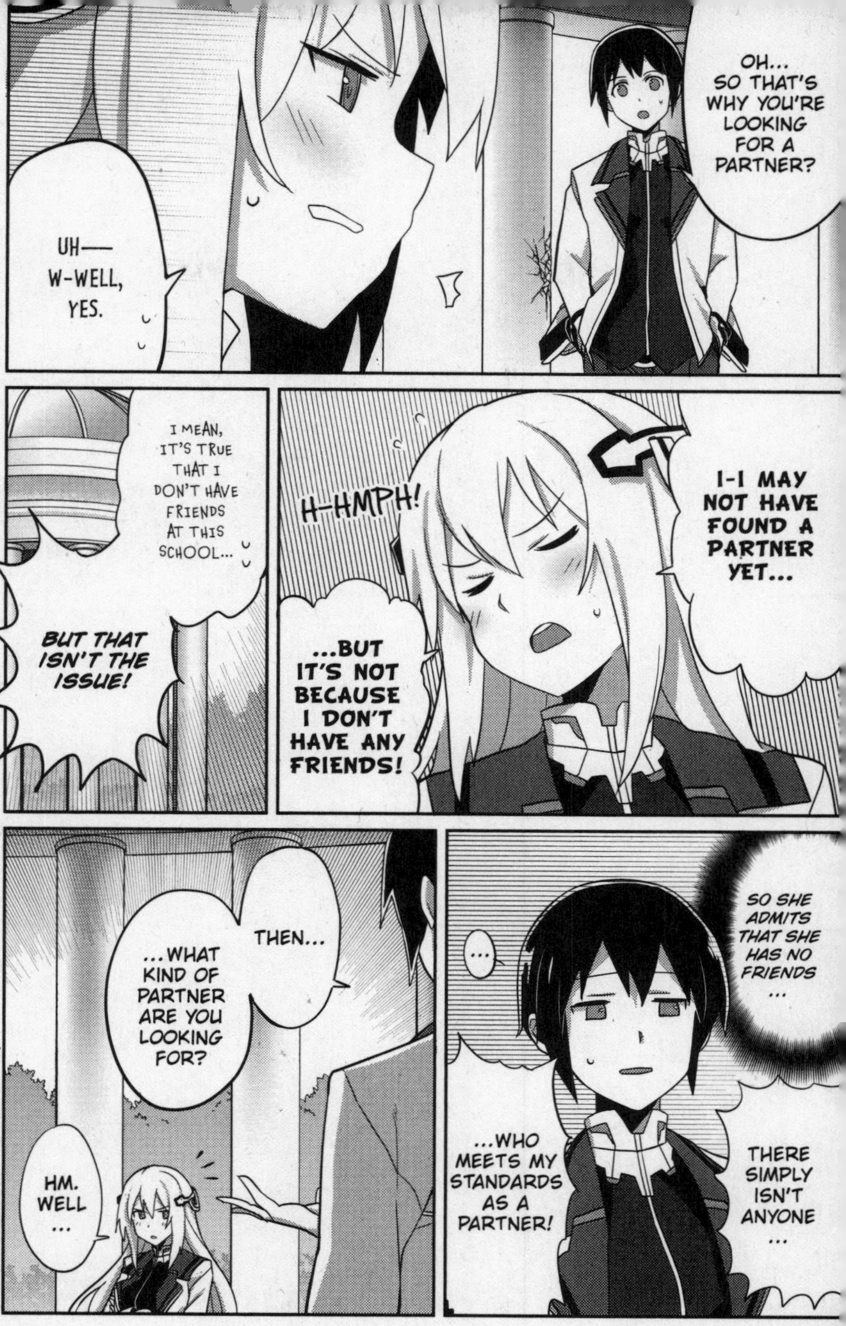

OH... SO THAT'S WHY YOU'RE LOOKING FOR A PARTNER?
UH— W-WELL, YES.
H-HMPH!
I-I MAY NOT HAVE FOUND A PARTNER YET...
...BUT IT'S NOT BECAUSE I DON'T HAVE ANY FRIENDS!
I MEAN, IT'S TRUE THAT I DON'T HAVE FRIENDS AT THIS SCHOOL...
BUT THAT ISN'T THE ISSUE!
...
SO SHE ADMITS THAT SHE HAS NO FRIENDS...
THERE SIMPLY ISN'T ANYONE...
...WHO MEETS MY STANDARDS AS A PARTNER!
THEN...
...WHAT KIND OF PARTNER ARE YOU LOOKING FOR?
HM. WELL...

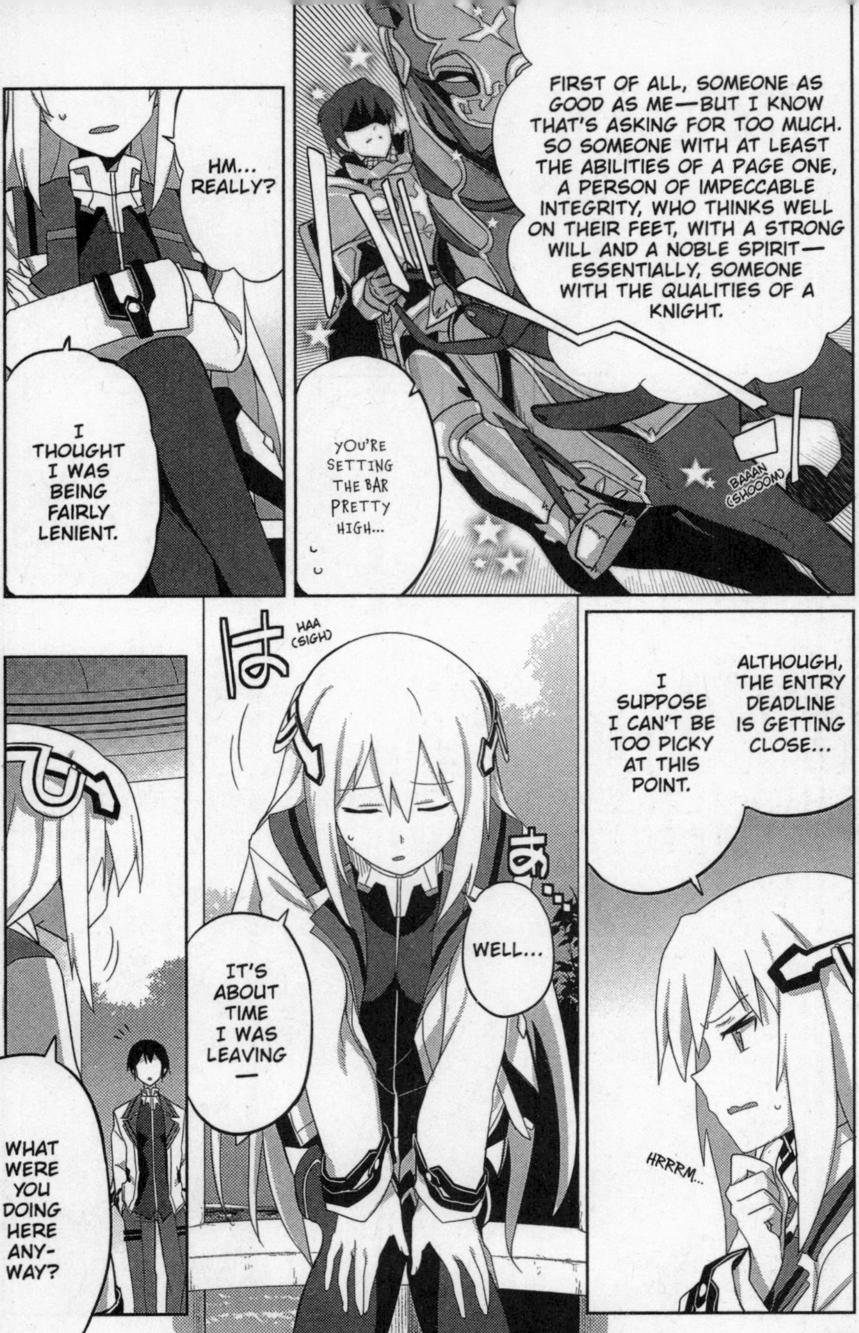
FIRST OF ALL, SOMEONE AS GOOD AS ME—BUT I KNOW THAT'S ASKING FOR TOO MUCH. SO SOMEONE WITH AT LEAST THE ABILITIES OF A PAGE ONE, A PERSON OF IMPECCABLE INTEGRITY, WHO THINKS WELL ON THEIR FEET, WITH A STRONG WILL AND A NOBLE SPIRIT—ESSENTIALLY, SOMEONE WITH THE QUALITIES OF A KNIGHT.
BAAAN (SHOOOM)
YOU'RE SETTING THE BAR PRETTY HIGH...
HM... REALLY?
I THOUGHT I WAS BEING FAIRLY LENIENT.
ALTHOUGH, THE ENTRY DEADLINE IS GETTING CLOSE...
I SUPPOSE I CAN'T BE TOO PICKY AT THIS POINT.
HRRRM...
は
HAA (SIGH)
あ…
WELL...
IT'S ABOUT TIME I WAS LEAVING—
WHAT WERE YOU DOING HERE ANYWAY?

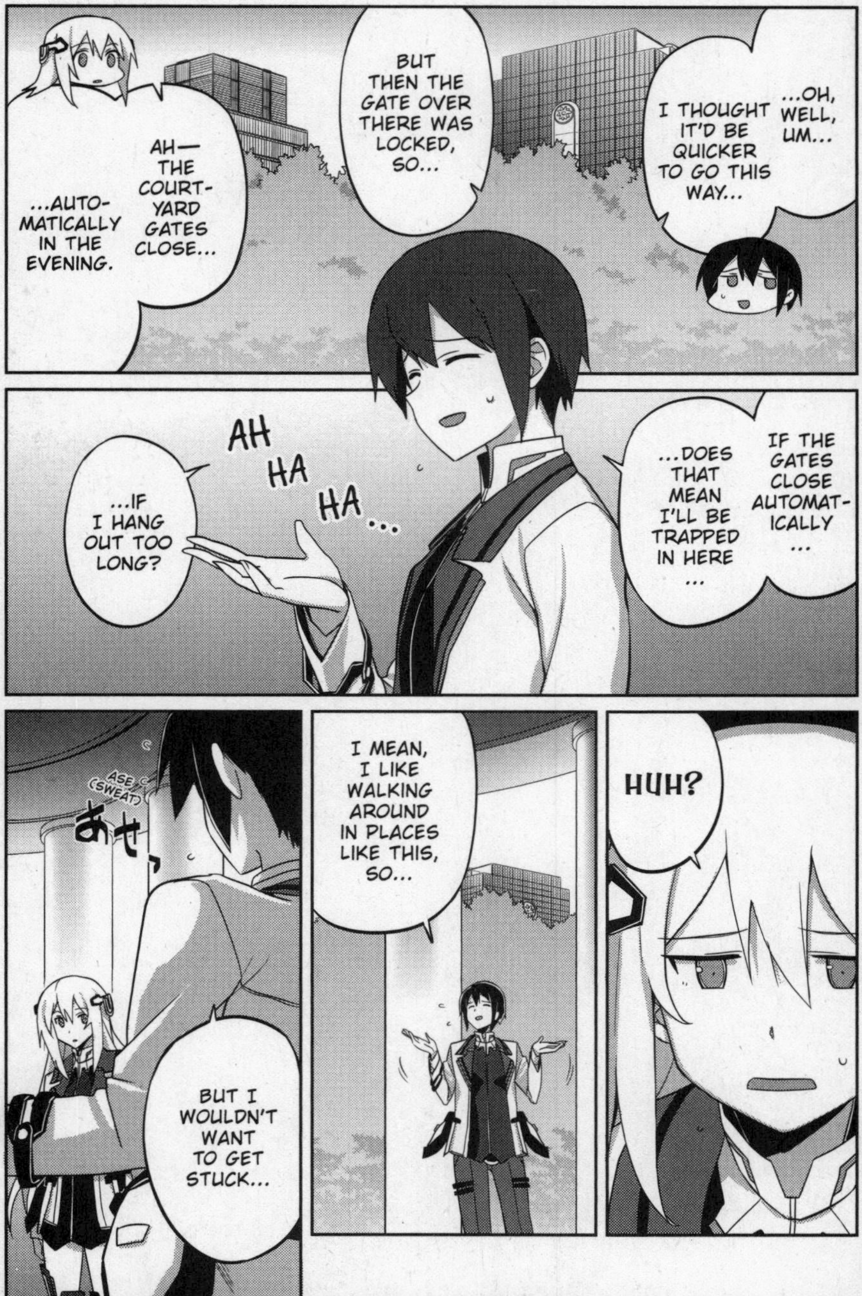
...OH, WELL, UM...
I THOUGHT IT'D BE QUICKER TO GO THIS WAY...
BUT THEN THE GATE OVER THERE WAS LOCKED, SO...
AH— THE COURT-YARD GATES CLOSE...
...AUTO-MATICALLY IN THE EVENING.
IF THE GATES CLOSE AUTOMAT-ICALLY...
...DOES THAT MEAN I'LL BE TRAPPED IN HERE...
AH HA HA...
...IF I HANG OUT TOO LONG?
HUH?
I MEAN, I LIKE WALKING AROUND IN PLACES LIKE THIS, SO...
ASE (SWEAT)
あせっ
BUT I WOULDN'T WANT TO GET STUCK...

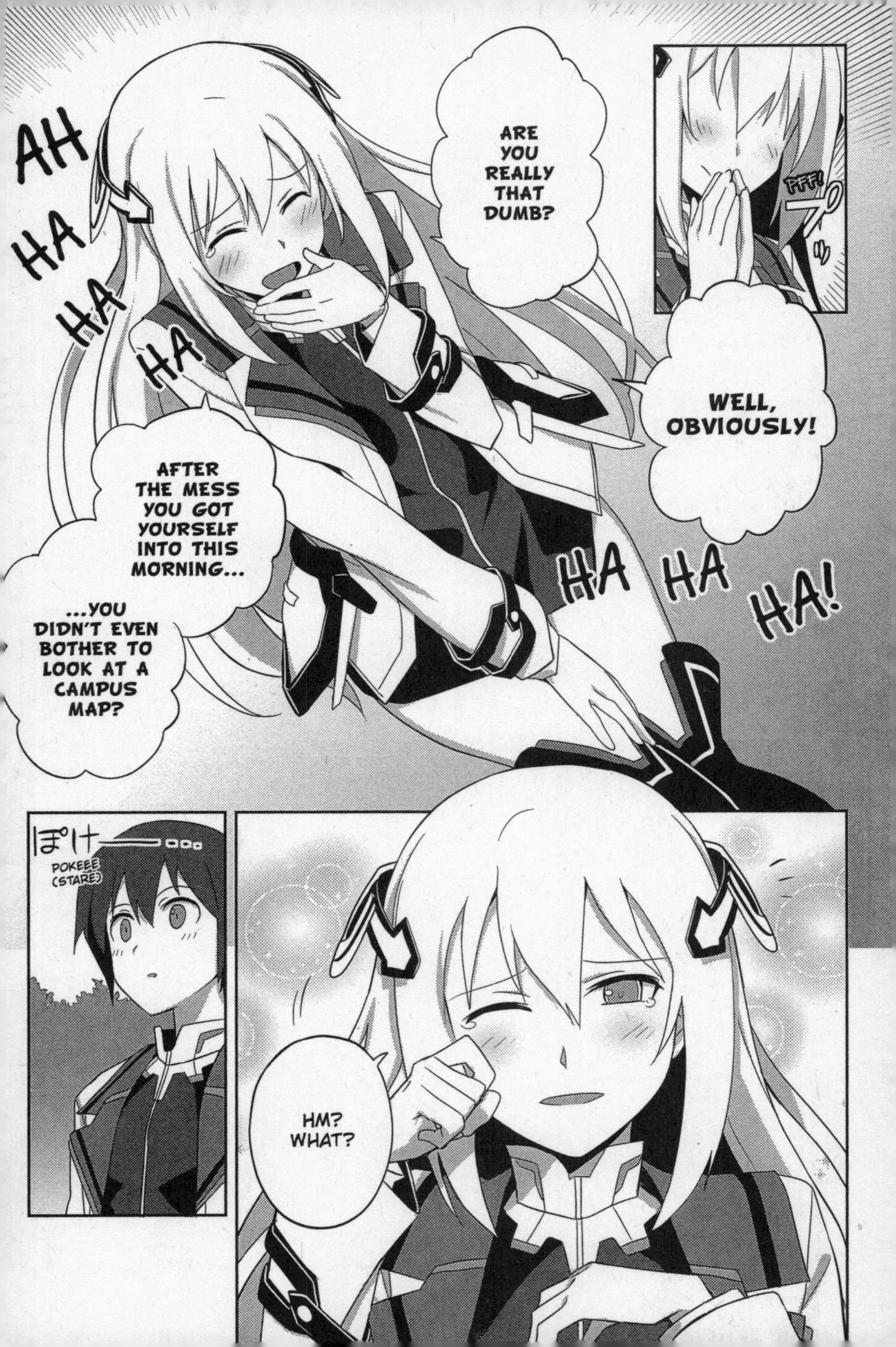
PFF!
ARE YOU REALLY THAT DUMB?
WELL, OBVIOUSLY!
AH HA HA HA
AFTER THE MESS YOU GOT YOURSELF INTO THIS MORNING...
...YOU DIDN'T EVEN BOTHER TO LOOK AT A CAMPUS MAP?
HA HA HA!
HM? WHAT?
ぽけー
POKEEE (STARE)

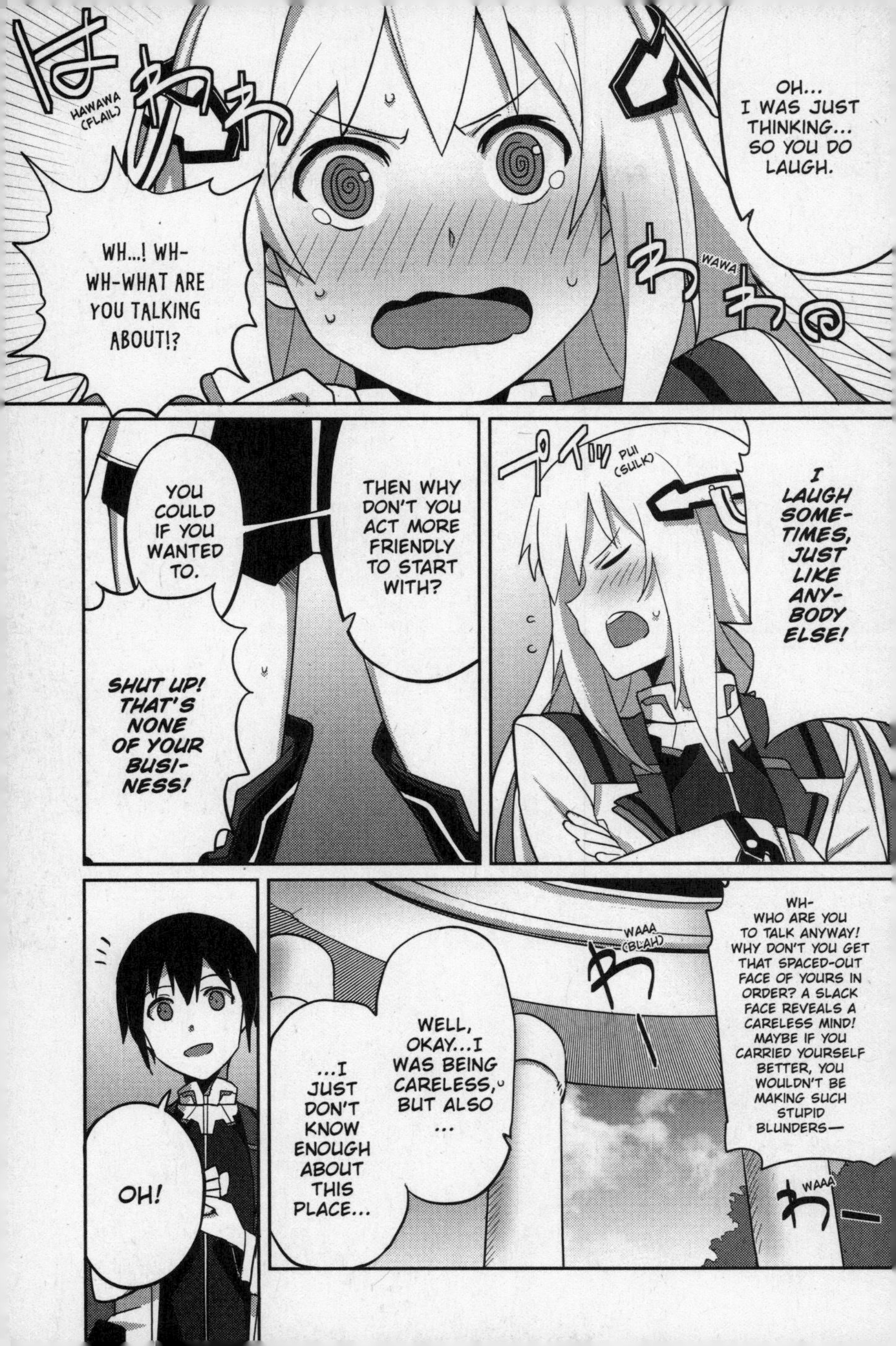

OH... I WAS JUST THINKING... SO YOU DO LAUGH.
WAWA
HAWAWA (FLAIL)
WH...! WH-WH-WHAT ARE YOU TALKING ABOUT!?
PUI (SULK)
I LAUGH SOME-TIMES, JUST LIKE ANY-BODY ELSE!
THEN WHY DON'T YOU ACT MORE FRIENDLY TO START WITH?
YOU COULD IF YOU WANTED TO.
SHUT UP! THAT'S NONE OF YOUR BUSI-NESS!
WAAA (BLAH)
WH- WHO ARE YOU TO TALK ANYWAY! WHY DON'T YOU GET THAT SPACED-OUT FACE OF YOURS IN ORDER? A SLACK FACE REVEALS A CARELESS MIND! MAYBE IF YOU CARRIED YOURSELF BETTER, YOU WOULDN'T BE MAKING SUCH STUPID BLUNDERS—
WAAA
WELL, OKAY...I WAS BEING CARELESS, BUT ALSO ...
...I JUST DON'T KNOW ENOUGH ABOUT THIS PLACE...
OH!

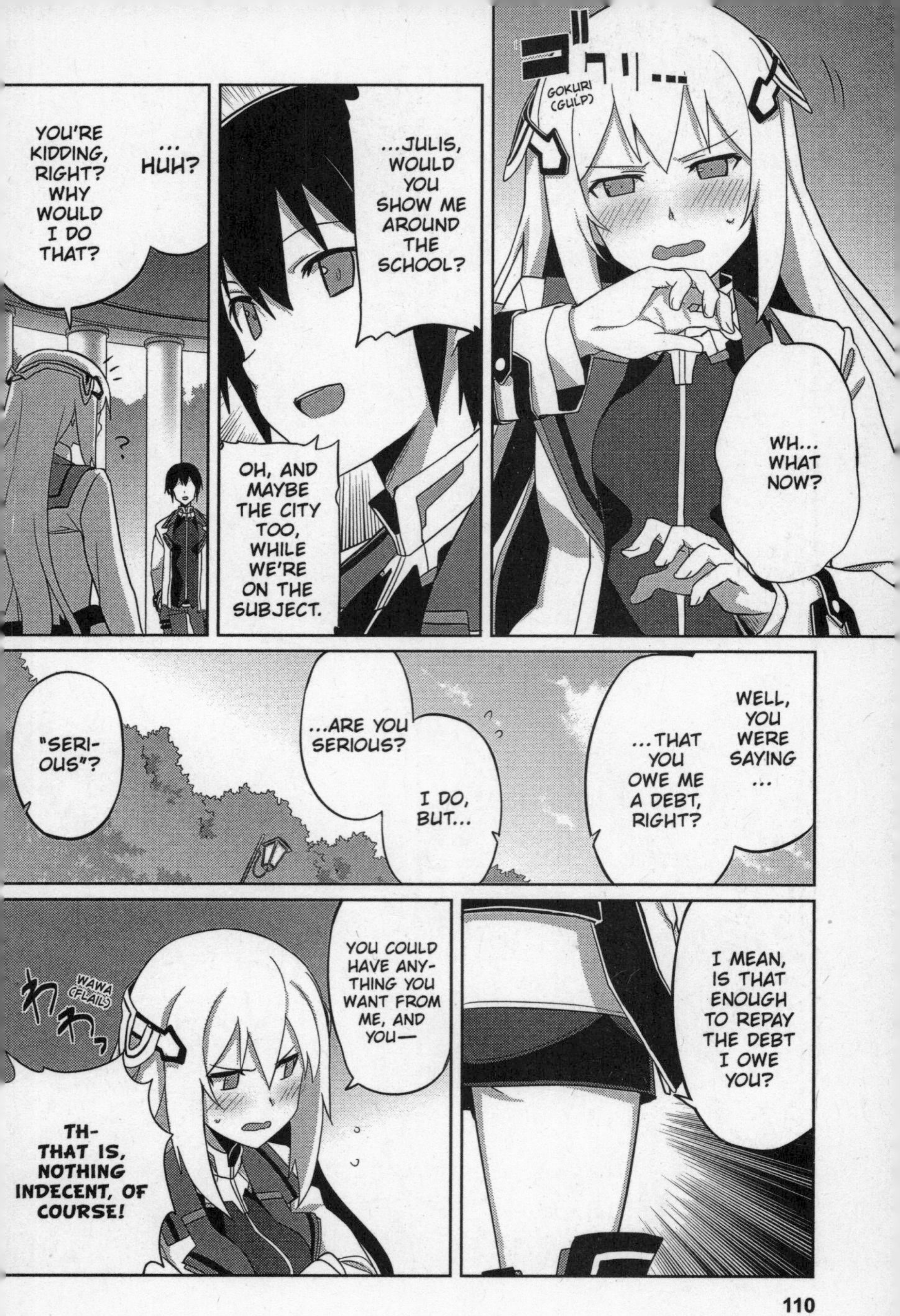
ゴクリ…
GOKURI (GULP)
WH... WHAT NOW?
...JULIS, WOULD YOU SHOW ME AROUND THE SCHOOL?
OH, AND MAYBE THE CITY TOO, WHILE WE'RE ON THE SUBJECT.
... HUH?
YOU'RE KIDDING, RIGHT? WHY WOULD I DO THAT?
WELL, YOU WERE SAYING ...
...THAT YOU OWE ME A DEBT, RIGHT?
I DO, BUT...
...ARE YOU SERIOUS?
"SERI-OUS"?
I MEAN, IS THAT ENOUGH TO REPAY THE DEBT I OWE YOU?
YOU COULD HAVE ANY-THING YOU WANT FROM ME, AND YOU—
わわっ
WAWA (FLAIL)
TH- THAT IS, NOTHING INDECENT, OF COURSE!

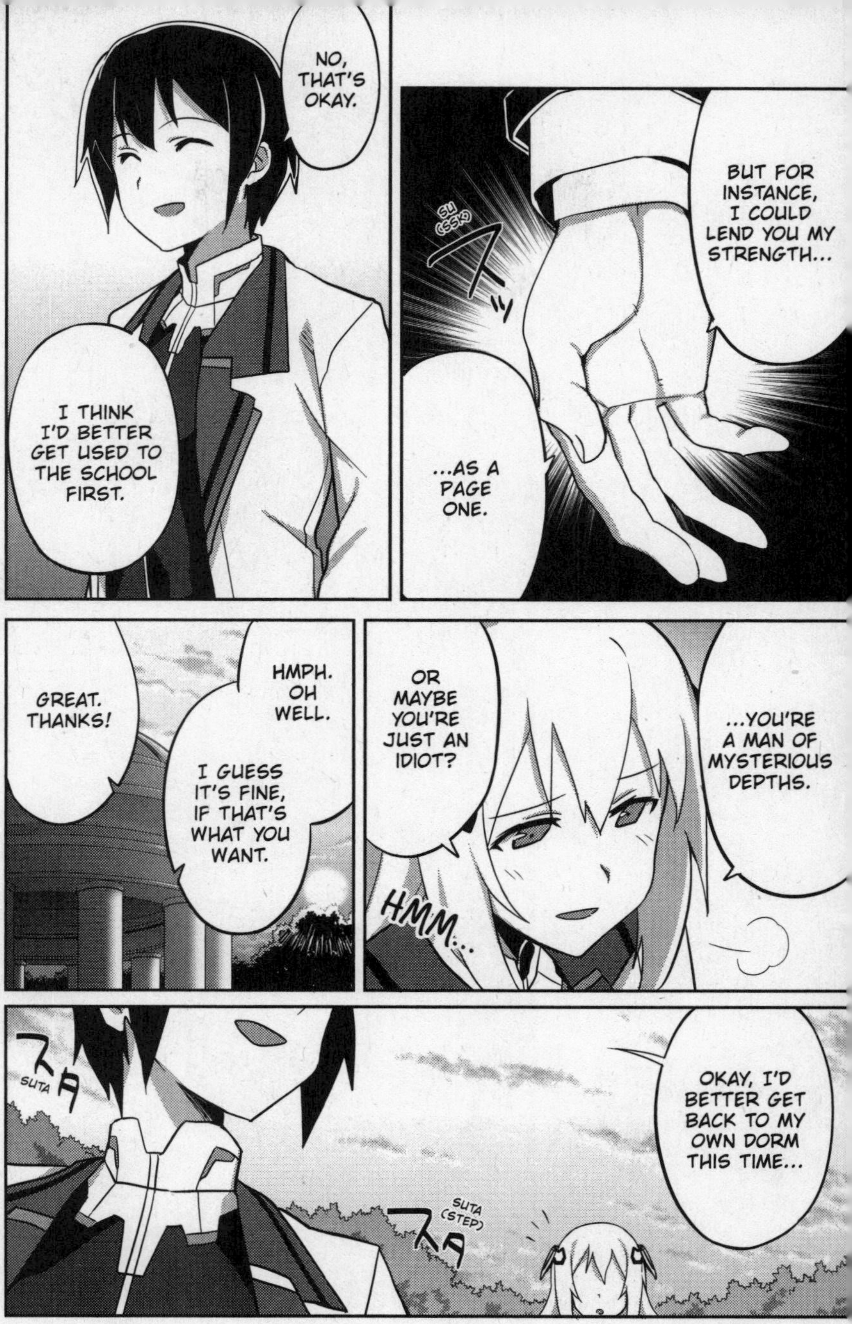
BUT FOR INSTANCE, I COULD LEND YOU MY STRENGTH...
SU (SSK)
...AS A PAGE ONE.
NO, THAT'S OKAY.
I THINK I'D BETTER GET USED TO THE SCHOOL FIRST.
...YOU'RE A MAN OF MYSTERIOUS DEPTHS.
OR MAYBE YOU'RE JUST AN IDIOT?
HMM...
HMPH. OH WELL.
I GUESS IT'S FINE, IF THAT'S WHAT YOU WANT.
GREAT. THANKS!
OKAY, I'D BETTER GET BACK TO MY OWN DORM THIS TIME...
SUTA (STEP)
SUTA

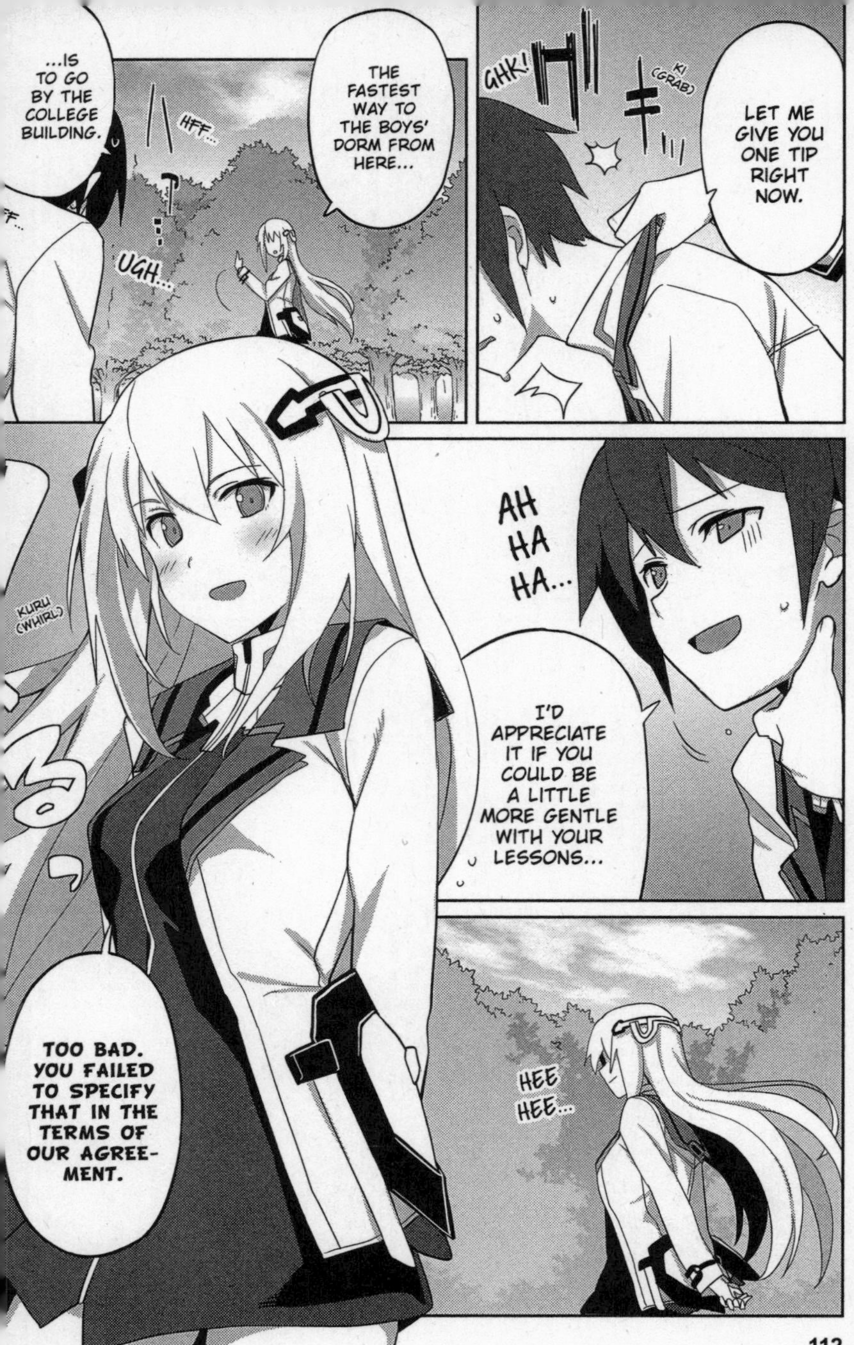
LET ME GIVE YOU ONE TIP RIGHT NOW.
KI (GRAB)
GHK!
THE FASTEST WAY TO THE BOYS' DORM FROM HERE...
HFF...
...IS TO GO BY THE COLLEGE BUILDING.
UGH...
FF...
AH HA HA...
I'D APPRECIATE IT IF YOU COULD BE A LITTLE MORE GENTLE WITH YOUR LESSONS...
HEE HEE...
KURU (WHIRL)
TOO BAD. YOU FAILED TO SPECIFY THAT IN THE TERMS OF OUR AGREE-MENT.

THE
ASTERISK WAR

THE
ASTERISK WAR

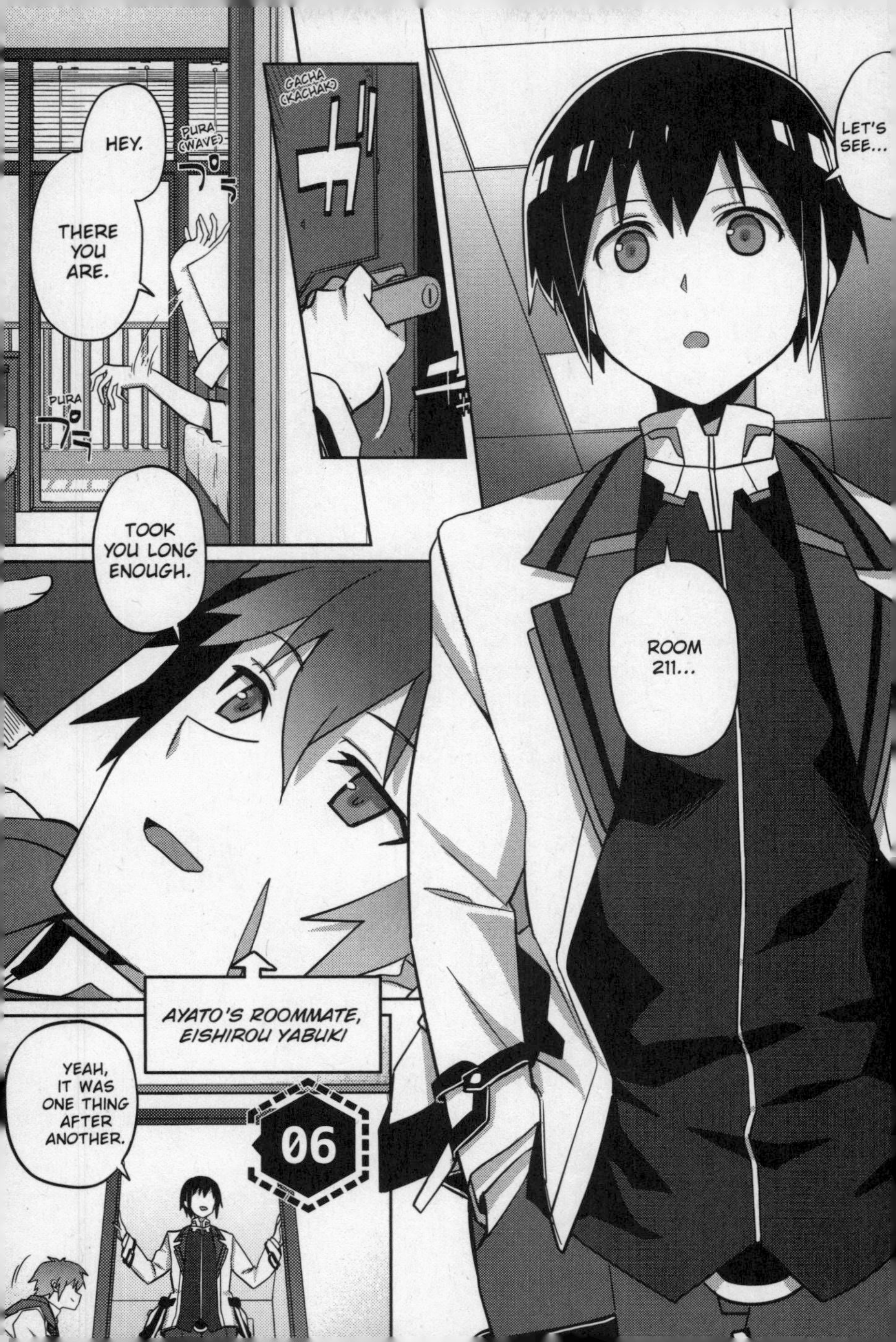
LET'S SEE...
ROOM 211...
GACHA (KACHAK)
HEY.
THERE YOU ARE.
PURA (WAVE)
PURA
TOOK YOU LONG ENOUGH.
AYATO'S ROOMMATE, EISHIROU YABUKI
YEAH, IT WAS ONE THING AFTER ANOTHER.
06

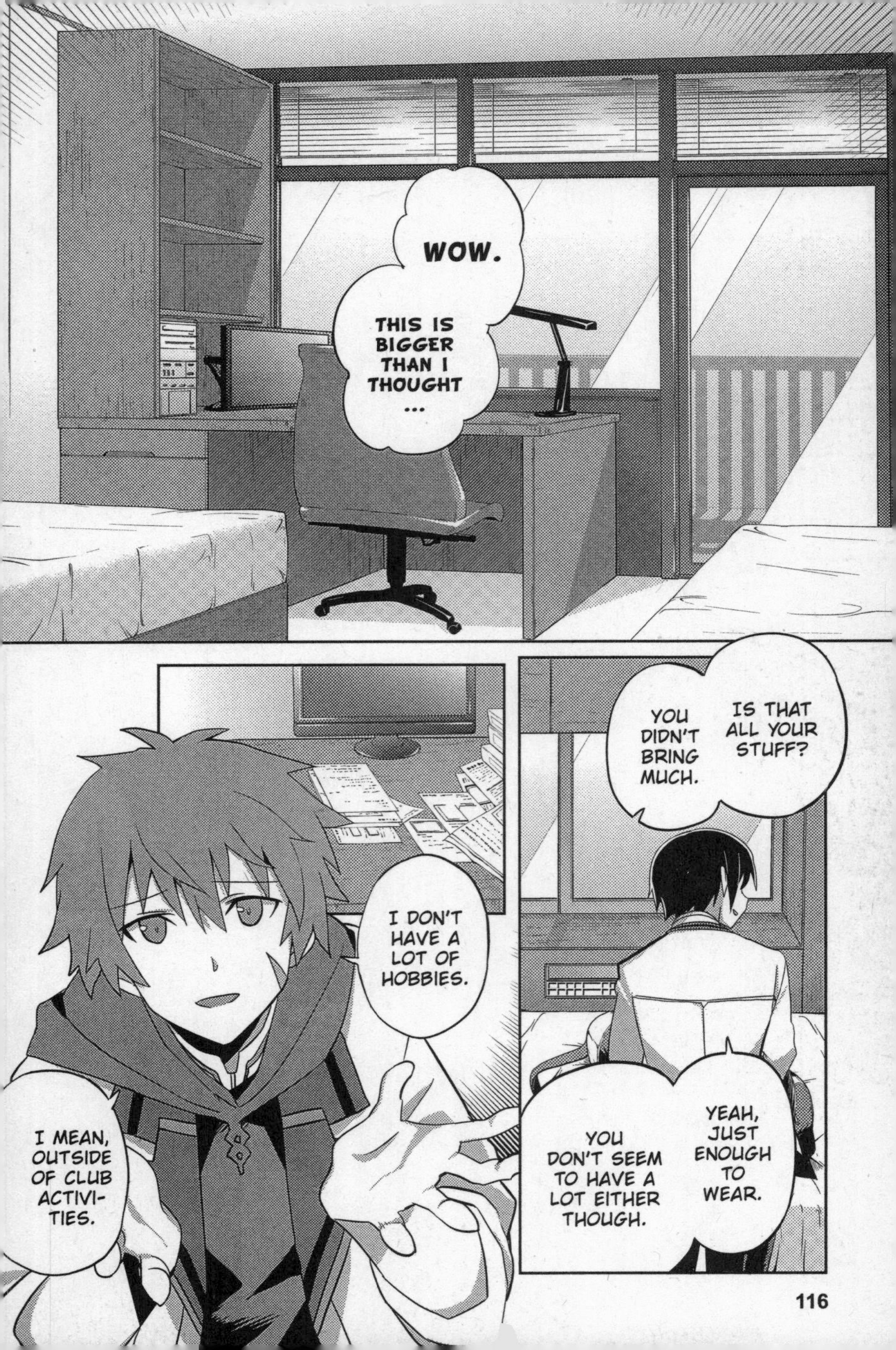
WOW.
THIS IS BIGGER THAN I THOUGHT...
IS THAT ALL YOUR STUFF?
YOU DIDN'T BRING MUCH.
YEAH, JUST ENOUGH TO WEAR.
YOU DON'T SEEM TO HAVE A LOT EITHER THOUGH.
I DON'T HAVE A LOT OF HOBBIES.
I MEAN, OUTSIDE OF CLUB ACTIVITIES.

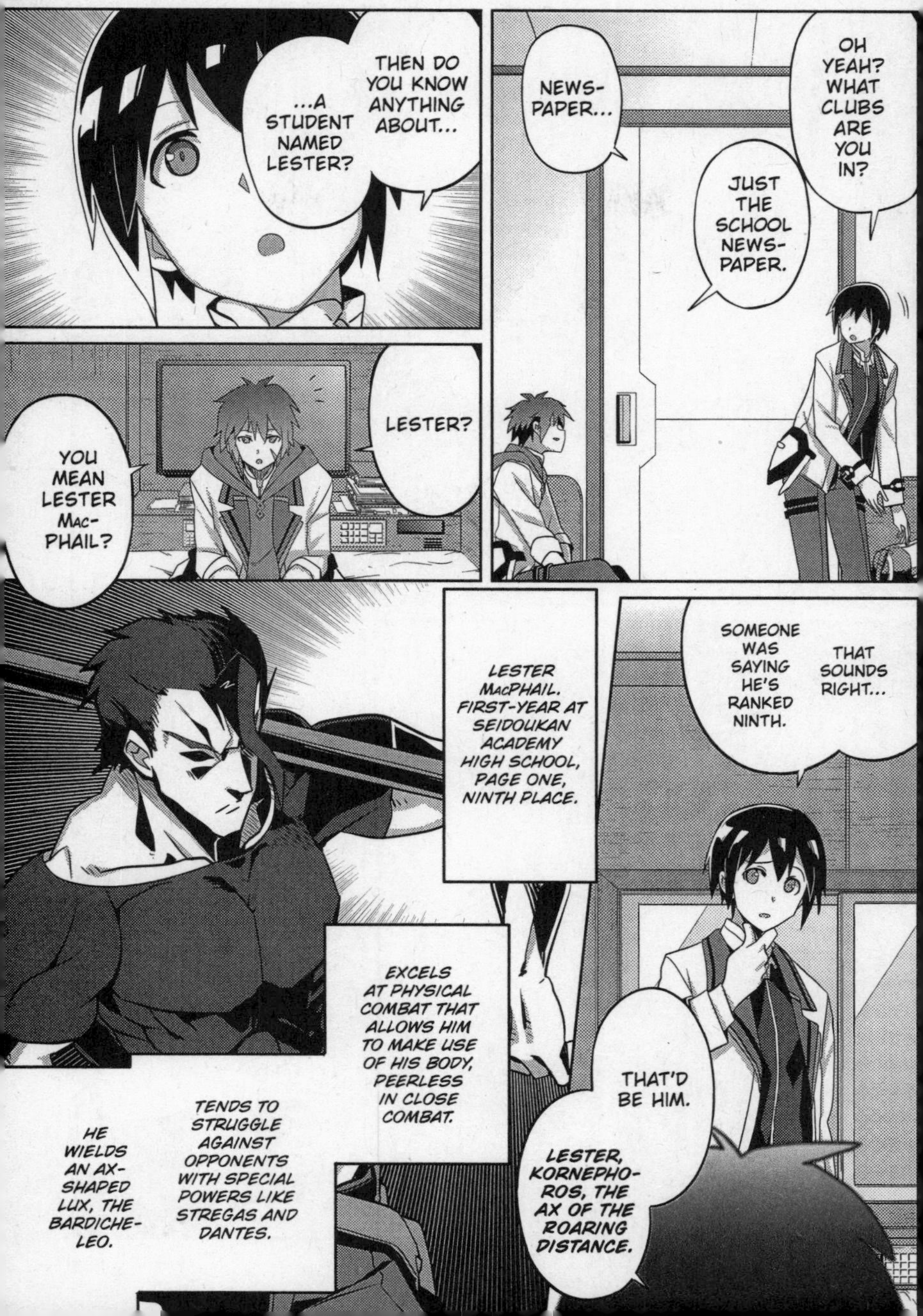

OH YEAH? WHAT CLUBS ARE YOU IN?
JUST THE SCHOOL NEWS-PAPER.
NEWS-PAPER...
THEN DO YOU KNOW ANYTHING ABOUT...
...A STUDENT NAMED LESTER?
LESTER?
YOU MEAN LESTER MacPHAIL?
THAT SOUNDS RIGHT...
SOMEONE WAS SAYING HE'S RANKED NINTH.
THAT'D BE HIM.
LESTER, KORNEPHOROS, THE AX OF THE ROARING DISTANCE.
LESTER MacPHAIL. FIRST-YEAR AT SEIDOUKAN ACADEMY HIGH SCHOOL, PAGE ONE, NINTH PLACE.
EXCELS AT PHYSICAL COMBAT THAT ALLOWS HIM TO MAKE USE OF HIS BODY, PEERLESS IN CLOSE COMBAT.
TENDS TO STRUGGLE AGAINST OPPONENTS WITH SPECIAL POWERS LIKE STREGAS AND DANTES.
HE WIELDS AN AX-SHAPED LUX, THE BARDICHE-LEO.

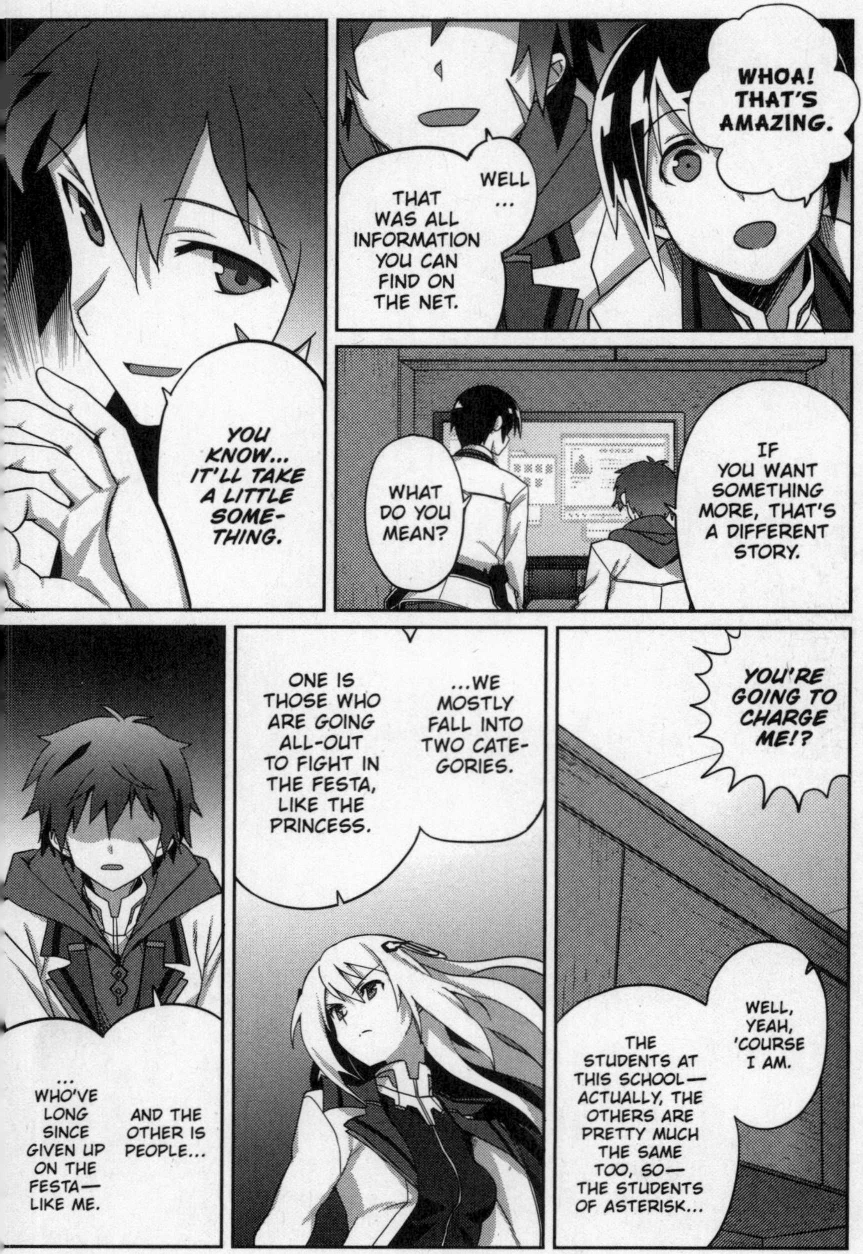
WHOA! THAT'S AMAZING.
WELL ...
THAT WAS ALL INFORMATION YOU CAN FIND ON THE NET.
IF YOU WANT SOMETHING MORE, THAT'S A DIFFERENT STORY.
WHAT DO YOU MEAN?
YOU KNOW... IT'LL TAKE A LITTLE SOME-THING.
YOU'RE GOING TO CHARGE ME!?
WELL, YEAH, 'COURSE I AM.
THE STUDENTS AT THIS SCHOOL— ACTUALLY, THE OTHERS ARE PRETTY MUCH THE SAME TOO, SO— THE STUDENTS OF ASTERISK...
...WE MOSTLY FALL INTO TWO CATE-GORIES.
ONE IS THOSE WHO ARE GOING ALL-OUT TO FIGHT IN THE FESTA, LIKE THE PRINCESS.
AND THE OTHER IS PEOPLE...
... WHO'VE LONG SINCE GIVEN UP ON THE FESTA— LIKE ME.

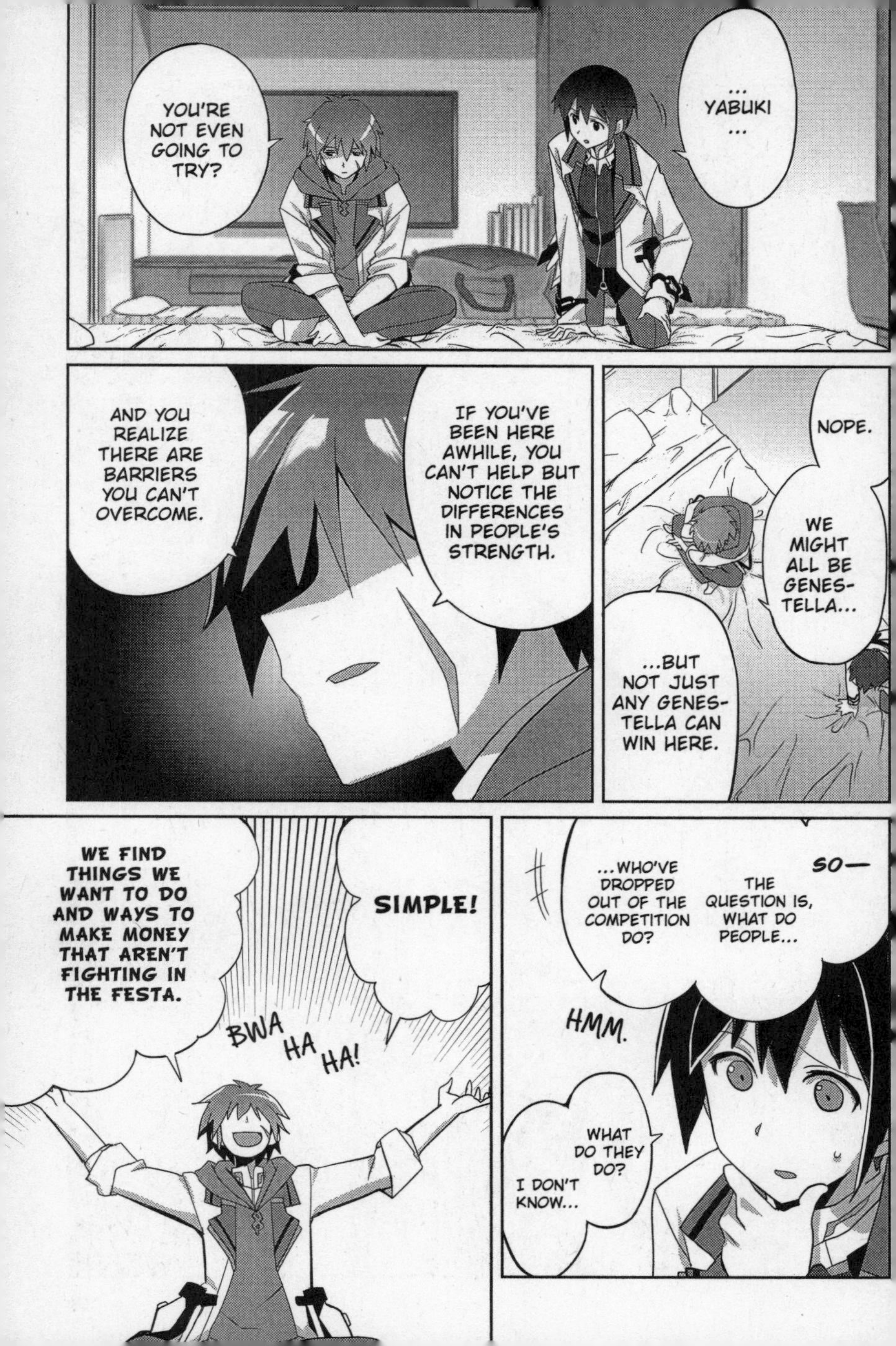
...YABUKI...
YOU'RE NOT EVEN GOING TO TRY?
NOPE.
WE MIGHT ALL BE GENES-TELLA...
...BUT NOT JUST ANY GENES-TELLA CAN WIN HERE.
IF YOU'VE BEEN HERE AWHILE, YOU CAN'T HELP BUT NOTICE THE DIFFERENCES IN PEOPLE'S STRENGTH.
AND YOU REALIZE THERE ARE BARRIERS YOU CAN'T OVERCOME.
SO—
THE QUESTION IS, WHAT DO PEOPLE...
...WHO'VE DROPPED OUT OF THE COMPETITION DO?
HMM.
WHAT DO THEY DO?
I DON'T KNOW...
SIMPLE!
WE FIND THINGS WE WANT TO DO AND WAYS TO MAKE MONEY THAT AREN'T FIGHTING IN THE FESTA.
BWA HA HA!

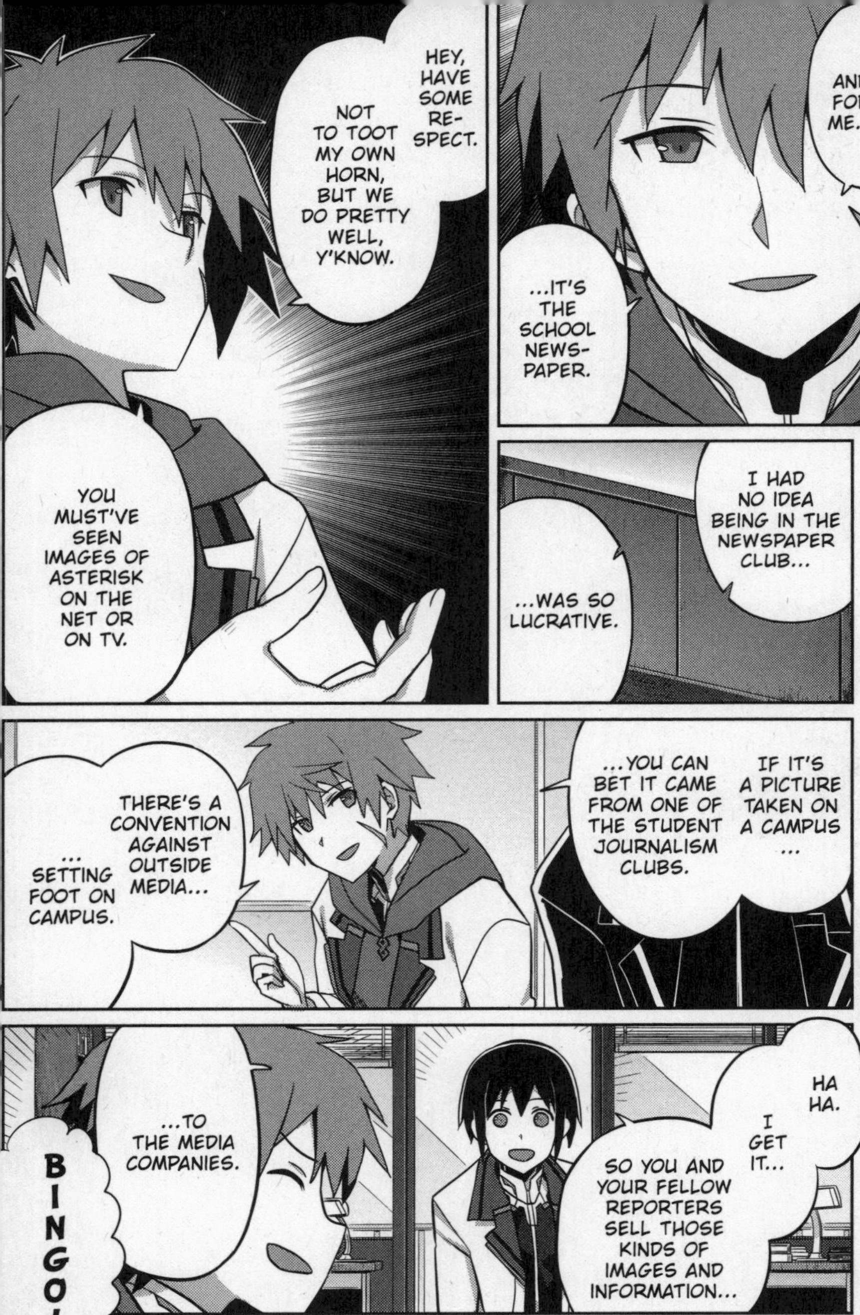
AND FOR ME...
...IT'S THE SCHOOL NEWSPAPER.
I HAD NO IDEA BEING IN THE NEWSPAPER CLUB...
...WAS SO LUCRATIVE.
HEY, HAVE SOME RE-SPECT.
NOT TO TOOT MY OWN HORN, BUT WE DO PRETTY WELL, Y'KNOW.
YOU MUST'VE SEEN IMAGES OF ASTERISK ON THE NET OR ON TV.
IF IT'S A PICTURE TAKEN ON A CAMPUS...
...YOU CAN BET IT CAME FROM ONE OF THE STUDENT JOURNALISM CLUBS.
THERE'S A CONVENTION AGAINST OUTSIDE MEDIA...
...SETTING FOOT ON CAMPUS.
HA HA.
I GET IT...
SO YOU AND YOUR FELLOW REPORTERS SELL THOSE KINDS OF IMAGES AND INFORMATION...
...TO THE MEDIA COMPANIES.
BINGO!

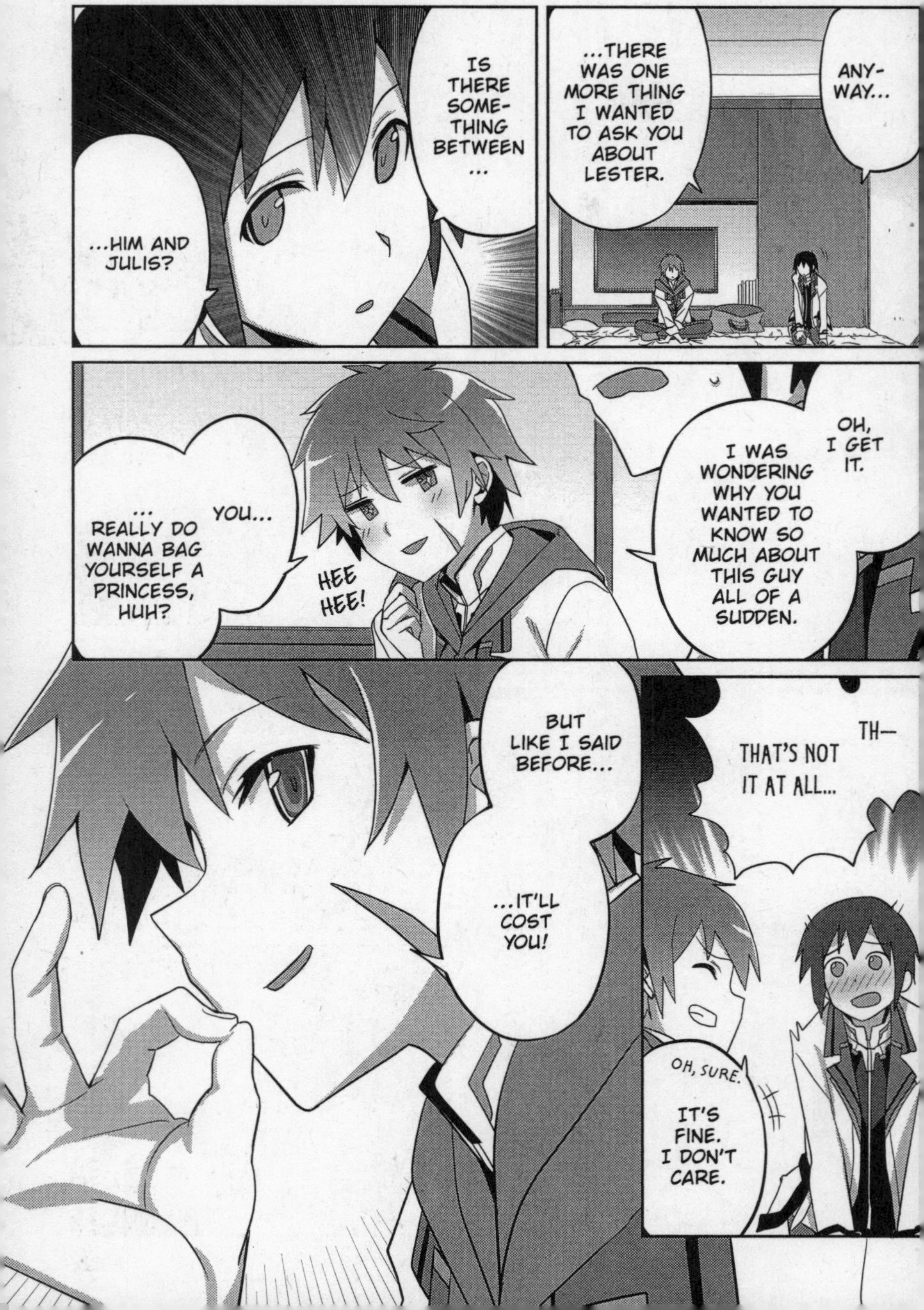
ANY-WAY...
...THERE WAS ONE MORE THING I WANTED TO ASK YOU ABOUT LESTER.
IS THERE SOME-THING BETWEEN ...
...HIM AND JULIS?
OH, I GET IT.
I WAS WONDERING WHY YOU WANTED TO KNOW SO MUCH ABOUT THIS GUY ALL OF A SUDDEN.
HEE HEE!
YOU...
... REALLY DO WANNA BAG YOURSELF A PRINCESS, HUH?
TH—
THAT'S NOT IT AT ALL...
OH, SURE.
IT'S FINE. I DON'T CARE.
BUT LIKE I SAID BEFORE...
...IT'LL COST YOU!

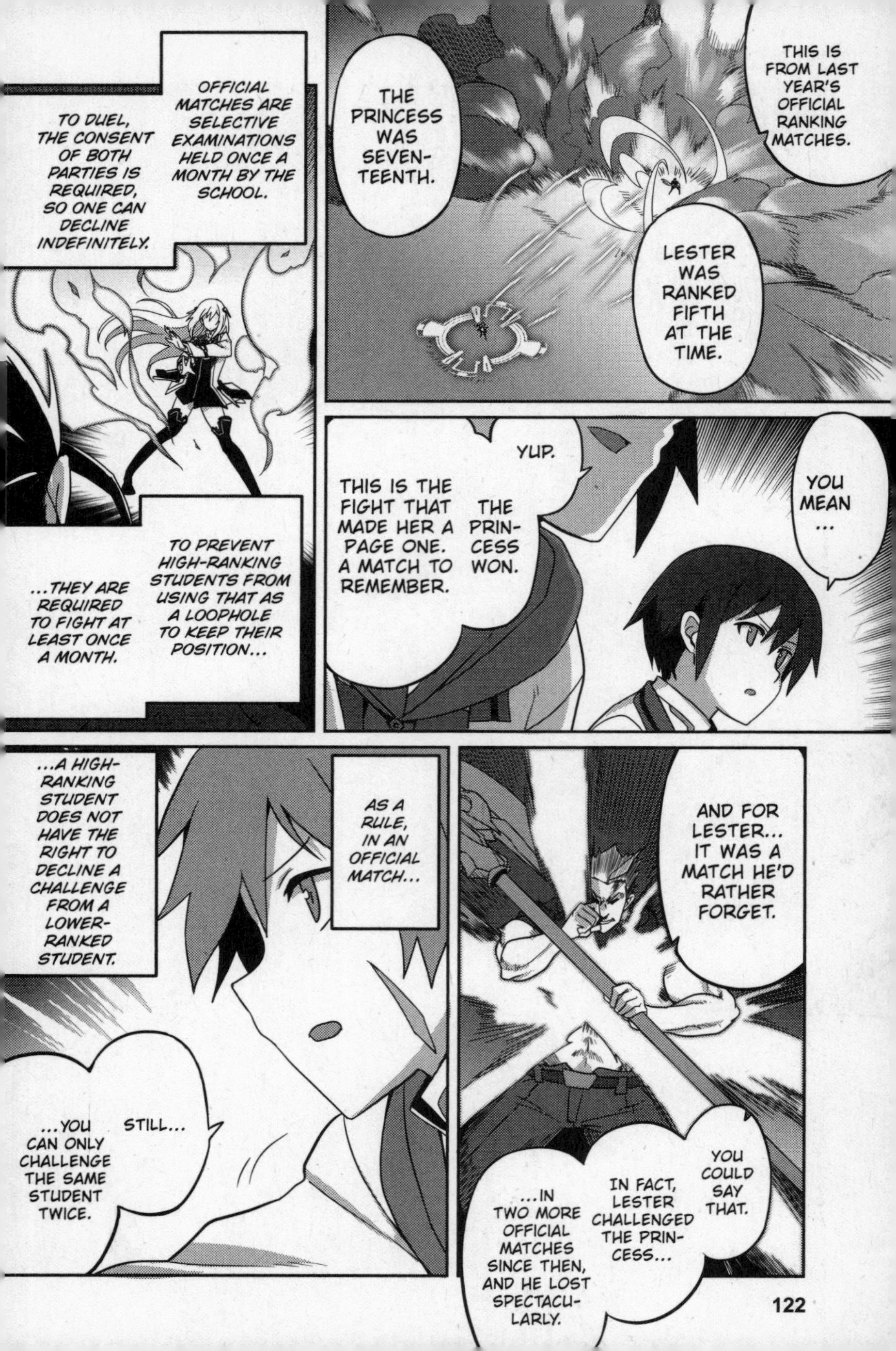
THIS IS FROM LAST YEAR'S OFFICIAL RANKING MATCHES.
LESTER WAS RANKED FIFTH AT THE TIME.
THE PRINCESS WAS SEVENTEENTH.
YOU MEAN...
YUP.
THE PRINCESS WON.
THIS IS THE FIGHT THAT MADE HER A PAGE ONE. A MATCH TO REMEMBER.
OFFICIAL MATCHES ARE SELECTIVE EXAMINATIONS HELD ONCE A MONTH BY THE SCHOOL.
TO DUEL, THE CONSENT OF BOTH PARTIES IS REQUIRED, SO ONE CAN DECLINE INDEFINITELY.
TO PREVENT HIGH-RANKING STUDENTS FROM USING THAT AS A LOOPHOLE TO KEEP THEIR POSITION...
...THEY ARE REQUIRED TO FIGHT AT LEAST ONCE A MONTH.
AND FOR LESTER... IT WAS A MATCH HE'D RATHER FORGET.
YOU COULD SAY THAT.
IN FACT, LESTER CHALLENGED THE PRINCESS...
...IN TWO MORE OFFICIAL MATCHES SINCE THEN, AND HE LOST SPECTACULARLY.
AS A RULE, IN AN OFFICIAL MATCH...
...A HIGH-RANKING STUDENT DOES NOT HAVE THE RIGHT TO DECLINE A CHALLENGE FROM A LOWER-RANKED STUDENT.
STILL...
...YOU CAN ONLY CHALLENGE THE SAME STUDENT TWICE.

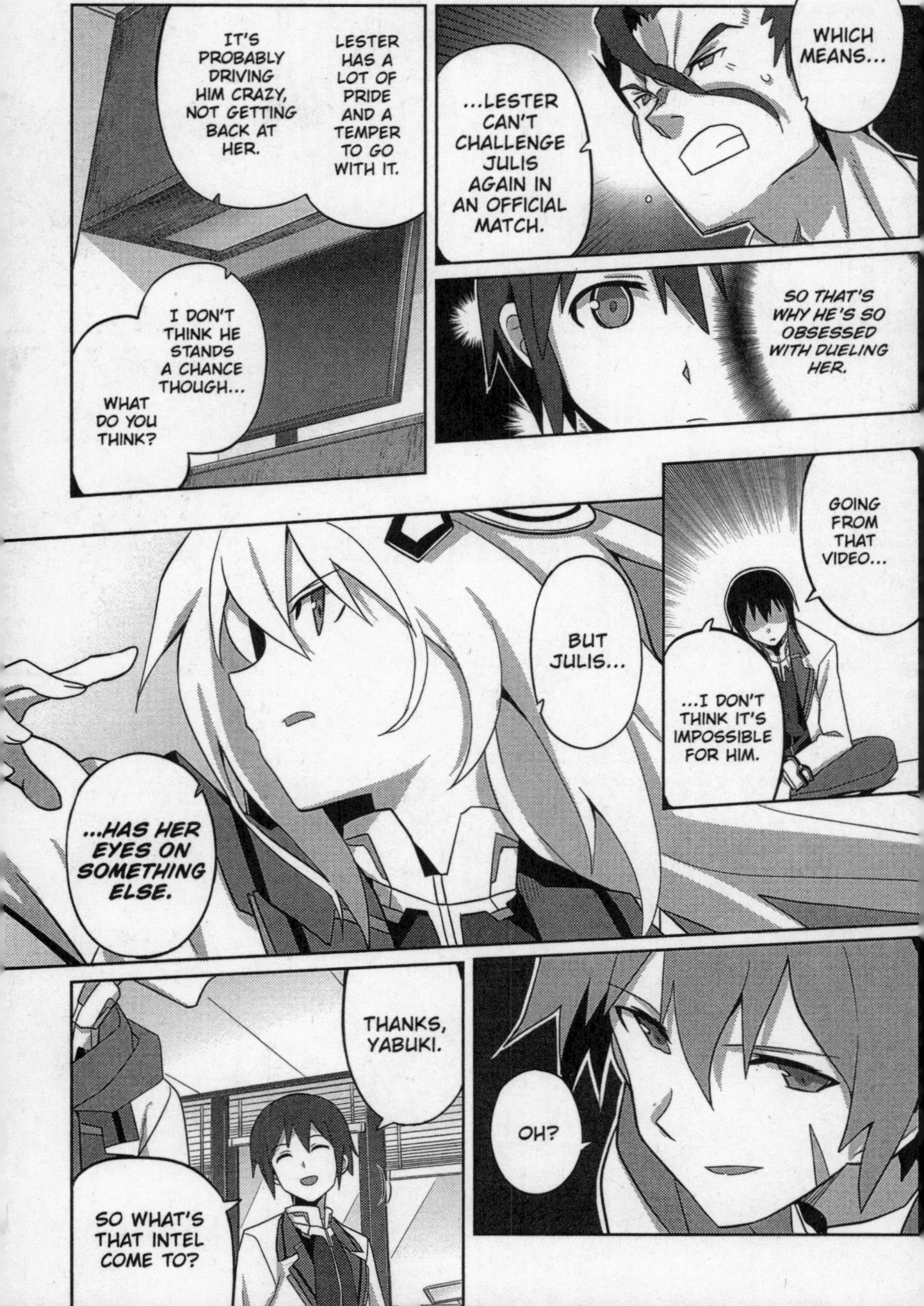
WHICH MEANS...
...LESTER CAN'T CHALLENGE JULIS AGAIN IN AN OFFICIAL MATCH.
SO THAT'S WHY HE'S SO OBSESSED WITH DUELING HER.
LESTER HAS A LOT OF PRIDE AND A TEMPER TO GO WITH IT.
IT'S PROBABLY DRIVING HIM CRAZY, NOT GETTING BACK AT HER.
I DON'T THINK HE STANDS A CHANCE THOUGH...
WHAT DO YOU THINK?
GOING FROM THAT VIDEO...
...I DON'T THINK IT'S IMPOSSIBLE FOR HIM.
BUT JULIS...
...HAS HER EYES ON SOMETHING ELSE.
OH?
THANKS, YABUKI.
SO WHAT'S THAT INTEL COME TO?

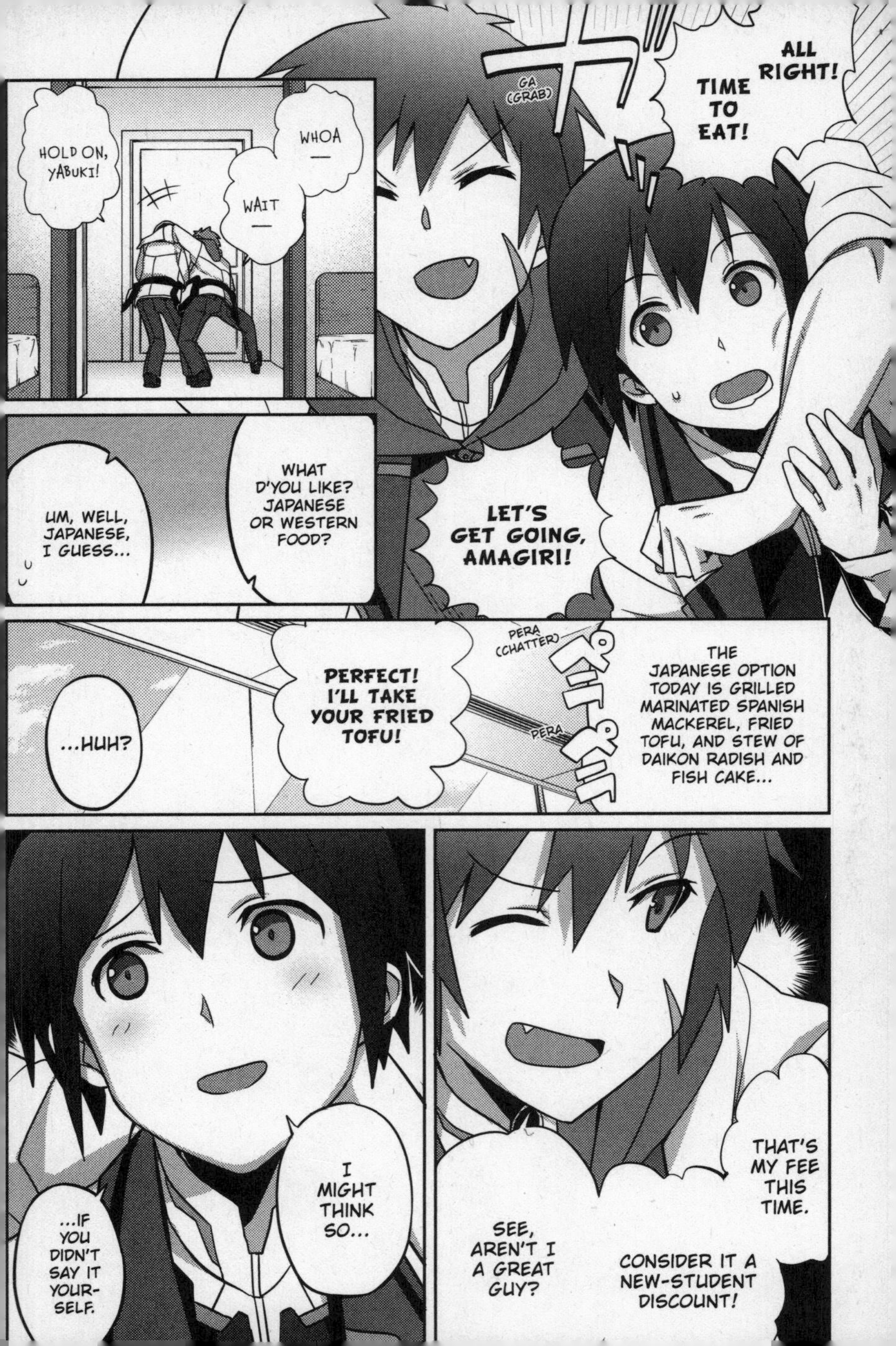

ALL RIGHT!
TIME TO EAT!
GA (GRAB)
LET'S GET GOING, AMAGIRI!
WHOA—
WAIT—
HOLD ON, YABUKI!
WHAT D'YOU LIKE? JAPANESE OR WESTERN FOOD?
UM, WELL, JAPANESE, I GUESS...
THE JAPANESE OPTION TODAY IS GRILLED MARINATED SPANISH MACKEREL, FRIED TOFU, AND STEW OF DAIKON RADISH AND FISH CAKE...
PERA (CHATTER)
PERA
PERFECT! I'LL TAKE YOUR FRIED TOFU!
...HUH?
THAT'S MY FEE THIS TIME.
CONSIDER IT A NEW-STUDENT DISCOUNT!
SEE, AREN'T I A GREAT GUY?
I MIGHT THINK SO...
...IF YOU DIDN'T SAY IT YOURSELF.

THE
ASTERISK WAR

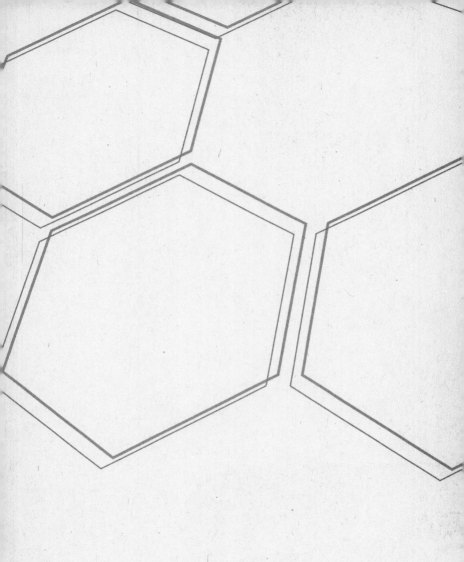

THE
ASTERISK WAR

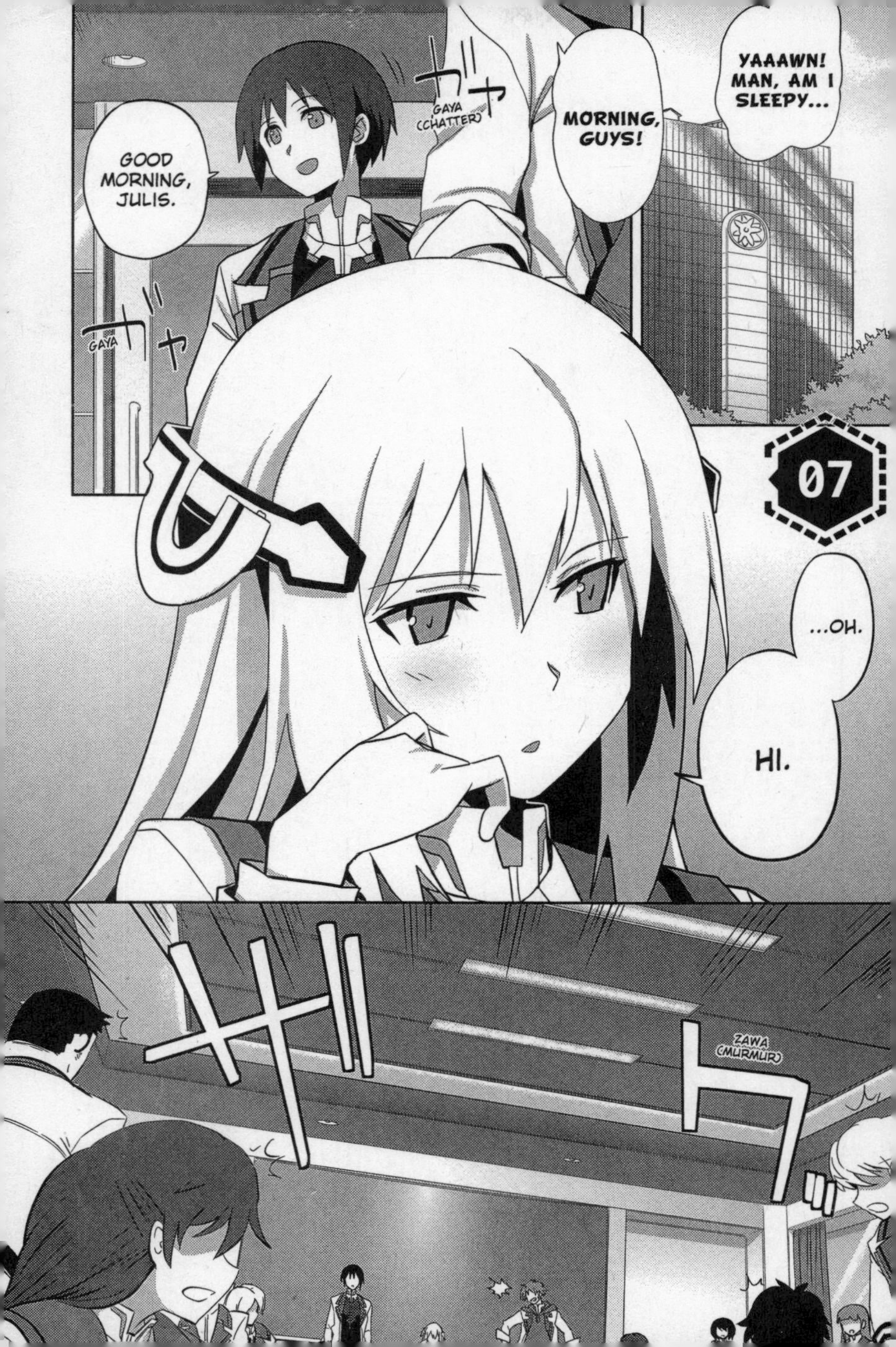
YAAAWN! MAN, AM I SLEEPY...
MORNING, GUYS!
GAYA (CHATTER)
GOOD MORNING, JULIS.
GAYA
07
...OH.
HI.
ZAWA (MURMUR)

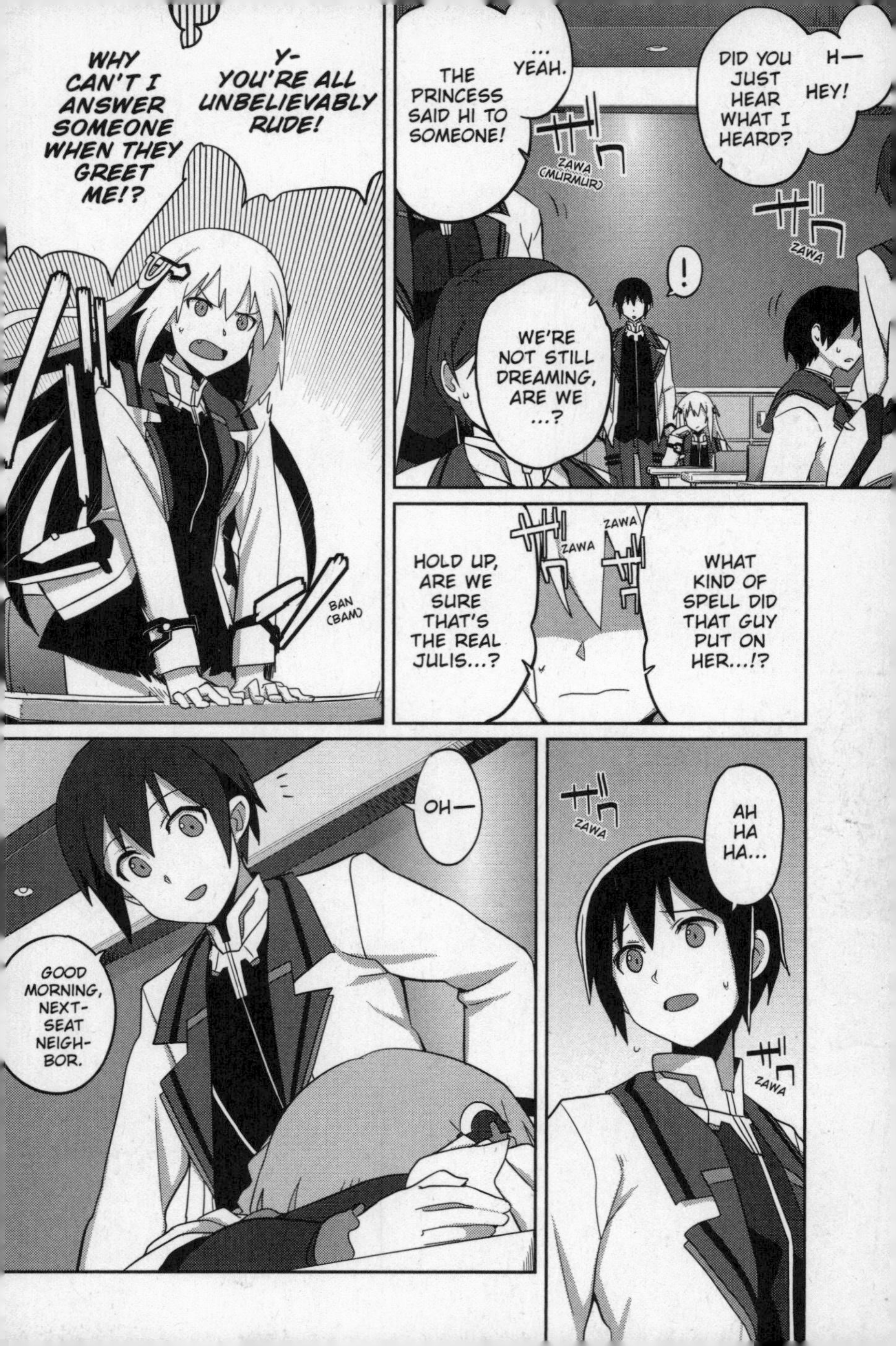
H— HEY!
DID YOU JUST HEAR WHAT I HEARD?
ZAWA
... YEAH.
THE PRINCESS SAID HI TO SOMEONE!
ZAWA (MURMUR)
!
WE'RE NOT STILL DREAMING, ARE WE ...?
WHAT KIND OF SPELL DID THAT GUY PUT ON HER...!?
ZAWA
ZAWA
HOLD UP, ARE WE SURE THAT'S THE REAL JULIS...?
Y- YOU'RE ALL UNBELIEVABLY RUDE!
WHY CAN'T I ANSWER SOMEONE WHEN THEY GREET ME!?
BAN (BAM)
ZAWA
AH HA HA...
ZAWA
OH—
GOOD MORNING, NEXT-SEAT NEIGHBOR.

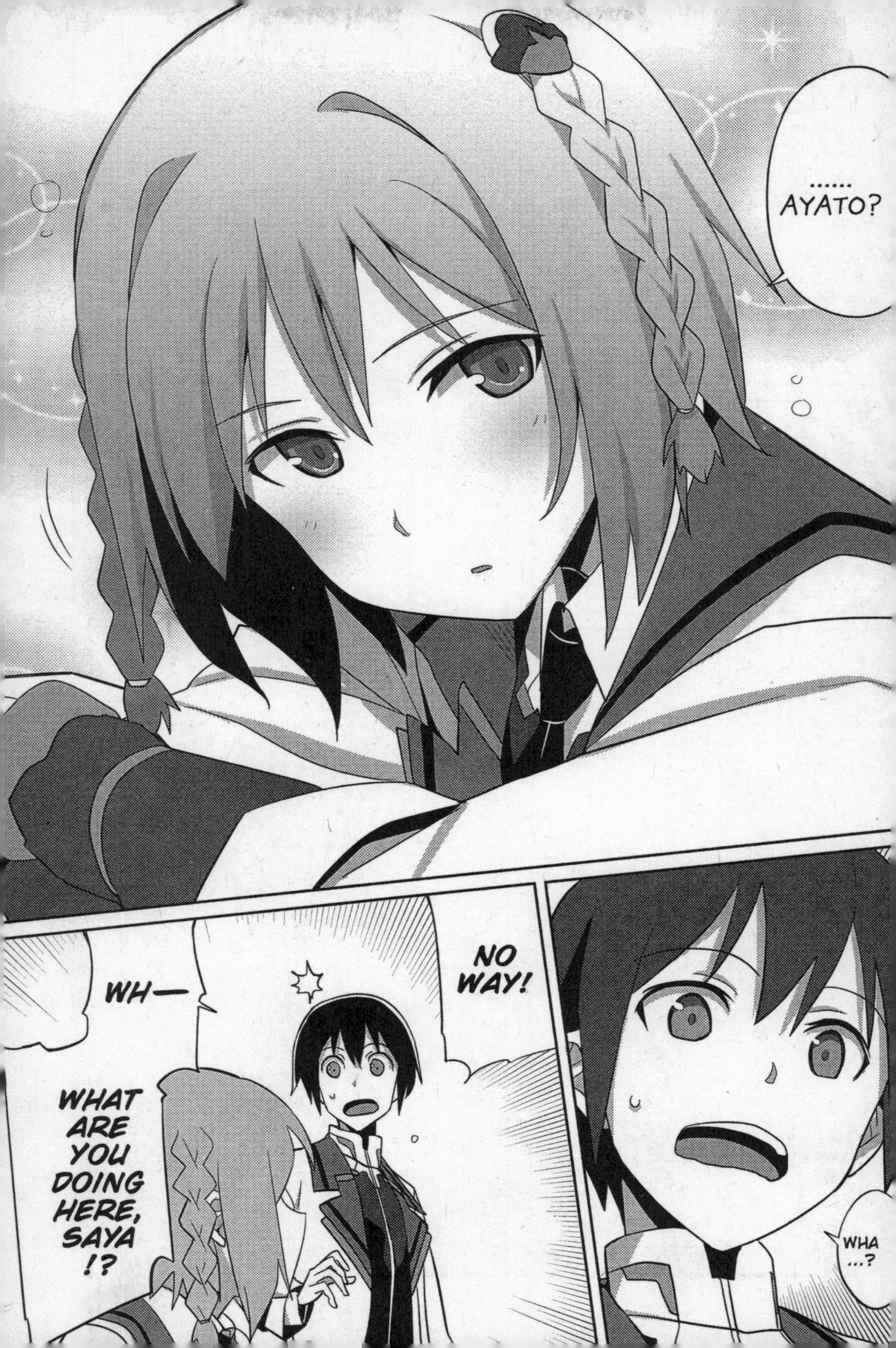

......
AYATO?
WHA
...?
NO WAY!
WH—
WHAT ARE YOU DOING HERE, SAYA!?

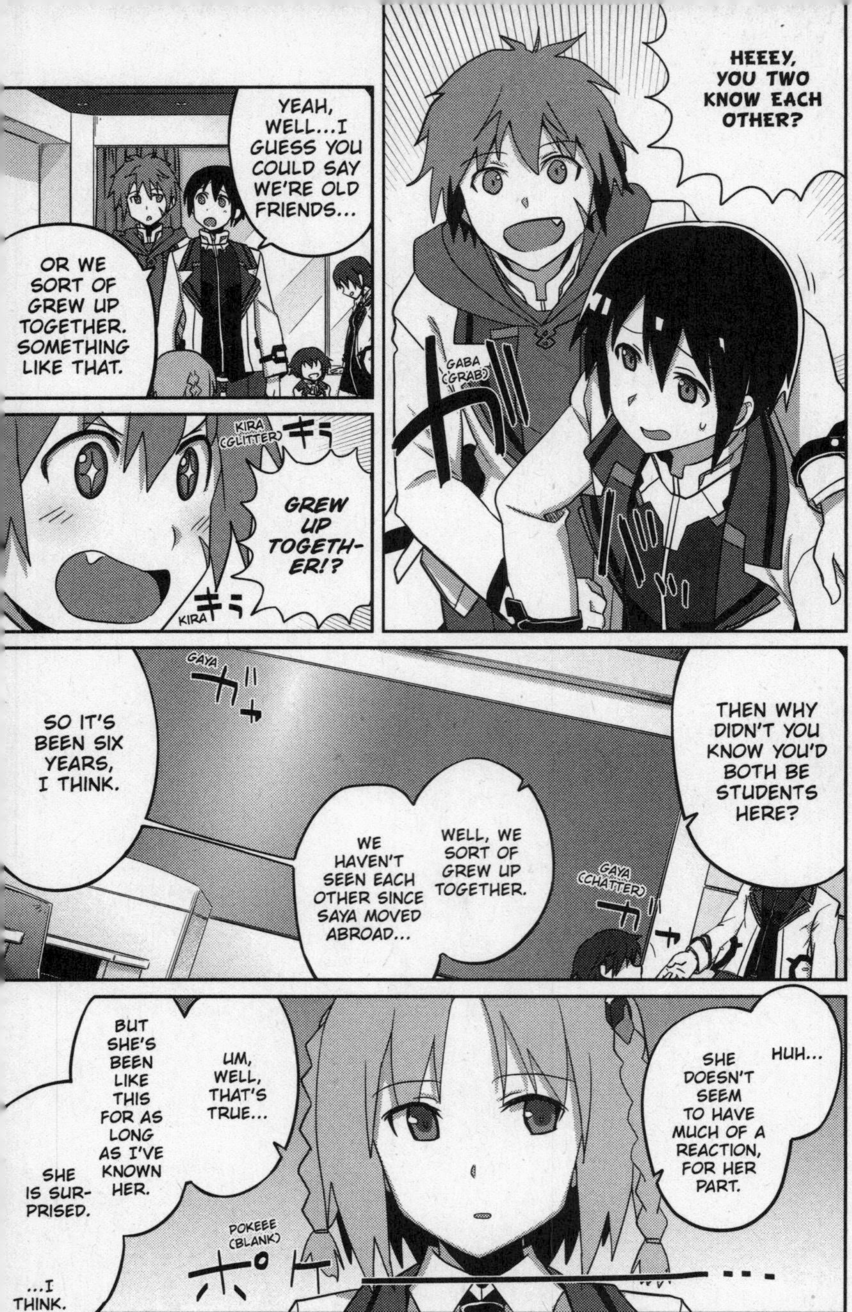
HEEEY, YOU TWO KNOW EACH OTHER?
GABA (GRAB)
YEAH, WELL...I GUESS YOU COULD SAY WE'RE OLD FRIENDS...
OR WE SORT OF GREW UP TOGETHER. SOMETHING LIKE THAT.
KIRA (GLITTER)
GREW UP TOGETH-ER!?
KIRA
THEN WHY DIDN'T YOU KNOW YOU'D BOTH BE STUDENTS HERE?
GAYA (CHATTER)
WELL, WE SORT OF GREW UP TOGETHER.
WE HAVEN'T SEEN EACH OTHER SINCE SAYA MOVED ABROAD...
GAYA
SO IT'S BEEN SIX YEARS, I THINK.
HUH...
SHE DOESN'T SEEM TO HAVE MUCH OF A REACTION, FOR HER PART.
UM, WELL, THAT'S TRUE...
BUT SHE'S BEEN LIKE THIS FOR AS LONG AS I'VE KNOWN HER.
SHE IS SUR-PRISED.
POKEEE (BLANK)
...I THINK.

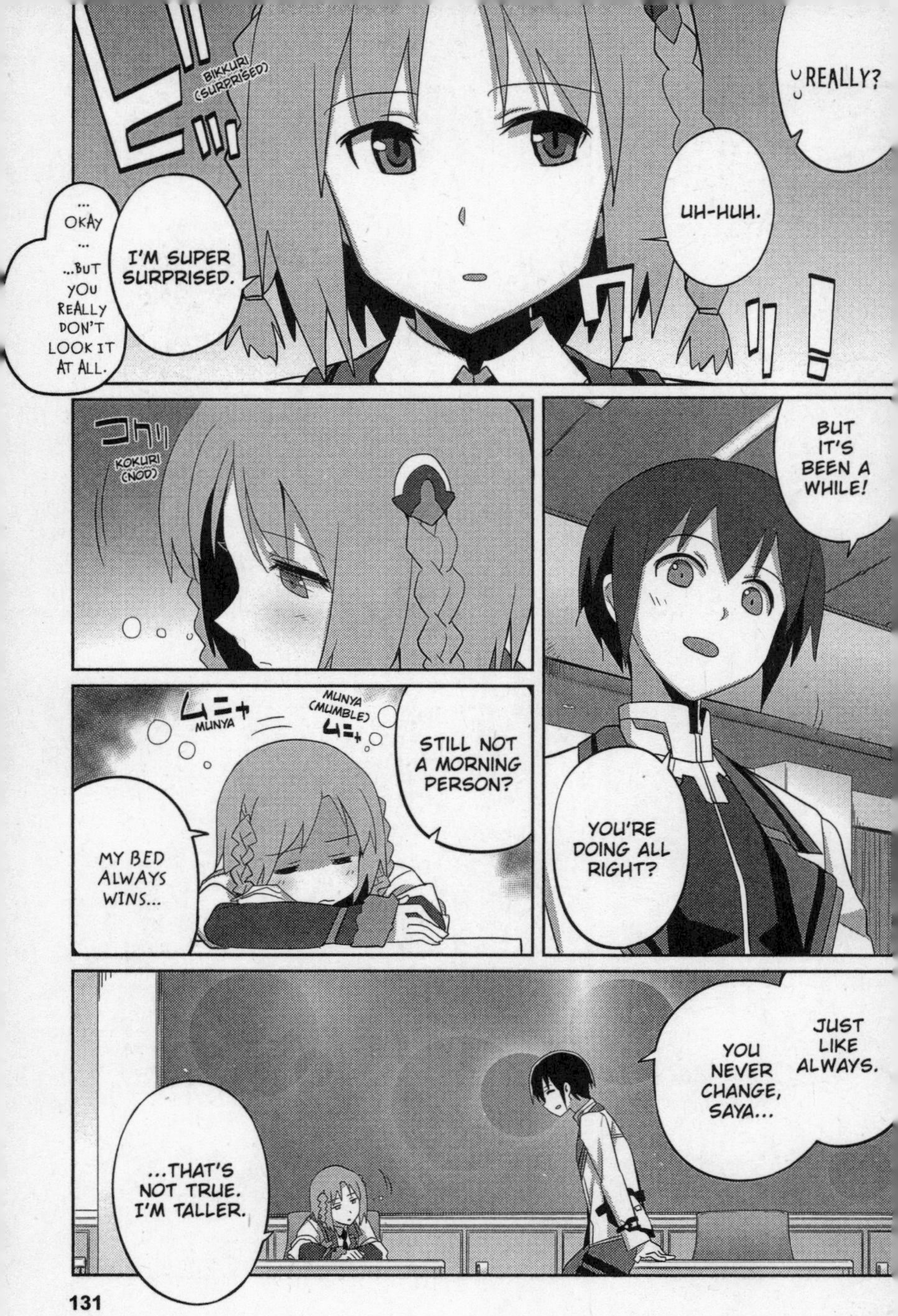
REALLY?
UH-HUH.
BIKKURI (SURPRISED)
I'M SUPER SURPRISED.
... OKAY ... ...BUT YOU REALLY DON'T LOOK IT AT ALL.
BUT IT'S BEEN A WHILE!
YOU'RE DOING ALL RIGHT?
KOKURI (NOD)
MUNYA (MUMBLE)
MUNYA
STILL NOT A MORNING PERSON?
MY BED ALWAYS WINS...
JUST LIKE ALWAYS.
YOU NEVER CHANGE, SAYA...
...THAT'S NOT TRUE. I'M TALLER.

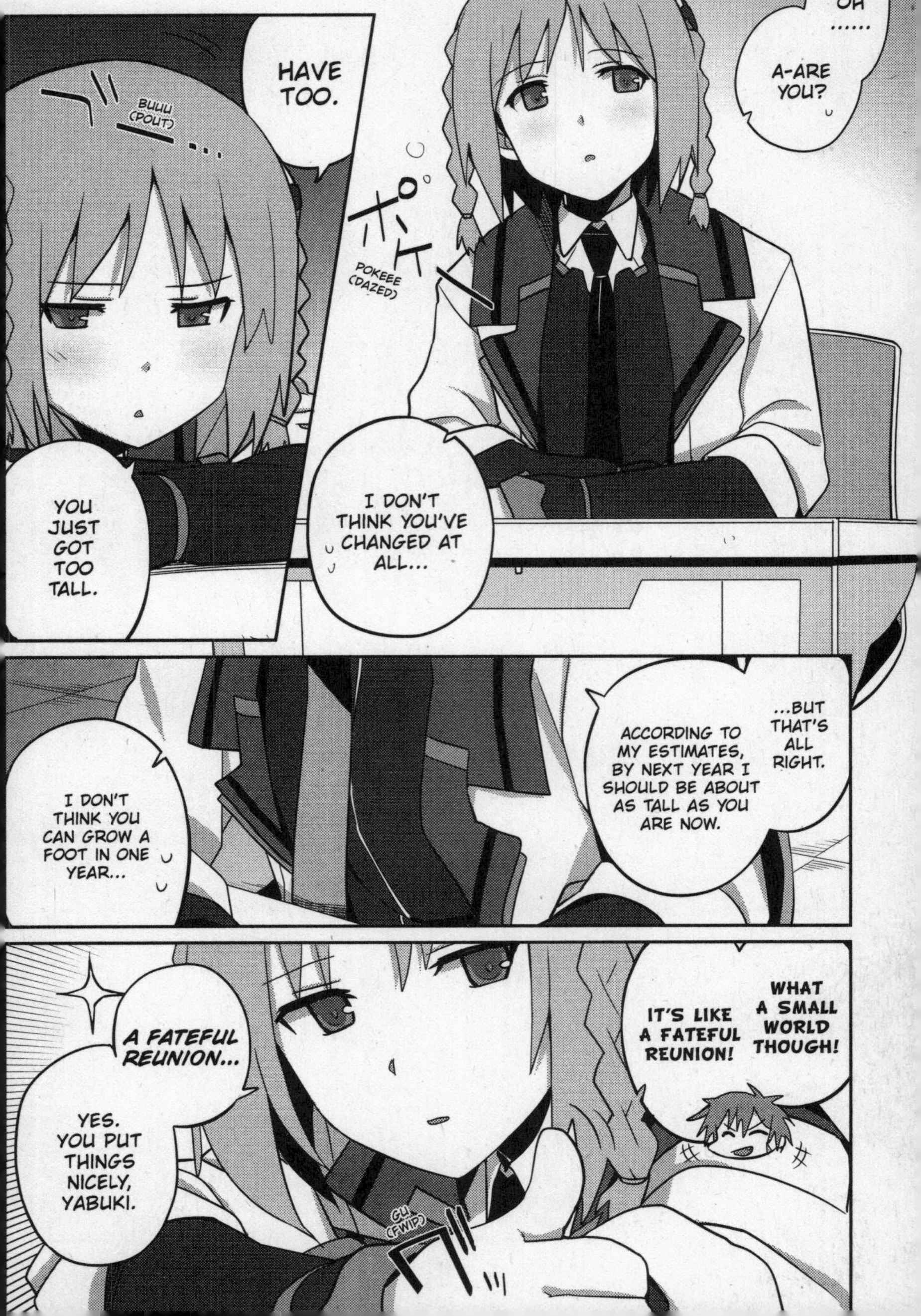
OH ...... A-ARE YOU?
POKEEE (DAZED)
I DON'T THINK YOU'VE CHANGED AT ALL...
HAVE TOO.
BUUU (POUT)
...
YOU JUST GOT TOO TALL.
...BUT THAT'S ALL RIGHT.
ACCORDING TO MY ESTIMATES, BY NEXT YEAR I SHOULD BE ABOUT AS TALL AS YOU ARE NOW.
I DON'T THINK YOU CAN GROW A FOOT IN ONE YEAR...
WHAT A SMALL WORLD THOUGH!
IT'S LIKE A FATEFUL REUNION!
A FATEFUL REUNION...
YES. YOU PUT THINGS NICELY, YABUKI.
GU (FWIP)

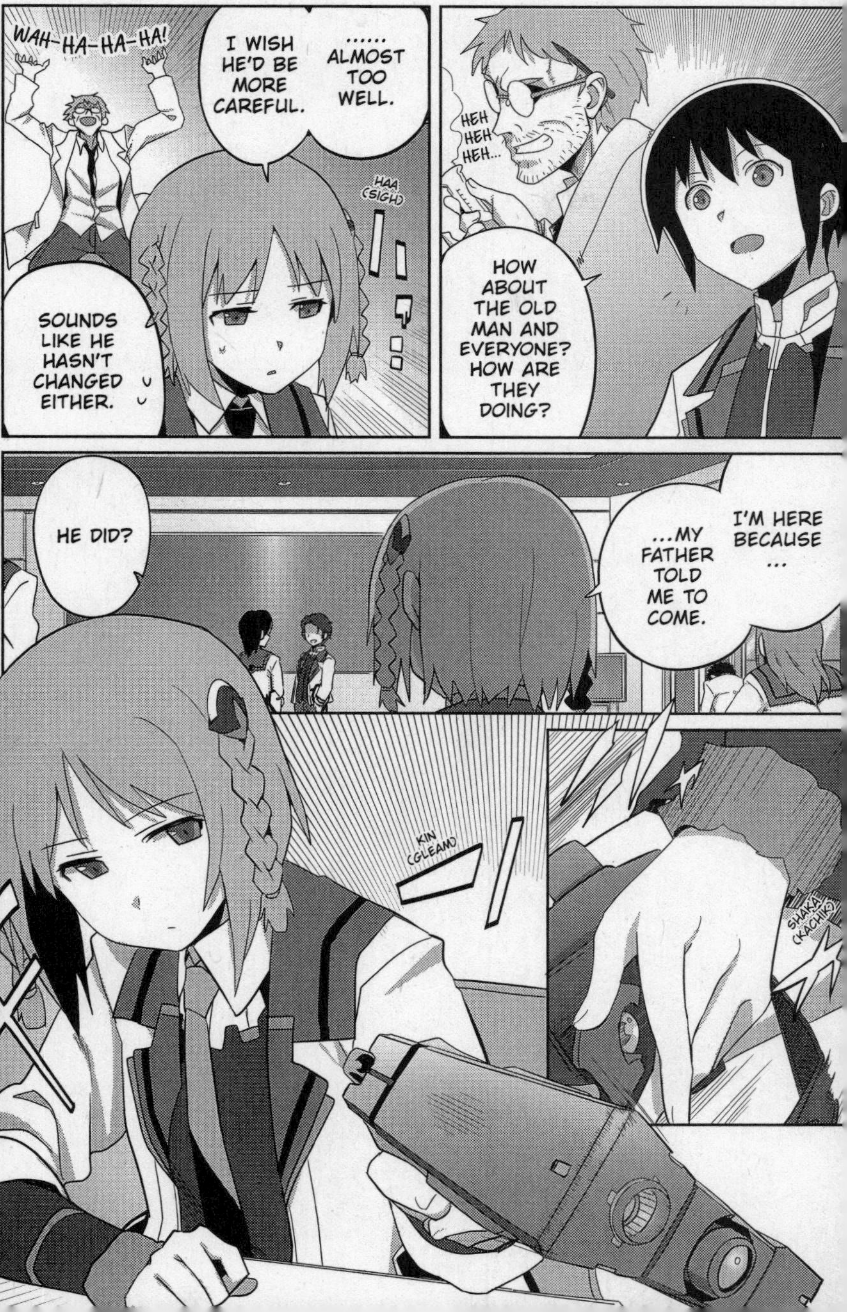
HEH HEH HEH...
HOW ABOUT THE OLD MAN AND EVERYONE? HOW ARE THEY DOING?
......ALMOST TOO WELL.
I WISH HE'D BE MORE CAREFUL.
WAH-HA-HA-HA!
HAA (SIGH)
SOUNDS LIKE HE HASN'T CHANGED EITHER.
I'M HERE BECAUSE ...
...MY FATHER TOLD ME TO COME.
HE DID?
SHAKA (KACHIK)
KIN (GLEAM)

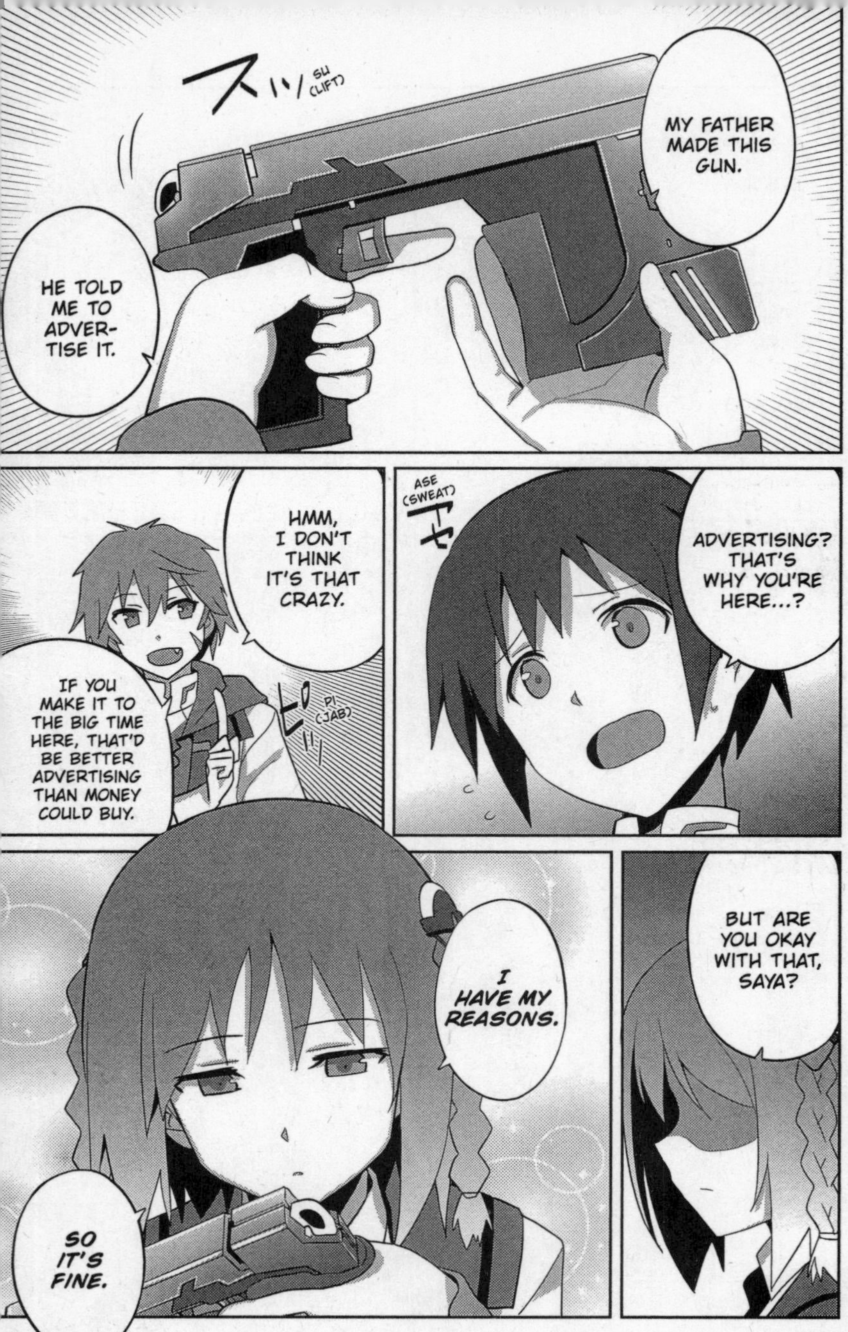

SU (LIFT)
MY FATHER MADE THIS GUN.
HE TOLD ME TO ADVERTISE IT.
ASE (SWEAT)
ADVERTISING? THAT'S WHY YOU'RE HERE...?
HMM, I DON'T THINK IT'S THAT CRAZY.
PI (JAB)
IF YOU MAKE IT TO THE BIG TIME HERE, THAT'D BE BETTER ADVERTISING THAN MONEY COULD BUY.
BUT ARE YOU OKAY WITH THAT, SAYA?
I HAVE MY REASONS.
SO IT'S FINE.

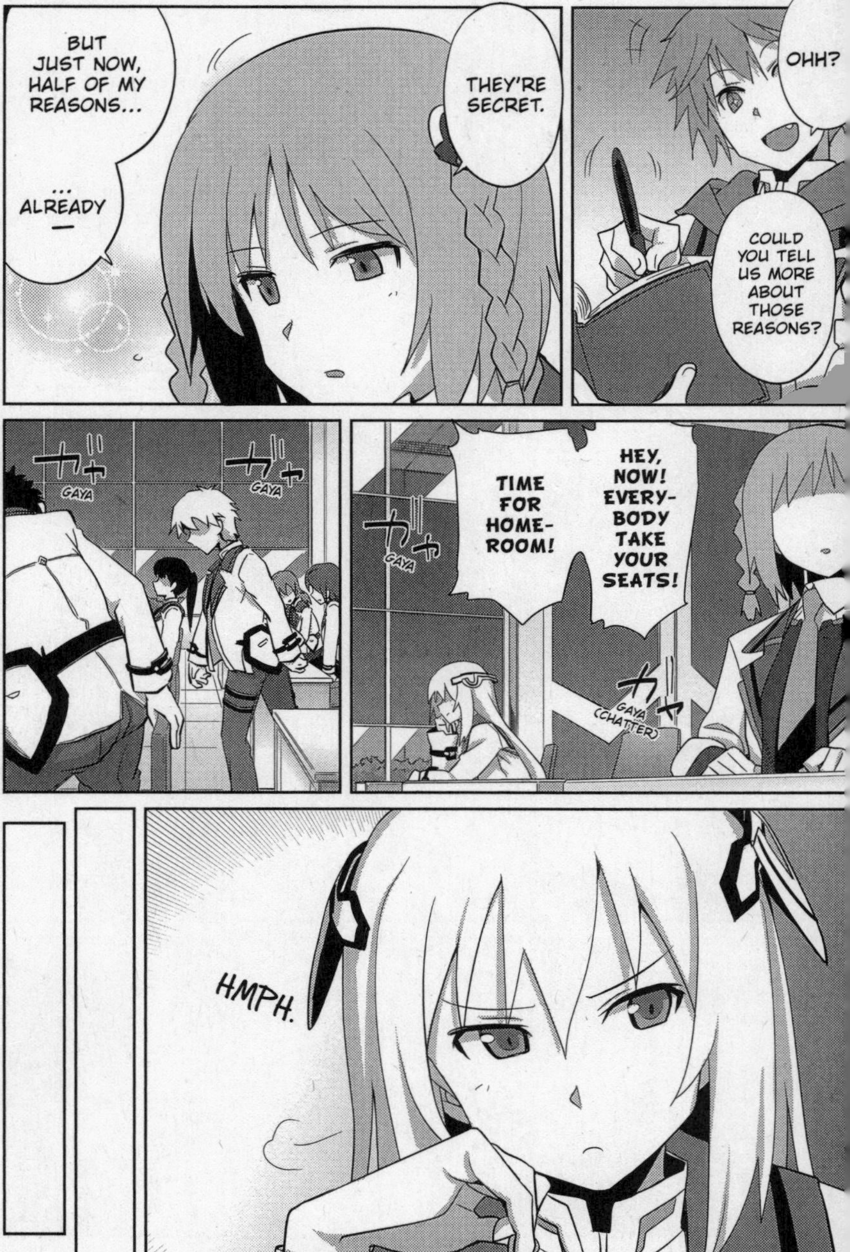
OHH?
COULD YOU TELL US MORE ABOUT THOSE REASONS?
THEY'RE SECRET.
BUT JUST NOW, HALF OF MY REASONS...
...ALREADY —
HEY, NOW! EVERYBODY TAKE YOUR SEATS!
TIME FOR HOMEROOM!
GAYA
GAYA (CHATTER)
GAYA
GAYA
HMPH.

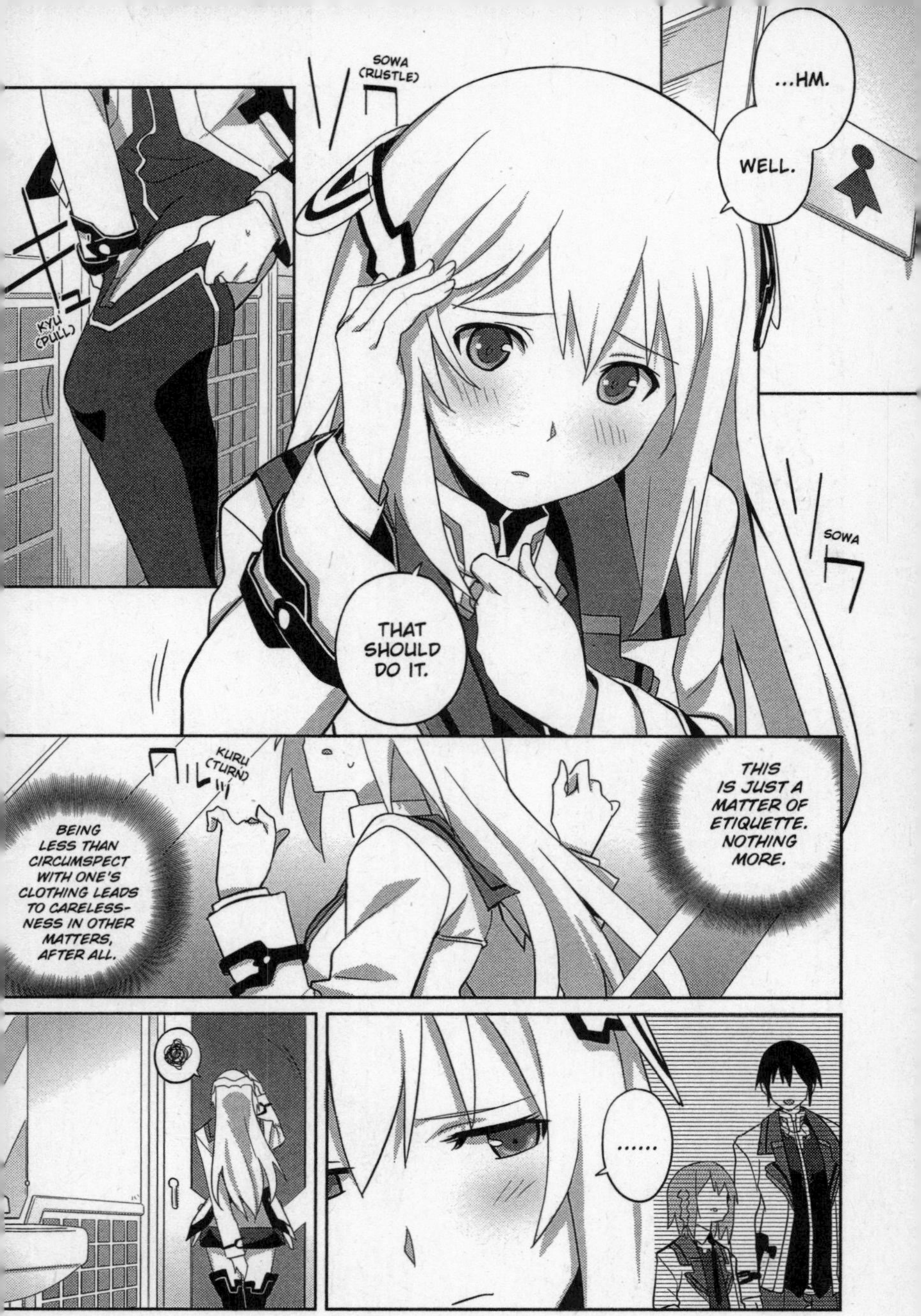
...HM.
WELL.
SOWA (RUSTLE)
SOWA
THAT SHOULD DO IT.
KYU (PULL)
THIS IS JUST A MATTER OF ETIQUETTE. NOTHING MORE.
KURU (TURN)
BEING LESS THAN CIRCUMSPECT WITH ONE'S CLOTHING LEADS TO CARELESS-NESS IN OTHER MATTERS, AFTER ALL.
......

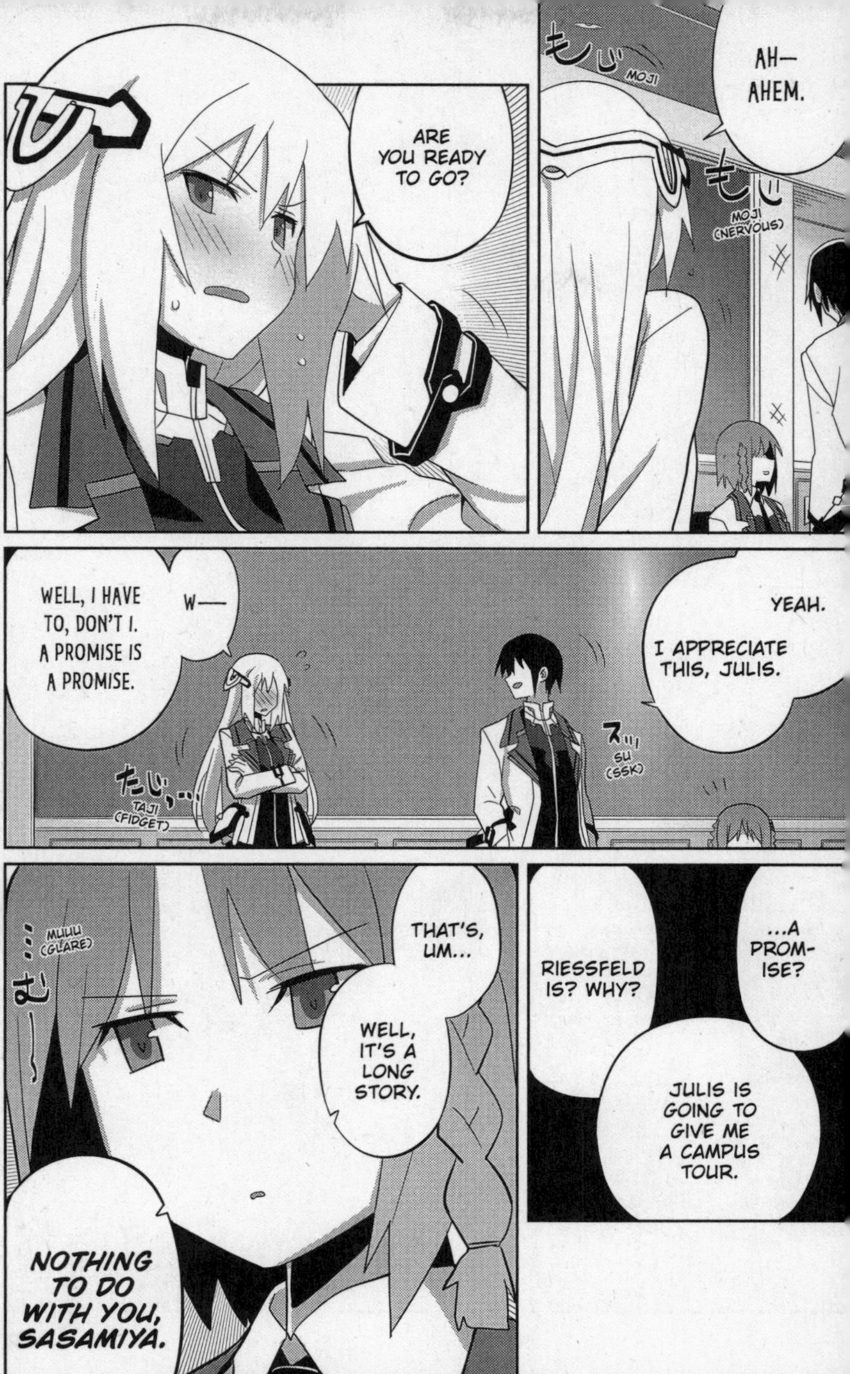
AH— AHEM.
MOJI
MOJI (NERVOUS)
ARE YOU READY TO GO?
YEAH.
I APPRECIATE THIS, JULIS.
SU (SSK)
W——
WELL, I HAVE TO, DON'T I. A PROMISE IS A PROMISE.
TAJI (FIDGET)
...A PROM-ISE?
RIESSFELD IS? WHY?
JULIS IS GOING TO GIVE ME A CAMPUS TOUR.
THAT'S, UM...
WELL, IT'S A LONG STORY.
MUUU (GLARE)
NOTHING TO DO WITH YOU, SASAMIYA.

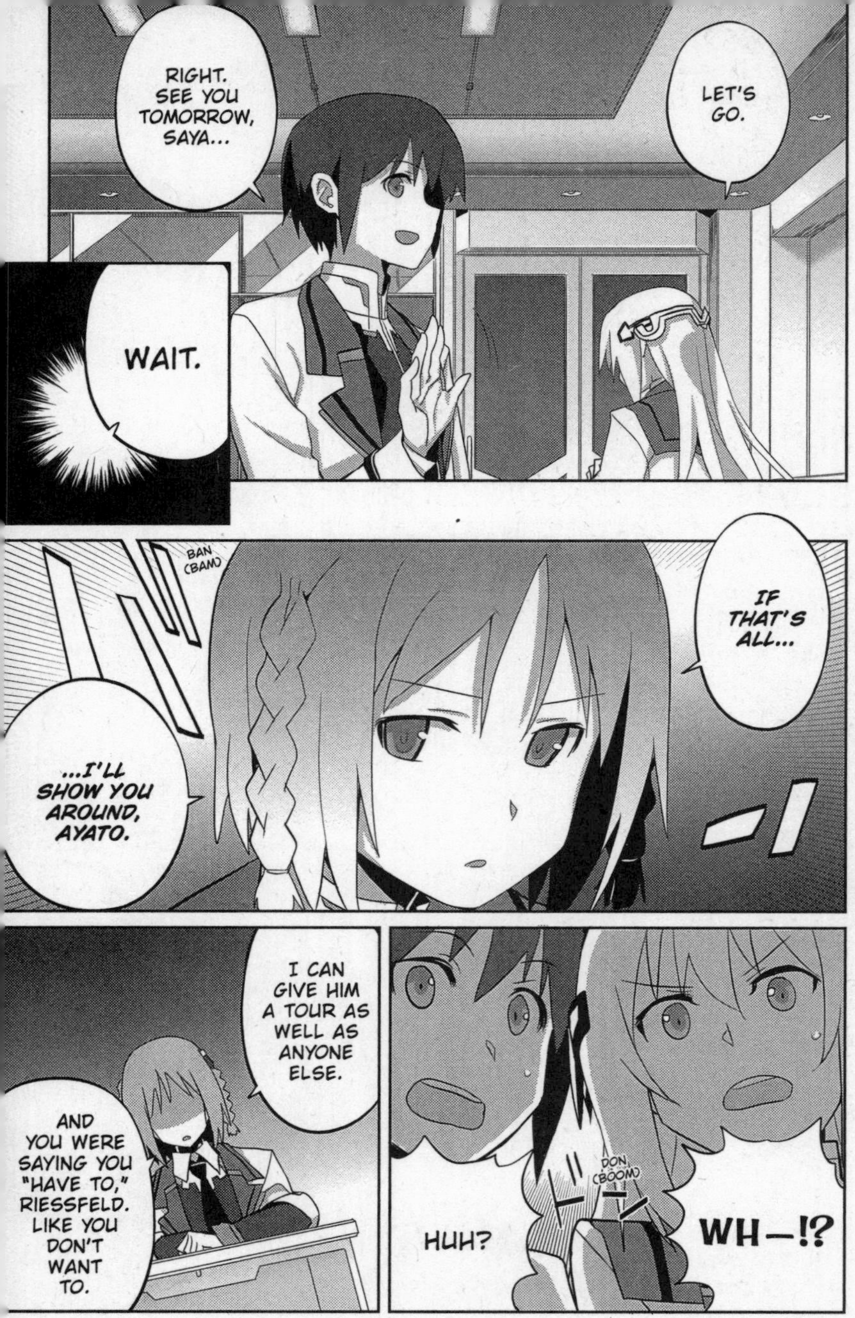
LET'S GO.
RIGHT. SEE YOU TOMORROW, SAYA...
WAIT.
IF THAT'S ALL...
BAN (BAM)
...I'LL SHOW YOU AROUND, AYATO.
WH—!?
DON (BOOM)
HUH?
I CAN GIVE HIM A TOUR AS WELL AS ANYONE ELSE.
AND YOU WERE SAYING YOU "HAVE TO," RIESSFELD. LIKE YOU DON'T WANT TO.

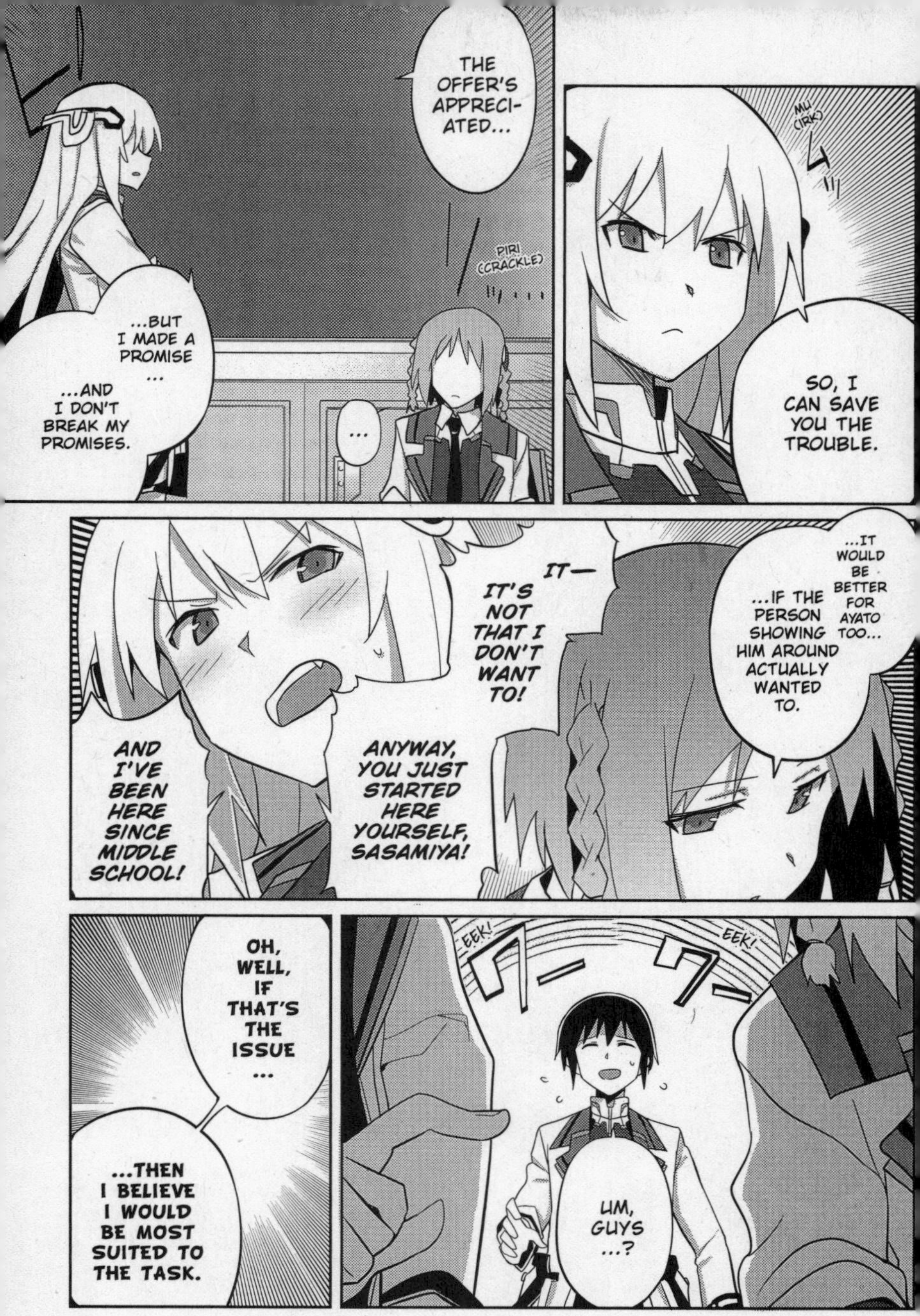
MU (IRK)
SO, I CAN SAVE YOU THE TROUBLE.
THE OFFER'S APPRECIATED...
PIRI (CRACKLE)
...BUT I MADE A PROMISE...
...AND I DON'T BREAK MY PROMISES.
...
...IT WOULD BE BETTER FOR AYATO TOO...
...IF THE PERSON SHOWING HIM AROUND ACTUALLY WANTED TO.
IT—
IT'S NOT THAT I DON'T WANT TO!
ANYWAY, YOU JUST STARTED HERE YOURSELF, SASAMIYA!
AND I'VE BEEN HERE SINCE MIDDLE SCHOOL!
EEK!
EEK!
UM, GUYS ...?
OH, WELL, IF THAT'S THE ISSUE...
...THEN I BELIEVE I WOULD BE MOST SUITED TO THE TASK.

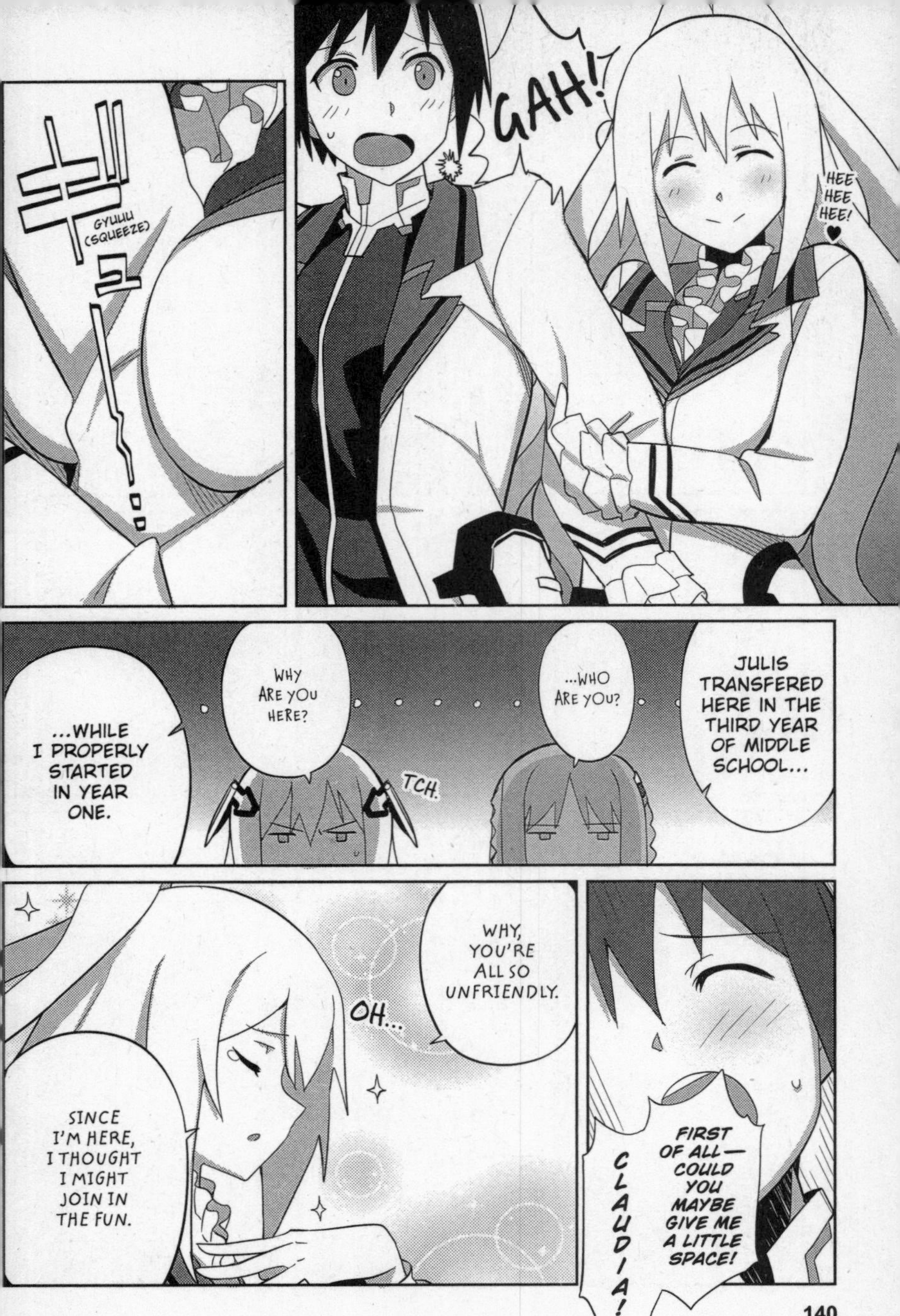
GAH!
HEE HEE HEE! ♥
GYUUU (SQUEEZE)
JULIS TRANSFERED HERE IN THE THIRD YEAR OF MIDDLE SCHOOL...
...WHO ARE YOU?
WHY ARE YOU HERE?
TCH.
...WHILE I PROPERLY STARTED IN YEAR ONE.
FIRST OF ALL—COULD YOU MAYBE GIVE ME A LITTLE SPACE!
CLAUDIA!
WHY, YOU'RE ALL SO UNFRIENDLY.
OH...
SINCE I'M HERE, I THOUGHT I MIGHT JOIN IN THE FUN.

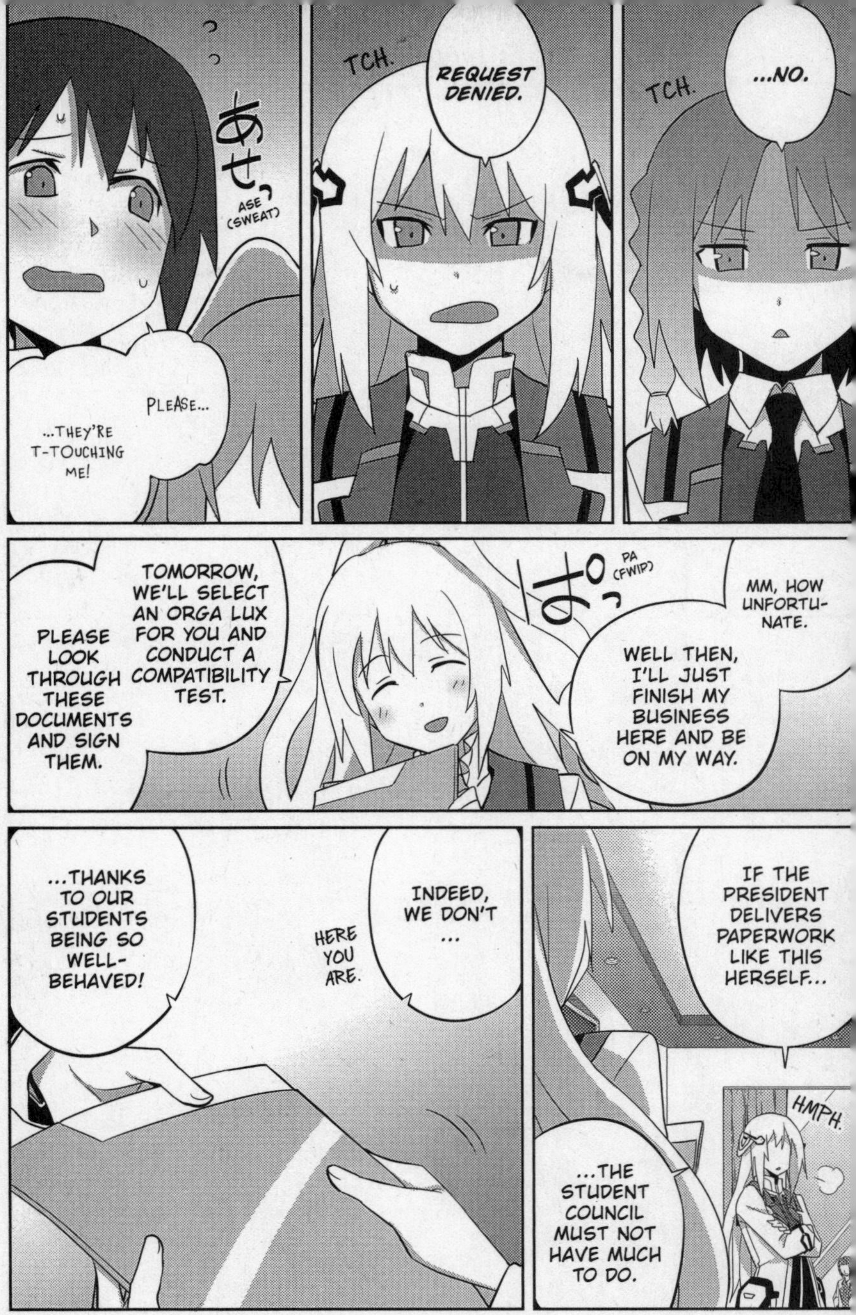
TCH.
...NO.
TCH.
REQUEST DENIED.
あせ
ASE (SWEAT)
PLEASE...
...THEY'RE T-TOUCHING ME!
MM, HOW UNFORTU-NATE.
WELL THEN, I'LL JUST FINISH MY BUSINESS HERE AND BE ON MY WAY.
ぱっ
PA (FWIP)
TOMORROW, WE'LL SELECT AN ORGA LUX FOR YOU AND CONDUCT A COMPATIBILITY TEST.
PLEASE LOOK THROUGH THESE DOCUMENTS AND SIGN THEM.
IF THE PRESIDENT DELIVERS PAPERWORK LIKE THIS HERSELF...
HMPH.
...THE STUDENT COUNCIL MUST NOT HAVE MUCH TO DO.
INDEED, WE DON'T ...
HERE YOU ARE.
...THANKS TO OUR STUDENTS BEING SO WELL-BEHAVED!

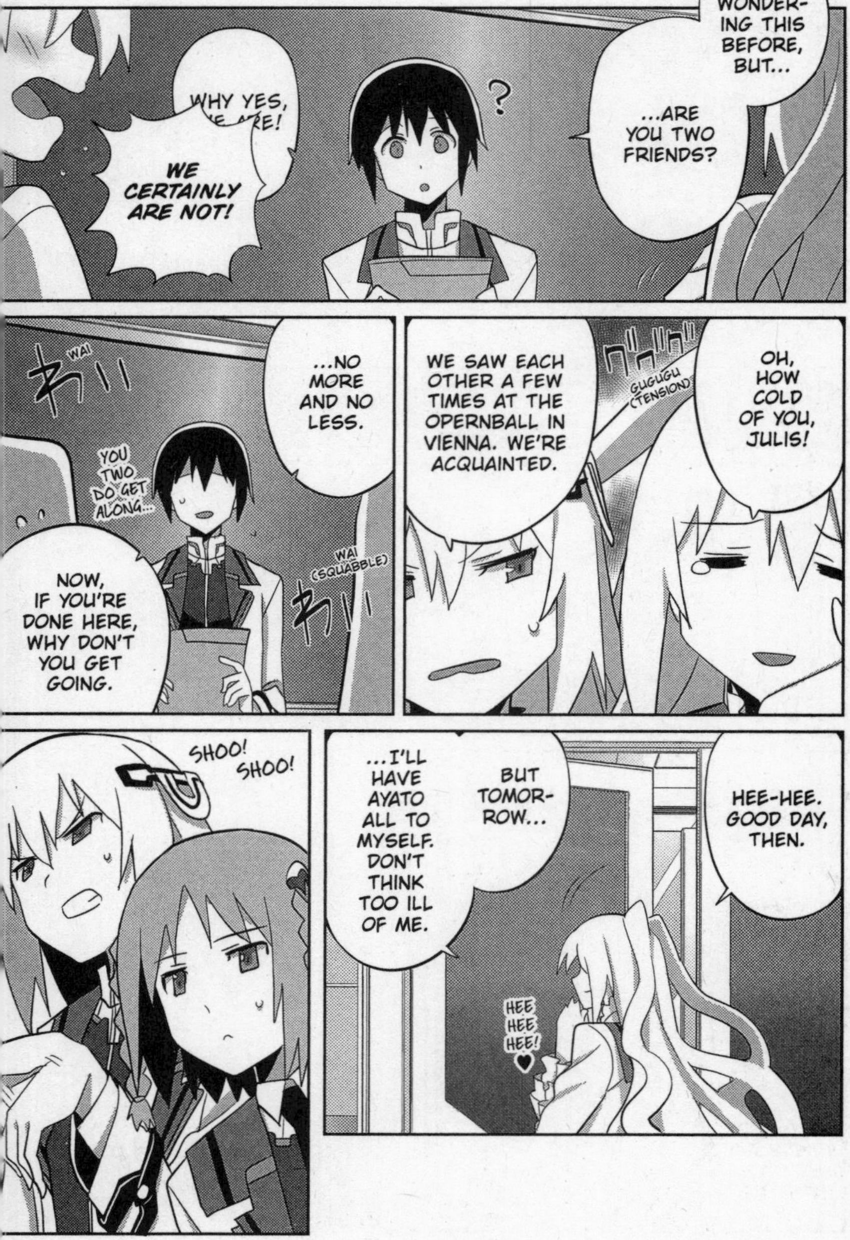
I WAS WONDERING THIS BEFORE, BUT...
...ARE YOU TWO FRIENDS?
WHY YES,
WE CERTAINLY ARE NOT!
OH, HOW COLD OF YOU, JULIS!
GUGUGU (TENSION)
WE SAW EACH OTHER A FEW TIMES AT THE OPERNBALL IN VIENNA. WE'RE ACQUAINTED.
...NO MORE AND NO LESS.
WAI
YOU TWO DO GET ALONG...
WAI (SQUABBLE)
NOW, IF YOU'RE DONE HERE, WHY DON'T YOU GET GOING.
HEE-HEE. GOOD DAY, THEN.
BUT TOMORROW...
...I'LL HAVE AYATO ALL TO MYSELF. DON'T THINK TOO ILL OF ME.
HEE HEE HEE!
SHOO! SHOO!

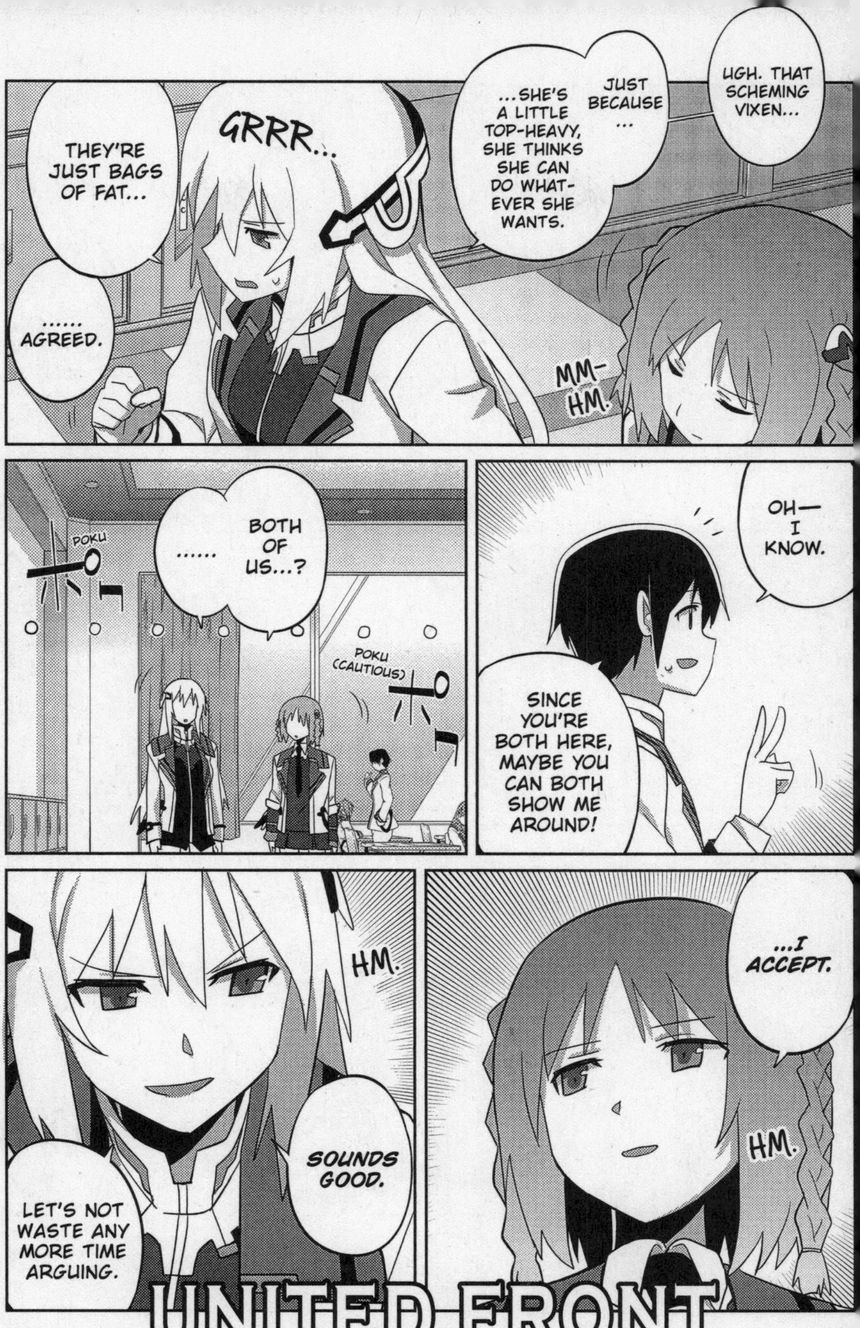
UGH. THAT SCHEMING VIXEN...
JUST BECAUSE ...
...SHE'S A LITTLE TOP-HEAVY, SHE THINKS SHE CAN DO WHAT-EVER SHE WANTS.
MM-HM.
GRRR...
THEY'RE JUST BAGS OF FAT...
...... AGREED.
OH— I KNOW.
SINCE YOU'RE BOTH HERE, MAYBE YOU CAN BOTH SHOW ME AROUND!
BOTH OF US...?
......
POKU (CAUTIOUS)
POKU
...I ACCEPT.
HM.
HM.
SOUNDS GOOD.
LET'S NOT WASTE ANY MORE TIME ARGUING.
UNITED FRONT

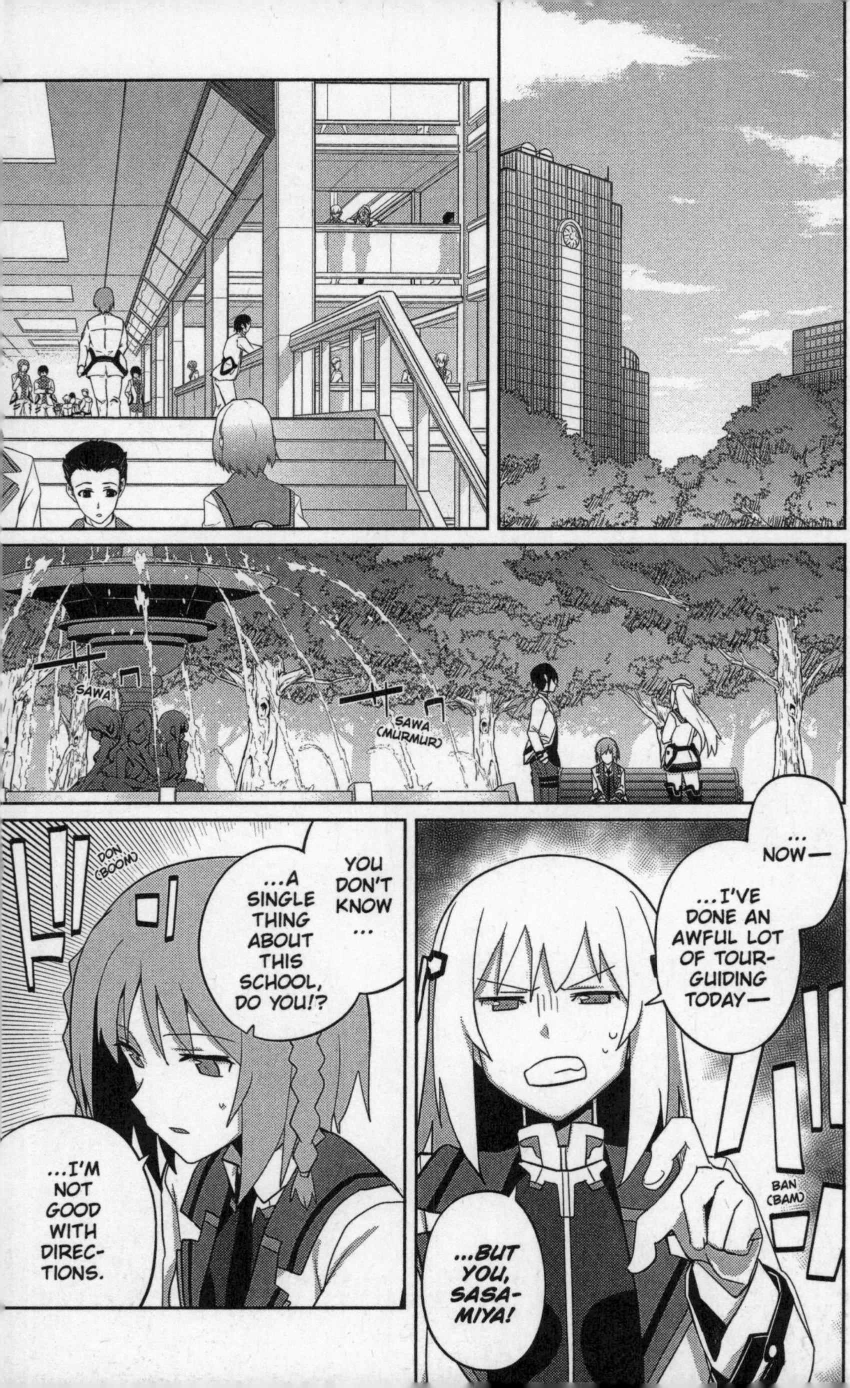
SAWA (MURMUR)
SAWA
...NOW—
...I'VE DONE AN AWFUL LOT OF TOUR-GUIDING TODAY—
BAN (BAM)
...BUT YOU, SASAMIYA!
YOU DON'T KNOW ...
...A SINGLE THING ABOUT THIS SCHOOL, DO YOU!?
DON (BOOM)
...I'M NOT GOOD WITH DIRECTIONS.

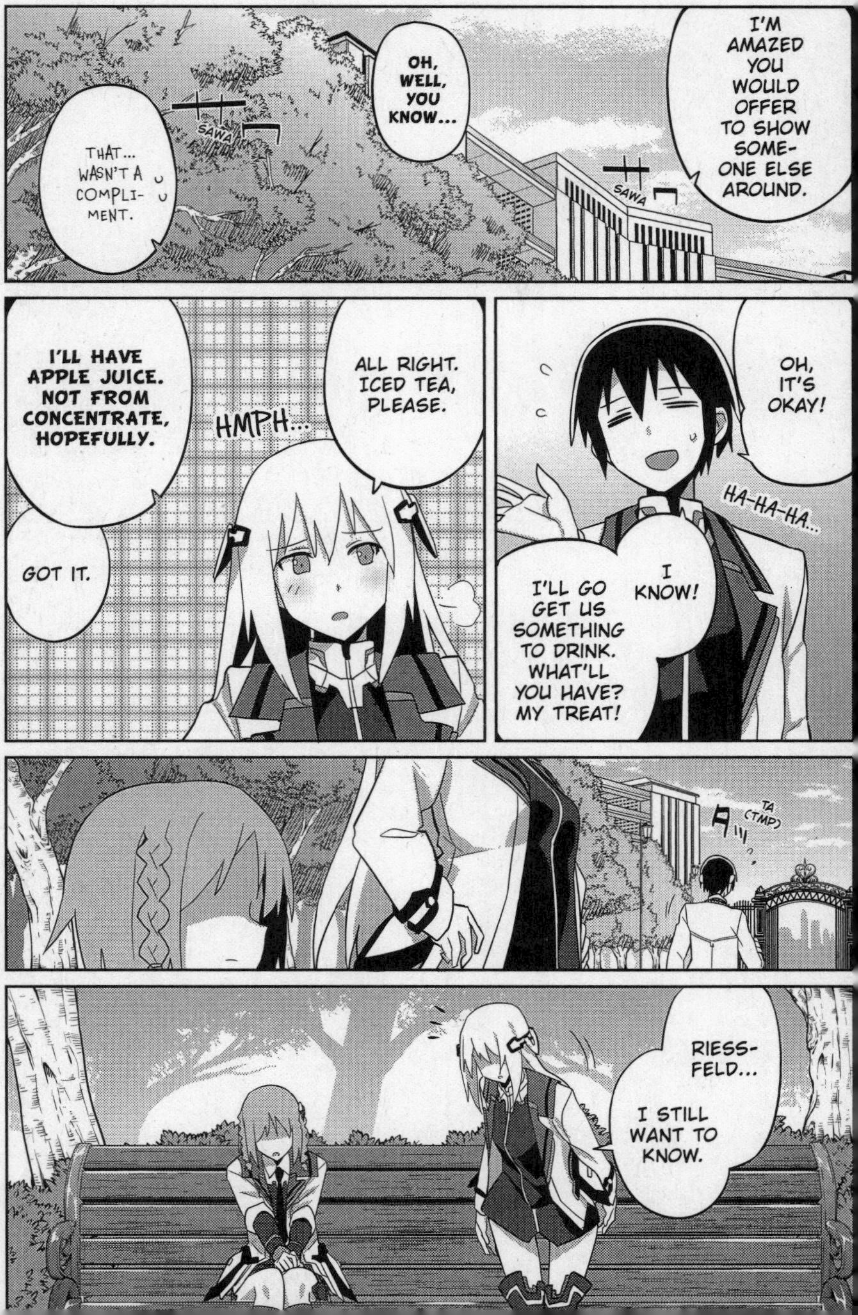
I'M AMAZED YOU WOULD OFFER TO SHOW SOME-ONE ELSE AROUND.
SAWA
OH, WELL, YOU KNOW...
SAWA
THAT... WASN'T A COMPLI-MENT.
OH, IT'S OKAY!
HA-HA-HA...
I KNOW!
I'LL GO GET US SOMETHING TO DRINK. WHAT'LL YOU HAVE? MY TREAT!
ALL RIGHT. ICED TEA, PLEASE.
HMPH...
I'LL HAVE APPLE JUICE. NOT FROM CONCENTRATE, HOPEFULLY.
GOT IT.
TA (TMP)
RIESS-FELD...
I STILL WANT TO KNOW.

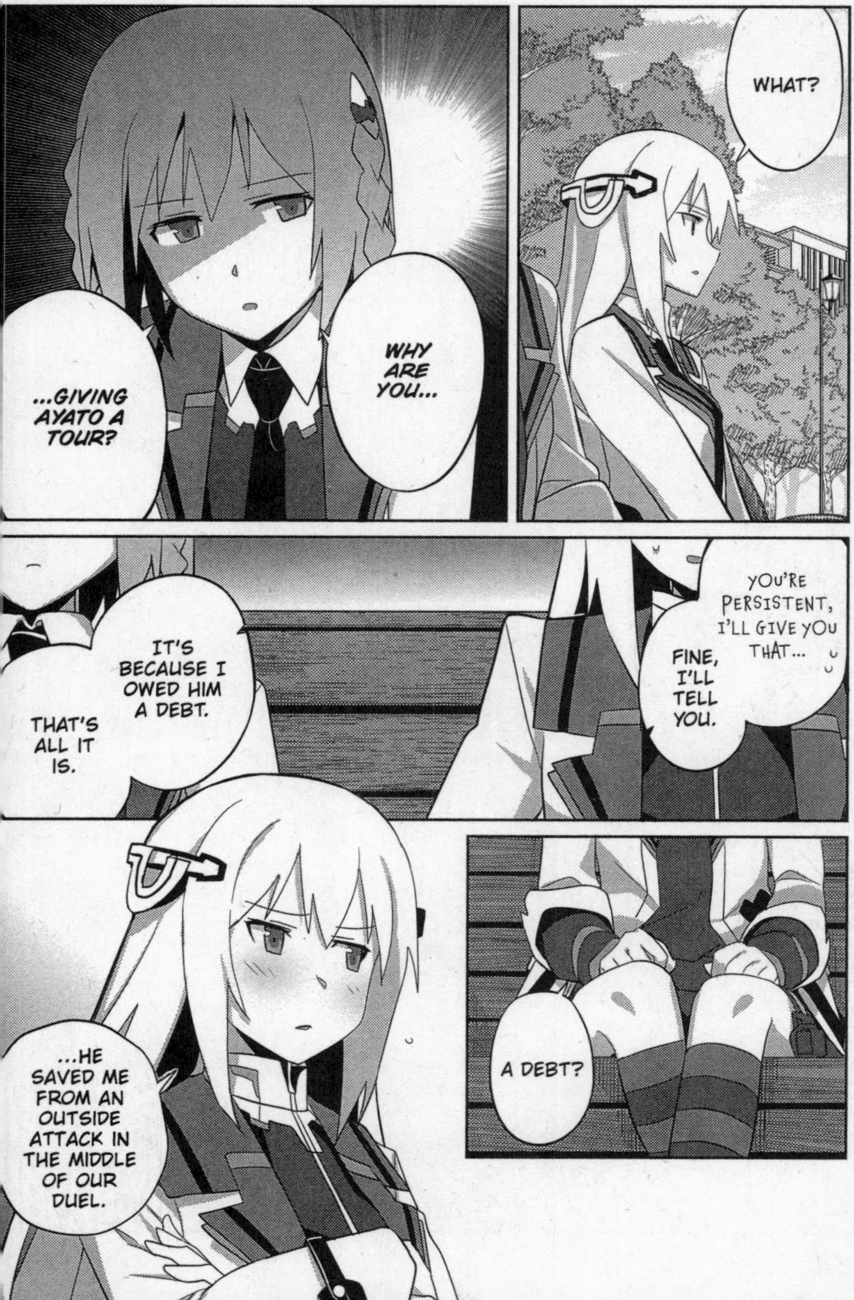
WHAT?
WHY ARE YOU...
...GIVING AYATO A TOUR?
YOU'RE PERSISTENT, I'LL GIVE YOU THAT...
FINE, I'LL TELL YOU.
IT'S BECAUSE I OWED HIM A DEBT.
THAT'S ALL IT IS.
A DEBT?
...HE SAVED ME FROM AN OUTSIDE ATTACK IN THE MIDDLE OF OUR DUEL.

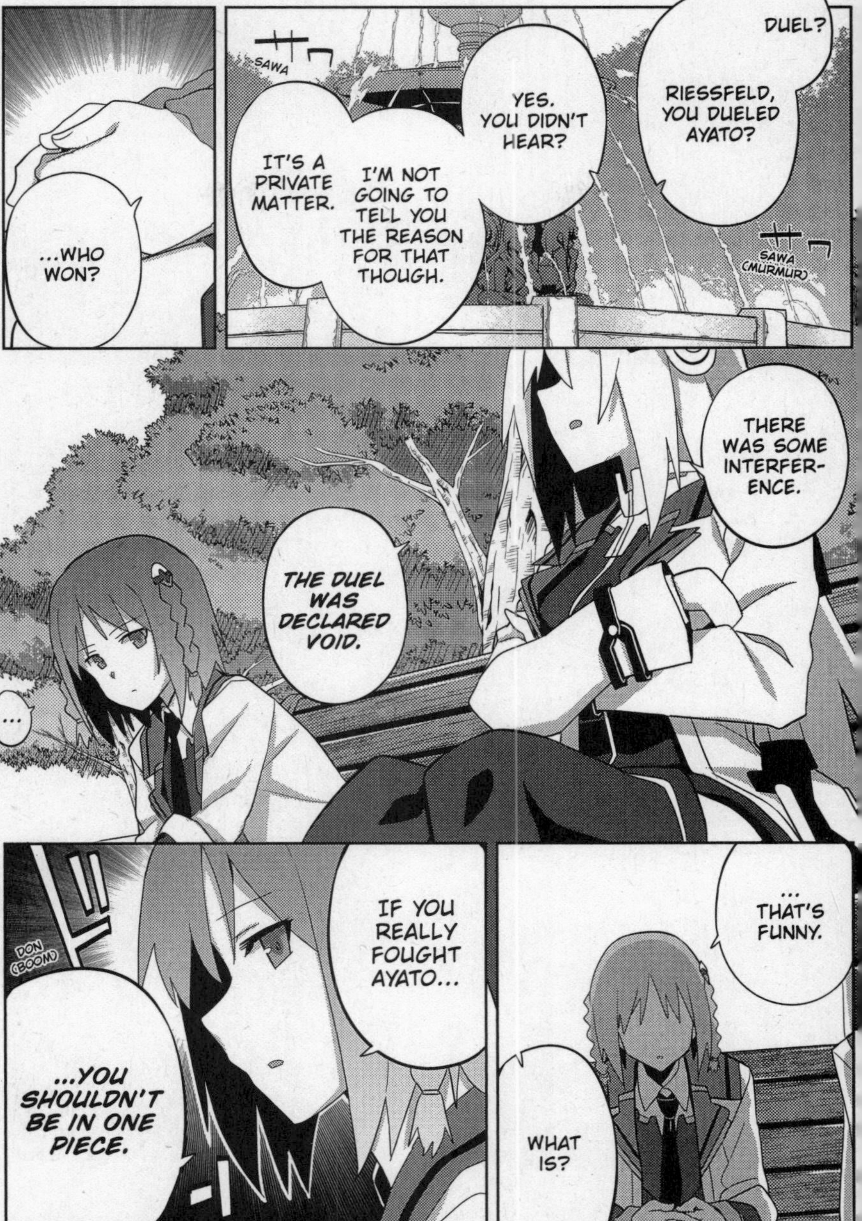
DUEL?
RIESSFELD, YOU DUELED AYATO?
SAWA (MURMUR)
YES. YOU DIDN'T HEAR?
IT'S A PRIVATE MATTER.
I'M NOT GOING TO TELL YOU THE REASON FOR THAT THOUGH.
SAWA
...WHO WON?
THERE WAS SOME INTERFER-ENCE.
THE DUEL WAS DECLARED VOID.
...
... THAT'S FUNNY.
WHAT IS?
IF YOU REALLY FOUGHT AYATO...
DON (BOOM)
...YOU SHOULDN'T BE IN ONE PIECE.

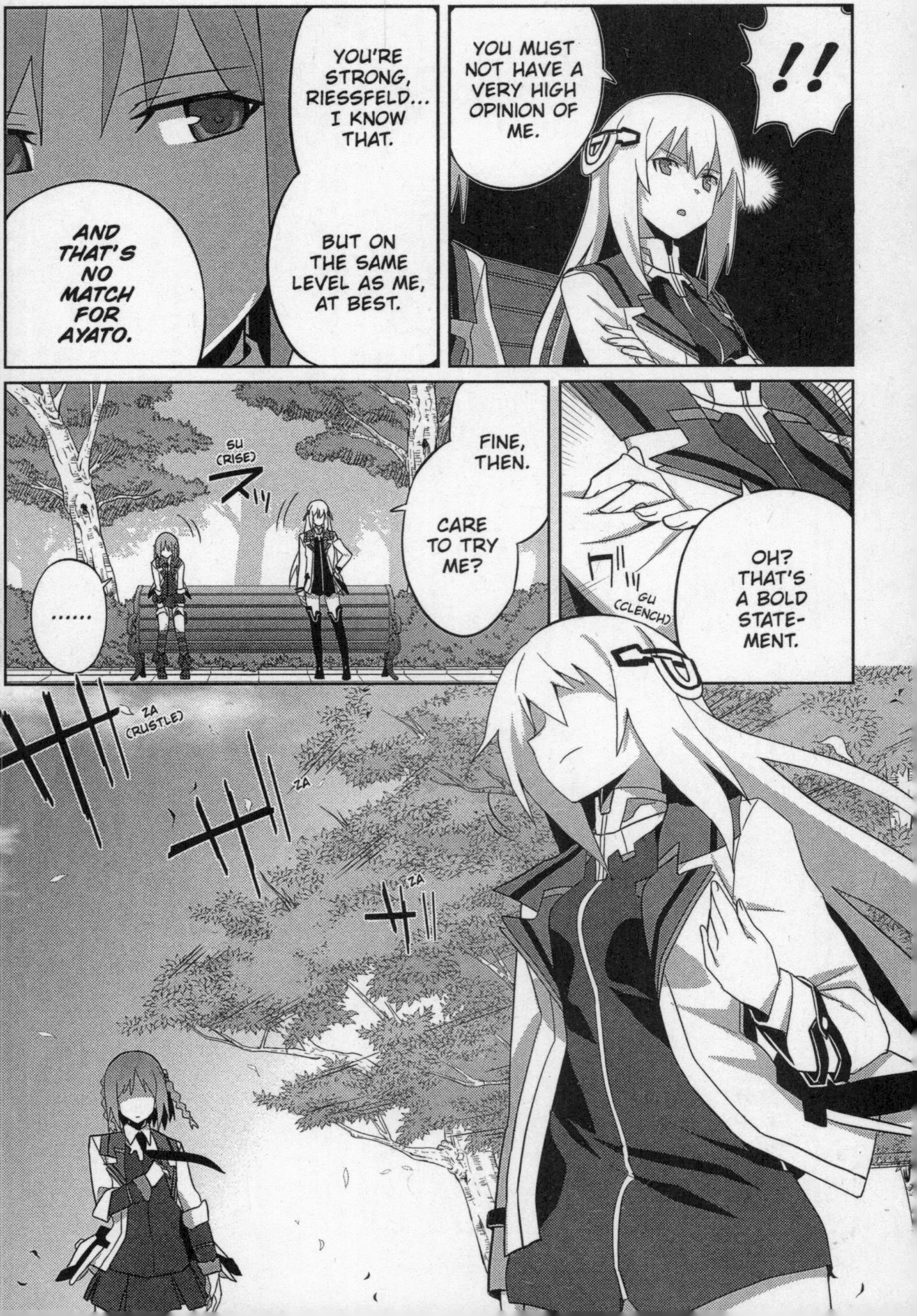
!!
YOU MUST NOT HAVE A VERY HIGH OPINION OF ME.
YOU'RE STRONG, RIESSFELD... I KNOW THAT.
BUT ON THE SAME LEVEL AS ME, AT BEST.
AND THAT'S NO MATCH FOR AYATO.
OH? THAT'S A BOLD STATEMENT.
GU (CLENCH)
FINE, THEN.
CARE TO TRY ME?
SU (RISE)
......
ZA
ZA
ZA (RUSTLE)

— TO BE CONTINUED...

BONUS AST #01.02. after_1

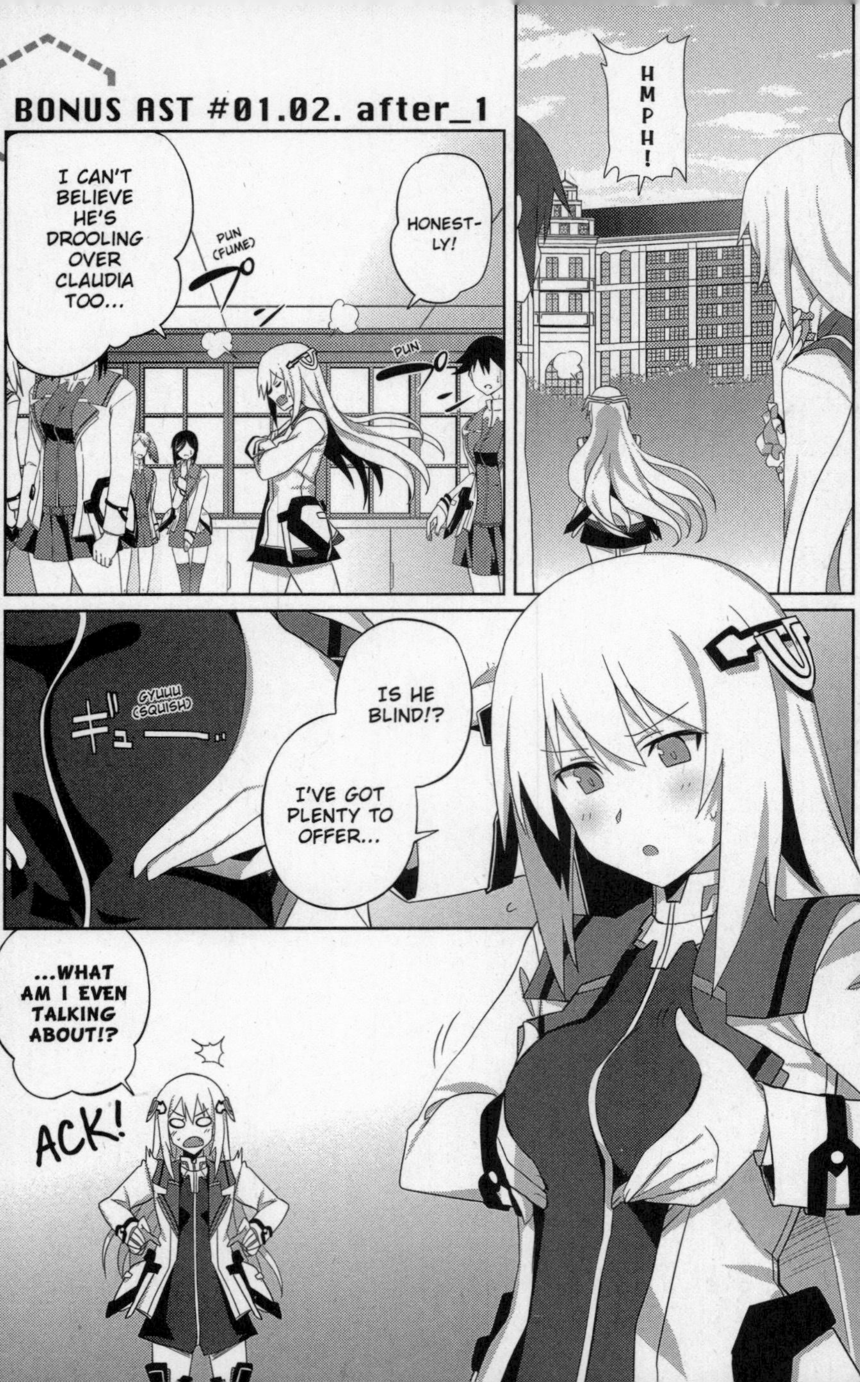
HMPH!
HONEST-LY!
PUN (FUME)
PUN
I CAN'T BELIEVE HE'S DROOLING OVER CLAUDIA TOO...
IS HE BLIND!?
I'VE GOT PLENTY TO OFFER...
GYUUU (SQUISH)
...WHAT AM I EVEN TALKING ABOUT!?
ACK!

BONUS AST #01.02. after_2

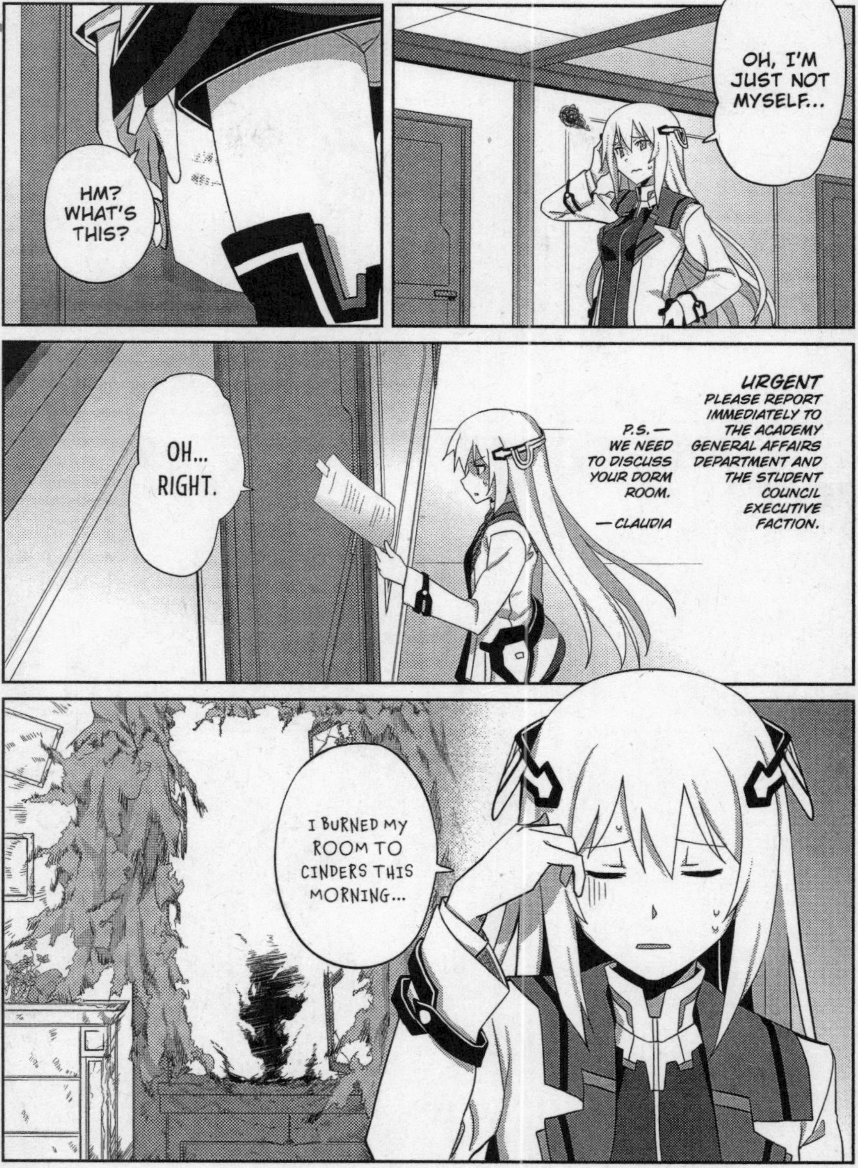
OH, I'M JUST NOT MYSELF...
HM? WHAT'S THIS?
URGENT
PLEASE REPORT IMMEDIATELY TO THE ACADEMY GENERAL AFFAIRS DEPARTMENT AND THE STUDENT COUNCIL EXECUTIVE FACTION.
P.S.— WE NEED TO DISCUSS YOUR DORM ROOM.
—CLAUDIA
OH... RIGHT.
I BURNED MY ROOM TO CINDERS THIS MORNING...

BONUS AST #03.04. after

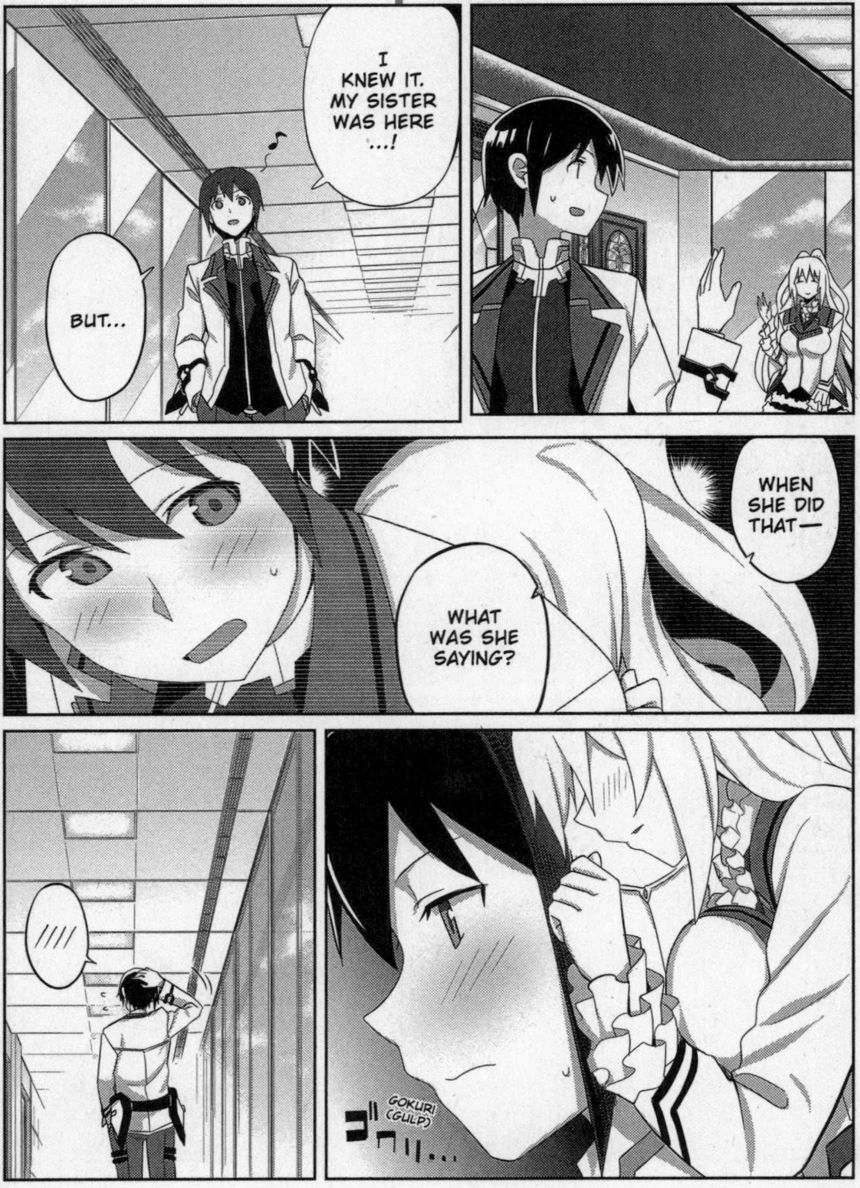
I KNEW IT. MY SISTER WAS HERE ...!
BUT...
WHEN SHE DID THAT—
WHAT WAS SHE SAYING?
GOKURI (GULP)
////

BONUS AST #05. after

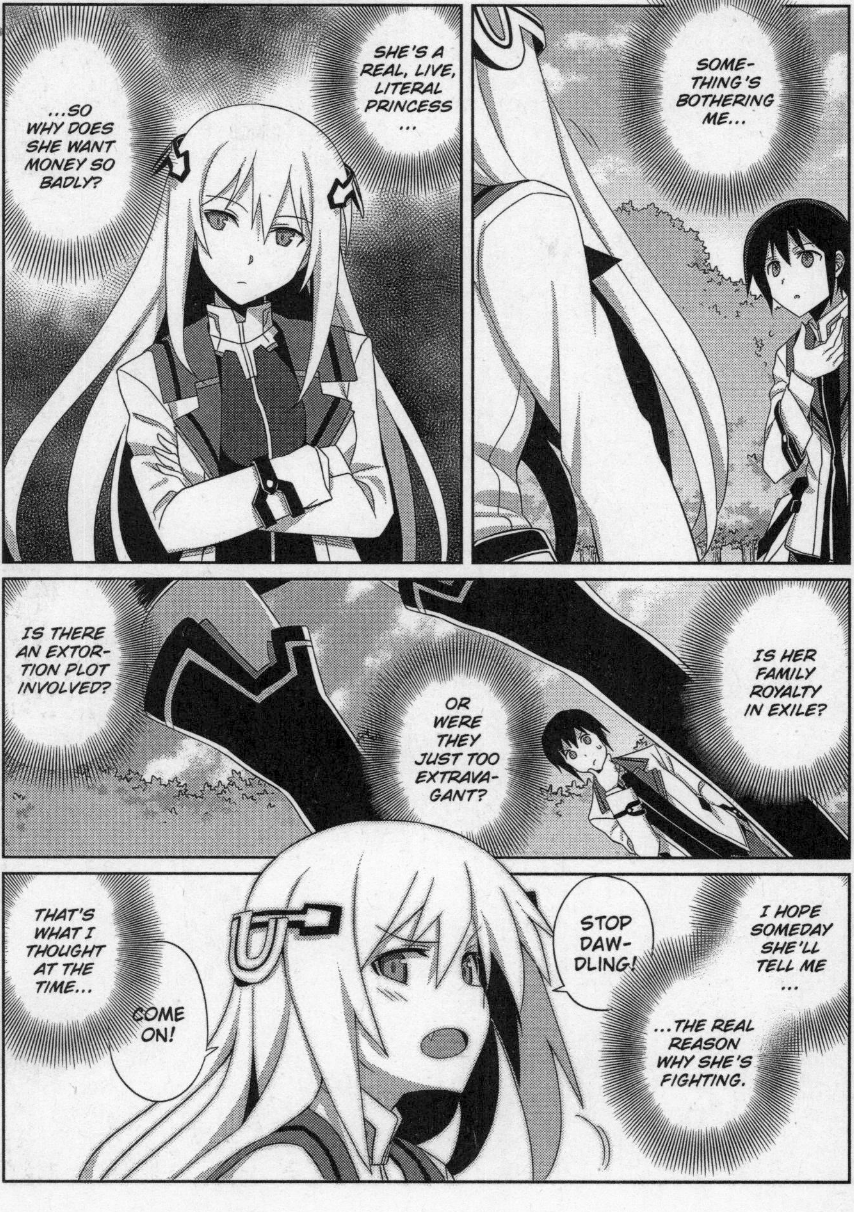
SOME-THING'S BOTHERING ME...
SHE'S A REAL, LIVE, LITERAL PRINCESS ...
...SO WHY DOES SHE WANT MONEY SO BADLY?
IS HER FAMILY ROYALTY IN EXILE?
OR WERE THEY JUST TOO EXTRAVA-GANT?
IS THERE AN EXTOR-TION PLOT INVOLVED?
I HOPE SOMEDAY SHE'LL TELL ME ...
...THE REAL REASON WHY SHE'S FIGHTING.
STOP DAW-DLING!
COME ON!
THAT'S WHAT I THOUGHT AT THE TIME...

BONUS AST #06. after

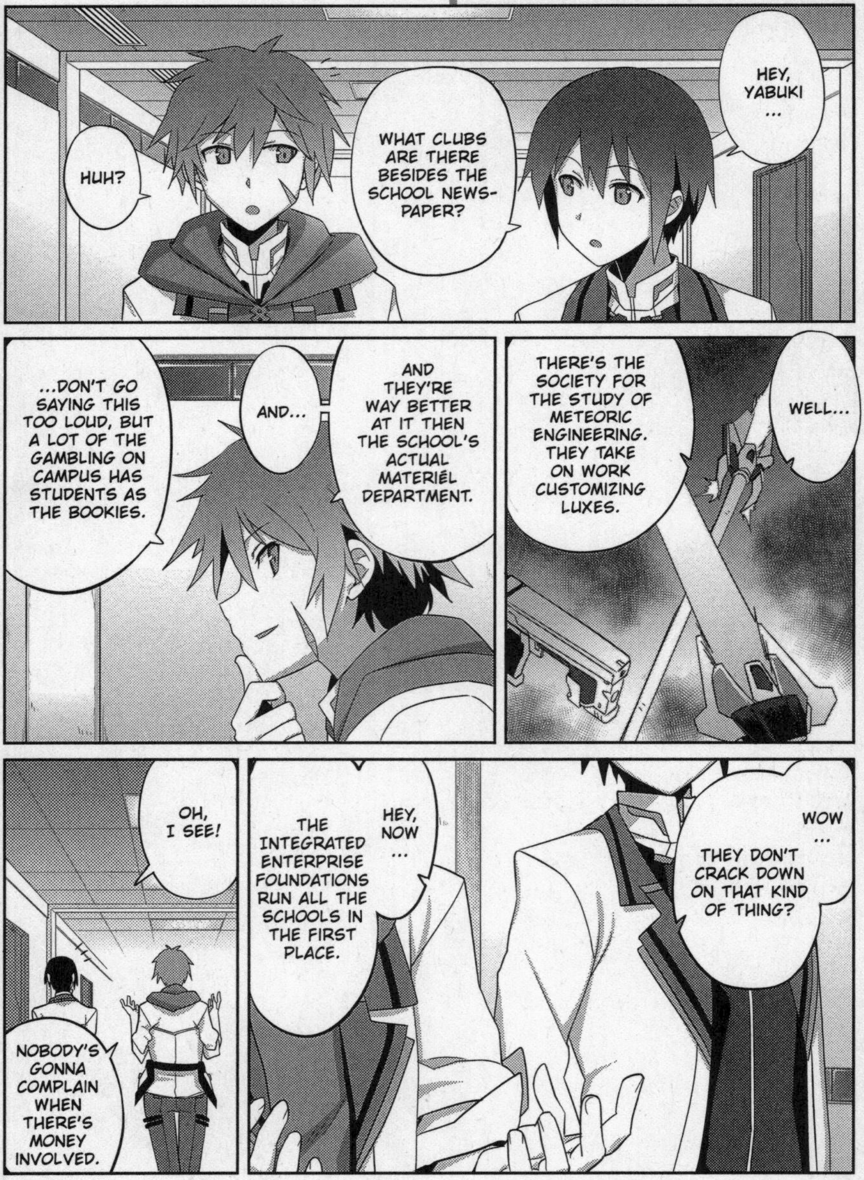
HEY, YABUKI ...
WHAT CLUBS ARE THERE BESIDES THE SCHOOL NEWS-PAPER?
HUH?
WELL...
THERE'S THE SOCIETY FOR THE STUDY OF METEORIC ENGINEERING. THEY TAKE ON WORK CUSTOMIZING LUXES.
AND THEY'RE WAY BETTER AT IT THEN THE SCHOOL'S ACTUAL MATERIÉL DEPARTMENT.
AND...
...DON'T GO SAYING THIS TOO LOUD, BUT A LOT OF THE GAMBLING ON CAMPUS HAS STUDENTS AS THE BOOKIES.
WOW ...
THEY DON'T CRACK DOWN ON THAT KIND OF THING?
HEY, NOW ...
THE INTEGRATED ENTERPRISE FOUNDATIONS RUN ALL THE SCHOOLS IN THE FIRST PLACE.
OH, I SEE!
NOBODY'S GONNA COMPLAIN WHEN THERE'S MONEY INVOLVED.

END

THE ASTERISK WAR

Comments from the Author and Character Designer

Author ◆ Yuu Miyazaki

Hurrah! The first volume of the manga is out!

Hi, I'm Yuu Miyazaki, the author of *The Asterisk War* novels. Ningen-san is bringing them to life as manga. What do you think? My highest hopes were exceeded! Ayato, Julis, and everyone else have a stylish charm all their own—unique from okiura-san's art too. The moment I laid eyes on the first illustrations for the comic, I was through the roof.

I hope everyone is as excited for the upcoming novels as the manga. Dear readers, please keep your eyes on both!

Character Designer ◆ okiura

Congratulations on the first volume of *The Asterisk War* manga!

I'm okiura, the illustrator for the original *The Asterisk War* novels.
I heard that there would be a manga adaptation, and when I saw Ningen-san's illustrations of Julis and Ayato, I thought, ecstatically, that it was like a beautiful crystallization of my own work, and I couldn't wait to read it.
From the storyboards and drafts too, it was obvious that the quality would be even higher than I'd expected...enough that maybe I'll end up using it for reference. LOL!

I hope you'll all be cheering for the original novels and the manga alike!

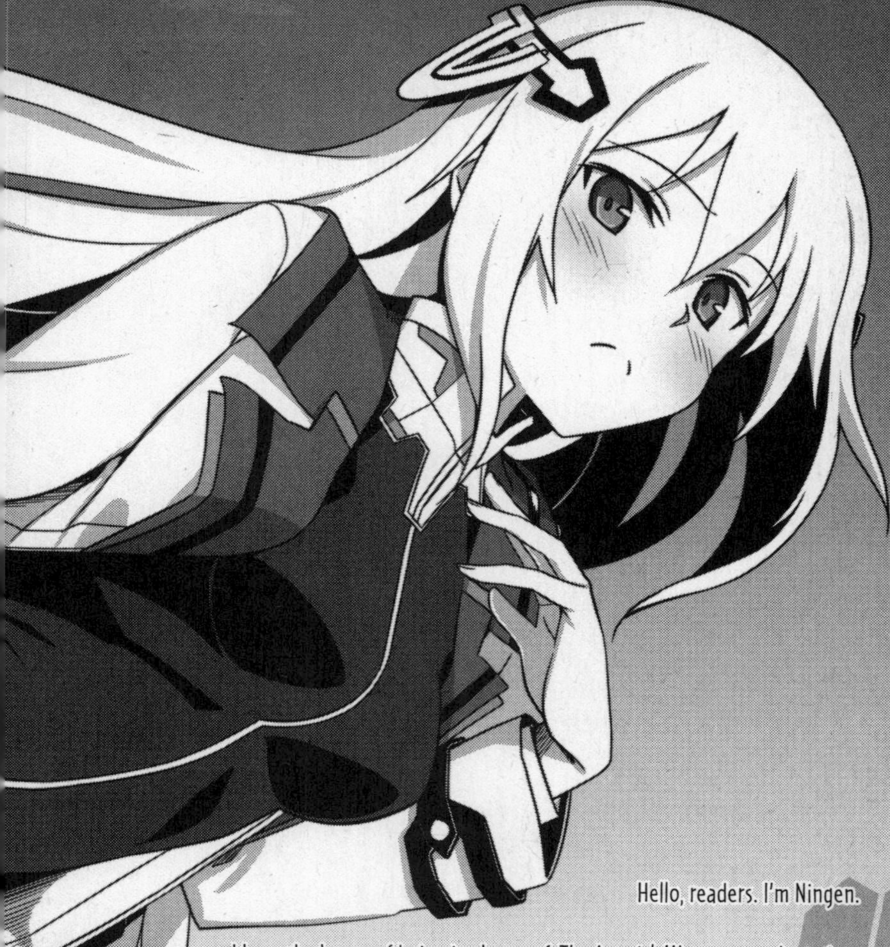

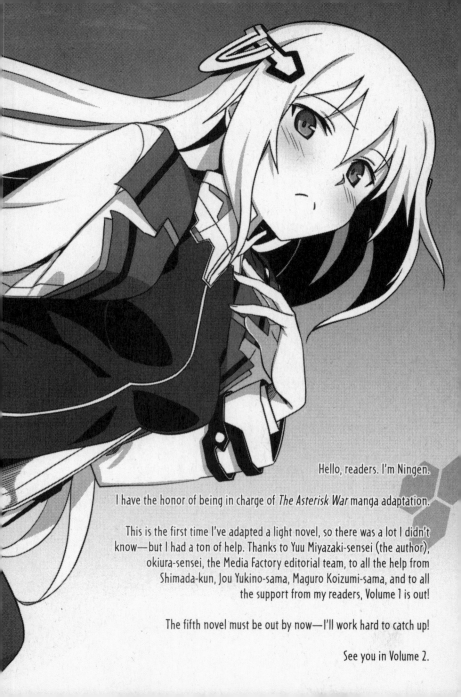

Hello, readers. I'm Ningen.

I have the honor of being in charge of *The Asterisk War* manga adaptation.

This is the first time I've adapted a light novel, so there was a lot I didn't know—but I had a ton of help. Thanks to Yuu Miyazaki-sensei (the author), okiura-sensei, the Media Factory editorial team, to all the help from Shimada-kun, Jou Yukino-sama, Maguro Koizumi-sama, and to all the support from my readers, Volume 1 is out!

The fifth novel must be out by now—I'll work hard to catch up!

See you in Volume 2.

Afterword

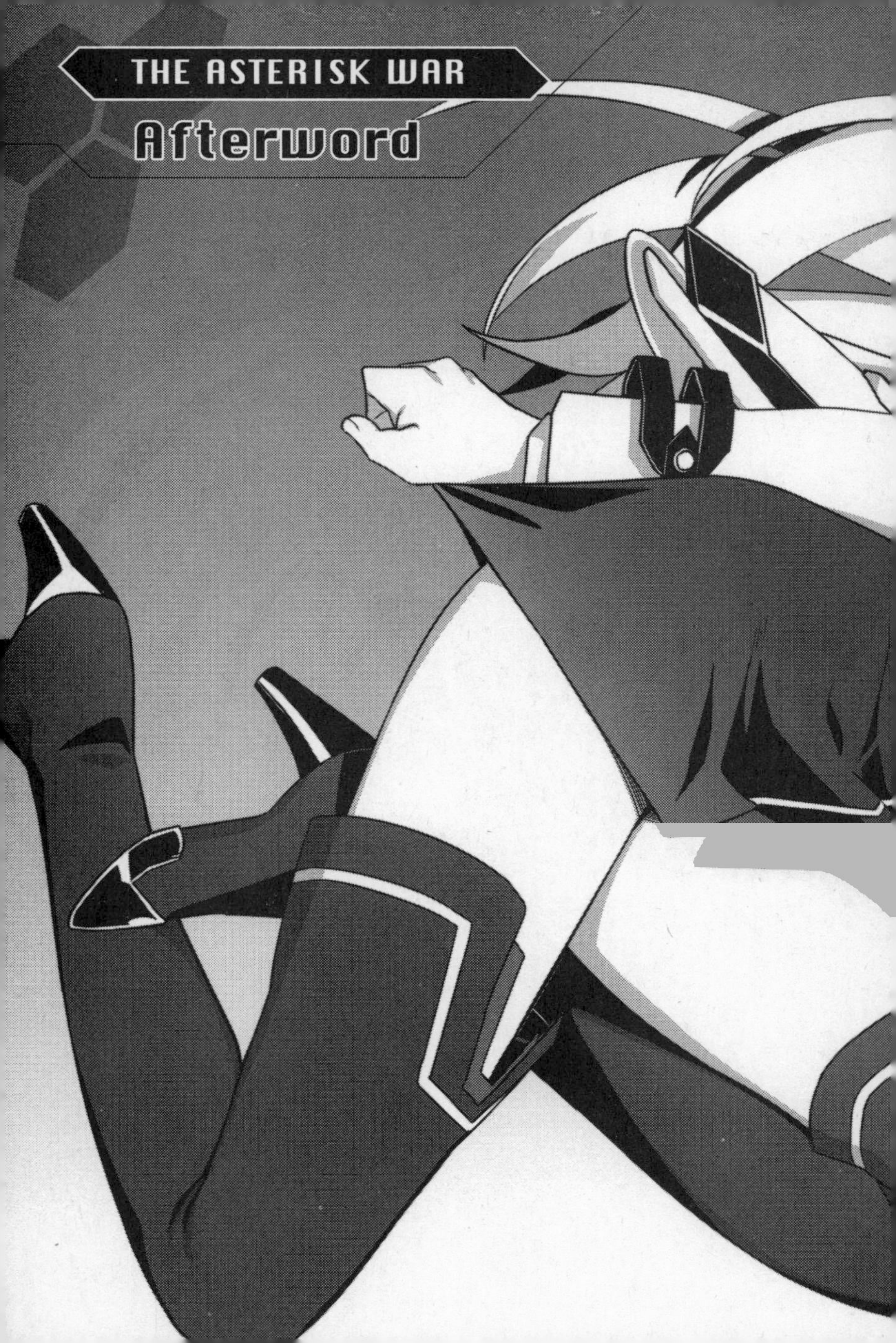

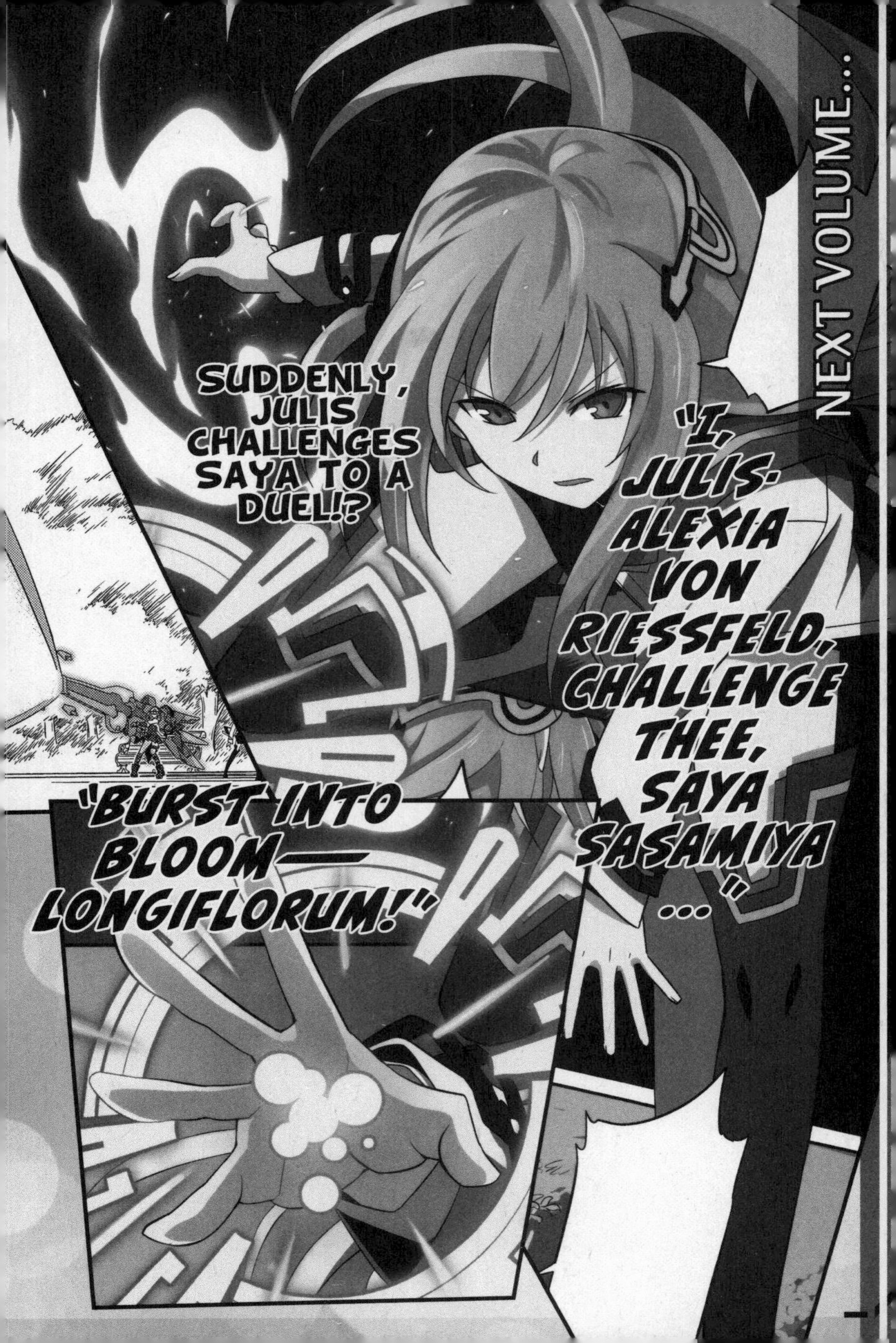
NEXT VOLUME...
"I, JULIS-ALEXIA VON RIESSFELD, CHALLENGE THEE, SAYA SASAMIYA..."
SUDDENLY, JULIS CHALLENGES SAYA TO A DUEL!?
"BURST INTO BLOOM—LONGIFLORUM!"

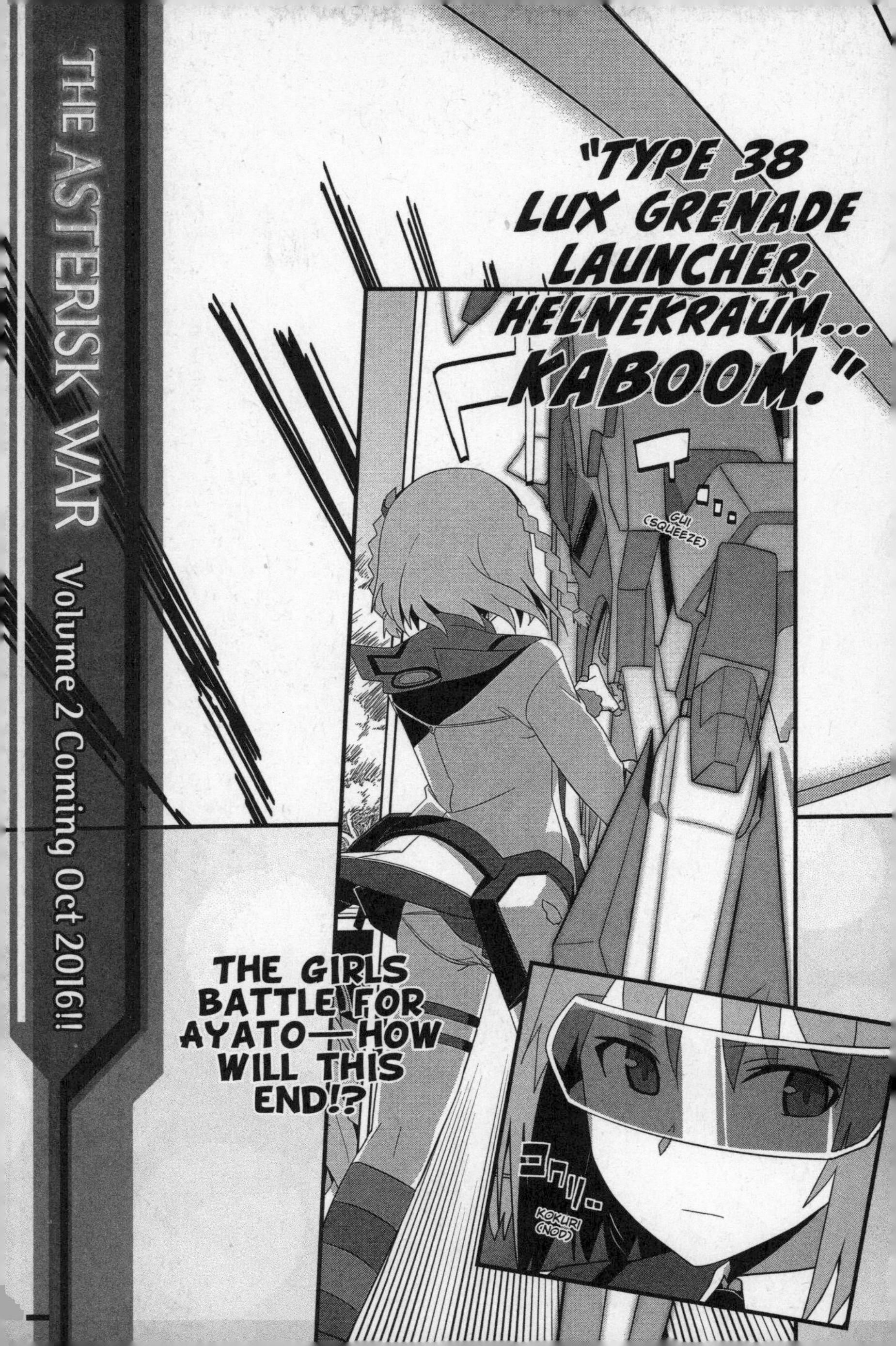
THE ASTERISK WAR
Volume 2 Coming Oct 2016!!
"TYPE 38 LUX GRENADE LAUNCHER, HELNEKRAUM... KABOOM."
GUI (SQUEEZE)
THE GIRLS BATTLE FOR AYATO—HOW WILL THIS END!?
KOKURI (NOD)

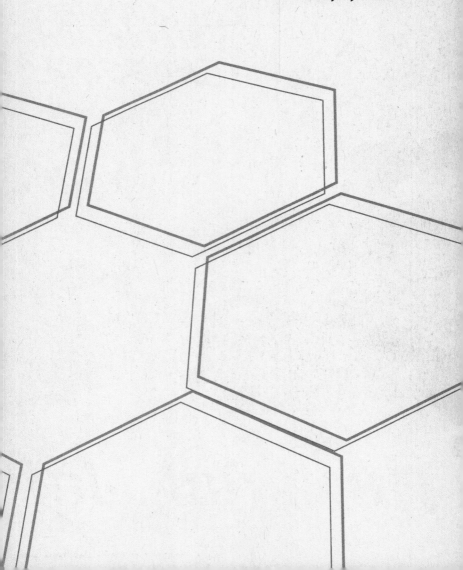

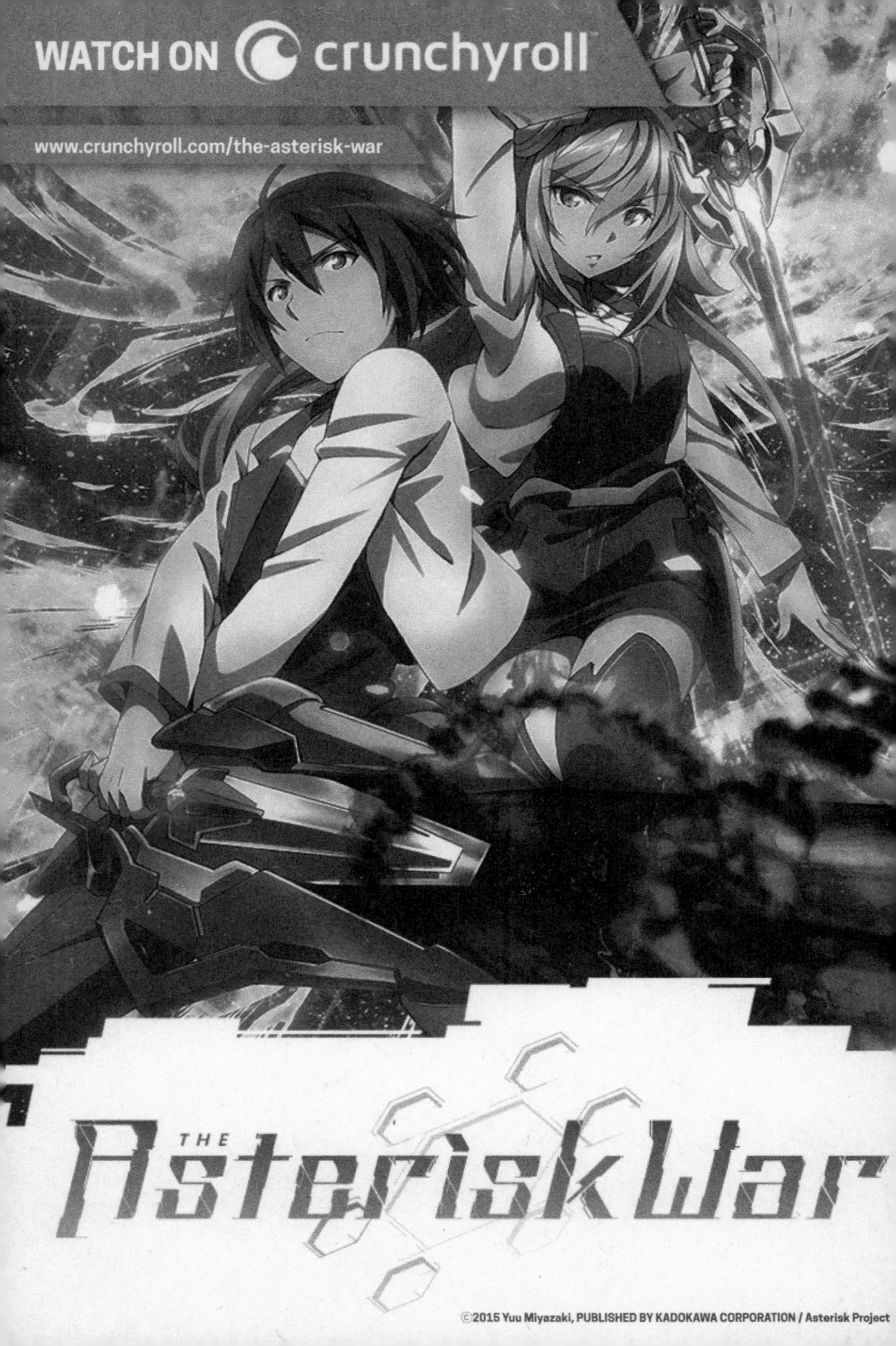
WATCH ON crunchyroll
www.crunchyroll.com/the-asterisk-war
THE Asterisk War
©2015 Yuu Miyazaki, PUBLISHED BY KADOKAWA CORPORATION / Asterisk Project

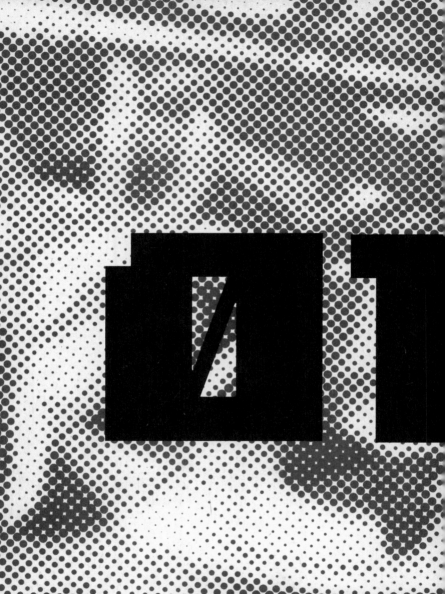

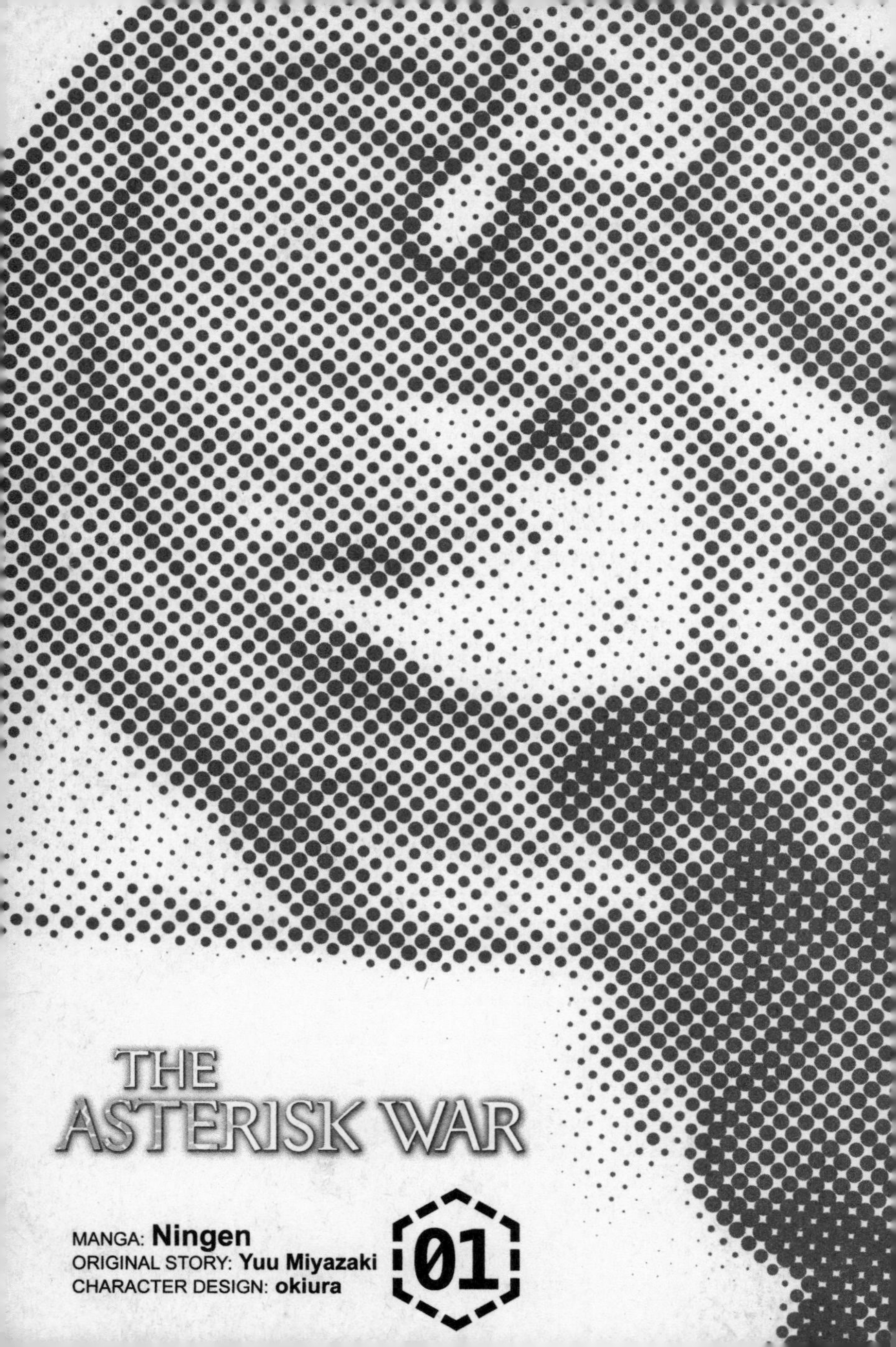

THE ASTERISK WAR

01

MANGA: **Ningen**
ORIGINAL STORY: **Yuu Miyazaki**
CHARACTER DESIGN: **okiura**

THE ASTERISK WAR 01

Ningen
Original Story: Yuu Miyazaki
Character Design: okiura

Translation: Melissa Tanaka   Lettering: Morgan Hart

THE ASTERISK WAR
© Ningen 2014
© Yuu Miyazaki 2014
First published in Japan in 2014 by KADOKAWA CORPORATION, Tokyo.
English translation rights arranged with KADOKAWA CORPORATION, Tokyo.
through TUTTLE-MORI AGENCY, Inc., Tokyo.

English translation © 2016 by Yen Press, LLC

Yen Press
1290 Avenue of the Americas
New York, NY 10104

Visit us at yenpress.com
facebook.com/yenpress
twitter.com/yenpress
yenpress.tumblr.com

First Yen Press Edition: July 2016

Yen Press is an imprint of Yen Press, LLC.
The Yen Press name and logo are trademarks of Yen Press, LLC.

The publisher is not responsible for websites (or their content) that are not owned by the publisher.

Library of Congress Control Number: 2016936539

ISBNs: 978-0-316-31528-9 (paperback)
       978-0-316-39874-9 (ebook)
       978-0-316-39875-6 (app)

10 9 8 7 6 5 4 3 2 1

BVG

Printed in the United States of America